THE MONEY MYTH

THE MONEY MYTH

School Resources, Outcomes, and Equity

W. Norton Grubb

Russell Sage Foundation ◆ New York

The Russell Sage Foundation

The Russell Sage Foundation, one of the oldest of America's general purpose foundations, was established in 1907 by Mrs. Margaret Olivia Sage for "the improvement of social and living conditions in the United States." The Foundation seeks to fulfill this mandate by fostering the development and dissemination of knowledge about the country's political, social, and economic problems. While the Foundation endeavors to assure the accuracy and objectivity of each book it publishes, the conclusions and interpretations in Russell Sage Foundation publications are those of the authors and not of the Foundation, its Trustees, or its staff. Publication by Russell Sage, therefore, does not imply Foundation endorsement.

Library of Congress Cataloging-in-Publication Data
Grubb, W. Norton.
   The money myth : school resources, outcomes, and equity / W. Norton Grubb.
      p.   cm.
   Includes bibliographical references and index.
   ISBN 978-0-87154-366-0 (alk. paper)
    1. Education—United States—Finance.   2. Public schools—United States—Finance.
   3. Education—Economic aspects—United States.   I. Title.
   LB2825.G838 2009
   370.110973—dc22   2008036248

Text design by Genna Patacsil.

RUSSELL SAGE FOUNDATION
112 East 64th Street, New York, New York 10065
10   9   8   7   6   5   4   3   2   1

The question of sufficient revenue lies back of almost every other [educational] problem.
—Ellwood Cubberly, *School Funds and Their Apportionment* (1905, 1)

I got a great big house on the hill here,
And a great big blonde wife inside it,
And a great big pool in my backyard
and another great big pool beside it.
Sonny, it's money that matters, hear what I say,
It's money that matters in the USA . . .
It's money that matters whatever you do.
—Randy Newman

Simple resource policies hold little hope for improving student outcomes.
—Eric Hanushek, "Assessing the Effects of School Resources on Student Performance: An Update" (1997, 141)

CONTENTS

W. NORTON GRUBB is professor and David Gardner Chair in Higher Education at the School of Education, the University of California, Berkeley. He is also the faculty coordinator of the Principal Leadership Institute.

In many ways, this book returns to concerns about school resources that started my research career nearly forty years ago. The examination in my dissertation of a problem in the "old" school finance—the issue of how district financing responds to state revenues—was incorporated into an early book with Stephan Michelson, *States and Schools*, which developed a conception of the differences among money, inputs, and outputs that was close to the analysis of money, resources, and outcomes developed in this book. I then joined the Childhood and Government Project at the University of California at Berkeley. Those were heady days. The California Supreme Court had just decided the *Serrano* case, throwing out the financing system based on property taxes. We all looked forward to more equitable financing, vast improvements for students in low-spending districts, and a future in which California would continue to be a leader among the states in education. The project's mission was to spread this strategy to all states: lawyers would stride across the land with the moral certainty of federal and state constitutions, school finance experts like me would improve the "minutiae" of finance formulas, and equitable and powerful schooling would spread to all children.

None of this came to pass. The *Rodriguez* decision in Texas demolished the strategy of using the U.S. Constitution as the basis for school finance cases. The *Serrano* case itself had to be relitigated several times, and its equalizing intent was subsequently undermined by other developments, including Proposition 13, which put a limit on property taxes. California began its long slide "from first to worst" among the states, weakened by a citizenry prone to harmful initiatives, a series of dreadful governors, a legislature afflicted by term limits and therefore lacking in any real understanding of educational problems, and now—as in much of the nation—a deep and seemingly unbridgeable divide in the electorate. Other states did indeed follow the *Serrano* case with litigation against inequitable school finance systems, but as clarified in chapter 11, these lawsuits had only fitful effects on funding and no effects in most states on the equity of outcomes. The dream that litigation could bring a new era of equity to education faded fast, and the excitement of working in this area faded as well.

Something else was missing from litigation efforts, as I came to understand only later. The litigation strategy, as well as more general legislative strategies to revise school finance, was built on the money myth—the idea that more money leads to improved outcomes, that the solution to any educational problem requires increased spending, and that, as Ellwood Cubberly put it a century ago, "the question of sufficient revenue lies back of almost every [educational] problem." Several beliefs developed in the nineteenth century—the idea of education as a panacea, the specific economic version of this idea I call the Education Gospel, and the money myth—have continued to exert great power over educators, even though they are overblown and sometimes just plain wrong. One ambition of this book, then, is to analyze the money myth more carefully, to clarify when it is right and when it is either wrong or misleading. This is not, of course, the argument that "money doesn't matter," and fiscal conservatives and anti-taxers should not take comfort from anything in this book. Of course money matters, since teachers cannot be paid, schools cannot be built, and computers and books cannot be bought without money. But, in a logical approach I use throughout this book, money is usually "necessary but not sufficient" (NBNS). It is therefore crucial to understand when it is necessary and when other kinds of resources—leadership, vision, cooperation among teachers, effective instruction, unbiased information about effective versus ineffective practices, stability, consistent district and state policies—are necessary as well.

In addition, the debates about constitutional principles and school finance formulas, the jousting over equity principles and the minutiae of school finance, never reached the classroom—that is, these debates never engaged with instructional issues, or imagined how teachers might teach differently, or modified the ways in which principals and districts organized schools. This provides yet another illustration of one of the many great divides in education—between, on the one hand, lawyers, economists, historians, sociologists, organization theorists, and policymakers, who are all concerned with macro perspectives on education but have little interest in classroom instruction and school conditions, and on the other hand, the teachers, principals, and curriculum and instruction specialists developing ways to teach math and English and social studies, who are focused on classroom interactions and are often unaware of macro and policy issues. The discussions of school finance did not address the fundamental *educational* issues of what needs to go on in classrooms and schools, nor the issues of resources rather than money—*effective* resources—that I develop in this book. Without bridging the great divide, it is impossible for litigation, accountability mechanisms, or any other policy approach to improve teaching and learning. So a second ambition of this book is to develop a novel approach to finance and resources that can bridge this particular great divide and show how the right resources at the classroom and school levels can improve learning, persistence in school, attitudes, and other important outcomes.

Another problem has been that the conceptions of equity underlying finance litigation and the "old" school finance are quite simple: equality of funding per student should displace earlier unequal patterns correlated with property value or income, an equity standard now often superseded by the weaker conception of adequacy. But in practice (never mind in theory), there have been many more conceptions of equity that have motivated education movements and reforms, and new approaches to finance and resources can help clarify these many theories and the implicit battles among them—the subject of chapter 6. These conceptions are static and cross-sectional, however, and recognizing the dynamic aspects of inequality—the ways in which initial differences among students in kindergarten are magnified over the many years of schooling—leads to new kinds of both qualitative and qualitative work, the subjects of chapters 7 and 8. So an elaboration of equity is a third ambition of this book.

Finally, a new approach to school resources is not simply a technical exercise in devising new funding formulas or better ways of tinkering with the minutiae of school finance, but is embedded in much larger approaches to what schools should be, as well as in approaches to the welfare state or the foundational state, as I argue in chapter 12. The greatest ambition of this book is to provide an alternative narrative or vision not only of school resource issues but also of what egalitarian schools could be. This vision is already apparent in many schools, some districts, and a few state policies that promote what I (awkwardly) label a complex/constructivist approach to schooling. It is possible that the politics of this country are inadequate to this change; indeed, the 2008 presidential election results indicate that the policies of change, equity, and deliberation—all crucial to the educational approaches in this book—can win over the politics of fearmongering, disinformation, atavism, divisiveness, and small-mindedness masquerading as "character." But changing schools in fundamental ways cannot happen without fundamental shifts in attitudes, policies, and politics.

I first put together an outline of new approaches to school resources in the summer of 1999 during a lovely month spent in Gloucester, England, writing in the mornings and hiking the Cotswolds in the afternoons. In expanding on this early version, I have incurred a series of debts to others. Luis Huerta provided extensive assistance in reviewing various strands of literature. Laura Goe came to Berkeley as a graduate student and immediately perceived that a specific program in California—the Intermediate Intervention/Underperforming School Program (II/USP), reviewed more carefully in chapter 9—provided a precise "natural experiment" that could be used to examine these new approaches to money and finance. Luis, Laura, and I published an early version of chapter 1 as "Straw into Gold, Revenues into Results: Spinning Out the Implications of the 'Improved' School Finance," published in the *Journal of Education Finance* in the spring of 2006. Thanks to assistant editor Robert Frost, Laura, Luis, and I published three other papers in that issue, creating a section devoted to these approaches; my individual paper was an early version of chapter 3.

In coming to understand the limits of money, students in the Principal Leadership Institute (PLI), of which I am the faculty coordinator, have been helpful in ways they may not recognize. Their experiences have revealed a central paradox of urban schools, for which these dedicated individuals are preparing to be leaders: such schools are places of not only incredible need but also incredible waste, in ways outlined in the "theory of waste" in chapter 1. Much of the evidence about the use and misuse of money and other resources, about the instability and chaos in all too many urban schools, and about the endless bureaucratic constraints that limit how schools can plan their resources comes from PLI students and graduates. While such evidence may seem anecdotal, in fact there is no other way to learn about the details of what happens deep within schools with the revenues and resources they are given.

A second strategy for testing these new approaches was to find data rich enough to measure a variety of school resources, not just the simple resources usually incorporated into education production functions. The NELS88 (National Educational Longitudinal Survey of the Class of 1988) data proved to be such a data set, and my greatest obligation is to Marcel Paret for meticulously programming the variables, merging NELS88 with other data (especially the "Common Core of Data" with information on finance patterns, the basis for chapter 3), and running endless regressions and multilevel models (ultimately unsuccessful) and growth equations. This statistical analysis is the basis of chapters 2, 3, 4, 5, and 7. In addition, Emmelie Geraedts prepared the tables in chapter 7 from the raw and nearly uninterpretable results, and Jane Valentino constructed a number of graphs that are useful in examining these longitudinal patterns (see chapter 7), though most of these graphs have not been included.

The idea of dynamic inequality developed in chapter 6 leads not only to growth equations like those in chapter 7 but also to qualitative research in schools, to determine what they do to narrow inequality over time. The analysis in chapter 8 of twelve schools in the San Francisco Bay Area was carried out with the help of Heather Kinlaw, Linn Posey, and Kathryn Young, who should properly be considered co-authors of this chapter.

Melissa Henne provided invaluable research assistance for chapter 10, especially in profiling the efforts of districts and states around the country to develop new approaches to policy, more in line with novel approaches to resources. Alison Cole reviewed the efforts at school-based budgeting around the country, the basis for the analysis of that promising practice in chapter 9. The funding for all these research associates has come from the David Gardner Chair in Higher Education, and I thank the anonymous donor of the chair for relieving me of the burden of being a professional beggar going hat in hand to foundations and grant sources.

I also thank colleagues for responding to endless questions about their areas of specialization: Dan Perlstein on historical issues, Cynthia Coburn on district-level developments, Bruce Fuller on policy developments and No Child Left Behind, and Russ Rumberger and Tom Timar.

Coming up with a title is always difficult since a good title summarizes an entire book in a simple phrase. The notion of "the money myth" emerged from a wonderful and wide-ranging dinner conversation with Ronnie Caplane, Kathleen Meagher, and Gail Saliterman, and I thank these wordsmiths for their willingness to understand the book and come up with an appropriate and memorable phrase. In the process my son Alex lost his bid to capture a share of the royalties by coming up with the winning title.

Barbara Fuller of Editcetera edited the second draft of the manuscript and helped enormously with improving the language, clarifying convoluted phrasing, and otherwise smoothing out my writing quirks. Her work also relieved my sweet wife of her usual chore of editing my bloated prose.

I should acknowledge the contributions of several anonymous referees, one in particular working on behalf of the Russell Sage Foundation, and others for the *Journal of Education Finance* and the *American Educational Research Journal*, which published an early version of chapter 2. Overall, however, I have found most current refereeing to be unhelpful at best and uncomprehending at worst, particularly among adherents of the "old" school finance who insisted quite incorrectly that my ideas were just variants of adequacy notions. I'm sure all authors complain that their precious ideas have been misunderstood, but I have been genuinely perplexed as well as aggravated by how small-minded and persnickety most refereeing has become.

Finally, I want to thank my beloved wife Rikki, who has the patience to put up with both my academic obsessions like writing books and the non-academic obsessions that overfill the walls of our home.

W. Norton Grubb
Berkeley, California
September 23, 2008

Introduction

Resources, Effectiveness, and Equity in Schools

ADEQUATE FUNDING has been a worry throughout the history of public schooling. During the first half of the nineteenth century, a prolonged effort took place to shift from voluntary support—charity schooling for the poor, private schooling for others—to tax-based support so that all children could attend school. Attempts to build a public school *system* put substantial financial strains on districts to allow longer periods of attendance, the abolition of tuition, high schools in addition to grammar schools, stone and brick buildings in place of log cabins, and decent privies. The demographics of the school population added its own demands, with migrations from rural to urban areas throughout the nineteenth century, waves of immigration in the 1830s and 1890s, the enforcement of compulsory education laws after 1900, and the rapid growth of high schools.

To meet the financial demands of the growing public school system, Horace Mann—often considered the father of public education—tried hard to convince districts and states to cough up enough money. He lambasted opposition to taxation as "embezzlement and pillage from children," while a contemporary complained about opposition to common schools as "hidebound conservatism, niggardly parsimony, sectarian bigotry, and political animosity."[1] Ellwood Cubberly, one of the first to identify variation in spending among rich and poor school districts as a barrier to equity, began his 1905 treatise with a similar complaint:

One of the most important administrative problems of today is how properly to finance the school system or a state, as the question of sufficient revenue lies back of almost every other problem. (1905,1)

The magnitude of the funding needs dwarfed many other problems: as immigrant and high school populations expanded enormously, the costs of city schools trebled between 1890 and 1910 (Tyack 1974, 183). It is no wonder that the administrative progressives—the champions of rationality who emerged during the Progressive Era—were consumed with funding and efficiency: the sheer volume of revenues needed to provide access to all who sought schooling and to keep schools open was overwhelming.[2]

The struggle for public funding continued, as the school-age population continued to expand and the high school moved from an elite to a mass institution. Keeping schools going during the Great Depression was particularly difficult as more youth, lacking employment options, enrolled in high schools just as tax bases (especially the local property tax base) declined. The solution, part of a century-long trend, was to turn to states for both property tax relief and additional school funding; over the 1930s, the proportion of revenues from states almost doubled, from 16.9 percent to 30.3 percent, and other efforts developed state earmarks to guarantee funds to education (rather than other local services). Even so, the increase in spending in the 1930s was the lowest of any decade over the last century (table I.1). These were all familiar battles over money; opponents of state funding included certain business groups and tax-cutting legislators whom supporters of education characterized as "pinchpenny politicians who want to save on education ... to have more money to squander on their friends and supporters" (Tyack 1974, ch. 2 and p. 82). As always in the battles over funding, the impulse to expand education—to fulfill views of education as a solution to every conceivable problem, as a panacea (Perkinson 1995), or as an element of faith (Grubb and Lazerson 2004)—conflicted with resistance to public spending.

In the mid-1950s, John Kenneth Galbraith (1958) coined the phrase "private wealth and public squalor" to describe the general hostility to government spending in the United States. Education reformers have provided many examples of squalor in the public sector, particularly in urban schools. These range from Jonathan Kozol's *Death at an Early Age* (1967) in the 1960s, describing inadequate facilities and indifferent teachers in city schools, to his reprise of this argument in *Savage Inequalities* (1992) in the early 1990s, to the documentation of horrendous bathrooms and dilapidated buildings in a recent court case, *Williams v. California*. One of the dominant stories or policy narratives around education has thus been a simple myth about money:[3] we need more money to extend schools (and now colleges and universities)

Table I.1   Total Expenditure per Pupil (ADA) in Public Elementary and Secondary Schools (Constant 2005–2006 Dollars)

School Year	Total Expenditure
1919–1920	$668
1929–1930	1,261
1939–1940	1,506
1949–1950	2,188
1959–1960	3,190
1969–1970	5,031
1974–1975	5,935
1979–1980	6,384
1984–1985	7,004
1989–1990	8,698
1994–1995	8,897
1999–2000	10,099
2000–2001	11,016

Source: National Center for Education Statistics (2006, table 167).

to all students, to improve schools and teachers, and to equalize the funding differences that allow squalor in some schools while others have every conceivable luxury. Every generation of reformers proposes new ways to fix the schools or reinvents old ways—"reforming again and again and again," as Larry Cuban (1990) has called it—and argues that we need more money to make the changes, what we might call "spending again and again and again."

Fortunately, in a country hostile to taxation, other narratives have developed to justify public spending. The vision of the nineteenth century was one of civic education that would prepare all students to be citizens, thus requiring common schools for all. Over the twentieth century, that narrative has been largely displaced by the view I have called the Education Gospel, which expresses the faith that schooling—especially schooling focused on preparation of the labor force—can resolve virtually all social and individual dilemmas (see Grubb and Lazerson 2004).[4] The document that began the current round of educational reforms—*A Nation at Risk*—opens with one version of the Gospel: "Our once unchallenged preeminence in commerce, industry, science, and technological innovation is being overtaken by competitors throughout the world." It went on to blame the schools for a "rising tide of mediocrity that threatens our very future as a Nation and a people." Since that manifesto, a raft of reports and proclamations have issued forth—*What Work Requires of Schools*, *America's Choice: High Skills or Low Wages!*, *Twenty-First-*

Century Skills for Twenty-First-Century Jobs, and the latest in this repetitive series, *Tough Choices or Tough Times*, from the *New* Commission on the Skills of
the American Workforce, all calling for more education and higher-order
skills to keep the nation competitive. While the Education Gospel is exaggerated in many ways and narrows the purposes of schooling, with detrimental consequences for learning, it has also served to justify public spending for both public and private goals. The result has been a contest between
two warring narratives—one skeptical about government spending and
hostile to taxation, the other promoting public education as a form of investment and salvation for the twenty-first century.

In these battles, the dominant concern has been money—money both as
an instrument to buy other school resources (teachers, books and computers, professional development, buildings) and as a symbolic commitment to
public education. When legislators try to demonstrate their support of education, they typically advocate increased spending. When advocates for equity have complained about wretched conditions in schools, the solution has
typically involved the redistribution of money. A great deal of educational
reform related to equity has been initiated by litigation—in the great battles
over school desegregation culminating in *Brown v. Board of Education*, and
then in the wave of school finance lawsuits that have sought to equalize
spending among districts since the *Serrano* case in California, now in a new
wave of lawsuits trying to establish adequate levels of spending. School finance as a field of study and practice—what I'll call the conventional or
"old" school finance—is concerned almost entirely with revenues and expenditures rather than with broader conceptions of resources or the effects of resources on schooling outcomes. Many of these discussions, from
Cubberly's book to the present, involve the technical details of funding
formulas rather than educational or instructional issues. As the lawyers behind the *Serrano* case complained, "Reforming zeal [has often been] dissipated in confrontation with minutiae" (Coons, Clune, and Sugarman
1970, 65).

Indeed, even when researchers have tried to move beyond money to the
resources that money might buy, they often have failed to do so. For example, the National Resource Council Committee on Education Finance produced a volume called *Making Money Matter*, potentially about how money
can be best used to support those resources that improve school performance. But while the volume examines a great deal of literature and wres-
tles with definitions of equity, productivity, and other crucial concepts, it
does not show how to use money effectively (Ladd, Chalk, and Hansen
1999). So a move away from the old school finance has proved difficult, even
conceptually, and state legislatures and school finance litigation continue to
struggle with revenues. This illustrates how dominant the narrative is: more
is always better, inadequate outcomes can be explained by inadequate rev-

enues, the solution to any educational problem requires increased spending, and, as Cubberly proclaimed, "the question of sufficient revenue lies behind almost every other problem" (1905, 1). We might also call this the myth of money, another one of the great faiths underlying our educational system that emerged from the nineteenth century—along with the conception of education as a panacea and the Education Gospel.

NEW APPROACHES TO SCHOOL RESOURCES

But money has never been the whole problem. Even as reformers struggled to expand tax support during the nineteenth century, some argued that taxation alone could not solve problems with educational resources such as mediocre teaching by untrained schoolmarms, decrepit physical facilities (log cabins and decaying privies), a limited variety of subjects, and poor-quality textbooks. During the 1890s, a dominant criticism involved the dreariness of schooling—the complaint that conventional classes were lifeless and boring, disconnected from life outside the school walls (Cremin 1961, ch. 2). This attack has continued, especially in round after round of critiques of the high school (Grubb 2008c) and in continued charges of the irrelevance of schooling to later life. By the 1950s, when the system of elementary/secondary education had stabilized, the dominant concerns shifted from the simple provision of schooling to issues of its quality. The attacks on "Life Adjustment Education," progressive education, and the weakness of science and math during the Sputnik crisis were all debates not about money, but about the curricula that money was being spent for. Evidently, spending more money on the wrong kind of education cannot produce the outcomes, either for individuals or for society, that we want.

Since the 1960s, several other challenges to the narrative or myth of money have emerged. One is simply that expenditures per pupil have increased—in real or inflation-adjusted terms—relatively steadily. As table I.1 indicates, spending per pupil vastly increased over the earlier years of the twentieth century. Recently, it has more than trebled since 1960, doubled since 1970, and increased by one-quarter since 1994–1995. Yet education is still beset by problems familiar from the 1960s: gross inequalities among students, dilapidated conditions in some schools, ineffective teachers, teacher shortages in some fields, the achievement gap among different groups of students. One implication is that simply increasing spending cannot resolve the problems of schools. Even if our expectation of schooling is a moving target—with increasing participation by young women, with demands on schools from children with disabilities and students just learning English, with the need for computers and multimedia centers as well as science labs—the apparent solution of spending more money seems unlikely to work. The constraints that Mann identified—"hidebound conservatism, niggardly parsimony"—remain at work, albeit at much higher levels of spending after 150 years.

Another challenge since the 1960s has been a deep question about the myth of money, especially the assumption that more money will improve quality and outcomes. In a widely cited 1966 report, *Equality of Educational Opportunity,* James Coleman and other scholars first linked schooling outcomes (specifically a vocabulary test measuring verbal skills) to simple inputs (including expenditures, the pupil-teacher ratio, and school facilities such as labs, libraries, and textbooks). The original intent was to document, especially for African American children, the lack of equal educational opportunity, an elusive concept that the report did not define but implicitly assumed to mean school resources equally distributed by race, religion, and national origin.[5] The great surprise, however, was that the school inputs included in the Coleman Report's statistical analysis proved to have only weak effects: instructional expenditure per pupil accounted for 0.1 percent of the variance in the scores of northern black students and 0.3 percent among northern white students. On the contrary, measures of family background—particularly parental education—proved to have substantial effects. Of course, educators have long recognized the effects of family background and wrestled with solutions ranging from early childhood programs to parental education to forms of compensatory education, introduced as part of Lyndon Johnson's War on Poverty. However, the Coleman Report provided the first statistical evidence of how powerful family background could be, especially compared to school resources including money. These two findings have since been simplified, or sloganized, into the notions that school resources do not make much difference (or "money doesn't matter") and that family effects dominate anything that schools can do. Such conclusions have become counters to the myth of money and standard defenses against school finance lawsuits, supporting the argument that equalizing money will not equalize outcomes.

One standard response to such dismal implications has been to replicate the Coleman Report. Outcomes have invariably been test scores, and inputs are those that can be readily measured—spending per pupil, pupil-teacher ratios, teacher experience, sometimes teacher knowledge as measured by test scores, and other school resources such as library books and science labs. These efforts are often referred to as education production functions, since they mimic the structure of production functions in economics that relate outputs to inputs without worrying about the production process itself—that is, about instruction and other activities within schools—so that the school remains a black box. Such equations have been estimated for many different data sources, and a large literature for developing countries reproduces many of the American conclusions.[6] When Eric Hanushek summarized this literature in 1989, he largely restated the negative conclusions of the Coleman Report. Only 13 of 65 studies found spending per pupil to be positively and significantly related to test scores; only 14 of 152 found class size to matter significantly. Teacher experience seemed a little more effective, but even here, only 40 of 140 studies found this variable to improve test scores. In sharp contrast to family background, which has powerful effects no matter how it is measured (Sirin 2005), the effects of school resources have been weak and inconsistent. Though there have been various rejoinders, the upshot of this long debate is the unhelpful conclusion that resources might matter under some conditions, though what those conditions are remains unclear.[7]

Something seems wrong here. Despite the faith of every educator, every parent, every resident of a high-spending district, and every policymaker that money matters and that certain resources (class size, teacher quality) also matter, evidence has been hard to come by. One challenge for a more effective approach to money and to school resources, then, is to identify what kinds of resources matter to outcomes and then to determine how those resources are related to funding—that is, to the question of what money can and cannot buy.

Moving Toward an Improved Approach to School Resources

My response to this challenge is both conceptual and empirical. An improved approach to school resources, presented in chapter 1, begins with a conception of waste, to illustrate that money can easily be spent to no purpose and that converting revenues into educational results is a serious challenge. This approach also clarifies that a wide variety of resources might matter to outcomes—not just the simple resources usually included in conventional production functions, such as the pupil-teacher ratio or the quality of teachers measured by experience and degrees earned, but also what I call compound resources, such as student placement in vocational or general tracks, which incorporate multiple effects; complex resources such as pedagogical approaches, which are difficult to change (especially in high schools) and cannot be readily bought; and abstract resources such as school culture and stability, which are embedded in multiple relationships within schools and which again cannot be bought in the same way that smaller class size can be. Money may be necessary for school improvement, but it cannot guarantee that improvement takes place, and it certainly cannot guarantee that compound, complex, and abstract resources are available, since they require inputs other than money—vision, leadership, understanding of what practices are effective and which are not effective, collaboration, and often support from district and state policies. Indeed, the logic of certain resources being necessary but not sufficient (NBNS) runs throughout this book, since it applies not only to money but also to many favorite reforms, of which class size reduction and smaller schools are perhaps the most prominent.

Finally, an advantage of improved approaches to school resources—or "the improved school finance" for short—is that exploring a wide range of school resources brings the discussion back to educational and instructional issues at the school level. These are the issues that ought to matter in education. Rather than dwelling on the technical minutiae of revenue sources and expenditure distributions, of funding formulas and grant structures, of manipulations of conventional educational production functions to squeeze a little more explanatory power out of them, the improved approaches in this book return to fundamental discussions of what can improve educational outcomes of many kinds.

The logic of money being necessary but not sufficient is similar to an old admonition of John Dewey, who consistently reminded us that debates framed in polar opposites—academic *versus* vocational education, behaviorist *versus* constructivist pedagogies, educational solutions *versus* economic reforms—often reflect false dichotomies. In his introduction to *Experience and Education* (1938, 17), he wrote: "Mankind likes to think in terms of extreme opposites. It is given to formulating its beliefs in terms of Either-Ors, between which it recognizes no intermediate possibilities." In discussing traditional and progressive pedagogies, Dewey lamented that "the problems are not even recognized, to say nothing of being solved, when it is assumed that it suffices to reject the ideas and practices of the old education and then go to the opposite extreme" (22). I will consistently return to this theme; for example, the idea that money is necessary but not sufficient (NBNS) is an example of a both-and approach, since often money *and* other resources (or vision, or direction) are necessary. The common conclusion about the powerful effects of family background on educational outcomes, analyzed in chapter 4, leads to other examples of both-and policies: both race-neutral or "color-blind" improvements *and* attention to racial and ethnic issues in schools, both educational reforms *and* non-education policy changes, are necessary for equity to be achieved, as I argue more fully in chapter 12. An analysis of policy issues at the school level and at the district, state, and federal levels, in chapters 9 and 10, reveals yet other versions of both-and policies: school-level reform without district support is unlikely to work well, and district initiatives that conflict with state and federal initiatives are no more likely to succeed.

When this conceptual approach is applied to a rich data set—the National Educational Longitudinal Survey of the Class of 1988 (NELS88), discussed in detail in chapter 2 and appendix A—many different school resources prove to make a difference, as do family characteristics and student resources. The conclusion that "school resources do not make a difference" is quite wrong, then, and has been the result of studies that are weakly conceptualized and dependent on impoverished data.

There are, to be sure, other traditions of analyzing the outcomes of schooling. One is the effective schools literature, which has examined unusually effective schools—some selected for unexpectedly high test scores and others selected by reputation—and tried to determine what contributes to their greater impact. One limitation of this approach—apart from weak methodologies for identifying exemplary schools and the unstandardized case study methods used to investigate schools—is that these studies either have been silent about funding or have failed to find any systematic relationship between effectiveness and funding.[8] Some authors have noted that some minimum spending level might be necessary; as John Gray concludes in the language of NBNS, similar to my own conclusion:

> Adequate levels of resources seem to be necessary but not a sufficient condition for a school to be effective. ... In twenty years of reading research on the characteristics of effective schools I have only once come across a record of an "excellent" school where the physical environment left something to be desired. (1990, 213)

Otherwise, the effective schools literature provides little help in solving the puzzles about the relationship of money to outcomes. Similarly, another tradition of analysis—a vast evaluation literature examining the effectiveness of specific practices ranging from early childhood education to tutoring to the use of time to specific curricula—proves useful in confirming the effectiveness or ineffectiveness of certain school resources, and it usually reinforces the results from the NELS88 data presented in this volume. But again, the links to revenues are usually left unexamined and the effects of money unclear.

One substantial advantage of using the NELS88 data, therefore, is that I am able to link these data with expenditure and revenue information to see when money makes a difference to the "purchase" of effective resources and when it fails to matter. It turns out that many effective resources—particularly complex, compound, and abstract resources—cannot be readily bought; that is, across schools in the United States, higher spending per pupil does not enhance these resources. Instead, they must be created or constructed by school leaders and teachers working cooperatively with one another, perhaps with additional funding but also with such abstract resources as collaboration, leadership, and stability. And the need to construct such resources collectively, rather than buying them in some marketlike transaction, leads in turn to the need for reorganizing schools so that they can engage in more collective decisionmaking—the subject of chapter 9.

The ancient philosophers were concerned with turning lead into gold, and the problem is similar for educators and policymakers trying to convert revenues—which are themselves useless, since dollar bills cannot themselves influence outcomes—into resources that might have meaningful effects. Luckily, the process for converting revenues into results is not magical, though it does require knowledge of which resources are effective and which are not, an understanding of which resources can be bought and which cannot, and knowledge of alternative school-level reforms, including alternative approaches to structuring schools and decisionmaking, as well as potential reforms at the district, state, and national levels, the subjects of chapters 9 and 10. In all these efforts, more money may be necessary, but it is rarely sufficient, and there is no substitute for identifying those effective resources that influence a variety of educational outcomes.

Conceptualizing Equity and Dynamic Inequality

The conversion of resources into educational outcomes is partly an issue of effectiveness and efficiency: if funds are wasted or misdirected, or if educators fail to understand which resources are most effective, then simply increasing revenues will not lead to improved results. But it is also an issue of equity. The evidence indicates that low-performing students suffer not as much from inadequate *revenues* as from inadequate *resources*, including ineffective teaching (defined in chapter 2), low-quality curriculum tracks (such as general and traditional vocational curricula), and detrimental school climates—again, the kinds of resources that cannot be readily bought with money alone. Therefore, the improved school finance is useful not only in determining what resources are effective but also in identifying the inequalities in resources that matter to variation in outcomes.

The other conceptual development of this book is a dynamic approach to inequality. Most of our conceptions of equity, and most measures of inequality, are cross-sectional: they compare two individuals or two groups at one moment in time. Discussions of the achievement gap usually compare the scores of white students with those of African American and Latino students at a given moment, for example, while diatribes against inequalities in funding compare the wretched resources in urban schools with the sylvan conditions in wealthy suburbs, or the spending in high-wealth and low-wealth districts in a particular year.[9] It is difficult to think about inequality over time, partly because our conceptions of equity are cross-sectional (as I will clarify in chapter 6) and partly because the longitudinal data necessary to document inequality over time are rarely available.

What really counts for many dimensions of adult life, however, is dynamic inequality—the inequality among students that develops over the long years of elementary, secondary, and then postsecondary education. Students start school with initial differences, many of them related to class or family background, and these differences widen steadily (at least in this country). By twelfth grade, the differences among individuals are enormous: some students have dropped out and are still reading at the elementary school level, while others have accumulated many AP credits and are about to enter the best universities in the world. So to understand differences at grade 12—the last year of the data used in this study—we need to understand the trajectory of development from earlier grades, and in theory we need to know about school resources not just in grade 12 but in every year extending back to kindergarten and even earlier. The concept of dynamic inequality presented in chapter 6 guides additional statistical work in chapter 7, where it becomes clear that trajectories from eighth to tenth to twelfth grade do indeed diverge rather than converge and that the factors causing divergence are some of the same school resources, family resources, and demographic factors identified in earlier chapters. The development of new conceptual approaches, together with a more powerful data set, therefore allows us to understand more about the determinants of both school effectiveness and dynamic inequality than do prior efforts using cross-sectional educational production functions. Then the concern with correcting dynamic inequality leads, in chapter 8, to investigating how a sample of twelve schools is trying to enhance the learning of low-performing students, as a precursor to understanding how to correct these inequalities in part III.

Inequalities in schooling outcomes in the United States have been a persistent concern among advocates for nearly two centuries, ever since the charity schools of the early nineteenth century were established to educate the children of the poor. The 1960s were another period when the War on Poverty incorporated many efforts to help low-performing children, including Head Start and Title I—the compensatory efforts that have recently been reborn as the Elementary and Secondary Education Act of 2001, commonly known as No Child Left Behind (NCLB). But what is sometimes difficult to fathom is how unequal schooling outcomes are in this country, compared not against some ideal of all children achieving proficiency (whatever that might be), but compared to other countries and international competitors. The shocking truth is that, when compared to other developed countries, the United States has the highest level of inequality in educational outcomes as measured by either the Program in International Student Achievement (PISA) data—test scores for fifteen-year-olds in language and math—or the International Adult Literacy Survey (IALS) data.[10] We also have the highest level of earnings inequality, as figure I.1 illustrates. These patterns are due to social and political choices, many of which emerge in this volume: high levels of inequality in *effective* school resources (in chapters 1 and 2), the special problems we have with

Figure I.1   Inequality in Earnings and Education

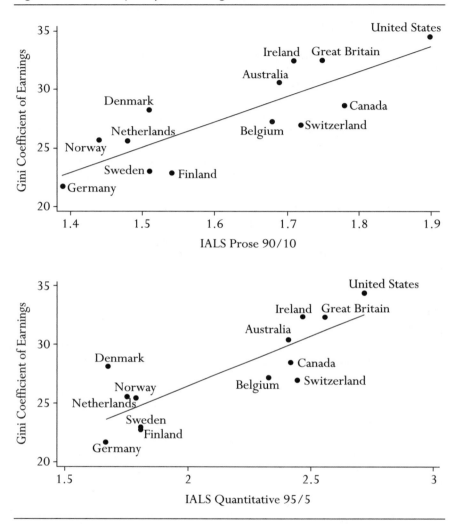

Sources: Inequality in earnings measured by the Gini coefficent is taken from Nickell (2004, table 9), which in turn comes from the Luxembourg Income Study data. Inequality in International Adult Literacy Survey (IALS) prose and quantitative literacy comes from the same source, taken from Organization for Economic Cooperation and Development (OECD 2001).

race and ethnicity in our educational systems (chapter 4), the varying commitment to schooling among students (chapter 5), the patterns of dynamic inequality that exacerbate differences over time (chapters 6 and 7), the fragmented and often ineffective policies for students who fall behind (chapter 8), and weak district and state policies despite some glimmers of improvement (chapters 9 and 10). In addition, a weak and deteriorating welfare state permits the substantial inequalities among families (chapter 12) that negatively affect schooling outcomes (chapter 4). In the United States, then, we have created a vicious circle between education inequality and social and economic inequality, each contributing to the other. Evidently other countries—especially the Scandinavian countries—have managed to create welfare and schooling systems in which inequality is much more moderate, creating a virtuous circle. I will not give a complete answer to why inequality of both kinds is so high in this country compared to others—this is not principally a book of international analysis—though there are more than enough reasons for high levels of inequality in both, and they generally reinforce one another.[11] But there is nothing inevitable about them, and the task we face—particularly if we believe the Education Gospel, with its emphasis on developing the skills of *everyone* in the country—is to moderate all these causes of inequality.

Exploring Ethnic and Racial Gaps

Statistical analysis clarifies not only what we can learn about the effectiveness of different resources but also what we do not yet know. The most troubling and enduring inequalities in this country have been the gaps in schooling outcomes for various racial and ethnic populations—gaps not only in the black-white test scores so frequently mentioned, but also in progress through high school, graduation from high school, and continuation to college (especially for Latinos and Native Americans). Even after considering many dimensions of family background (or class), all the variation we can identify in school resources, and other aspects of student behavior and engagement, racial and ethnic differences persist. These remaining and unexplained differences—what I call racial and ethnic residuals—require some interpretation, at least if we are ever to reduce the various racial and ethnic gaps that have been the subject of so much concern. With the help of the qualitative literature on schools, I conclude in chapter 4 that various forms of mistreating students may be responsible for much of this residual, including forms of correction and discipline, the tendency to ignore racial-minority students, lower expectations, and various forms of disparagement. This perspective leads in chapter 9 to proposals for a number of policies that would confront racial and ethnic issues directly—rather than start with a racial-ethnic analysis of achievement gaps and then pretend that the correctives need not consider race and ethnicity, as has usually been the case.

THE SPECIAL PLIGHT OF THE HIGH SCHOOL

The data used in this book describe students in eighth, tenth, and twelfth grades.[12] It covers the transition from middle school into high school and then the years when students are completing, or failing to complete, their high school program. The high school is a crucial juncture in the education system, the point at which differentiation and tracking create very different futures for students—elite colleges for a few, lower-status regional universities and community colleges for many more, unskilled work for some, and dropping out for an estimated 20 to 30 percent of students.[13] It has long been considered one of the most troubled levels of K–12 education, so any analysis that can illuminate potential strategies for making high schools more effective as well as more equitable is a boon, particularly as high schools wrestle with the need to increase passing rates on exit exams and improve rates of completion. Furthermore, the high school is one of the points in the educational system where there seems to be a sharp increase or "burst" in inequality, and reforming the high school is therefore crucial to resolving the problem of dynamic inequality.

Critiques of the high school started as early as the period after 1910, but complaints and commentary seem to have reached a crescendo recently: no fewer than twelve commission reports appeared in 2004 alone, and more are coming out all the time.[14] High school dropout rates have become more worrisome: the economic penalty for dropping out has increased; dropouts have a difficult (though not impossible) time getting back into the educational and economic mainstream; and dropout rates are clearly higher for black, Latino, Native American, immigrant, and working-class students. Many reformers have noted that, after nearly a century of calls for reform, the high school today looks much as it did in the late nineteenth century: dominated by conventional academic subjects; structured by Carnegie units devised in 1906; focused on preparation for college; largely insulated from real-world experiences; and as boring to most students as it was in the 1890s (Cremin 1961, ch. 1). Of course, there have been changes: the occupational purposes of high schools have become much more dominant (Grubb and Lazerson 2004); the distractions of youth culture have expanded; and racial-ethnic and class diversity has increased enormously from the early years of the twentieth century, when the high school was a decidedly elite institution. But from an educational standpoint, everything seems much as it was then, an "industrial-era institution" preparing students for a twenty-first-century world. Similarly, the historian Larry Cuban (1993) has noted how little teaching methods in high schools have changed over the past century, with behaviorist methods of information and fact transfer continuing to dominate, despite evidence in chapter 2 and from other sources that traditional methods of teaching are much less effective than innovative, constructivist, or balanced methods.[15]

However, proposals for what to do about high schools vary enormously, not surprisingly in a country where views about education are so different and schooling itself is so unequal. One camp concentrates on sticks: a number of proposals have called for new and more rigorous exams, or "benchmarks," keyed to "the knowledge and skills required for college and workplace success" by the American Diploma Project—as if the requirements for all colleges and workplaces were uniform. The most recent report invoking the Education Gospel, *Tough Choices or Tough Times*, proposes a board exam at the end of tenth grade that would direct students toward a community college, a four-year degree in a regional college, or further high school preparation leading to an elite four-year college. But it is unclear how this would enhance student motivation, make the high school a more engaging or personable place, or remedy the inequities that now exist in high school tracks and placement rather than reinforcing them with yet another testing mechanism.

Other camps have proposed different types of carrots, or efforts to transform high schools into more engaging experiences. Ideas include creating small schools where the environment is more personalized and students are better known and can be given closer attention; establishing "pathways" around themes (either broadly occupational or interdisciplinary) that would create more coherence and smaller schools-within-schools;[16] enhancing more engaging approaches to learning, including project-based learning and other active or participatory teaching; creating activities, such as internships and service learning, that get students out of the high school and into the world of adults; and ensuring adequate support services for students at risk of dropping out. The conclusions I reach in chapters 2, 4, and 5 about the effects of school resources, family resources, and the actions of students themselves clarify that many of the existing proposals stand little chance of improving high schools because they pay no attention to the school resources and practices that contribute to higher levels of learning and steady progress through high school. So the results in this book can help determine which approaches to high school reform have some chance of success and which are likely to fail, the subject of chapter 9.

I sometimes label the late-nineteenth-century approach to the high school the "default" model, because reforms revert to this familiar approach unless there is consistent pressure from teachers and leaders with a different vision, steady financing, stability in personnel, and consistent support from unions, parents, the district, the state, and other influences. The default approach is also the legacy of administrative progressivism, with its emphasis

on standardized quantities of schooling like Carnegie units, uniform procedures, a conventional curriculum with some differentiation to handle the diversity of students, and an assembly-line approach to schooling large numbers of students in impersonal ways. Many developments of the past fifteen
years, including more standardized testing, accountability at state and federal levels, and now high school exit exams, represent the full flowering of
administrative progressivism. But an alternative vision of the high school can
emerge, differentiated into alternative pathways or clusters or schools-
within-a-school, with richer goals as well as access to college, more collaboration among teachers and administrators, greater interaction with activities outside the school walls, and more attention to the nature of teaching
than now exists. The evidence in this book supports such an alternative,
though such reforms may prove difficult because the default model is so en-
trenched. I return to these different models of schooling in the final chapter.

THE PLAN OF THE BOOK

I use a variety of evidence throughout this book. Much of it is based on statistical analysis of the NELS88 data, although, to accommodate both readers
comfortable with statistical analysis and those with more policy and qualitative interests, I have tried to concentrate in the text on substantive conclusions and keep the technical details in the notes and appendices for those
who want to see it. Evidence corroborating these statistical results comes
from many sources: from the literature evaluating specific educational practices and approaches to teaching; from assessments of current school reform
models; from extensive ethnographic literature on how families influence
their children's preparation for schooling; and from problems that have
emerged in district, state, and federal policies that purport to improve education or redress inequities. These different forms of evidence have consistent implications and support narratives or visions of schooling that differ
significantly from conventional approaches to resources, inequality, the nature of the high school, and appropriate policies.

Part I: Implications of the Improved School Finance

Part I of this book develops the ideas of the improved school finance and
then applies these ideas with a powerful data set, the National Longitudinal
Survey of the Class of 1988. By and large, part I is analytic and descriptive,
leaving the normative and policy implications of these findings for part III.
Chapter 1 begins with observations of how often money is wasted in
schools—especially, I fear, in urban schools. This perspective clarifies that
the conversion of revenues into effective resources, or of wasted resources
into effective practices, is not a trivial task. The effects of money itself and

simple resources like credentialed teachers and class size are inadequate ways of describing what goes on within schools; in addition, compound, complex, and abstract resources must also be considered. Families and communities are resources for students, as the extensive literature on family background attests. Students themselves are also resources in the process of learning; their attitudes, behavior, and responses to distractions such as employment and television all affect how they take advantage of school resources and how much they benefit from schooling. Chapter 1 concludes with an elaborated model describing these influences on outcomes, opening up the black box of schooling.

Chapter 2 describes the NELS88 data, including the variety of compound, complex, and abstract resources derived from these data. The chapter then presents the basic effects of different resources, showing how many school resources are effective and creating in the process a complex agenda for high school reform (to which I return in chapter 9). Multiple outcome measures—some describing test scores; some measuring progress through high school, including graduation; and some reflecting student attitudes, such as educational aspirations, that are important for future decisions— indicate that the effects of school resources are far from uniform. Some resources affect all outcomes, whereas others influence test scores but not progress, or progress but not test scores. One implication is that the many existing analyses confined to the examination of test scores understate the potential of educational resources and improvement.

In chapter 3, I shift back to the money side of the problem, asking how levels of expenditures and patterns of revenues affect—or fail to affect—the resources identified as effective in chapter 2. By and large, expenditures affect simple resources, but only rarely the compound, complex, or abstract resources that are so influential. Instead, administrators and teachers need to work together to *construct* these latter types of resources at the school level. The vision to which this leads—of a collaborative high school, with leadership distributed among administrators, teachers, and others, and a greater concern with instructional issues—is very different from the nineteenth-century version of top-down management, efficiency concerns, isolated teachers, and the traditional approaches to instruction that emerged from administrative progressivism.

Chapter 4 examines the effects of family background, taking advantage of the different measures possible with NELS88. These measures clarify which family characteristics are important (especially parental education and aspirations for children) and which are surprisingly weak (such as income and family composition). In addition, the effects of demographic variables, including racial and ethnic variables, are presented. Because the causal mechanisms underlying these findings are sometimes ambiguous, the chapter also explores the qualitative literature on the effects of family background, noting the consistency between qualitative and quantitative findings. In the conclusion, I point out (as others have done) that equity in educational outcomes requires equalization of *both* educational resources *and* family resources, an issue I take up again in chapter 12.

In chapter 5, I address the role of students as resources, an "input" into schooling that is often ignored. The results will be unsurprising to parents and teachers alike. Conventional advice—do your homework, don't get into trouble, run with the right crowd, don't work too much outside of school but do participate in extracurricular activities—is all correct, since these behaviors affect various educational outcomes. Furthermore, student values about schooling and life goals can affect outcomes as well—particularly the view that schooling is primarily a route to better occupational opportunities, the foundation of the Education Gospel—clarifying another mechanism by which influences from beyond the school walls can affect outcomes. The chapter concludes with a discussion of steps that high schools can take to enhance student motivation, engagement, and ability to benefit from instruction.

Part II: Dynamic Inequality and the Effects of School Resources over Time

Part II looks at the problems of equity and dynamic inequality and what they imply for understanding schooling outcomes. Chapter 6 first presents an array of equity concepts, based on the distinctions among access, funding, resources, and outcomes of the improved school finance, partly to argue that battles over equity are often debates over different conceptions of what equity means. I then develop conceptions of dynamic inequality and dynamic equity, to move away from the cross-sectional conceptions that dominate most work on equity in schooling, including the old school finance.

This leads in turn to estimating, in chapter 7, growth models or trajectories that confirm two predictions associated with dynamic inequality. The first is that there is substantial divergence in test scores from eighth to tenth to twelfth grades associated with familiar influences like family background and race, ethnicity, and gender. The second is that a "burst" of inequality is associated with moving from middle school into high school. In addition, the results discussed in this chapter confirm that the school resources identified as effective in chapter 2 influence not only *levels* of outcomes but also *growth rates*—again supporting the idea that school resources make a great deal of difference to outcomes.

In chapter 8, I shift from quantitative to qualitative analysis of dynamic inequality and examine how twelve schools have wrestled with students who have fallen behind grade-level norms. These schools have acted in ways that vary enormously, both in nature and in scope, with many fragmented and uncoordinated efforts. Despite this variation, most follow a small number of rationales, or theories of action. Many depend on specific interventions or curricular programs of doubtful effectiveness, especially when judged by the NELS88 results. Overall, the efforts that schools and districts are making to counter inequality over time are fragmented and ineffective, though a few schools are pursuing strategies of greater promise. The chapter concludes by clarifying what a goal of dynamic equity would require of schools.

Part III: Implications for School Practice, Education Policy, and Litigation

Part III outlines the implications of all this work for school practice; for education policy at the district, state, and federal levels; and for the litigation that has played such an important role in school reform. Chapter 9 summarizes the implications of the preceding chapters about the ways in which high schools could marshal resources to enhance educational outcomes. A series of "natural experiments," for which schools have been given additional funding, clarifies that schools have wasted much of this funding or spent it in ineffective ways, confirming the theory of waste developed in chapter 1. The results discussed in chapters 2 and 7 imply that wasteful practices need to be replaced by a series of compound, complex, and abstract resources, some of which affect many outcomes, some of which are necessary to improve learning and test scores, and some of which improve progress through high school but not learning. In addition, the analysis of the racial-ethnic residual from chapter 4 implies the need to address racial and ethnic issues head on; the several ways in which chapter 9 illustrates how to do this constitute other kinds of complex resources. One implication, particularly given the collective nature of most resources, is that schools need to be restructured and decisionmaking procedures need to be changed if collective decisions are to be made and money spent wisely. The last section of chapter 9 outlines how this might happen, including implications for the preparation of teachers and principals.

Chapter 10 explores the policies that districts, states, and the federal government could adopt that would enhance the ability of schools to make effective choices about resources. The dominant strategies for districts and states emerging from administrative progressivism have included additional funding in the interests of equalization, categorical funding to increase purchases of resources considered especially worthwhile or effective (like computers, or books, or professional development), and various requirements, of which state and federal accountability are recent examples.[17] However, improved approaches to school resources indicate that the incentives to improve cannot work unless schools have the capacity to mobilize resources in new ways. The improved school finance therefore provides a clear conception of capacity-building—one that increases the varied resources that have been identified as effective *and* that reorganizes schools so that they can make these decisions collectively. Then the challenge for districts, states, and even the federal government is to support this form of capacity-building. Recent evidence from reforming districts indicates a number of ways in which some districts have managed to enhance the capacities of schools. And just as reforming schools often follow the approaches of distributed leadership and internal accountability, similar approaches to *district* organization and decisionmaking create more support for reforming schools. The chapter goes on to explore how states and the federal government might remedy the problems of dynamic inequality, since individual schools cannot by themselves resolve some of these problems, particularly transitions among levels of schooling and the resulting "bursts" in inequality.

In chapter 11, I discuss litigation, which has been an important method for pursuing educational equity and for reforming school finance. The first section poses a central dilemma about litigation: while it often works in the sense of overturning inequitable or racist or exclusionary practices, it is also a confession that conventional political or legislative solutions do not and cannot work. But when litigation requires either legislation or cooperation to be implemented appropriately, we get right back to the political settings that created the need for litigation in the first place. Not surprisingly, then, litigation is often ineffective over the long run. In the realm of school finance, evidence from the past three decades indicates that litigation has led to improved equity in *expenditures* in a few states, but it has not successfully achieved equity in important school *resources* or equity in *outcomes*. The implication, particularly in light of the resources that matter in the improved school finance, is that current litigation efforts will remain relatively ineffective unless a new kind of relationship is forged between litigators and educators—a relationship that is just barely visible in three recent court cases.

The conclusion draws together the implications of this book for effectiveness and equity. Overall, the results indicate that several shifts in thinking about schools, especially high schools, would be valuable. One shift is from the conventional myth of money and the "old" school finance to a conception of the improved school finance, with its broader conception of resources. Because many of the resources are collective, a second necessary shift is a new vision of how schools are structured, how decisions are made more collectively, and how leadership is distributed among a variety of teachers and administrators—rather than the model derived from administrative progressivism in which leadership and power are held by the principal, usually acting under the district's direction. A third shift, specific to the high school, is one from the "default" model to one that allows for more variation, more innovative and experiential teaching, more integration across subjects and collaboration across teachers, and more connections with the world outside the high school. These all imply basic reforms in the default conception of schooling that emerged from administrative progressivism, reforms that are concerned with effectiveness more than with efficiency, with the quality of instruction more than with administrative uniformity, with constructivist or balanced instruction more than with the conventional behaviorist teaching that has been so resistant to change in the high school.

In addition, the conclusion examines briefly the kinds of non-educational policies necessary to counter the effects of inequality among families and communities. This is in some way a digression from the emphasis in this book on school resources and school reforms. But having introduced families as resources for schooling, and students and their commitment as other resources, it would be irresponsible not to mention some of the non-educational policies of the welfare state that might moderate the inequality in earnings in figure I.1 or those dimensions of family inequality explored in chapters 4 and 5.

Establishing new conceptions of educational practices and new narratives is hard work. It requires the collaborative effort of many individuals, from teachers to state and federal policymakers to researchers. The default approaches to schooling are powerful, and any relaxation of effort is likely to lead to backsliding as schools revert to older visions and myths. But with a shift to a different vision, schools have new opportunities to become both more effective and more equitable, a combination that otherwise will remain elusive.

Part I

Implications of the Improved School Finance

Chapter 1

Moving Beyond Money: The Variety of Educational Resources

DESPITE THE demands of generations of reformers for more funding, there are too many puzzles in the myth of money to ignore. The substantial increases in spending throughout the last century have neither reduced the need for reforms nor eliminated many inequalities in resources and outcomes. States and districts have poured substantial sums into reforms, but some of these funds have accomplished little; some expensive initiatives have been ineffective, and sustaining real reform has been difficult. A long series of efforts to demonstrate the effects of conventional resources—smaller class size, greater teacher experience, more overall spending per pupil—have generated ambiguous results, sometimes leading to the facile conclusion that money and school resources do not make a difference. Arguing again for more money might lead simply to more spending increases without the resolution of underlying problems.

So it is inadequate merely to debate the level and distribution of funding, as the "old" school finance has usually done. Instead it is necessary to develop an *improved* approach to school resources—including not just money but all of the conditions, practices, and personnel within schools that might enhance outcomes—as well as an improved approach to judging the effectiveness of school resources.[1] To do this, I first review in this chapter the dominant literatures examining resources and their effectiveness. Next I turn to more practice-based and anecdotal evidence about waste in schools to develop a conception of why waste seems so pervasive, particularly (it seems) in urban schools.

I then examine how we might conceptualize the effective use of resources, introducing a set of precepts or conditions quite different from the assumptions of the "old school finance. With these precepts in mind, I distinguish between funding—expenditures per pupil, for example—and resources, or those inputs to schooling that dollars can only *potentially* buy. Furthermore, I distinguish among *simple* resources (like class size), *compound* resources (like class size reduction plus staff development), *complex* resources (like pedagogical approaches), and *abstract* resources (like school climate and stability). A final precept is that students are themselves resources and that several of their characteristics contribute to their own and their peers' learning.

The idea of expanding the conception of educational resources well beyond funding is based partly on the conceptions about the causality of resource effects that are discussed in the third section of this chapter. The purpose is to reframe old questions in new ways and to establish a revised perspective that leads to different kinds of research, practice, and policy. While some of them are not particularly novel, the extent of these perspectives has been limited.[2] Most analyses of school resources still concentrate on dollars spent rather than on how resources are used, even when they attempt to determine *how* money matters (see, for example, Ladd, Chalk, and Hansen 1999). Principals and other school leaders seem to pay little attention to the educational efficacy of their spending decisions (Boyd and Hartman 1988), and leadership preparation programs include very little about how to spend money effectively. Some popular reforms like class size reduction cost huge sums but pay little attention to how changes might affect student learning; as a result, they often fail to accomplish anything. So it is worth continuing to define effective resources and clarifying the links (often tenuous to nonexistent) between spending and effective resources, since improved approaches to school resources will dominate only when most educators, policymakers, and researchers embrace them.

Few educators like to think much about money. It is dross, or straw, or filthy lucre that impedes thinking about loftier goals like educating all children to the limits of their potential. But money is also necessary if we are to produce the educational results that educators and parents and policymakers want; no one can build a schoolhouse or hire a teacher or buy a textbook without money. The provision of the bare minimum resources to create schools is no longer the issue, as it was in the nineteenth century; greater effectiveness and equity are now more important. The conversion of revenues into educational outcomes should not be magical, like Rumpelstiltskin helping the miller's daughter spin straw into gold. Rethinking school resources requires moving away from alchemy toward a clearer understanding of the requirements for effective school spending.

CONVERTING RESOURCES TO RESULTS: OPENING THE BLACK BOX

Several areas of research have wrestled with the effectiveness of school re-sources, particularly attempting to link education outcomes to inputs. Like production functions in economics, educational production functions are an effort to describe this connection, both conceptually and empirically—at least since the Coleman Report of 1966 linked educational outcomes (read-ing scores) to inputs—but without being precise about the process of "pro-duction," that is, about the nature of teaching and learning.

The most common production function can be simply represented as a simple equation:

$$\text{schooling outcomes} = f(\text{school resources, family background}) + u \quad (1.1)$$

where schooling outcomes potentially include more than test scores, school resources includes expenditures per pupil but potentially many other kinds of simple, compound, complex, and abstract resources, family background reflects the myriad effects of families and communities, f represents a func-tion (usually linear) linking school resources and family background to out-comes, and u is an error term representing what is unexplained by school resources and family background. This particular model of schooling does little to describe what happens within schools; as many have noted, it leaves the learning process as a black box with various external influences on it—as in figure 1.1. Resources are those that can be readily measured—spend-ing per pupil, pupil-teacher ratios, teacher experience, sometimes teacher "ability" or knowledge as measured through test scores, and other school re-sources like library books and science labs. Outcomes have invariably been measured only by test scores. Such equations have been estimated with many different data sources, and a large literature for developing countries reproduces many of the American conclusions.[3]

The finding that the effects of resources are statistically insignificant more often than not has often been interpreted crudely as showing that "school re-sources don't make a difference." After various technical debates, the upshot has been the relatively weak statement that money and other resources might matter under some conditions (Hanushek 1997; Hanushek et al. 1994). This suggests that the challenge in developing alternative approaches is to specify the conditions that make resources effective—and by exten-sion, that some resources (including money) may be necessary but not suffi-cient (NBNS).

However, a careful rereading of Hanushek's summary results suggests

Figure 1.1   The "Black Box": Conventional Production Functions

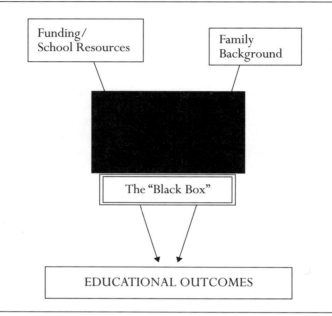

Funding/
School Resources

Family
Background

The "Black Box"

EDUCATIONAL OUTCOMES

Source: Author's compilation.

why so many studies have found simple school resources to be ineffective. If instructors continue to teach the same way in smaller classes, then class size reduction may have no effect; indeed, a random-assignment study of smaller classes in Toronto found that few teachers changed their behavior (Shapson et al. 1980), reinforcing the findings of Richard Murnane and Frank Levy (1996), who examined fifteen classrooms in Austin, Texas. Similarly, if some experienced teachers become skilled while others are burned out and are detrimental to students' learning (Henry et al. 2008)—a common problem facing principals with an aging teacher workforce—then without ascertaining the practices among experienced teachers, experience may have no effect on average. If teacher education is concerned with content knowledge but fails to improve pedagogical practices, as has been a special problem for high school teachers oriented toward their disciplines (Cuban 1993), then it might not influence the quality of instruction. So resources are likely to be NBNS, and the conditions for sufficiency can be examined only by looking *inside classrooms* to determine the nature of instruction—to see whether experienced teachers seem burned out or sophisticated and whether or not teachers in smaller classes teach in different ways to encourage improved participation from students. The a priori reasons for thinking that these simple resources are effective turn out to be weak once we recognize the complexities of schools and classrooms.

A second problem is that even those studies that find resources to be effective cannot tell *why* resources might make a difference. For example, Ronald Ferguson's analysis of Texas districts found that having teachers with high scores on a test of general knowledge led to higher test scores among their students, but the author acknowledged that "we can only speculate what teachers with high scores do differently from teachers with low scores" (1991, 477). Possible explanations for the success of smaller classes in a Tennessee experiment have included greater teacher morale, more teacher-student interaction, more student participation, greater effectiveness of small classes in socializing young children to school, and improvements in student engagement (Finn, Pannozzo, and Achilles 2003). The reason behind success matters a great deal. For example, if smaller classes enable teachers to socialize their students better, then resources should be concentrated in the early grades. If instead small classes create more student engagement, then middle and high school grades—when motivation and engagement flag for many students—might benefit more from smaller classes.

Overall, then, the approach of simple production functions, embedded in equation 1.1 and figure 1.1, has generated a number of puzzles and few clues about why some school resources might not matter. But both the conceptual approach to the effectiveness of resources and the resulting empirical research need to be elaborated before we can understand much more about what creates effective schools.

THE POLITICAL ECONOMY OF WASTE: IMPLICATIONS FOR RESOURCE USE

Contrary to the assumptions of most reformers and to the myth of money that additional spending automatically leads to improved outcomes, other insights emerge from observations about the ways in which education funds are misspent. Many forms of waste come up routinely in discussions among teachers, principals, and reformers, though not in most school finance literature.[4] Here are some examples:

1. Funds can be embezzled or spent to hire incompetent friends and relatives.

2. Funds can be spent on inputs that have no effect—sometimes for incompetent teachers and other staff (a problem in every organization), sometimes for what economists call rents (like increases in salaries that do not call forth greater teacher effort or reduce turnover), and sometimes for

worthless inputs like textbooks, supplies, or computers that remain unused by teachers who did not want them.

3. Resources can be used without changing practices—as when weak and old-fashioned forms of staff development fail to change how teachers teach, or when reforms fail to change long-established practice.

4. Funds can be spent on purely symbolic practices, for public relations value rather than for effectiveness. For example, a new retention program may be established or a new superintendent hired simply to assure parents that everything possible is being done, not because these practices are effective.

5. Resources can be spent on well-intentioned but ineffective practices—adopting simple-minded forms of "technology," for instance, or following the reform du jour which turns out to have no effect on learning. Alternatively, resources may be spent on practices with the potential for improvement, but the schools neglect the crucial features that make them effective. For example, after-school and tutoring programs are likely to be effective when instructors are well trained, where there is a coherent vision of their purpose, when the programs are connected to regular classrooms, and when they use motivating approaches to teaching—but not when schools throw students who are lagging in classrooms together with untrained high school graduates who have no instructional plans and no connections to regular classrooms. An after-school program turns out to be a compound and complex resource rather than a simple practice of hiring a few aides and tutors.

6. Resources may be spent on changes with potential long-run benefits—like improving school climate, changing the approach to instruction within a school, or developing committed teacher-leaders. Then, if other changes take place—a new principal or superintendent is hired, a different reform du jour is adopted, turnover occurs among teachers, the state shifts its priorities—the resources spent earlier are effectively wasted. This implies that, with changes that take some time to develop, the stability of personnel and reforms is itself a resource, though one that is usually overlooked. Indeed, instability breeds more instability, since teachers and principals are likely to burn out at schools with too much commotion; stability is therefore a precarious resource.

7. Spending resources piecemeal may fail to lead to coherent change. This happens, for example, when schools spend money without an overall plan, when they have to spend money quickly at the end of the year, when categorical grants are used for peripheral changes that do not improve a school's core teaching or further a central vision, or when materials or staff development funds are allocated to individual teachers to spend independently rather than to a schoolwide priority.

8. Resources may be spent on changes that are necessary but not by themselves sufficient—purchasing computers without providing teacher training

and maintenance, alleviating chaos (or creating a positive school climate) without improving teaching, reducing class sizes without sufficiently training teachers, or hiring instructional aides without putting them to good use.

9. All too often, it seems, principals and other school leaders (like school-site councils) are ignorant of the resources they have, of the funds over which they have control, and of ways of thinking about money, resources, and the relationships between the two. Their preparation programs usually neglect any broad ways of thinking about resources and treat finance and budgeting (if they are treated at all) as technical issues of what budget codes to use and how to use various spreadsheets.[5] Many districts provide little discretionary funding to schools, so principals have few incentives to invest time in learning about their budgets and resource alternatives. Even when they instigate school-based budgeting (SBB), districts usually train principals in the spreadsheets and computer tools necessary for submitting their budgets, not in how to think about which resources are effective and how to enhance them. Many urban principals are overwhelmed by discipline issues, angry parents, and district demands and too distracted to pay much attention to resources (or to instruction, for that matter); an appalling number of them unload budgeting chores onto administrative assistants.[6] But it is hard to know how to eliminate waste, how to identify ways of reallocating resources to more effective uses, or how to institute reforms that require additional resources if principals are ignorant about the resources in their schools.

10. Particularly in urban schools, including the schools that are trying to narrow inequality, a good deal of spending at the margin represents second-chance efforts, that is, programs to teach students the academic capacities they failed to learn the first time around. On the one hand, the existence of so many second-chance programs in the United States is heartening because they provide individuals with several chances to succeed—another dimension of the American Dream. However, second-chance programs almost by definition operate under difficult circumstances. Some students have experienced mistreatment or failure in earlier schooling that makes them resistant to "more of the same." Peer effects work in counterproductive ways, since second-chance programs bring together groups of students who have not done well, rather than mixing them with more successful and higher-performing students. And for high schools, teaching basic academic, conceptual, and personal skills in short periods of time to students who have not learned them in eight years of regular schooling is self-evidently difficult: such programs are often asked to make many years of gains in one year or less. So it is not surprising to find that many second-chance efforts are ineffective despite the amount of money involved; the review of such school efforts in chapter 8 only reinforces this point. As educators, we can only be ambivalent about second chances; the best alternative would be not to need them.

The reasons for waste surely vary among schools and districts, but they generally fall into four groups. First, in the first three categories described here, spending money leads to no change; second, in the next five categories, practices change, but the changes are in the end ineffective, for reasons varying from a choice of the wrong reform to lack of planning to expenditures that are NBNS. In the case of principal ignorance about budgets and resources, these administrators lack the technical competence to reallocate resources from conventional practices, from the historic or "default" uses of money to more effective uses. And the ambiguity of second-chance solutions is simply a structural feature of schools that are trying hard (if often unsuccessfully) to "leave no child behind." The challenge is to use funding *both* to change practices *and* to make the kinds of changes that matter to outcomes.

Third, in positing a simple relationship between revenues and schooling outcomes, as in figure 1.1, there are special problems with non-instructional expenditures. Some of these (for transportation and safety measures) are necessary but can never enhance learning. The goals they promote (student safety, for example, or simply getting students to school) are crucial to parents and children but are rarely included among educational outcomes. Other goals (like improving the physical conditions of schools) can lead to increased learning if students have been bothered by heat, cold, noise, poor lighting, disgusting bathrooms, or crumbling buildings (Corley 2002; Sandel 2002) or if instructors have been constrained by inadequate space or inadequate lab equipment. But beyond some point, increasing these expenditures is unlikely to further increase learning. Administrative spending is widely excoriated as "bloat," necessarily wasteful, but some administrative spending is necessary to keep schools functioning. Furthermore, under special conditions (NBNS, once again), more administrative resources can enhance effectiveness; for example, multiple principals at a school may increase attention to instruction and to student support services (Grubb and Flessa 2006). The frequent calls for principals to become instructional leaders also imply that increased spending for administration may, if used in particular ways, improve learning and motivation. Some non-instructional resources, including extracurricular activities and certain student support services, are intended to strengthen motivation and progress through high school (see Marsh and Kleitman 2002; National Research Council 2004, ch. 6), but they do not affect learning and may therefore be viewed as ineffective in research limited to test scores. So some non-instructional resources are necessary, and others under the right conditions enhance student engagement, but they may also become forms of waste. An obvious implication is that measures of outcomes other than test scores may be critical, since some resources may affect outcomes like motivation, persistence, and progress rather than test scores.

Finally, there are problems about short-run versus long-run effects that are both difficult to detect and may lead in the end to waste. Usually reformers believe that their innovations have long-run effects—for example, that a tutoring program for third-graders or coaching for fifth-grade teachers or Reading Recovery (as its name implies) has permanent effects. But long-term research is expensive, especially for random-assignment research, so we know very little about long-run effects. If a reform has only short-run effects, *and* if there are no follow-up reforms, then funds spent on it are wasted over the long run. I return to this problem in chapter 6 when I examine the question of short-run versus long-run effects on learning trajectories and dynamic inequality (see especially figure 6.3).

What is troubling about public schools is not that they occasionally misspend resources, as every institution and every family does, but that they seem structured to do so. The sources of waste identified here arise not primarily from venality or stupidity or carelessness (though these characteristics may be found in any organization), but from several structural features of public education.

First, public education (like most public activities) is driven by conventional interest group politics—a struggle for scarce public resources based on the power of interest groups rather than on the rightness of the cause. The constituency for jobs is often more powerful than that for improved educational performance, and so battles over the level and distribution of spending (on teachers, for example) rather than over the promotion of learning often dominate educational politics—the kind of problem that causes participants to comment that education ought to be above politics. (Unions are often considered to be special culprits here.) In addition, education seems especially prone to symbolic politics, like the state and federal policy rhetoric around holding schools accountable, the practices of "naming and shaming" low-performing school, and the rhetoric in the federal No Child Left Behind (NCLB) Act that "all children can learn." These tactics cannot by themselves improve educational outcomes; they are instead designed to show taxpayers—and especially the anti-taxers expressing "hidebound conservatism and niggardly parsimony"—that policymakers are demanding more of schools and students. Ironically, symbolic policies may themselves waste resources and degrade effectiveness—for example, when students who are retained fail to learn any more the second time in a grade and end up dropping out, or when state and federal accountability measures undermine learning, or when the general expansion of state, federal, and court mandates makes it impossible for schools to operate as effectively as they could (Wise 1979).

Second, some characteristics of schools as organizations make it difficult to impose changes on schools and teachers. Loose coupling, or the ability of teachers to pursue their own agendas when the classroom door is closed, makes it difficult to require or mandate reform. The relative independence of teachers means that the curriculum and instruction and methods vary from class to class, from school to school, from district to district. As students move through the system, they find themselves in inconsistent classrooms, often repeating material from earlier grades or lacking the prerequisites for what they are supposed to be learning. Of course, state standards are supposed to eliminate such variation, but they often fail to do so—creating not only inconsistency and waste but also greater inequalities over time. Reforms that require jointly necessary changes, rather than piecemeal reform, are particularly difficult under the conditions in many schools where disagreements over goals and pedagogies, instability in personnel, and inconsistencies in conceptions of roles may prevent making a series of coordinated decisions. The potential lack of agreement leads in turn to inconsistency or misalignment as different participants stress different aspects of reform or try to use resources in different ways. And organizational inertia, or the difficulty in changing organizations with long-standing practices and conservative cultures, means that a great deal of energy and many resources are necessary to change schools. In the current fiscal climate, the lack of slack resources—time and energy for teachers to reexamine their own practices or for school leaders to institute reforms rather than just respond to daily crises—inhibits teachers and administrators from changing practices. Ironically, then, especially low levels of resources may lead to *less* effective schools not only by reducing the resources (like teachers, staff development, or materials) that money can buy but also by reducing the "invisible" or abstract resource of cooperation—a resource that proves crucial to reforming instruction in schools. The inertia of all institutions constrains even the best-designed reforms.

Third, the pedagogical complexity of schooling can lead to a different inconsistency or misalignment within classrooms. For example, teachers skilled in more constructivist or "balanced" teaching methods are not effective if students have been prepared only in behaviorist classrooms. As another example, students who think of their education in highly instrumental and vocationalist terms may themselves thwart the efforts of instructors to develop deeper understanding (see Cox 2004; Pope 2001). If there needs to be an equilibrium between teachers' approaches and students' expectations, then neither is effective without the other. More generally, where there are differences among the four basic elements of the classroom—teacher practices; student understanding of schooling and pedagogy; the curriculum, including elements coming from outside the classroom; and the larger institution, including school-level administrators and also district, state, and federal pressures—instruction is compromised in one way or another.[7] This is another version of NBNS: imposing a new curriculum without preparing teachers, or shifting pedagogy without resocializing students, is unlikely to be effective.

Fourth, the history of schools imposes its own weight. Most revenues (more than 80 percent of total expenditures) are locked up in salaries and benefits covered by contracts and cannot be changed at all in the short run; even in the long run, changes cannot take place without bitter political battles (especially battles with unions). Other resources that are embedded in school buildings and land are difficult and expensive to reconfigure. The dominant conceptions of "school" limit the abilities of reformers to shift resources too wildly; this is a problem even in charter schools, where nonstandard practices may cause resistance from parents accustomed to more conventional conceptions of school. Furthermore, without continuous effort, reforms are likely to collapse back to the default model of schooling, as has happened with proposals to experiment radically with deschooling or experiential education. In practice, then, incremental budgeting reigns, with only marginal changes from year to year. Many reforms end up being more of the same, and if the old configurations of resources were not particularly effective, the new ones will not be either.

Finally, school finance litigation, which has been such a powerful attempt to alter spending patterns, is necessarily a crude instrument of policy. Courts can forbid practices but often cannot (or will not) specify what *should* take place. The remedies that legislatures have developed in response usually reallocate dollars through changes in finance formulas—the minutiae of school reform—without providing much direction about finding effective uses of these dollars. This has reinforced a tendency to see the problem as one of spending levels and redistribution—consistent with the money myth—rather than as one of effectively using the resources that exist. To be sure, a few states have responded to school finance lawsuits by revising state policy substantially rather than just by changing spending patterns, and such efforts might help districts and schools to spend money wisely. But only with the recent *Williams* case in California have litigation remedies been stated in terms of potentially effective *resources* rather than *dollars*.

The Special Case of Urban and Low-Income Districts

So it is easy to develop a conception of resource use that identifies the deeply rooted structural conditions—political, organizational, pedagogical, historical, and legal—that undermine the effective use of funding. Furthermore, my working hypothesis—meriting much more investigation, to be sure—is that these conditions are worse in urban and low-income districts. The issue is not one of simple funding levels, since urban districts on the whole have slightly higher expenditures per pupil than do suburban districts. In

2003–2004, for example, central-city schools spent $7,812 per pupil compared to $7,542 in suburban schools (and $7,268 in all public schools). At the same time, this slightly higher level of spending did not lead to more real resources: central-city schools had higher numbers of students per teacher (15.0 versus 14.6), lower teacher salaries ($45,400 versus $46,100), a higher proportion of schools with temporary buildings (37.7 percent versus 34.4 percent), and a higher proportion of schools using common spaces for instruction (21.3 percent versus 19 percent).[8]

Rather than overall inadequacy of funding, urban districts suffer from multiple problems that make it more likely that they will waste resources and fail to translate the funding they do have into effective resources. One includes the sharper political disagreements and lack of consensus about supporting public schools that Clarence Stone (2001) has labeled the lack of civic capacity. The many battles over mayoral control of schools provide obvious examples of reforms simply stopping while basic governance issues are resolved. Political disagreements often take racial forms because different racial and ethnic groups compete for resources and attention, a less serious problem in more homogeneous suburban and rural areas, and greater numbers of advocacy groups contend for influence over urban schools compared to suburban and rural areas. Resource-starved communities in low-income central cities are more likely to view schools as sources of employment; this perspective undermines the commitment to learning as the sole purpose of schooling and then leads to calls to "put schools above politics." Union conflicts seem to be especially bitter in urban communities, perhaps because bread-and-butter unionism focused on salaries and employment conditions predominates over professional unionism, which is focused more on professional issues like instruction.[9] Symbolic politics is likely to be especially acute because the depth of problems and racial conflicts make real solutions difficult and symbolism attractive. Instability and turnover—of teachers and principals and district administrators and policies as well as of students—make institutional change more difficult. The lack of consensus within schools, tense personal relationships (see, for example, Ballou 1998; Payne 1997; Payne and Kaba 2001), and the absence of slack resources appear to be worse than in suburban or rural schools. The pedagogical issues in teaching low-income students, as well as large numbers of immigrant and special education students, are especially difficult, while teachers are more likely to lack experience and credentials.

The problem is not only that funding and other resources are inadequate to the educational and non-educational needs of urban students, but also that structural conditions may make urban districts unable to do as much with the resources they have. These are conditions under which more funding might well be ineffective and the reform of structural conditions may be necessary before money can be spent effectively.

AN IMPROVED APPROACH: MOVING AWAY FROM INEFFECTIVE SPENDING

There are several ways out of the dilemma of ineffective spending, including both research-based and practice-based possibilities. If we knew with some certainty what practices are effective, then we could concentrate funds on specific uses and reforms. This is the impulse behind the enormous and growing literature on "what works," starting with the Obey-Porter Comprehensive School Reform Demonstration legislation of 1997, which provided federal funds for "proven practices," and continuing with the What Works Clearinghouse of the Institute of Education "Sciences" (IES). This logic also motivates the allocation of categorical funds for specific (and presumably effective) practices ranging from Head Start to school lunches; the efforts of foundations to replicate successful models; and the creation by reformers of networks of schools that move their promising practices to scale, from Comer schools, which provide a variety of community supports, to "Accelerated Schools" to small schools. It is also the impulse underlying the research I report in this book, since the school resources identified in chapters 2 and 7 as effective then lead to recommendations for school, district, state, and federal policy in part 3.

But coming up with a list of "proven practices" has been both difficult and contentious. One effort to identify what works—the inventory of the American Institutes for Research (AIR 1999) of twenty-four schoolwide reforms—reported "substantial" evidence of success for only three of these school reforms. Of those three, one ("High Schools That Work") had no comparative research; another ("Direct Instruction") was evaluated only by standardized tests well suited to its emphasis on specific skills and has since been challenged by other research; and a third ("Success for All") has had highly contentious evaluations. The effectiveness of the major federal programs—particularly Chapter I and bilingual education—has been extremely controversial, the latter for political as well as technical reasons. The methodology of evaluations involves endless debates, and the current efforts of the Institute of Education "Sciences" to promote random-assignment research over other quantitative and qualitative methods have been controversial. At the same time, because controlled experiments in education are so difficult and have always been resisted (Cook 2000), hard-nosed analysts can always claim that some aspect of student or school selection is responsible for any positive results. The networks of reforming schools all acknowledge that the fidelity of reform varies enormously, making it difficult to distinguish the effectiveness of the reform idea from the quality of its implementation. Finally, the need for "proven practices" raises the unavoidable question of what we want education to be. Do we want to measure outcomes

with standardized tests of grammar facts and decontextualized math problems, or with analytic writing and problem-solving abilities? Do we want to
concentrate on a sparse set of cognitive outcomes—reading and math—or
do we want schools to develop a range of competencies or "intelligences"
(Gardner [1983]1993)? The notion of "proven practices" cannot be disentangled from discussions about what education is all about; indeed, the need to
cast "proof" in quantitative terms requires unambiguous outcome variables.
So the search for "what works" will surely continue, but it is hard to imagine
marshaling universally accepted proof.

In the absence of "proof," we have usually placed resources in the hands of
people who might know what is effective. Conventionally, school boards
have been given this power, though they usually delegate authority to superintendents. Sometimes, in site-based budgeting, the decisionmakers are
principals, or principals with school-site councils. In other cases, as in
vouchers and choice mechanisms, parents are given more control, if only
through choice and exit. Recently states have played more active roles, with
state tests for students or teachers, state standards and curriculum guides,
staff development and pre-service education requirements. The federal government has resources too, and in some legislation Congress has expressed
its conception of effective resource use—the Obey-Porter legislation, or
the requirement to integrate academic and vocational education in vocational education, or the Reading First program in No Child Left Behind, or
the What Works Clearinghouse with its insistence on experimental or quasi-
experimental evidence. Courts often intervene, particularly in desegregation cases and special education. But each of these implicit decisions about
who can best decide the effective use of resources has its own limitations.
Principals, school-site councils, school boards, superintendents, districts,
and state and federal policymakers are all distracted from instructional concerns by other political and administrative issues (Cuban 1988); they may
have limited information about instructional alternatives, they may hold on
dearly to simple and favorite solutions (class size reduction, instructional
aides) despite contrary evidence; or they may have different priorities for
outcomes, returning us to the structural problems identified in the theory of
waste. And the implicit delegation of power to so many levels of government
as well as the courts has led to the "bureaucratization of the American classroom" (Wise 1979): no one has complete authority, and the search for effective resources is often drowned in other agendas.

So neither the research-based approach to finding "what works" nor the
practice-based approach of identifying who might make the best resource
decisions can extract us from the structural problems associated with spending money effectively. A Deweyan distaste for either/or solutions might suggest that some synthesis is preferable to either alternative—for example, a
search for varied evidence about what works under what conditions, to-

gether with resource decisions by those at the school level who are most familiar with the conditions of students and their communities. Such an approach might also allow educators to confront both the central questions of improved approaches to school resources: how resources are spent at the school and classroom levels and whether they are spent on effective practices. But in searching for some way forward, there is no substitute for confronting the reasons why resources often go for naught.

PRECEPTS FOR AN IMPROVED APPROACH TO SCHOOL RESOURCES

Earlier sections of this chapter, based on interpretations of research and on the implications of practice, provide a number of guidelines for an improved approach to school finance and the use of resources. We can usefully break these into four primary precepts:

1. *Understanding how effectively or ineffectively resources are used requires observation in the classroom.* One obvious conclusion is that it is necessary to enter the classroom and the school—through classroom observation and measurement—in order to see how resources are used. Otherwise, it is impossible to distinguish a skilled and experienced teacher from a burned-out and experienced teacher; to see what changes in instruction have been caused by class size reduction, or staff development, or new standards, or a new curriculum, or any other change; or to see whether resources that are not easily measured—strong leadership, for example, or consistency of pedagogical approaches—are present.

2. *Funding must result in changes that affect outcomes of interest.* A second conclusion is that effective spending requires a two-stage process. Contrary to the forms of waste identified in the previous section, funding must first result in changes, and *then* those changes, to avoid being ineffective, must affect outcomes of interest. The decision for any school, then, is to first ascertain those practices within schools and classrooms that enhance learning or educational progress, and then to allocate resources (including but not limited to money) to ensure that these practices are carried out, rather than using resources in ways that are ineffective or fail to change practice.

3. *Many resources are necessary but not sufficient.* A third conclusion is that many resources are necessary but not sufficient (NBNS). Class size reduction requires an adequate supply of able teachers, computer use requires the professional development of teachers, changes in teacher practices should be accompanied by changes in student conceptions of learning, and so on.

This conclusion leads in turn to thinking of resources in four categories. *Simple* resources are components of expenditure per pupil and can usually be recognized from the simple identity:

$$\text{Expenditure per pupil} \equiv (\text{teachers/pupils}) \, (\text{average teacher salary}) + \text{admin\$/pupil} + \text{materials\$/pupil} + \text{capital outlays/pupil} + \ldots \quad (1.2)$$

where expenditure per pupil is disaggregated into components like the teacher-pupil ratio T/P, the average teacher salary (itself a function of credentials and experience), and other expenditures like administrative costs per pupil, materials costs per pupil, capital outlays per pupil, and so on. Conventional production functions like equation 1.1 usually include only simple resources defined in this way. Often schools try to introduce changes based on simple resources—smaller classes, better-credentialed teachers, specific curriculum materials for a new program, more computers, or multimedia resource centers (the replacements for libraries). Some of these reforms then run into trouble when it turns out that a simple resource by itself is inadequate to enhance learning—for example, when reducing class size or adopting a new curriculum or introducing a multimedia center requires professional development to enable teachers to take full advantage of these resources. The failure to recognize the need for a compound rather than a simple resource not only wastes resources but also makes the process of reform suspect if teachers are subjected to "reforming again and again and again." If certain resources are NBNS, then it becomes necessary to identify *compound* resources.

Some resources, which I call *complex*, are difficult to introduce into a school and cannot be readily bought, as simple resources can be. These include such practices as the strong leadership of the effective schools literature or the shift to more constructivist or "balanced" pedagogies. These resources are complex not only because they cannot be simply bought, but also because the mechanisms necessary to create them are lengthy and complex, like improving the quality of instruction using classroom observation and feedback (Tharp and Gallimore 1988, ch. 10).

Finally, *abstract* resources may be particularly hard to detect and measure, and their relationship to funding is uncertain. For example, it is hard to know how to buy stability, and while curricular coherence might benefit from staff development, it surely requires much more than money can buy. Similarly, the quality of relationships between teachers and students, a constant refrain of teachers, surely influences the quality of learning (confirmed for early childhood programs by Mashburn et al. 2008), but it requires careful teacher selection, preparation, attention to school climate, perhaps classroom observation and feedback—and none of these is easily bought. Abstract resources are often embedded in the web of relationships within schools and thus require the cooperation of many participants; like complex resources, they may require some funding, but money is not the key resource. Many kinds of abstract resources have been mentioned by reformers, including school climate, coherence of curriculum (Newmann et al.

2001), trust (Bryk and Schneider 2002), pedagogical consistency, alignment of views about reform, and the stability among students, teachers, school leaders, and district administrators and their policies. When I return in chapter 9 to a more collective approach to schools, this feature of abstract resources will emerge as an important characteristic.

4. *Students themselves can be classroom resources.* A fourth conclusion, starting from the observation that teacher and student expectations about instruction may not be consistent, is that students are themselves resources in the classroom (also emphasized by Cohen, Raudenbush, and Ball 2003). Students come to school with different personal and intellectual resources, reflecting differences in their prior cognitive preparation (at home or in previous schooling); in their motivation and engagement; in their approaches to discipline and schoolwork; in their conceptions of what constitutes learning; in the distractions of work, television, and other forms of contemporary culture; and in their peers. We might call this resource "student connectedness to schooling," or SCS, since there is a substantial literature on different dimensions of connectedness (Libbey 2004; Nasir, Jones, and McLaughlin forthcoming), though closely related labels include "motivation and engagement," or the phrase I used in earlier writing, "student ability to benefit from instruction." Connectedness to schooling is, of course, an abstract resource, often embedded in the relationships between students and school personnel (especially teachers), though it can be measured in various ways—as in table 1.1 and in chapter 5.

Family background surely influences student connectedness to schooling, though student motivation can also be enhanced by early childhood programs, the efforts of teachers to socialize children in the early grades, the quality of prior schooling, family literacy and parent participation, efforts to institute instructional practices (like constructivist and conceptual teaching), and organizational forms (like small schools) that enhance motivation and engagement through guidance and counseling, school services, and the like (National Research Council 2004). Conversely, student connectedness may be undermined by the impersonal conditions prevalent in many high schools; the mistreatment of students (especially black and Latino students); conditions leading to student resistance (Willis 1977); black students' notions that school success is "white" and therefore reprehensible (Fordham and Ogbu 1986); preferences for fun and games or adolescent mating rituals during high school; or more serious health and mental health conditions like drug and alcohol abuse, pregnancy, or depression. And instructional conditions may respond to a student's connectedness to schooling. For example, teachers may respond positively to motivated students and negatively to those who are disruptive; they may give up on students with poor attendance or those who do not do their homework; and they may have little patience for those employed a great deal, even if family circumstances re-

Table 1.1   Variation in Resources

Variable	Coefficient of Variation
Financial resources	
Current expenditures per pupil (adjusted)	.234
Instructional expenditures per pupil (adjusted)	.244
Percent state revenue	.415
Percent federal revenue	1.107
Parental contributions per pupil (adjusted)	3.190
Simple resources	
Pupil-teacher ratio	.427
Low teacher salary	.159
High teacher salary	.213
Teacher certified	.366
Teacher education	.321
Compound resources	
Teacher experience in secondary education	.545
Teacher teaching in field of preparation	.294
Planning time	.370
Staff development	.530
Student in general education	1.416
Student in vocational education	2.886
Student in remedial education	1.717
Complex resources	
Teacher time use	.765
Conventional teaching	.239
Innovative teaching	.497
Teacher control	.183
Teacher sense of efficacy	.194
Teacher innovation	.951
Conventional math teaching	.255
Innovative math teaching	.421
Abstract resources	
Positive school climate	.234
Negative events	1.483
College pressure	.244
Staff responsibility	.193
Principal control	.221
School attendance rate	.059
Percent school lunch	1.037
School problems (administration-reported)	.523

Table 1.1   *Continued*

Variable	Coefficient of Variation
Family background	
Mother's education less than high school	2.899
Mother's education college	1.511
Mother's occupation low-status	1.480
Mother's occupation professional	1.288
Income per dependent (unadjusted)	.993
Income per dependent (adjusted)	.758
College savings	1.651
Parental aspirations low	2.024
Parental aspirations high	1.229
Family changes	2.859
Student changed school	2.571
Student language not English	2.995
Student connectedness	
Homework	.737
Television	.606
Use of counselor	.940
Attendance problems	.996
Total absences	.824
Behavior problems	4.169
Hours of employment	.999
Extracurricular activities	1.163
Outside activities	1.400
College-oriented peers	.332
Dropout-oriented peers	4.266
Gang activities	2.799

Source: NELS88, second follow-up, senior year. See appendix A for variable definitions and sources. Adjusted variables are corrected for cross-section price differences.

quire it. Student-centered teachers adjust their instruction to students with varying backgrounds and interests.[10] As I review in chapter 4, middle-class parents are more likely to instill in their children the attitudes and behaviors—independence, initiative, facility in speaking with adults, "interpersonal competence"—that teachers prize, at least in college-bound tracks. Schools provide different levels of resources through tracking or teacher assignments to students with lower levels of preparation—sometimes allocating more compensatory resources for struggling students and sometimes more resources for high-performing students (Brown 1988; Gamoran 1988).

As a working hypothesis, it seems likely that many of these resources are more unequally distributed among schools and among students than are expenditures per pupil, and that compound resources are more unequally distributed than are simple resources.[11] While the existing literature contains a smattering of evidence confirming this hypothesis (see, for example, Alexander 2003; Lankford and Wyckoff 1995), table 1.1 presents more complete results based on the National Educational Longitudinal Survey of the Class of 1988 (NELS88) data. These figures describe the variation among individual students in many resources, as measured by the coefficient of variation (the standard deviation divided by the mean). The resources included in this table are largely those included in the analyses of chapters 2 and 3, and therefore the school resources described are only those found to be effective in enhancing one outcome or another. The coefficient of .234 for expenditure per student—the most enduring target of equity reformers—is among the lowest levels of inequality in the table, and the variation in instructional spending per pupil is about the same. Not surprisingly, parental contributions per student are much more unequal than are total expenditures per pupil, as high-income parents are better able to contribute to school foundations. Inequality in both low and high teacher salaries is about the same as inequality in spending, but other simple resources—the pupil-teacher ratio, teacher certification, and teacher education levels—are more unequal.

When we shift our attention to compound, complex, and abstract resources, inequalities are (with the exception of the school attendance rate) much higher still. In particular, the resources linked to innovative instruction—teacher use of time, overall innovative teaching, innovative math teaching (and innovative science teaching as well), teacher innovation as noted by the principal—are highly unequal, at least as compared to the distribution of spending per pupil. Some abstract resources are about as unequal as spending (like the existence of college pressure, positive school climate, and the extent of staff responsibility), but negative events in school, school problems as reported by the principal, and the proportion of the student body who receive free or reduced-price school lunch—a reflection of overall student socioeconomic status—are all highly unequal. So to understand the inequality of school resources, it is necessary to consider a much wider range of resources than has been customary.

When we turn to nonschool resources, inequalities are markedly higher. Every dimension of family background is much more unequally distributed than virtually any school resource. The coefficient of variation for family income per dependent (adjusted for cross-sectional cost differences), often used as a summary measure of inequality, is .758, much more than the inequality in school spending per pupil, but the other dimensions of family background are more unequally distributed than income—coefficients are well above one and sometimes above two for measures of parental education, aspirations for children, college savings, and occupational status. These results confirm the notion that the variation across families and across the elements of family background that affect schooling outcomes is much greater than the variation in school resources, however measured (see also Downey, von Hippel, and Broh 2004). Finally, the measures of students as resources—the measures of their connectedness to schooling—are more unequally distributed than most school resources, in part because they are linked to unequal family backgrounds.

From an equity standpoint, then, it is inadequate to consider just spending patterns and simple resources. The largest inequalities among students prove to be found in other school and nonschool resources, clarifying the importance of an improved approach to resources. And so concern with the inequities in schooling inputs, including compound, complex, and abstract resources, needs to go well beyond the concern with simple resources that has dominated school finance discussions.

REVISING THE MODEL OF SCHOOLING "PRODUCTION"

Based on these precepts, then, a revision of the simple model of school "production," as in equation 1.1, is necessary. While conventional production functions treat the educational process as a black box, an improved approach should start to examine the ways in which resources are used and open up the black box. The simplest approach is to specify a two-step process in which revenues influence instructional conditions and school resources, including simple, compound, complex, and abstract resources within classrooms and schools, and these instructional conditions in turn enhance learning and other outcomes of various kinds. They might include both instructional resources related to teaching and non-instructional conditions like extracurricular activities that keep students in school (Marsh and Kleitman 2002), student support services like health and mental health services, and different forms of guidance and counseling (NRC 2004, ch. 6). Slightly more formally,

$$\text{School resources} = g(\text{expenditures/pupil}, \ldots) + e \qquad (1.3)$$

$$\text{Schooling outcomes} = h(\text{school resources, family background}) + u \qquad (1.4)$$

where e and u are error terms, reflecting the fact that the independent variables on the right-hand side of each equation are unlikely to explain all of the variation in the dependent variables. The first of these equations describes the way in which expenditures are (or are not) translated into classroom and school conditions related to learning. The second describes the effects of instructional and non-instructional conditions on valued outcomes, both cognitive and noncognitive. The conventional production function (equation 1.1) is a reduced-form version of equations 1.3 and 1.4 in which equation 1.3 is substituted into equation 1.4 to yield equation 1.1, conflating two different causal processes.

A further elaboration is to introduce the role of student connectedness to schooling. This may be influenced by family background, as well as by instructional school resources that enhance motivation and engagement, or

$$\text{Student connectedness} = j(\text{school resources, family background, ...}) + v \qquad (1.5)$$

where v is another error term. Because student connectedness to schooling and instructional conditions may influence one another, the growing system of equations now includes a simultaneous relationship between school resources and student commitment. Finally, we might include state and federal policies related to instructional standards, assessment, exit requirements, and other school operations intended to affect instructional conditions and therefore outcomes. Now the model looks like figure 1.2, in contrast to the simple production function of figure 1.1. The final equation describes the effects on outcomes of all these resources: a variety of school resources (simple, compound, complex, and abstract); many dimensions of family background; measures of student connectedness to schooling; and other external policies.[12]

$$\text{School outcomes} = k(\text{school resources, family background, student commitment, other external policies}) + w \qquad (1.6)$$

Now the school is no longer a black box, since figure 1.2 allows us to specify any number of causal processes that operate inside schools. School revenues affect outcomes only indirectly, through their *potential* influences on school resources, as well as their *potential* effects on student connectedness to schooling. The effects of family background are still exogenous, or external to the conception of how schools work, though family effects operate in three distinct ways—directly on schooling outcomes, through mechanisms I explore in chapter 4; indirectly through their influence on their children's commitment to schooling, examined in chapter 5; and potentially through their effects on school resources, if parents or voters pressure schools to invest in certain resources.[13] The reduced-form equation corresponding to equations 1.3, 1.4, 1.5, and 1.6 is still equation 1.1, indicating how many different causal processes are conflated in the conventional production function.

Figure 1.2   The Black Box Exposed: How Resources Impact Student
Achievement

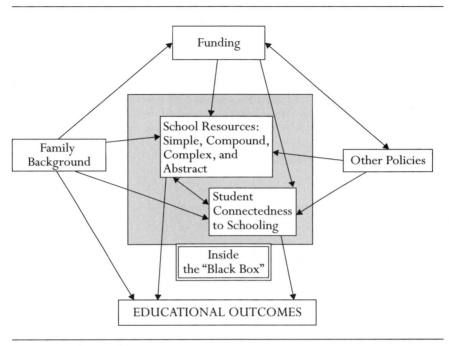

Source: Author's compilation.

Finally, this approach moves well past the emphasis on school finance formulas and the other minutiae of the old school finance and considers instead
a wide variety of the most important educational issues. Funding formulas
and both the adequacy and equity of funding are still important, of course,
but many other issues of causality and effectiveness within the black box are
just as important.

Particularly since this model of schooling is more complex than the simple input-output relationships of figure 1.1, there are some inevitable problems with causality. One is that the relationship between school resources
and student connectedness to schooling is a reciprocal interaction. However, for purposes of estimating equations that describe educational outcomes, this complication is irrelevant since both student connectedness to
schooling and school resources are strictly exogenous to outcomes. Second,
Dan Goldhaber and Dominic Brewer (1997) have raised the possibility that
the variables describing the schooling process that are unavoidably omitted

might bias the effects of the variables included, though their results imply that such bias does not exist.[14] In addition, I have included many more measures of school resources than are used by them or others estimating production functions, further minimizing the danger of bias.

Finally, some researchers have cautioned against a causal ambiguity that no one has resolved: it is possible that some outcomes determine resources rather than resources determining outcomes. In many cases, however, there is an ample literature clarifying the nature of the causal effects in figure 1.2. For example, the effects of family background have been the subject of enormous amounts of ethnographic literature, and the effects of approaches to instruction are the subject of research showing the importance of balanced instruction (see introduction, note 15). In other cases, however, this kind of "wrong-way" causality is more plausible. For example, if experienced teachers are able to pick the classes they teach, then experienced and innovative teachers may choose to teach high-performing students headed for college so that student performance determines pedagogical approaches rather than the other way around. If teachers believe (incorrectly) that low-performing and unmotivated students need drill-based pedagogical approaches, then low performance will lead to conventional teaching practices. For many school resources, this kind of causality is ruled out by the other variables included, particularly the tenth-grade test scores incorporated into some of the equations reported in chapters 2, 4, and 5. For example, the negative effects of different track placements in general and vocational tracks persist even when low performance on tenth-grade tests and measures of connectedness to schooling are included, implying that tracking causes outcomes, not that outcomes—including earlier test scores and motivation—cause track placement. In the absence of any better ways to disentangle causal mechanisms,[15] I include a wide array of explanatory variables to strengthen the assumption that every other researcher has made—that resources determine outcomes rather than the other way around.

Many problems with data can make estimating equations that correspond to figure 1.2 and equation 1.6 difficult. Measures of multiple school resources and student connectedness to schooling are often unavailable. Almost all studies of educational outcomes have relied on test scores only, though the effects of school resources on *different* school outcomes is an important issue, requiring data on many outcomes. In addition, the logic of resources being necessary but not sufficient requires a more careful specification of the interactions among variables and of compound and abstract resources rather than simple resources. The effects of non-instructional conditions are particularly complex: some (like guidance and counseling) are intended to enhance student connectedness to schooling, while others (like efforts to enhance the school climate) are intended to improve instructional conditions in the schools—again asking for data with multiple outcomes.

Finally, improved approaches to school resources—which ask us to be more precise about the mechanisms by which multiple resources affect schooling outcomes—require more careful thought about exactly how family background affects the processes internal to schools. Family background is often crudely measured (by free or reduced-price school lunch eligibility, for example); I will instead examine many different dimensions of family background or class in chapter 4. For example, family background might reflect the financial resources of middle-income students, the cognitive benefits of growing up with well-educated parents, or the expectations and motivation provided by professional parents, and each of these describes a different causal mechanism. So the model of figure 1.2 is useful in several ways: as a process of conceptualizing the varied causal mechanisms underlying outcomes; as encouragement to focus the attention of researchers and educators on the array of important school resources; and finally, as a model for statistical analysis.

NEW RESEARCH AND NEW NARRATIVES FOR SCHOOLING

An improved approach to school resources can be useful only if it leads to different kinds of empirical research to ascertain what resources are most effective and how to mobilize such resources—or conversely to determine how schools and districts make decisions about resources, whether effective or ineffective. Several avenues for research follow from this approach. One is to examine "natural experiments," when schools receive substantial infusions of money, to see how these funds are used to enhance certain resources over others. This has happened, for example, when states have responded to lawsuits by increasing their aid to districts, as in Kentucky, New Jersey, and Texas (Yinger 2004); in state pilot projects designed to increase funding and other resources to low-performing schools, as in California's Immediate Intervention/Underperforming Schools Program (II/USP) grants and more recently in the High Priority Schools Grant Program; and in some individual districts, for example, in the Chicago schools in 1990 as part of the Chicago School Reform Act (Hess 1999). I review some evaluations of such "natural experiments" in chapter 10, where I examine state and district policies, and in chapter 11, where I analyze the effectiveness of school finance litigation. These natural experiments and self-conscious reforms provide opportunities to see how additional resources are spent and then to ask whether these changes might improve learning and other schooling outcomes or whether they are dissipated or wasted. They provide additional empirical evidence about waste, corresponding to the conceptual categories of waste developed earlier in this chapter.

In addition, the method of effective schools research—that is, examining the practices of schools judged to be unusually effective—remains attractive. As one example, Karen Miles and Linda Darling-Hammond (1998) used the measure of above-average and improving student performance to search for effective schools that also enhanced the ability of teachers to work with one another and to know their students well, particularly by replacing nonclassroom aides and specialists with classroom teachers to reduce class size. After observing classrooms to see the instructional effects of these changes, they concluded that the particular use of time, not just the amount of time on task, is important. Unfortunately, the effective schools research method has generally failed to examine funding, and so this line of research currently provides little insight into the relationship between funding and resources.[16] However, researchers might examine schools with higher than expected outcomes to see how resources are used differently within those classrooms and schools—essentially the approach Alfred Hess (1999) takes in examining Chicago schools.

Yet another research approach—the tactic followed in this book—is to estimate equations like those represented in figure 1.2 to replace the standard educational production function in equation 1.1 and figure 1.1. Some research has already done this. Stephen Raudenbush, Randall Fotiu, and Yuk Fai Cheong (1998) used National Assessment of Educational Progress (NAEP) data to determine that four dimensions of instructional conditions enhance math scores: the school's disciplinary climate, advanced course offerings, the preparation of math teachers in mathematics, and the emphasis on math reasoning. Although they did not estimate versions of equation 1.3 to examine the effects of revenues on instructional conditions, they did examine the variation in these resources and found differences by parental income and race. Similarly, Goldhaber and Brewer (1997) used NELS88 data to estimate the effects of teacher characteristics like experience and certification—all simple resources—as well as teachers' college majors, their classroom practices (or instructional conditions) like control over discipline and teaching techniques, and the use of small groups, questioning, and problem-solving. Although some teacher practices led to higher math scores, teacher characteristics like education and experience proved to be unrelated to higher scores, implying that buying expensive characteristics does not generally lead to more effective practices. Marta Elliott (1998) also used NELS88 data with a model similar to equations 1.3 and 1.4 to examine the effects of spending on "opportunities to learn," measured by teacher qualifications, pedagogical strategies, and classroom resources like science and computer equipment. Expenditures affected math and science scores both directly and indirectly, through their effects on increasing the likelihood of having educated teachers using effective pedagogies—a compound resource.

Efforts to move beyond simple production functions have not been common, however, partly because the data necessary for expanded measures of resources, as well as for outcomes beyond test scores, are usually unavailable. However, NELS88, used in the research of Goldhaber and Brewer (1997) and Elliott (1998), has a particularly rich set of variables drawing on questionnaires given to teachers, students, administrators, and parents. In chapter 2, I introduce the NELS88 data and present the results of estimating equations like equation 1.6, which allow me to ascertain which of the many school and nonschool resources affect schooling outcomes. Chapter 3 turns to equations like equation 1.3 to describe the effects of revenue and expenditure patterns on instructional conditions, specifically on those instructional conditions known to be effective in enhancing outcomes. Chapter 4 examines the effects of family background in greater detail, and chapter 5 analyzes students as resources, as measured by dimensions of students' connectedness to schooling.

One hope of an improved approach to school resources is that the dominant money myth—that more money is usually more effective than less money, and that the solution to any educational problem requires increased spending—might be replaced with a more accurate if more complex vision. The improved school finance is at least a candidate to replace the older myth of money and the old school finance. Without abandoning the importance of spending levels and equity, it emphasizes effectiveness in a manner consistent with current interest in accountability and with what works. It responds to the historical concern about efficiency (see, for example, Callahan 1967), since it explicitly links resources to results. And by focusing on instructional conditions within schools and classrooms as well as on revenues, it is consistent with recent reforms that emphasize the inner workings of schools and classrooms and the pedagogies and cultures appropriate to enhanced learning.

But new ideas and narratives do not come to dominate practice and policy unless they attract widespread allegiance, including support from research (or evidence in general) and from teachers and administrators, policymakers, and parents. This is why I stress the implications of improved approaches to school resources for several different groups of participants in chapters 9, 10, and 11: only when there is some consistency in perspective and practices can a new vision come to govern.

There are also barriers to any new narrative. The theory of waste I outlined earlier in this chapter describes potential barriers to the more effective use of resources that are by turns political, organizational, pedagogical, and historical. The nature of politics is a particularly serious barrier, since the preoccupation with dividing the spoils—a politics geared to the old school finance and interest group democracy—is hostile to concerns about effective practice. Part of changing a policy narrative, therefore, is changing the politics that supports it, a subject to which I briefly return in chapter 12. In addition, policy narratives are often distinguished by their simplicity, and it is possible that a complex conception—like one that encourages attention to a wider variety of resources—will prove too complex and too varied to be widely accepted. Finally, old habits die hard, and it will be difficult to introduce these perspectives to the vast numbers of administrators, teachers, policymakers, parents, and researchers in ways that make them stick and then to prevent backsliding into old ways of thinking. But the alternatives are grim: without the changes necessary to move beyond the conventional analysis of money, spending for education will keep escalating without much improvement to show for it.

Chapter 2

Multiple Resources, Multiple Outcomes: Testing the Improved School Finance with the National Educational Longitudinal Survey of the Class of 1988

THE CHALLENGE for improving schools, based on the approach presented in chapter 1, is to identify which school resources—now broadly defined as simple, compound, complex, and abstract—are effective. In this chapter, I discuss the rich data from the National Educational Longitudinal Survey of the Class of 1988 (NELS88) that enable me to do that. I present basic conclusions from the data and describe the powerful effects of school resources—most of them compound, complex, or abstract—on a variety of educational outcomes. I also clarify how existing analyses often understate the potential of educational resources. Some resources affect all outcomes; some affect learning, as measured by test scores, but not progress through high school; and some affect progress but not test scores. So confining educational outcomes to test scores, as do virtually all efforts to estimate educational production functions like equation 1.1, misses the powerful effects of some resources.

To improve schooling outcomes, then, we must not only identify effective resources of all types but also determine ways to enhance those resources. In chapter 3, I examine which resources require additional funding and which must be developed in other, more complex ways—for example, by combining teacher participation with strong instructional leadership from principals and assistant principals.

Although many researchers and many educators have tried to understand what school resources might be effective, the research underlying this chapter differs from prior work in at least four ways. First, it rests on a more complex model of the schooling process, illustrated by figure 1.2, which suggests what relationships are important. Second, rather than confining the analysis to the simple school resources that result from spending, it also includes compound, complex, and abstract resources. Third, NELS88 is a considerably richer data set than prior studies have used, and it enables me to measure a large number of different school and nonschool resources rather than a restricted set. And finally, rather than focus exclusively on math and English test scores, NELS88 makes it possible to construct many different outcome measures—twenty-nine in all, though I present here the results for only twelve.

The next section describes the NELS88 data, the variables corresponding to the model of schooling in figure 1.2, and the estimation issues. In the following section, I analyze the effects of different school resources before going on to examine different types of outcomes, contrasting a *common* view that resources influence all outcomes in roughly the same way with a *differentiated* view that different resources affect different outcomes. I conclude with a summary of the implications for reform and policy, suggesting that many current policies are detrimental.

This chapter answers questions with long histories to them—especially questions of whether and how schools make a difference. In chapter 3 it will be possible to examine the role of money in enhancing (or failing to enhance) these effective resources and to determine when funding makes a difference and when it does not.

THE NELS88 DATA AND THE CREATION OF VARIABLES

Because NELS88 data go well beyond simple resources and include information on many school resources, as well as information on many measures of family background and student connectedness to schooling, they are admirably suited to the estimation of expanded production functions. The study initially drew a random sample of schools with eighth grades and randomly sampled eighth-graders within those schools in 1988. The students were questioned again in the tenth and twelfth grades (the first and second follow-ups), two years after they had completed high school (the third follow-up), and six years after that (the fourth follow-up, in 2000). Parents received questionnaires in the base year and again during the second follow-up, and teachers and administrators associated with grades 8, 10, and 12 were also questioned, with much more detailed information collected in grades 10 and 12. In addition, high school transcripts were collected during the senior year. I confine the analysis presented here to information collected as of the twelfth grade, except that I obtained data on students' initial enrollment in a two- or four-year colleges from the third follow-up.

To be sure, the NELS88 data are now old in the sense that these students graduated sixteen years ago, in 1992. Much has taken place since then, including the rise of state and federal accountability, the rise of adequacy lawsuits, and renewed concern about high school quality and completion rates, and it is possible that responses to some of these pressures have changed the nature of high schools since the years around 1990. Improvements in access to math (and presumably science) among young women have increased their test scores so that their scores are now equal to those of young men (Hyde 2008); as a result, some of the gender patterns discussed briefly in chapter 5 are obsolete. But it seems unlikely that the other patterns have changed much: the racial and ethnic differences in test scores have not changed very much (Fuller et al. 2007), and the class-related patterns associated with race and ethnicity have surely not diminished; the high school remains the most resistant to reform of any level of the educational system, and the many critical reports continue to stress the same problems (Grubb 2008c). Furthermore, the question for research is not whether there have been changes overall, but whether subsequent developments have changed the *relationships* among funding, school resources, and outcomes, and this seems even less likely. Finally, there is a practical reason for continuing to use the NELS88 data, especially compared to the more recent Education Longitudinal Study of 2002 (ELS:2002). ELS:2002 began a longitudinal study of tenth-graders as of 2002, but it has much less information on school resources and family conditions than did NELS88. Subsequent analysis should reexamine these NELS88 conclusions in light of ELS:2002, but it is helpful to start here by examining new approaches to school resources with the richest data set possible.

NELS88 includes many outcome measures: test scores for math, reading, history, and science; measures of progress through high school, including credits earned, high school completion, and progression to college[1]; and many measures of attitudes and values. Including test scores in our test-besotted age is obligatory, and it allows for comparisons with other research results. While the four subject test scores analyzed in this study are highly correlated with one another (with correlation coefficients of about .75), the effects of school resources on the four scores differ in interesting ways. These test scores are based on item response theory (IRT) models, which are particularly appropriate for examining test scores over time (Seltzer, Choi, and Thum 2003; Seltzer, Frank, and Bryk 1994). They are also free of gender and racial-ethnic bias, since they have been investigated with differential item functioning (DIF). In general, the tests are multidimensional— for example, the math tests include questions related to both knowledge and reasoning, while the science scores encompass basic knowledge, reasoning, spatial-mechanical reasoning, and quantitative science rather than being tests of basic knowledge and computational ability.[2]

A second set of outcomes includes measures of progress through high school such as passing algebra 1 (a gatekeeper course), credits accumulated, completion of a standard academic program usually required for admission to college (four years of English, three of math, and so on), receipt of a high school diploma, and enrollment in a two- or four-year college after high school. This second set of outcomes may in fact be more important than test scores, especially in a period when employment opportunities have been eroding for high school dropouts. The final set of outcomes includes such attitudes as educational and occupational aspirations, which may affect other school and nonschool decisions—in particular, low aspirations often put a ceiling on continued attendance. In every year of data collection, students were asked whether they would continue their education past high school, another perception that often limits what students do. Appendix A describes more fully the outcome measures, with the specific questions from which they were derived. Altogether I created twenty-nine dependent variables, though I report on only twelve of them to save space.[3] Although these outcomes are positively correlated with one another, most of them, aside from the four tests, are not highly correlated—that is, it is possible to make progress through high school with mediocre test scores, or to drop out even with adequate test scores, or to complete high school and still not progress into postsecondary education.[4] Of course, these outcome measures, while much broader than test scores, do not exhaust the valued outcomes of schooling. The civic, cultural, familial, and occupational benefits of schooling have been widely promoted (if often eclipsed by the occupational emphasis of the Education Gospel), and these could also be related to school resources. But here I confine myself to educational outcomes because the debate I address involves the relationships among funding, school resources, and educational outcomes, not the debate about the overall effects of schooling in the world outside the school.

Because NELS88 collected data from teachers, students, and administrators, it provides considerable information on many measures of school resources. Simple school resources include the pupil-teacher ratio and low and high teacher salary levels, adjusted for cost differences across districts and over time. The pupil-teacher ratio is the ratio of all pupils to the number of all teachers, not a measure of average class size, since many high schools have resource teachers and coaches whose presence affects the pupil-teacher ratio but not class size; I interpret the pupil-teacher ratio as a reflection of the relative numbers of adults in a school, a measure of personalization. Salaries are likely to be proxies for quality, because districts that pay higher real salaries can attract a larger pool of applicants and choose higher-quality teachers, however they may define quality. Compound resources include experience teaching in secondary schools, a more powerful predictor than overall teaching experience or experience in the current school; a measure of whether an instructor teaches in his or her field of preparation; the amount of time devoted to planning for teaching; and the amount of staff development. Track placement—student placement in the general track, the vocational track, or remedial courses—is a compound resource because such tracks include the influence of teacher expectations, content, and peers, which are all difficult to disentangle.

Among the complex variables, I have included a number of measures related to instruction: the amount of time devoted to administration, discipline, and conventional lecture as distinct from discussion, projects, or labs; the principal's assessment of whether teaching is overall conventional and behaviorist or more innovative and constructivist; the teacher's sense of control over her classroom, averaged over the several teachers that a student has; the teacher's sense of efficacy; whether the teacher thinks that the department encourages innovation; and measures of conventional versus innovative teaching in math.[5] Abstract resources include students' estimates of a positive climate; the principal's report of negative events like fights, theft, drug and alcohol problems, and gangs; the extent of college pressure within the school; the extent of principal (versus district) control; and, to reflect other dimensions of climate, the overall school attendance rate, as well as the proportion of students receiving subsidized school lunches. Exogenous variables include types of schools, school size, and the presence or absence of several state and district requirements. Appendix A provides more detail about the specific questions in NELS88 from which these variables were constructed.

Information in NELS88 from students and parents also provides many dimensions of family background. Because the NELS88 data permit measurement of ten different dimensions of family background, I am able, for example, to disentangle the effects of parental education from income from occupation.[6] In addition, I include standard demographic variables of race and ethnicity (describing white, African American, Latino, Asian American, and American Indian students), gender, and physical disability. The inclusion of such variables, while universal, is inherently troublesome because it can say nothing about the causal links between, for example, racial status and outcomes. In chapter 4, therefore, I consider several possible interpretations of such racial-ethnic measures.

Student commitment to schooling is measured by variables (most of them self-reported by students) that reflect the attention that students pay to their schooling rather than to distractions such as television, work, or gangs. These variables include measures of attendance, completion of homework, hours of watching television, hours of employment, parenthood (whether a student has a baby), self-reported behavior problems at school, the aspirations of a student's peer group, and initiative in seeking help from counselors or tutors. In addition, since school-based extracurricular activities reflect students' allegiance to schooling, which in turn affects their continued enrollment and progress (Marsh and Kleitman 2002), the data include measures of extracurricular activities. A different measure reflects activities outside of school that may be educational even though they do not affect ties to schooling; these include such activities as membership in service and political organizations, church involvement, and volunteer work.

For test scores, I also present a second specification that includes test scores in tenth grade. A student's ability to benefit from subsequent instruction may be a function of what he or she already knows, or as Lauren Resnick (1989) has said, "Knowledge begets knowledge"—a high level of factual and procedural knowledge (in tenth grade, for example) leads to better understanding of concepts, which in turn leads to acquisition of more knowledge (in twelfth grade). In plain English, students who have done well in school are likely to continue doing well as they build on previous knowledge. Similarly, in equations describing attitudes like educational and occupational aspirations, I also include the same variable measured in tenth grade, since prior attitudes may continue to affect the attitudes measured later. Although including variables measured in tenth grade has several advantages, it also complicates estimation procedures and the interpretation of results over time.[7]

Constructing specific measures for resources and schooling outcomes has been a lengthy process of identifying the questions included in various NELS88 questionnaires that correspond to different conceptual constructs of the improved school finance. Appendix A presents the NELS88 questions from which all variables were developed and describes the procedures used to treat missing data, weighting procedures, and the estimation of standard errors. While there are statistical techniques to create composite variables from multiple questions, I have preferred to formulate variables on the basis of a priori conceptual concerns rather than to let a software program formulate variables that would then be difficult to interpret.[8]

Overall, my strategy has been to exploit the richness of the NELS88 data, both for a variety of outcomes and for potential explanatory variables. In particular, one crucial question—what school practices make a difference?—cannot be answered without examining a large number of practices thought to be effective. This approach has the obvious disadvantage of producing numerous results, with patterns that are sometimes difficult to summarize. But the alternative, in conventional production functions, has been to use overly sparse specifications because of data limitations, and that cannot help us understand the complexity of how schools work.

The results in this chapter, as well as in chapters 3, 4, 5, and 7, depend on statistical estimation of equations like 1.6, reflecting the causal mechanisms in figure 1.2. I have tried to make these results as user-friendly as possible by presenting them as easily interpretable beta coefficients whose magnitudes can be readily compared across equations and across variables, and I have relegated many of the statistical details to the notes and appendices. However, those who are regression-averse and who trust my own reading of the results should skip the following section and move directly to the section on "Implications for Policy and Practice," where I have summarized the substantive results in the plainest and least technical English I can muster.

The Overall Effects of School Resources

An initial and powerful conclusion is that including the variety of school and nonschool resources implied by the improved school finance, and described in figure 1.2, makes a great deal of difference to many results—to the explanatory power of equations, to the estimates of coefficients, and to conclusions about which school and nonschool resources affect outcomes. Table 2.1 presents a simple measure of explanatory power—R-squared, measuring the proportion of variance in schooling outcomes explained by the variables included in each equation—for a variety of specifications.[9] The most basic specification is a simple production function like equation 1.1, including only demographic variables; simple school resources, including the pupil-teacher ratio and high and low teacher salary levels; and a single measure of family background, income per dependent. Explanatory power is low: between 12 and 19 percent for the four test scores, and much lower for the three attitudinal variables—educational aspirations, occupational aspirations, and whether a student plans to continue education past high school. Then, in specification 2, adding complex, compound, and abstract school resources increases explanatory power substantially—from 16 to 45 percent for math scores, for example, and from 13 to 34 percent for reading, a larger increase in explanatory power than for any other set of variables (with a single exception). Variables for family background and for student connectedness to schooling add somewhat less to explanatory power, in specifications 3 and 4, respectively. The exception is high educational aspirations: not surprisingly, the influence of parental aspirations on children's aspirations is very high. Adding all three kinds of variables—school resources, family resources, and student resources—increases explanatory power even further, and the addition of a lagged dependent variable in specification 6 increases R-squared between .01 and .05 points. By the criterion of explanatory power, then, school resources are the most important of all independent variables, since they add more explanatory power to simple production functions than any other set of variables.

Furthermore, failing to include a rich set of school resources, family resources, and student resources biases the coefficients of those variables that

Table 2.1   Explanatory Power (R-squared) of Different Sets of Independent Variables

	Specifi-cation 1	Specifi-cation 2	Specifi-cation 3	Specifi-cation 4	Specifi-cation 5	Specifi-cation 6
Dependent Variable						
MATHTS	.16	.45	.34	.35	.53	.58
SCITS	.19	.37	.32	.33	.45	.48
READTS	.13	.34	.28	.29	.43	.47
HISTTS	.12	.32	.26	.28	.41	.44
HIEDASP	.04	.15	.40	.16	.44	.45
HIOCASP	.06	.15	.16	.11	.21	.22
CONTED	.02	.16	.13	.10	.22	.23

Source: Author's computations.
Specification 1: basic production function
Specification 2: adding school resources to specification 1
Specification 3: adding family background to specification 1
Specification 4: adding student connectedness to schooling to specification 1
Specification 5: adding school resources, family background, and student measures to specification 1
Specification 6: adding an instrumented lagged dependent variable to specification 5

are included in the basic or simple production function. For example, in specifications for math test scores, the coefficient on family income is .167 in the simple production function, .031 when additional family background measures are included, .023 in specification 5, and an insignificant .003 in specification 6. Similarly, the coefficient of teacher salary drops from .087 to .044 when other school resources are included, and to .032 and .012 in specifications 5 and 6, respectively. So limitations in the data used to estimate most production functions result in both low explanatory power and seriously biased coefficients: the variables that can be included—usually simple school resources and a single measure of family background—have effects that are systematically *over*estimated compared to what they are when a richer set of variables is included. Impoverished data sets cannot be trusted, therefore, to accurately describe the effects of school resources.

THE VARIETY OF SCHOOL EFFECTS

To examine the effects of all school resources, table B.1 in appendix B presents the coefficients of thirty-seven school resources, for twelve of the twenty-nine outcome variables, corresponding to equation 1.6.[10] In addition, for those seven dependent variables with consistent data over time, I include a second specification that includes a dependent variable for the previous period (tenth grade), estimated with an instrumental variables technique, in order to capture the possibility that student ability to benefit from instruction is reflected in past test scores and attitudes as well as by current resources.[11] The coefficients presented in this table are beta coefficients, which describe the standard deviation change in the dependent variable associated with a one-standard-deviation change in the independent variable. Because these coefficients are pure numbers, they can be compared with each other. A beta between .04 and .08 is of moderate importance; betas over .08 indicate relatively powerful relationships. I include symbols for significance at 1 percent, 5 percent, and 10 percent. For those unfamiliar with reading regressions, the upper left-hand coefficient of −.025 means that an increase of one standard deviation in the pupil-teacher ratio decreases math test scores by .025 standard deviations, and the effect is statistically significant—that is, we can be relatively sure that sampling error is not responsible for the negative effect.

Simple Resources

Among simple resources, one of the most contested has been the pupil-teacher ratio.[12] With more pupils per teacher, math scores (but not other scores) drop significantly, and students are less likely to complete a standard academic program and to continue to a four-year college. Surprisingly, students are *more* likely to graduate and to go to a community college (a second-chance outcome) with more pupils per teacher. This result suggests that students at schools with impersonal conditions are likely to graduate with incomplete academic programs and therefore to attend community rather than four-year colleges. In addition, class size may have indirect effects on other school resources; in more detailed results, Jennifer Rice (1999) shows that class size itself affects the use of time, with teachers in large classes spending less time on innovative instructional practices, small groups, and individuals and more time on order—consistent with the negative effects on test scores of teacher time use described later.[13]

Higher teacher salaries, as the only proxy available for better-quality teachers, are associated with higher scores on three of the four tests (all except science) and also with improved occupational aspirations, intentions to continue in schooling, and accumulation of credits. These multiple effects suggest that efforts to attract and retain teachers through higher salaries do generate positive outcomes.

Overall, however, the effects of these simple resources are not especially powerful. The highest of these coefficients is .041, a modest effect; most of the significant effects are closer to .03. If researchers concentrate on simple resources, then, it is easy to see why they might conclude that "school resources do not make a difference," despite the results reported in table 2.1. Greater explanatory power proves to come from the compound, complex, and abstract school resources not usually measured.

Compound Resources

One effective compound variable is teachers' experience at the secondary school level, which combines experience with tenure specifically at that level. This variable has more consistent and larger effects on test scores than any other measure of experience does, including total experience teaching and teaching experience in the current school. Teaching the subject matter of an individual's undergraduate major also enhances four test scores, though the effects are small; these findings replicate those of Richard Ingersoll (2004) about the greater effectiveness of in-field teaching. In addition, more planning time for teachers increases all test scores, but its effect on other outcomes is sporadic. Staff development has no effects on learning, and other effects are marginal; it is possible that this reflects the domination in the early 1990s of "old" forms of staff development, like Friday afternoon one-shot events, rather than the "new" forms of continuous staff development focused on pedagogical content knowledge (Little 2006).

The most powerful and consistent effects of any school resource are those related to track placement—placement in a traditional vocational, general, or remedial track. The vocational programs described in the NELS88 data are likely to be traditional vocational education aimed at entry-level occupations rather than the new approaches to occupational education that developed over the 1990s, variously referred to as "education through occupations" (Grubb 1995), programs preparing for "college and careers" (Stern 1999), "theme-based" approaches (National Research Council 2004), and "pathways" through high school (Oakes and Saunders 2008, including Grubb 2008c). The general track is usually viewed as a watered-down version of the academic track; despite efforts to eliminate the general track, it has evidently persisted.[14] While sometimes "chosen" by students, tracks are often determined for students through testing and counseling, and tracking gets its bad name from evidence that working-class students and African American and Latino students have in the past been assigned to vocational tracks against their will. Curriculum tracks are effectively compound resources because lower tracks usually combine lower-level content, teachers with lower expectations of students, often teachers with lower levels of experience or less competent teachers, peers with lower aspirations, and sometimes lower student ambitions, thereby depressing performance in multiple ways.

Consistently, outcomes for students in the general or vocational track are worse compared to outcomes for those in the academic track, and placement in a remedial program has still more powerful negative effects (even after considering the effects of tenth-grade test scores).[15] This finding holds for a wide range of outcomes, including all test scores, educational and occupational aspirations, most measures of progress through high school, and enrolling in four-year colleges. This is consistent with the existing literature on vocational tracking, which has found consistent evidence of lower standards and reduced likelihood of graduating from high school, without any compensating benefits in the form of better employment.[16] The negative effects of the general track are consistent not only with prior research but also with the role of the general track as a weak alternative to the academic track.[17] The negative effects for those who have taken remedial coursework suggest that, while remedial efforts could provide low-performing students with intensive interventions and imaginative alternatives to conventional teaching, remediation usually takes the form of dreary drill-oriented teaching on basic skills. It is possible that other forms of tracking have beneficial effects—after all, such practices as bilingual education and advanced placement (AP) courses are forms of tracking that provide additional resources to some groups of students—but the dominant forms of high school tracking do not.[18] These negative effects confirm the value of replacing such tracks with more demanding curricula through academic tracks, programs that integrate more academic education with occupational offerings, or theme-based magnet schools or schools-within-schools.

The example of tracking provides a good example of the school resource issues underlying specific practices. What makes tracking acceptable and even desirable in gifted classes, or AP classes, or programs using bilingual or bicultural approaches to second-language learners is that the students tracked into these practices are provided *additional* resources, whether of content, teacher attention, expectations, or breadth of approaches. What makes tracking in traditional vocational education and general education so detrimental to outcomes is the fact that these students receive *lesser* resources, of several different kinds. And in the middle, where new practices spring up that differentiate students—for example, the multiple pathways that could replace traditional vocational and general tracks (Oakes and Saunders 2008)—the equity argument usually turns on whether new practices will provide students with more motivating curricula, innovative teaching, and greater options in the future ("college *and* careers"), or whether they will stigmatize students, provide them with inferior teachers, and eventually limit their options. In these and many other cases, specific practices are really compound resources, and determining whether they enhance resources on the whole or undermine them is almost always debatable.

Complex Resources

Complex resources are difficult to create and difficult or impossible to buy with money. Many variables related to teaching and pedagogy are complex resources and are notoriously difficult to change at the high school level

(Cuban 1993). Given the endless battles over approaches to teaching—the math wars, the reading wars, the intervention wars described in chapter 8, the many forms in which proponents of behaviorist or teacher-centered or skills-oriented instruction have contended with advocates for constructivist or student-centered or conceptual approaches—it is perhaps surprising to find that a number of variables related to pedagogy and teacher attitudes influence test scores consistently. The teacher's use of time (TimeUse) affects several outcomes: more time spent on discipline, tests, and administrative tasks reduces test scores, while a greater proportion of time used for group work, individual instruction, and labs enhances learning. Teachers' perceptions of their own efficacy improve learning, and their perceptions that their departments encourage innovation enhance scores. Innovative and constructivist teaching, particularly in math, enhances test scores, while conventional and behaviorist teaching leads to lower scores. Students with teachers who report being in control of their classrooms and their teaching have higher test scores (except in history), more credits earned, and a greater likelihood of enrolling in four-year colleges—indicating that current efforts to constrain teachers by requiring them to use scripted and behaviorist curricula are counterproductive. Most of these effects hold for test scores but not for attitudes or measures of progress, reflecting (not surprisingly) the influences of instruction on learning but not on persistence or other valued outcomes. Innovative math teaching is especially powerful, and its effects extend to enhanced completion of an academic program, continuation to four-year college, and (in a result not shown in table B.1) a greater proportion of academic credits. Innovative math teaching may be particularly effective overall either because it lowers the barriers to taking math (usually considered a gatekeeper) or because it signals an effort to improve teaching schoolwide, given that math teachers are usually the most resistant to change.

None of these effects is overwhelmingly large: none is as large as the effects of placement in different tracks, and most of the statistically significant coefficients range between .02 and .047. On the other hand, many of these practices are correlated with one another. Schools that make sustained efforts to improve instruction often try to eliminate time spent by teachers on administrative tasks and other distractions from instruction; they promote work in groups (such as departments) to share teaching methods, encourage innovation, and learn how to move away from conventional or behaviorist teaching toward more constructivist or "balanced" teaching; and they involve teachers in the development of curriculum and instruction, thereby enhancing teachers' sense of participation and efficacy. Students in schools that follow this general approach would therefore benefit from the positive effects of many of these complex resources, and the aggregate effects of these approaches to teaching might be as high as a beta of .12, comparable to the effects of tracking. As a group, then, these variables related to con-

structivist or balanced instruction and pedagogy are among the most powerful school resources.

Overall, these results confirm the research on effective teaching, particularly as summarized by the National Research Council in the areas of reading, math, science, and history and in high school students' motivation and
engagement in their school. In reading, for example, effective teaching requires *both* some elements of phonics (including attention to how spoken
words are represented alphabetically as well as to vocabulary and fluency,
the emphases of most phonics approaches) *and* rich and varied reading with
students extracting their own meaning from a variety of texts, a combination often described as a "balanced" literacy approach (Snow, Burns, and
Griffin 1998). In subjects like math, science, and history, effective learning
requires not only a deep foundation of factual knowledge but also an understanding of facts within a conceptual framework and the knowledge of how
to organize those facts to facilitate both retrieval and application. The conventional teaching of facts and procedures without conceptual frameworks,
without understanding student preconceptions about how the world works,
and without providing a meta-cognitive approach in which students recognize and monitor their own progress is unlikely to lead to deep understanding (Donovan and Bransford 2005). Similarly, in its investigation of motivation and engagement among high school students, another NRC panel
stressed that motivation is greater when students have some autonomy in selecting tasks and methods of learning; when educational environments are
structured with clear, meaningful purposes, allowing students to see the
connections between schooling and other activities; when students face a
curriculum that is challenging and has a strong emphasis on achievement;
and when students have several paths to competence (NRC 2004). But these
conditions for effective teaching are violated when schools or districts adopt
scripted or semiscripted curricula that constrain teachers in how they teach;
when curricula stress phonics but not comprehension and the development
of meaning from rich texts; and when teachers emphasize routine drill to
the exclusion of more innovative methods—confirming the implications of
the NELS88 results for complex resources. Finally, these dimensions of
teaching in both the NELS88 results and NRC reviews go far beyond what
has been included in the concept of "qualified teachers" in the No Child Left
Behind Act, which stresses certification; evidently, *effective* teaching requires
pedagogical approaches that are nowhere addressed in NCLB and that have
been actively discouraged by the time pressures of accountability.

Abstract Resources

A school's culture or atmosphere or climate is made up of many dimensions
that can be observed through ethnographic work or measured by asking students or teachers about the school, but that are otherwise invisible—and

these dimensions certainly are not among the simple resources that can be readily bought with increased funding. Various measures of a school's climate are among these abstract resources. A positive climate as reported by students, incorporating both academic dimensions (like "teaching is good") and non-academic characteristics ("there's real school spirit," "the school is safe") increases test scores, while negative events like stealing, drug-dealing, physical threats, and fights depress students' test scores in math, reading, and history, reduce the likelihood that they will complete academic programs, and lower their occupational and educational aspirations. Furthermore, a high overall attendance rate at a school—a measure of general attachment to schooling among all students—enhances learning, as measured by all four test scores.

A greater concentration of low-income students depresses learning, aspirations, and completion. In chapter 5, we will see that a student's peers influence outcomes in positive and negative ways (particularly regarding the likelihood of attending college or dropping out), as we might expect. The results presented here regarding school composition indicate that the overall composition of the school matters, beyond the peers with whom any individual student associates. A high proportion of low-income students may increase demands on student services and detract from instructional concerns, or it may intensify negative peer effects as a school becomes predominantly poor; because low incomes are correlated with low performance, a high school dominated by low-income students may experience lower levels of learning (see table 6.2 and the associated text) or engage in "hidden remediation" (Grubb and Associates 1999, ch. 5). Low rates of attendance may force teachers and administrators to focus on absences and motivation, with learning and advancement given secondary priority, or high absenteeism may reflect some other dimension of the climate or atmosphere of the school (for example, particularly unengaging or demeaning teaching) that is driving students away. These results clarify that there are *school* effects on students as well as *peer* effects, so that student achievement and advancement are not wholly determined by an individual's own resources. Finally, these results clarify that physical location and housing patterns—not usually seen as aspects of school resources—influence schooling outcomes, because housing patterns concentrate low-income students in "urban" schools. When I consider the nonschool policies that might support schooling outcomes in chapter 12, I incorporate housing and locational policies into the conception of the welfare state.

These results clarify that several abstract resources make a substantial difference to learning, to progress through high school, and to attitudes, particularly occupational aspirations and students' perceptions of whether they will continue in education past high school. However, many other abstract resources, articulated and investigated by others, cannot be measured with the NELS88 data, rich as they are: trust among individuals in schools (Bryk and Schneider 2002; Payne 1997), since some schools have such hostile and distrusting relationships that reform proves impossible; the coherence of the curriculum (Newmann et al. 2001), since some high schools adopt so many little programs and random interventions that students are subject to conflicting messages about learning; and consistency among teachers, students, the curriculum, and institutional pressures on the school (Lampert 2001), particularly since unacknowledged differences in approaches to learning among teachers, students, and the curriculum can erode learning.[19] If it were possible to measure these other abstract resources, they too might prove to affect outcomes.

Another abstract resource, particularly scarce in urban schools, is stability. Some students move around a great deal, largely as a result of housing problems. Such movement affects the learning not only of moving students as they stop and start different curricula (Rumberger and Larson 1998), but also that of other students as teachers interrupt their teaching to introduce new students to the class and to the new curricula. In addition, teachers are likely to move among schools, especially with some of the most able teachers abandoning the difficult working conditions in urban schools for suburban schools. The higher turnover of principals in urban schools, often accompanied by changes in priorities and curricula, has negative consequences for reform; as evidence, the high-performing Chicago schools described in chapter 9 have principals with longer tenure. And finally, urban superintendents also turn over at a high rate, with new district personnel bringing new priorities and programs to schools and therefore becoming another source of instability. Turnover often leads to substantial waste when changes in priorities require abandoning previous programs and plans, but instability also makes it virtually impossible to sustain reforms since new teachers and new principals and new priorities displace earlier efforts. No one has succeeded in quantifying the multiple dimensions of stability and examining their overall effects on student learning and progress, but this is surely an abstract resource that distinguishes the most chaotic urban schools from stable schools that are able to make steady progress on reform. Overall, then, these results probably *under*estimate the effects of school resources, since measures of other abstract resources like stability and consistency might increase the explanatory power of school resources.

Exogenous Effects

Finally, several dimensions of school structure and exogenous or external influences on schools might affect student outcomes. Among different types of schools, private religious schools enhance the likelihood that students will complete the academic program and enroll in a four-year college, but at the expense of lowering overall high school completion—suggesting that these schools tend to eliminate weak students. Nonreligious private schools in this sample do not appear to be elite schools; students attending them complete fewer credits and are less likely to complete the academic program than students at all other schools. Public magnet schools and schools of choice have no significant effects. While these results as of 1992 predate the current interest in charter and choice schools, they are consistent with more recent findings that charter schools are no more effective on average than conventional schools (Carnoy et al. 2005).

The effects of school size are complex. Size appears to have nonlinear effects, largely for test scores. Contrary to expectations that scores might be highest at a school with a modest level of enrollment—see, for example, Lee and Smith (1997), who show maximum test score *gains* at enrollments between 600 and 900—the NELS88 data show *minimum* scores at high school enrollment levels of 571 students for math test scores, 532 for science scores, 315 for reading scores, and 498 for history scores. The average enrollment in this sample is 1,105, with a range from 8 to 4,252; evidently, students at relatively small schools have lower test scores on average, and those at large high schools have higher test scores once other variables have been considered. When tenth-grade test scores are included in these equations, however, school size becomes insignificant.[20] Similarly, in the growth models of chapter 7 examining test scores over time, school size has no significant effect. However, Lee and Smith fail to include a range of school resources among their independent variables. Based on the NELS88 results, size affects outcomes not directly but indirectly, through effects on teacher innovation, in-field teaching, the likelihood of negative events, and teacher experience in the current school, all of which reach maxima (or minima, in the case of negative events) at school sizes between 645 and 971 students.[21] Once these other variables have been considered, little evidence remains that size itself enhances progress through high school. Overall, there is no strong argument in these results for smaller high schools, reinforcing the point made by others that small school size does not have a positive effect unless that size enhances the school resources—innovation, in-field teaching, school climate, teacher turnover, and experience—that do make a difference to outcomes.

State and district exam requirements have no significant effects, except that competency tests reduce the rate of students attending four-year colleges and increase community college enrollment, usually viewed as a second-best alternative.[22] However, these measures for 1992 predate the elaboration of state testing and accountability schemes of the past decade, and it is inappropriate to make too much of these findings.

The Explanatory Power of School Resources

The last row of table B.1 presents R-squareds, describing the explanatory power of these equations—the proportion of the variance in the outcome measures that can be explained by school resources, measures of family background, and student connectedness to schooling. These are quite high (.40 and over) for test scores and quite substantial (.30 and over) for most other variables. Two of the three attitudinal variables presented here—high occupational aspirations and the intention to continue education—have much lower explanatory power, around .21. The explanatory power is quite low only for enrolling in a two-year college (R-squared is .07), perhaps because this is a second-chance or residual option combining two contradictory effects: students who follow this option have generally done better than dropouts and those not enrolling in any postsecondary education, but worse than those enrolling in four-year colleges. Overall, the explanatory power of these equations is quite respectable and confirms that a rich enough data set can explain a substantial fraction of the variation in schooling outcomes.[23] Of course, as the lack of comprehensive NELS88 data on stability makes clear, creating perfectly comprehensive data, either qualitative or quantitative, to describe all possible dimensions of school resources would be difficult. But overall, these results suggest that impoverished data, like those used to estimate simple production functions, yield impoverished results, such as the misleading conclusion that "schools don't make a difference"; only richer and more varied data allow us to specify the many ways in which school resources do make a difference.

Many school resources have significant but not overwhelming effects. Most of the statistically significant coefficients in table B.1 are in the range of .02 to .06; few are quite large (except for those on different curriculum tracks, which are often above .10). Furthermore, there is little evidence of interactions among these school resources—for example, there is little evidence that having innovative teachers and staff development has powerful synergistic effects, or that certain approaches to teaching students of lower socioeconomic status have more powerful effects.[24] The result is a description of schooling in which many potentially independent sources influence outcomes. This is a statistical version of the common claim that there is no "silver bullet" in school reform. Instead, multiple resources are necessary for substantive reform.

Overall, these results firmly reject the simplistic notion that "schools don't make a difference." School resources increase explanatory power more than any other set of variables. Many dimensions of teaching practice, especially innovative and constructivist or balanced methods, are quite effective; school climate makes a great difference to a variety of outcomes; and the compound effects of track placement are powerful, even after controlling for a large number of selection and self-selection mechanisms. Collectively, these results confirm that a variety of compound, complex, and abstract resources—not just the simple resources usually included in production functions—are effective. They also provide considerable guidance for reforming high schools, a subject to which I return in chapter 9.

BEYOND TEST SCORES: THE DIFFERENCES AMONG EDUCATIONAL OUTCOMES

While most research that examines schooling outcomes has concentrated on test scores, other outcomes measured in these NELS88 results include progress through high school and movement into college—a crucial determinant of employment, earnings, and many other dimensions of adult life—as well as attitudes and values that may shape future decisions. One question is what conclusions are skewed and what findings are lost when research and accountability programs look only at test scores. In a recent paper, Russell Rumberger and Greg Palardy (2005) distinguish between a *common* view of schooling, in which inputs and resources influence outcomes in roughly the same ways, and a *differentiated* view, in which different inputs affect different outcomes. To the extent that differentiated patterns dominate, reliance on test scores only obscures how schools work and may lead to misstatements about "what works."

Of course, both common and differentiated patterns may operate at the same time. Some variables in the NELS88 results affect most outcomes. Among school resources, track placement—in a general, vocational, or remedial program—has consistently negative effects on outcomes, not a surprising result given the multiple influences reflected in tracks. School climate (including the prevalence of negative events) also affects outcomes consistently. In addition, seeking help from counselors affects a wide variety of outcomes. Whether this measure reflects student initiative or the value of the counseling encounter itself is unclear, but it does indicate—somewhat surprisingly—the value of a school resource often thought to need strengthening.[25]

Among measures of family background, maternal education—especially high levels of education—affects all test scores, progress as measured in almost every way, and enrollment in four-year colleges. Similarly, parental aspirations for children—particularly low aspirations—influence virtually all outcomes. Among the variables that reflect student connectedness to schooling, four different measures of engagement in the academic agenda of schooling—amount of homework completed, amount of employment, attendance problems, and (to a somewhat lesser extent) amount of television watching—influence a wide variety of outcomes. In addition, participation in outside activities influences all outcomes.

Relatively few variables affect all outcomes, however, and this finding suggests that the *differentiated* view of school resources is more accurate. Teacher salaries (as a proxy for quality, presumably), teacher attitudes, instructors who teach in their field of preparation, pedagogical innovation, and constructivist or balanced practices enhance test scores consistently, as we might hope, but they do not affect student values and aspirations, and their effects on progress through high school are sporadic. Indeed, in most high schools, where teachers face 150 to 180 students a day, it is unreasonable to think that teachers could have much influence on outcomes other than classroom learning because enhancing progress or attitudes might require closer connections to students than is possible in the large anomic high school.

The effects of variables that have attracted a great deal of attention—the pupil-teacher ratio and staff development and planning time—are similarly mixed: more planning time enhances test scores but not aspirations or progress, whereas having more pupils per teacher reduces the rate of progress, completion, and enrollment in four-year colleges but does not reduce test scores (except for math). This result suggests that more planning time leads to more instructional support but may not affect the personalization of the high school, while the personalization reflected in the pupil-teacher ratio affects progress and completion but not learning. Seeking help with academic subjects and participating in extracurricular school activities enhance progress but not test scores. Somewhat surprisingly, both climate measures (a positive climate and negative events) affect test scores and attitudes but not progress; one explanation is that the measure of positive climate emphasizes dimensions related to learning, while negative events distract students from learning but do not prevent them from attending classes and accumulating credits.[26]

These results indicate that, aside from improving those school resources that influence most outcomes, high schools can choose reforms that *either* improve test scores *or* improve progress and completion. Those that improve test scores must focus on instructional improvement, especially through constructivist or balanced practices, whereas resources that make the school a more supportive place—fewer students per teacher, more counselors and help with academic work, extracurricular activities—influence progress but not learning. Ideally, high schools could improve both kinds of resources and all types of outcomes.

Overall, then, most of the *differentiated* resources affect test scores but not progress, or progress but not test scores. These findings are consistent with evaluations of several whole-school reforms. For example, the Talent Development model of high school, with its ninth-grade Success Academy, has increased attendance and credits earned, but the effects on math scores have been slight and on reading scores insignificant (Kemple, Herlihy, and Smith 2005). Career academies—schools-within-schools that integrate academic and vocational preparation and some work-based internships—have enhanced measures of motivation and engagement but not test scores (Kemple and Snipes 2000; NRC 2004, ch. 7). The Puente program, an effort to increase college-going among minority students, has increased educational aspirations, knowledge about the college application process, and enrollment in the academic courses required for college, but not grade point averages (Gándara, Gutierrez, and Molina 1998). Similarly, choice programs in San Diego have helped with racial and ethnic integration but generally have not increased test scores (Betts et al. 2006). In their efforts to enhance student motivation and engagement by creating smaller learning communities where teachers and students know one another better and by developing curricula of greater interest for self-selected students, these programs have improved attendance and course-taking, but they have not (except perhaps in the Talent Development model) invested much in enhancing instructional approaches.

Conversely, a few programs have emphasized reforming instruction, particularly through long-term staff development focused on pedagogical content knowledge (Little 2006). For example, a reform called First Things First has tried both to reshape instruction, through intense staff development and enriched language and math curricula, and to create greater support for students through small learning communities and a system of family advocates. Results indicate that this program has increased standardized test scores as well as student attendance and graduation (Quint et al. 2005). This evaluation suggests that reforms should pay explicit attention to both instructional improvement and supportive measures that enhance progress.[27]

Overall, then, high schools display a mixture of common and differentiated educational processes: a few powerful resources influence virtually all outcomes, but most resources affect some outcomes but not others. Based on this finding, studies that evaluate reforms based only on test scores are partial at best and misleading at worst, since some reforms may effectively enhance motivation, engagement, and progress—all valuable results, surely—while failing to improve learning. Schools that want to improve a variety of outcomes—learning as well as progress and attitudes toward future schooling and life courses—need to develop a wide variety of resources.

IMPLICATIONS FOR PRACTICE AND POLICY

To summarize the results in this chapter, particularly for nontechnical readers, the results clarify first and foremost that school resources make an enormous difference to explaining outcomes. In fact, compared to an equation describing a simple production function (that is, figure 1.1), the set of variables describing school resources increases explanatory power substantially more than do family background or student connectedness to schooling. This clarifies that the conclusion often drawn from simple production functions—that "schools don't make a difference," or that we do not know how schools make a difference to student outcomes—is simply incorrect. The moral is that impoverished descriptions of schools and impoverished data sets with few measures of what goes on inside schools cannot possibly capture the variety of school effects; only a comparatively rich data set like NELS88 can capture the richness of schooling. And there are many school resources that are unmeasured even in a rich data set like NELS88, including abstract resources like stability and trust; if it were possible to create an even richer data set—the "dream" data of an enterprising principal or researcher conversant with schools—we could anticipate that even more school resources would be found effective. Of course, this should not be surprising to teachers or principals or anyone else who has spent some time in schools. But it means that the strenuous efforts to explain why schools *might* not make a difference, or to find "silver bullets" or better evidence in favor of certain cherished reforms—class size, or teacher credentials, or teacher experience—are misguided, since many resources make a difference.

A second important conclusion is that a variety of school resources matter. The pupil-teacher ratio—really a measure of adults per students and personalization rather than class size—makes a difference, as many would expect, as do teacher salaries. But a variety of compound, complex, and abstract resources are more powerful than these simple resources, and therefore the tendency to emphasize simple resources, particularly in policy discussions, is misleading. Among compound resources, several descriptions of teaching conditions—teacher experience specifically in secondary education, teaching in one's field of preparation, and planning time— are important, and the effects of placement in a general, traditional vocational, or remedial track—combining teacher expectations, curriculum content (or its lack), peer effects, student ambition, and sometimes school selection mechanisms—are consistently powerful. Among complex variables, a variety of resources describing innovative and constructivist (or balanced) instruction improve learning, just as advocates since John Dewey have claimed, while conventional teaching and the use of class time for administration and maintaining order impede learning. And many abstract resources matter as well, many of them reflections of school climate and peer effects (as captured by the school's average attendance rate and school lunch subsidies). So confining our analyses to simple resources, or trying to figure out how to allocate funds to enhance simple resources only, cannot improve schools; as Eric Hanushek (1997, 141) has said, "Simple resource policies hold little hope for improving student outcomes."

While many school resources have significant effects on outcomes, none of these effects is overwhelmingly large by itself—with the exception of placement in a general, traditional vocational, or remedial track. A school, then, is a combination of many different influences—teachers and their approaches to instruction, aspects of climate and peers, forms of internal stratification like tracking, and certainly some simple resources, each with small to moderate effects. School improvement requires getting a large number of practices "right." Good schools pay attention—because of leadership, teacher selection and staff development, consistency between students and teachers (and parents), support services, the internal organization of schools—to a large number of practices. Dismal schools seem to be able to pay attention to few such practices. In addition to having obvious implications for improving schools with mediocre outcomes, the "model" of schools described here makes clear that evaluating discrete practices can never provide powerful answers about how to reform schools because no specific practice has the power to improve outcomes substantially.[28]

Finally, the valued outcomes of schooling include more than test scores. Even in this test-besotted age, making progress through high school, especially graduating and going on to college, is as important as the extent of learning, and students' aspirations and plans to continue school after high school are important because they may place upper limits on attainment. But for purposes of reform, the crucial finding is that school resources differ in their effects on specific outcome measures. Some of them have *common* effects and influence almost all outcomes in expected ways; these include track placement, school climate, and having a high number of students who seek counselors. But most school resources have *differentiated* effects. Teacher salaries (as proxies for quality), teacher attitudes, teacher planning time, instructors who teach in their field of preparation, pedagogical innovation, and constructivist or balanced practices enhance test scores consistently, but they do not influence students' values, and they rarely affect student progress through high school. The resources that suggest a more personalized school environment—the pupil-teacher ratio, seeking help with academic subjects, participating in extracurricular activities—influence progress through high school but not test scores. High schools can certainly invest in those resources with common effects, but if they are to enhance learning, they must also improve the quality of teaching. Similarly, if they are to enhance progress, including graduation, reformers should make schools into more personalized environments that provide a variety of supports for students, but they should not hope that such environments (or schools-within-schools, or small schools, or learning communities) will themselves improve learning.

Finally, the NELS88 results suggest several approaches to high school reform. First, schools should concentrate on developing resources that affect virtually all outcomes. This would mean replacing vocational and general tracks with more demanding curricula—for example, with the college-prep curricula supported by those in favor of College for All[29]; or with curricula that integrate academic and broadly occupational curricula, thus providing more choice and more obvious relevance to students; or with a variety of "pathways," both occupational and non-occupational.[30] It would also require replacing remedial efforts—emphasizing material that students have already covered, using drills and other ineffective behaviorist techniques—with intervention methods that are more constructivist, more enriched with applications, projects, and problems, and more like upper-track courses in techniques and content. The most uniformly powerful reforms would also create a school climate conducive to learning and would provide more counseling—in more efficacious forms than is usually the case—to support students. Schools would look for ways to reverse the negative effects of the most powerful aspects of family background (particularly low parental education and aspirations for children) and of student behavior (failure to complete homework, poor school attendance, general problems with getting into trouble, frequent television watching, employment, and pregnancy).

Then reform efforts should recognize that many school resources have differentiated rather than common effects. Some reforms increase attachment to schooling, such as smaller pupil-teacher ratios, more help with academic work, extracurricular activities, smaller learning communities, enhanced student choice, and increased student interest in the curriculum as its relevance is improved. These reforms increase progress and completion but are unlikely to improve test scores and, presumably, other measures of learning. Improving learning requires increasing instructional capacities and teacher innovation, characteristics that have been particularly resistant to change in high schools (Cuban 1993). One mechanism for achieving this reform is professional development focused on pedagogical improvement (Little 2006). Higher salaries might also help with teacher retention, as might better working conditions, such as increased voice in decisionmaking, better student discipline, and support from administrators (Ingersoll 2004). In the best of all worlds, high schools would undertake both kinds of reforms, though in the pinched funding of the past decade, they may be forced to choose and may in particular be forced to avoid those reforms—higher teacher salaries and reduced pupil-teacher ratios—that are the most expensive, instead concentrating on reforms that cost relatively less but require more consensus and cooperation to construct.

Unfortunately, current policies are hostile to many of the reforms that might improve high schools the most. Some of the current pressures for academic achievement have positive consequences—for example, efforts to replace general and traditional vocational tracks; the ethic of College for All, which enhances the importance of completion and progress to postsecondary education; and the adoption of accountability measures focused on low-performing students. But many current policies have made it more difficult for high schools to respond appropriately to these incentives. Test-based accountability and exit exams create pressures to enhance test scores in the short run. As I show in chapter 8, these tests and exams often lead to small intervention programs using remedial strategies and scripted curricula that are antithetical to innovative teaching and teacher control. The emphasis on reading and math test scores as the only measure of outcomes has forced schools to pay attention to a limited range of results rather than to the broader set of aspirations, values, and progress through high school that are crucial for many purposes. The conceptions of "qualified teachers" in the No Child Left Behind Act, focusing on certification, are thoroughly inadequate: the instructional approaches that improve learning in these NELS88 results are completely omitted in NCLB. Fiscal pressures work against the provision of counseling and other forms of student help, which have always been relatively marginal in high schools, as well as extracurricular activities; subtle forms of parent participation and parent education programs to enhance students' expectations are also unlikely to be developed in an era of fiscal pressure. Finally, federal policies since the Reagan administration have weakened the welfare state, including the non-educational policies that could moderate the effects of family background.

Overall, then, the current policy climate has not been supportive of the reforms that might improve both test scores and other outcomes. Until the policy wheel turns, improving the capacity of high schools to meet increased demands will continue to be difficult.

Chapter 3

When Money Does Matter: Explaining the Weak Effects of School Funding

IN THE PREVIOUS chapter, I identified the school resources that enhance a variety of schooling outcomes. This was the first task required of improved approaches to school resources. The second task is to understand better what role money plays in enhancing these effective resources—whether, as the myth of money implies, increased spending increases effective resources and then outcomes, or whether this relationship is more complex and checkered. In this chapter, I apply the NELS88 data to equation 1.3, or the causal path between revenues and school resources in figure 1.2. I look at where increased spending makes a difference, where it fails to do so, and how we might construct more effective schools in the future.

In analyzing when money might matter, the most critical question is whether increasing expenditure per student—the conventional measure of high and low spending—increases various effective school resources.[1] In addition, more detailed patterns of expenditures and revenues may affect resources. For example, various conditions are often attached to the use of state and federal revenues: state revenue often comes in the form of funds for categorical expenditures only on specific resources—textbooks or counselors or computers—and federal revenues are largely earmarked for certain groups like low-income students, English learners, and special education students. It is possible, therefore, that the sources of revenue as well as overall revenue levels may affect spending on effective resources. In addition, to test the common view that non-instructional spending is "bloat" that fails to contribute to outcomes, I examine whether the *proportion* of instructional versus non-instructional funding influences outcomes. Finally, contributions through private foundations set up by parents may enhance effective school resources, on the theory that parents spend their own money to enhance the effectiveness of schooling.

As in chapter 2, the results reported in this chapter rely on tables of regression coefficients, and those readers who are uninterested in following the details should skip the rest of this section and continue with the summary in "Revising the Money Myth." Appendix table B.2 presents coefficients on the five measures of expenditures and revenues, in regressions following equation 1.3.[2] As in the prior chapter, the numbers presented are beta coefficients, which describe the standard deviation change in the dependent variable associated with a one-standard-deviation change in the independent variable. The magnitudes of these pure numbers can be compared with each other to make statements about relative magnitude. I again include symbols for significance at 1 percent, 5 percent, and 10 percent.

SPENDING PER STUDENT: HOW EFFECTIVE IS IT?

The most powerful effects of expenditures per pupil are on simple resources, not surprisingly: the pupil-teacher ratio, low and high teacher salaries, and teacher experience in secondary education. The effects of such expenditures are all substantial, with beta coefficients ranging from $-.234$ for the pupil-teacher ratio—that is, increased spending decreases the number of students per teacher—to $.472$ for the highest teacher salary in a district. The effects of expenditures on other effective school resources, however, are much smaller. Higher spending increases teacher experience in secondary education (really a compound resource describing experience at a particular level), presumably by increasing salaries and reducing turnover. Increased spending also positively affects the amount of teacher planning time and student use of counseling, two resources that cost additional money in obvious ways—for teacher salaries and counselors. Furthermore, higher spending reduces the likelihood of conventional teaching in math and science. Although the reason for this finding is not transparent, improving the quality of teaching usually involves *sustained* professional development that requires spending for teacher release time, materials, and sometimes outside consultants (Little 2006). Finally, a number of positive but statistically marginal effects of additional spending—on more extracurricular activities, more teacher control over instruction, and an improved school climate—are less important because of relatively small beta coefficients.

However, a few of these results have the "wrong" sign. Higher expenditures appear to *reduce* teacher collaboration and *reduce* school attendance rates.[3] Higher spending reduces the likelihood of conventional teaching but also enhances the likelihood of the most innovative teaching—perhaps implying that increased spending leads to more balanced instruction that draws on both pedagogical approaches. So the effects of revenue patterns are not always clear.

Ineffective Use of Funding

If funding is used for resources that are not effective at increasing student achievement or progress, then the overall relationship between money and outcomes will also be weaker. Vocational education provides an example: although traditional vocational education is generally more expensive than other types of education, and more spending per student increases the likelihood of a student being in a vocational track (see table B.2), this spending has uniformly negative effects on outcomes—so schools with vocational education are spending more to get worse results. (This is also true for some other expensive practices, such as continuation and alternative schools and some forms of special education.) As long as more money is sometimes necessary for *ineffective* practices, the overall relationship between funding and outcomes can never be strong. The same is true, indirectly, for other kinds of spending: schools often spend money on ineffective forms of professional development, on ineffective counseling, and on planning time in which nothing much takes place. So the results in table B.2 show the *average* effects of both effective and ineffective uses of expenditures per pupil, but in any particular school the expenditures on these resources may support either effective or ineffective forms.

What is more noticeable in table B.2 is how many effective resources are *unaffected* by expenditures per student. The likelihood of teachers teaching in their field of preparation, the amount of staff development, the overall sense of efficacy among teachers, the extent to which departments encourage innovation, approaches to teaching math, and negative dimensions of school climate are all unaffected by spending per pupil. These complex and abstract resources cannot be simply bought, in the way a lower pupil-teacher ratio can be simply by hiring more teachers; instead, they must be constructed at the school level, by teachers and leaders working together to change approaches to instruction, or school climate, or innovation. If it were possible to obtain data on other abstract resources—particularly the dimensions of trust, coherence, and stability—it seems likely that these resources would also be unrelated to simple spending levels, since again they do not require expensive outlays as much as they require vision, leadership, and collaboration.

These results provide a second answer to the puzzle of why the relationship between overall spending per pupil and student outcomes is so low: not only is some funding wasted, but also some effective resources are unrelated to spending levels, while a few ineffective resources (like traditional vocational tracks) cost more. The result is to weaken the effects of spending on virtually all student outcomes.

The Implications of Instructional and Non-Instructional Spending

In addition, not all funding enhances instructional resources; some supports non-instructional programs that might have little or no positive effect on outcomes, particularly learning outcomes. Non-instructional spending covers such things as administration, maintenance, transportation, and food services—all are necessary to maintaining schools but do not directly enhance the resources that affect instruction. This form of spending has often been derided as "administrative bloat," assuming that administrators inflate their own activities at the expense of instructional improvement. If this "bloat" does take place, then we might expect to see the proportion of funding spent on instructional versus non-instructional needs positively related to effective school resources, particularly those related to improving learning and test scores.

Devoting a higher proportion of expenditures to instructional purposes has several positive effects, particularly a reduced likelihood that students will be in the general track, teachers' greater sense of control, increases in teacher salaries (almost a tautology, of course), and fewer negative events (like fighting, alcohol, and drugs) in schools. The effect on students' use of counseling is also positive, if marginal. The negative effects on staff development reflect the classification of staff development as a non-instructional category, even though it may enhance the quality of instruction—providing a good example why non-instructional expenditures should not be automatically dismissed as "administrative bloat." These modestly positive results reinforce the preference among parents and policymakers for spending on instruction and the hostility toward "bloat."

But I should caution against a too-facile labeling of administrative expenditures as "bloat," since the category of administrative spending is not precise enough to disentangle administrative waste—ineffective or even counterproductive district personnel, for example—from the use of resources for more effective principals and alternative approaches to the principalship (in the effective schools literature and research on multiple principals). The recent emphasis on principals as reform and instructional leaders has argued that some approaches to administration can be highly productive, even if it costs more to provide the district support and training to develop these kinds of school leaders. Similarly, the rare practice of having coprincipals, something that costs a small amount of additional money, can enhance the attention not only to instruction but to non-instructional supports and to teachers and parents.[4] So it is generally necessary to understand precisely what non-instructional expenditures refer to and how they might affect desirable outcomes before deciding whether they are wasteful. These are again cases in which increased spending—for example, to increase the pool of applicants from which a district might choose principals, to pay for a second principal, or to provide sustained professional development and induction programs for new principals—is necessary but not sufficient, since districts must also have a clear vision of what kinds of principals to hire.

The Effects of Revenue Sources

Public schools in the United States are funded with a mixture of local, state, and federal funds, as well as some parental contributions (especially where public funds are limited). All too often, however, state and federal revenues come with conditions that prevent them from being used most effectively—for example, in the practice of categorical grants, state and federal funds are restricted to being spent on specific resources. This poses the question of whether the proportion of funding from state, federal, and parental sources affects the resources that are "bought."

State Funding

Over time, the proportion of revenue from state sources has increased as a result of both efforts to equalize spending across districts and state efforts at reform. But as the results in table B.2 indicate, many of the effects of relatively higher state revenues are counterproductive. More state spending reduces teacher salaries, even though increasing salaries is an effective policy in the sense that it enhances outcomes like math, reading, and history scores, academic credits, and plans to continue past high school. This result may reflect the uncertainty associated with categorical funds: because they may change from year to year, districts and schools often avoid spending categorical revenues on personnel, including teachers, since any funding cutbacks would make it necessary to let teachers go.

In addition, proportionately higher state revenues *reduce* the extent of teacher innovation and collaboration and reduce teacher perceptions of their efficacy, perhaps because states are taking over the direction of instruction when they increase state revenues; if so, this would indicate that states are using their policies to constrain teachers rather than to foster more professional approaches. For example, the widespread practice of authorizing specific curricula and textbooks reduces the possibilities for teacher innovation. Relatively more state revenues reduce the likelihood of teachers teaching in their own fields, perhaps again a reflection that teachers become interchangeable parts with scripted and semiscripted curricula. Students report less supportive climates where state revenues are higher, perhaps another reflection of more rigid and test-driven approaches. These results suggest that the steady increase in state revenues over time has been a mixed blessing: it has certainly brought some increases in spending levels and some equalization of spending levels in some states, but it has also come with constraints that reduce the effectiveness of its use. Once again we see that what counts is not only the level of spending per student but the specific resources that money buys.

Federal Funding

Federal revenues also often come with restrictions, being earmarked largely for programs for certain groups of students—the educationally disadvantaged for Title I, students with disabilities for special education funding, and recent immigrant students and English learners for bilingual education funding. A higher proportion of funding from federal sources increases teacher planning time, the use of counselors, and in-field teaching. However, like state revenues, higher federal revenues also have counterproductive effects. Federal spending reduces teacher salaries, again probably reflecting the reluctance of schools and districts to use external funding for personnel and salaries. Finally, a higher proportion of federal spending—which encompasses funding for vocational education—increases enrollments in traditional vocational tracks, as we might expect, although this is hardly a benefit to students.

Overall, then, except for modest effects of federal revenues on teaching in-field and on planning time, increasing the proportion of revenues coming from state or federal sources has largely negative impacts on effective resources.

Parental Spending

We might expect to see parental contributions enhance effective resources if parents are knowledgeable about what resources are effective or if they have strong beliefs about effectiveness. Parental contributions decrease the prevalence of the general track (even after considering the effects of family background)—a curriculum widely viewed as a watered-down version of the academic track—but they fail to decrease the pupil-teacher ratio, one of the most popular reforms. Aside from enhancing teacher collaboration modestly, these sources of revenue appear to reduce certain effective resources: teacher control, innovative math teaching, teacher planning time, and extracurricular activities. Again, these results may reflect a different causal mechanism if parents in schools with mediocre teaching, little planning time, and few extracurricular activities try to raise more money. Overall, however, the effects of parental contributions on resources that improve students' achievement and progress are weak and uneven. They may, of course, fund field trips, music and arts, and other forms of "enrichment" that make life in schools more pleasant and varied, but they do not appear to help resources lead to other improved outcomes. One possible implication is that the current alarm about the fundraising by middle-income parents and its potential disequalizing effects is unwarranted, because the translation of the resulting revenues into effective resources is uncertain.

THE EFFECTS OF OTHER INFLUENCES WITHIN SCHOOLS

The equations underlying the results in the previous section, following equation 1.3 and figure 1.2, include a variety of other variables describing school characteristics to measure the potential effects on the school resources of different types of schools (private versus public, charter and magnet schools versus conventional schools); of schools with different racial and socioeconomic composition, in case families influence resource use within schools; and of schools with various types of internal governance regarding teacher and principal decisionmaking and relations with districts. These results are not reported in the appendix B tables because most coefficients are insignificant; instead, I report here on the few significant patterns in these results.

The Positive Effects of Internal Accountability

A number of observers and researchers have argued that schools are much better able to reform themselves, and to respond to demands from external accountability, if they follow an approach variously described as internal accountability (Carnoy, Elmore, and Siskin 2003); distributed leadership (Spillane 2006); organic management (Miller and Rowan 2006; Rowan 1990); and in the business literature, "High Involvement Management" (Lawler 1998). These approaches emphasize somewhat different aspects of school organization, but they are similar in replacing top-down management with more collective decisionmaking, distributed among teachers, administrators, and other stakeholders and embedded in various school-site councils and other decisionmaking groups. They focus on principals and other administrators as instructional leaders first and foremost (rather than as administrators or managers) who work with teachers to improve instruction. In place of isolated teachers focusing only on their own classrooms, such models encourage more collegial participation in the development of curricula, approaches to teaching, and the school climate in general. If these observations are correct, then we might expect to see schools that follow these approaches experiencing improved instruction, teachers' greater sense of efficacy, improved school climates, and other effective resources. These approaches to organizing schools are attractive because they allow for the enhancement of certain collective resources—complex and abstract resources in particular—that influence outcomes, and I shall return to the importance of such organization in chapter 9.

In a few cases, a pattern of significant coefficients emerges. Teachers report higher levels of control over their teaching—an effective resource enhancing test scores—in schools where there are fewer administrative and district controls, where there is greater teacher participation in decision-making, and particularly where administrators report good principal-teacher relations ($\beta = .466**$); these results confirm the value of distributed leadership (Spillane 2006). Staff development increases in schools that employ capable and strong principals and that have more coherent policies as reported by teachers ($\beta = .300**$), reinforcing a finding of Fred Newmann and his colleagues (2001) about the value of coherence. Not surprisingly, administrator-reported efforts to engage in school reforms increase the amount of staff development. External control—for example, by the district or state—*reduces* students' sense of a supportive environment, implying that efforts to restrict school autonomy are counterproductive. A measure of the coherence of the school curriculum significantly affects a number of teacher resources, including pedagogy and the stability of teachers, though it fails to affect school climate. All these findings indicate the value of enhancing control at the school level and internal alignment, which are abstract resources for which money is certainly NBNS. Other abstract resources, like principal leadership, teacher commitment, and district support, may also be important.

Overall, then, results support the hypothesis that school-level control, distributed leadership, strong principals, and more coherent policies enhance effective resources, and some of the individual coefficients are relatively high.[5] However, these results are not especially uniform, and the low explanatory power of many of these equations—given in the penultimate column of table B.2—indicates that, even with a rich data source, we know relatively little about how schools choose the resources they use.

Student Characteristics and Commitment to Schooling

In addition, the characteristics of students have various effects on school-level resources. When more students report unstable family conditions, peers with behavior problems, peers likely to drop out, and peers involved with gangs, the school climate is generally less positive and supportive and the incidence of negative events like fighting is higher, while reports of college-bound peers have the opposite effects. Administrators' reports of school problems respond to several dimensions of student background: school problems are greater in schools with more Latino and African American students, with more students from one-parent families, and with students whose native language is not English. Even after controlling for various other measures of family background, the presence of African American students reduces some effective resources, including teachers' sense of control and the schoolwide attendance rate, while a higher proportion of Latino students reduces teachers' sense of efficacy. None of these results is particularly surprising, but they indicate that students and their behavior affect the climate of schools, thereby influencing the educational outcomes of their peers. Furthermore, these results imply that schools with high proportions of such students require greater resources of various kinds—money, effective leadership, external support, and more elaborate forms of student support, including guidance and tutoring. The need for additional resources in such schools emerges repeatedly in the claims of advocates for "high-need" schools. The weighted student funding formulas used in some districts, which allocate more revenue per student to schools with more low-income and immigrant students, is a partial recognition of the revenue requirements of high-need students.

However, despite the rich array of variables in table B.2, the explanatory power of the results is disappointing, as reported in the next-to-last column of the table. Explanatory power is high only for simple school resources, including the pupil-teacher ratio, teacher salaries (powerfully affected by spending per pupil), and school climate as reported by administrators (strongly affected by student backgrounds). Explanatory power is otherwise low to moderate, in the range of 4 to 25 percent. In particular, variables reflecting pedagogical approaches, teachers teaching in the field of their degree, teacher attitudes, teacher planning time, staff development, access to counseling and extracurricular activities, and teacher experience in the same school all have R-squareds of .16 or lower, indicating that a great deal of variation in both support for teachers and services for students is random, as far as we can tell from these data.

Furthermore, some variables that advocates have championed are almost never significant in their impact on effective resources. Magnet schools and schools of choice do not enhance effective resources. The size of high schools and therefore small schools make virtually no difference to these results, confirming a common contention that size may affect pupil-teacher contacts or school climate but has little direct effect on outcomes. State and district exit exams and competency tests are almost completely ineffective in explaining the variation in effective resources; evidently these forms of external accountability fail to drive schools to use resources more effectively, and indeed they may have *negative* effects on resource use. Teacher observation, a personal favorite because of its ability to enhance conversations about instruction (Grubb 2000) and because it has emerged as a powerful way for principals to monitor and then improve instruction, has distinctly mixed effects: it reduces teachers' sense of autonomy ($\beta = -.089**$) while enhancing their sense of efficacy ($\beta = .057*$), but has few other significant effects. Evidently, several school practices that have been promoted by advocates as paths to more effective schools do not have especially powerful effects on the resources known to enhance outcomes.[6]

From the poor explanatory power of many of these equations I conclude that, even with much more detailed data than usual, we lack powerful explanations for what shapes the resource decisions of schools and districts, particularly when it comes to *effective* resources.[7] One reason is that many schools may simply be unaware of what the most effective resources are. As I show in chapter 8, based on a limited sample of twelve schools, many schools make resource decisions in random and haphazard ways, getting information about supposedly effective practices from doubtful sources and failing to understand false claims about "proven practices." Second, schools rarely have significant control over the way they use funds and other resources: decisions are often determined by districts, by district-level bargaining agreements, and by historical patterns of spending, and the political and symbolic issues that surround educational spending, rather than issues of effectiveness, often consume districts, especially urban districts. Moreover, in most districts aside from those that adopt school-based budgeting, schools do not have enough resources under their control to make it worth investing in the information and decisionmaking procedures that would enhance effective resources. Under these conditions, the characteristics of the schools that we might expect to enhance resource use have little effect, just as these NELS88 results indicate.[8] The policy implication of these results is that, in order to think more carefully about the effectives of resources, schools must have enough discretionary funding to make these decisions matter, without district or state interference, and sufficient expertise about effectiveness to make wise choices. Without these conditions, not surprisingly, the only strong effects of money are on simple resources.

REVISING THE MONEY MYTH

To summarize the effects of funding and revenue patterns on effective resources, these results indicate once again the usefulness of distinguishing simple resources, derived from the identity in equation 1.2, from compound, complex, and abstract resources. The effects of spending on simple resources are powerful and direct: decreasing the pupil-teacher ratio requires hiring more teachers, which requires more funding per student, as does increasing the salary structure of a district or (to a lesser extent) the experience levels of teachers in secondary education. Greater expenditures also make possible more planning time and allow increased access to counselors and extracurricular activities—again, school resources that obviously cost money—but these effects are much smaller. For the most part, then, districts with higher expenditures per student invest them in simple resources, ignoring a greater variety of effective practices. On the contrary, overall expenditures per pupil have few and inconsistent effects on other resources, particularly those related to the quality of instruction and to measures of school climate. While simple resources—such as additional teachers and increased salaries—can be bought, communities of educators must work together to construct most other resources. Even when additional money may be necessary, other factors are crucial—for example, school autonomy, collegial decisionmaking, and distributed leadership, all of which we might also consider abstract resources.

Other dimensions of funding and revenue patterns have even weaker effects on effective resources. Increasing the fraction of spending on instructional rather than non-instructional spending ("administrative bloat") does have some positive effects, especially on enhancing teacher control and reducing the likelihood of students being in a vocational or general track, but these results must be interpreted with caution since some specific forms of administration spending, which generally cannot be disentangled from other kinds of spending, may have positive effects on outcomes. Higher proportions of state and federal revenues increase overall spending levels and the equity of spending but have largely negative influences on resources, since these revenues come with conditions that constrain schools from enhancing teacher collaboration, innovation, and control. A few measures of internal accountability and distributed leadership affect effective resources, especially teacher control over instruction, professional development, and the coherence of the curriculum, but these effects are also relatively small and sporadic. Under current conditions—most schools having little discretionary revenue, districts and states constraining much of what schools do, and schools (most with very little expertise in effective practices) often making spending decisions in haphazard ways—the incentives and conditions necessary for more effective use of resources is simply missing.

Finally, an unpleasant but unsurprising finding is that student characteristics influence school resources. Unstable family conditions, behavior problems, gangs, higher dropout rates, students from one-parent families, immigrant students, and higher proportions of African American and Latino students all influence certain resources negatively. This is a statistical way of stating the more conventional (and often derogatory) description of "urban" schools, and it clarifies what it means to say that such students and schools are high-need: these schools need additional resources to overcome the negative effects of their students on such resources as teacher control and efficacy, school climate, and attendance. In chapters 4 and 5, I return to these aspects of student background and come up with different interpretations of class and racial effects. But as schools are now constituted, the composition of their student bodies influences certain resources.

With these results, we now have a more complete understanding of the money myth and of why money doesn't matter that much for so many educational outcomes. Some money is simply wasted, as I argued in chapter 1 and as other evidence presented in part III will illustrate. Sometimes more money is necessary for resources that actually weaken outcomes, most obviously in the case of conventional vocational programs, but also when schools spend money on the wrong kind of professional development, on textbooks and curriculum materials that follow conventional pedagogies, or on remedial programs that substitute low-content drill for a richer curriculum. Very often money is necessary in conjunction with other resources to create compound resources—new curricula (or computers or class size reduction) plus professional development, the abolition of ineffective tracks plus the creation of more ambitious "pathways," counselors plus student initiative. And most important of all, some effective resources cannot be bought and increased spending does not lead to higher levels of such resources, again weakening the connection between spending and outcomes. Instead, complex and abstract resources must be constructed by teachers and leaders working collectively at the school level without much money but with certain other resources (leadership, collaboration, and vision).

Of course, these conclusions do *not* mean that money doesn't matter, or that it would not matter much more under the right incentives and conditions at the school level. Increasing spending does enhance simple resources, as well as compound resources with identifiable costs like counselors and professional development, and very often complex and abstract school resources require small amounts of additional funding. The conclusion that money doesn't matter is not correct, and fiscal conservatives and opponents of funding equalization should not take comfort from the complexities of an improved approach to school resources. But money by itself is not enough to ensure greater effectiveness.

We can now understand why policies driven by the myth of money have never been reliable ways of enhancing outcomes. The long history of efforts to expand state aid to schools, starting in the early twentieth century, has certainly led to schools with better physical facilities, teachers with higher salaries, and many new programs for particular groups of students. But there is no reason to think that these funds have supported more effective resources in general, and indeed the fraction of revenues from states generally has negative effects on resources. The similarly long history of efforts to equalize funding—either by manipulating school finance formulas or more recently through litigation that in turn redistributes funding—has led to sporadic equalization of spending but done nothing to equalize outcomes (as I will argue at greater length in chapter 11). Similarly, efforts to allocate more funding to low-performing students and schools has dominated federal policy in Title I, yet constant debates about the effectiveness of Title I and now NCLB provide yet another illustration that additional funding may have scant effects on outcomes. The development of accountability mechanisms as part of state aid and the No Child Left Behind Act has created incentives to spend money effectively but has not always given low-performing schools and districts the capacity to do so—as we will see in chapter 8, where I examine a sample of schools to see what they are now doing to reduce inequality, and in chapter 10, where I examine state and federal policy. A large number of policies have been predicated on the myth of money, yet this approach proves to be inadequate.

To be sure, some approaches to school reform have tried directly to enhance specific school resources that we can identify as effective. A number of reforms have tried to enhance the quality of instruction through professional development of the "right" kind, often focusing explicitly on constructivist or balanced approaches to teaching. For example:

- First Things First has tried both to enhance instruction, through intense staff development and enriched language and math curricula, and to create greater support for students through small learning communities and a system of family advocates (Quint et al. 2005).

- The DiME (Diversity in Mathematics Education) program is an extensive and lengthy effort to change teachers' views and practices about instruction, content, and the capacities of students, in ways consistent with effective teaching.[9]

- Math teachers at Railside School banded together to develop their own innovative math curricula, based more on exploration of mathematical concepts than on routine drill of mathematical procedures (Boaler and Staples 2008).

- Schools that have developed professional learning communities usually collaborate to improve teaching practices by discussing student work, observing in each others' classrooms, and making instructional practices a central focus of discussion.

Other attempted reforms include a wide range of efforts to create smaller high schools and more supportive schools, thus enhancing some of the resources that reduce dropout and contribute to progress through school. Some have tried to replace general tracks and traditional vocational education with more demanding curricula, particularly in the High Schools That Work of the Southern Regional Education Board; these schools have either replaced the general track with academic tracks or tried to integrate academic and occupational education. Other schools have created theme-based curricula or pathways, or, like Comer schools and full-service schools, they have expanded the range of supportive services beyond conventional counseling and tutoring. These are all examples of schools focusing on particular kinds of school resources, shifting from ineffective to more effective patterns of resource use. When I turn more explicitly to policies at various levels in chapters 9 and 10, these kinds of reforms concentrating on certain school resources—resources that are arguably or demonstrably more effective—provide us with alternatives to the narrative of money as ways of improving outcomes.

The real value of the improved school finance, then, is that it can direct our attention away from funding issues to the crucial questions of what resources are most effective in enhancing schooling outcomes. Then the problem becomes one of increasing these particular resources, using funding as appropriate but remembering that funding may be NBNS. Other elements of schools—appropriate leadership, vision, capacity building, internal accountability, teacher support and improvement—may be even more powerful in making schools effective.

Chapter 4

Families as Resources:
The Effects of Family Background and
Demographic Variables

SCHOOL RESOURCES are not the only inputs that matter to outcomes. At least since the charity schools for the poor of the early nineteenth century, educators have noticed that the families from which children come—poor or rich, immigrant or native-born, working-class or middle-class, black or white—influence their prospects. As noted by DeWitt Clinton, one of the early supporters of charity schools in New York, the children of the poor would, except for the intervention of the schools, be "brought up in ignorance, and amidst the contagion of bad example, are in imminent danger of ruin" (Kaestle 1983, 84). The efforts to develop the common schools of the nineteenth century—publicly supported schools that would provide a common curriculum to all students—were also premised on the idea that some children would otherwise escape schooling because of the inattention of their parents; as a result, serious efforts were made "to persuade the indifferent and careless to send their children to school" (117), efforts later expressed in compulsory attendance laws and their enforcement. The differentiation of schools after 1890 was explicitly based on observations about the varying "needs" of children from different family backgrounds; as two educators commented in 1906:

> It is obvious that the educational needs of children in a district where the streets are well paved and clean, where the homes are spacious and surrounded by lawns and trees, where the language of the child's play-fellows is

pure, and where life in general is permeated with the spirit and ideals of America—it is obvious that the educational needs of such a child are radically different from those of a child who lives in a foreign and tenement section. (Elson and Bachman 1910, 360)

And the efforts to incorporate immigrant children into public schools have almost always focused on "Americanizing" them, or replacing their foreign ways and family effects with the American norms of the schools; as one educator declared about immigrant parents:

They must be made to understand what it is we are trying to do for the children. They must be made to realize that in forsaking the land of their birth, they were forsaking the customs and traditions of that land; and they must be made to realize an obligation, in adopting a new country, to adopt the language and customs of that country. (Tyack and Cuban 1995, 237)[1]

These were largely concerns about equality of access—about making sure that all children were included in schooling, one of the simplest concepts of equity developed in chapter 6. But educators also noticed that family background affected school performance as well, so simply incorporating all children into schools did not create other forms of equity—equity in learning, or years of schooling completed, or anything else about education that mattered to adult outcomes. The Coleman Report (Coleman et al. 1966) found a substantial influence of family background, especially parental education, and modern social science has confirmed these effects: virtually every examination of schooling performance has found substantial advantages to families of higher standing, whether measured by income, occupation, parental education, or some other dimension (Sirin 2005).

The continued influence of family background is rooted in many aspects of the relationships between families and school, including a transformation in the ways families can influence their children's future. In the nineteenth century, before schools played much of a role in occupational attainment, families could ensure their children's future by passing on occupations directly: sons inherited businesses from their fathers, or fathers arranged promising apprenticeships for their sons. But over the course of the twentieth century, educational institutions became vocationalized, or oriented toward preparation for future vocations, and indeed they became the only route to certain high-status occupations (especially the professions). In this process, the direct link between families and adult status became weaker and the link through schooling became stronger (Grubb and Lazerson 2004). Today families no longer sponsor their children's future success directly, by and large, but indirectly—by preparing them for schooling and sustaining their performance through formal education; by choosing schools for their children to attend and influencing those schools on behalf of their children; and by supporting both financially and emotionally their children's participation in postsecondary education.

But the increased motivation for parents to sponsor their children through successful schooling does not explain why some parents have been more able than others to do so. Do these patterns, consistent as they are, reflect the income advantages of middle-class families—their ability to provide richer experiences, better preschool programs, after-school activities, private schools or access to communities with the best public schools, and supplements to schooling like computers or tutoring or (at the high school level) private college counseling? Do these patterns reflect the educational advantages of well-educated parents—the kind of informal education that takes place in the early years, the education at the dinner table, the ability to provide children with advice and to run interference for them as they make their way through bureaucratic institutions? Or do they reflect the ways in which schools react to students from different backgrounds—expecting more of some and less of others, treating some with respect while demeaning or neglecting others?

In this chapter, I use the rich data of NELS88 first to explore the effects of family background on schooling outcomes, identifying many different dimensions of family background that might explain outcomes. Next, because the *causal* relationships underlying these *statistical* relationships are not always transparent, I examine some of the enormous qualitative literature on the effects of parents to explain what these results might mean.

Then I turn to racial and ethnic patterns of outcomes. In the United States, with its long history of strained and sometimes violent racial relationships, issues of family background have almost always been racialized. Current discussions about inequality in outcomes are invariably led by evidence about the achievement gap, and this is virtually always described as the gap in test scores between black and white students (or the Latino-Anglo gap, especially in progress through schooling). And because race or ethnicity and other dimensions of family background overlap, it has always been difficult to know whether racial-ethnic issues are to blame, or whether class dominates race, or whether it might be necessary to address both of these dimensions of family background in different ways. Not surprisingly, some of the achievement gap attributed to race and ethnicity can be explained by differences in school resources and other components by class differences. But at the end of all this analysis, there remains a stubborn racial-ethnic gap that cannot be explained in any other way—what I call the racial or demographic residual. If we as a society are to make schools effective for all students, or if we aspire to close the many racial-ethnic gaps, then we need first to explain the racial residual, as I do in this chapter, and then identify what might be done to eliminate it—a set of recommendations I reserve for chapter 9.

The implications of all this for school reforms and policy initiatives are not straightforward—just as the implications of finding certain school resources to be more effective than others are not straightforward. Some dimensions of family background can be more readily changed than others—income patterns, for example, are conceptually (though not politically) easy to change through tax and transfer policies, while the language of a child's family cannot be changed (though its consequences can be modified). Some racial dimensions of inequality can be manipulated with conventional policies—policies related to the assignment of teachers, for example, or to school climate—while others require that specifically racial dimensions of inequality be confronted head on, something that public schools have always been reluctant to do.

In the search for reasons explaining the outcomes of low-performing children, sometimes parents have been blamed, and sometimes schools have been blamed (Deschenes, Cuban, and Tyack 2001). This has often led to debates over what policies should be stressed—whether it is necessary to "fix" families or to narrow the inequalities among families that generate unequal schooling outcomes, or whether we should "fix" schools instead, focusing on school reform alone. In this either-or debate, the possibilities for creating coherent "both-and" policies—focusing *both* on school reform *and* on the dimensions of family background related to schooling outcomes—have often been forgotten. When I reflect in chapter 12 on the variety of policies necessary to create equity, I stress policies well outside of education—in health and housing, income support, labor market regulation, community development and locational policies—that are *complementary* to school reforms, a Deweyan both-and rather than either-or approach to reform that recognizes how important families are to schooling.

THE EFFECTS OF FAMILY BACKGROUND

Like school resources, family background can be measured in many different ways, with varying causal interpretations.[2] The NELS88 data collection included extensive questionnaires to parents that enabled researchers to construct a broad array of family background measures.[3] I include maternal education as a set of three dummy variables for low, medium, and high levels of schooling since parents, and especially mothers, are the first and most enduring teachers of children. Maternal occupation is represented by two dummy variables: one for unskilled occupations and one for professional and managerial occupations. In my interpretation, parents in professional and managerial occupations are more likely to give students access to information about the relationship between schooling (or skills) and occupations and also are more likely to provide children with certain positive attitudes toward schooling that are beneficial to their commitment, whereas those in unskilled occupations are much less likely to pass on these beneficial attitudes and information. An additional effect of occupational status might be that parents in professional or managerial positions have increased stature, power, and confidence in encounters with school officials. Income per dependent (to reflect differences in family size) is also included, adjusted for cost differentials across districts and over time to reflect differences in purchasing power. In addition, a dummy variable describes whether parents have saved for college, a dimension of wealth specific to the quest for postsecondary education. Parental aspirations for their children, as reported by students, are also measured.

Family structure is reflected in a variable for female-headed households, which is conventionally thought to measure less attention from parents, less support of schooling, and the greater stresses on mothers in such families. The presence of family changes—divorce, separation, remarriage, or new cohabitation—is considered, reflecting stability and instability in family life; substantial ethnographic and journalistic evidence indicates that changing or unstable families are less likely to pay attention to children (DeParle 2004; LeBlanc 2003). A variable denoting families whose native language is not English is incorporated to examine the potential problems that English learners may have, both on standardized tests in English and in progress through high school. Finally, religious affiliation is measured because of the reportedly stabilizing influence of religion, especially in African American and Latino families.

Because the correlations among these different measures of family background are relatively low, collinearity is not a problem.[4] That is, the different measures of family background are relatively independent of one another, and their effects can be distinguished from one another, which would not be the case if they were highly correlated.

Parental Background and Values

The results for different measures of family background are presented in appendix table B.3, for the same twelve outcome measures described in chapter 2. Again, those who are coefficient-averse should skip the presentation of these detailed results and go to the section entitled "A Summary of the Quantitative Findings."

The most consistent and powerful effects are those of maternal education. More education is always better than less. However, the effects are nonlinear, because having a mother with at least a bachelor's degree is particularly beneficial, affecting all test scores, aspirations, and several measures of progress through high school (total credits earned and completion of an academic program) as well as progression to a four-year college. Middling levels of schooling (some college) make little difference except to accumulating credits, aspiring to continue education, and going to a four-year college (although some college experience for a mother also has small positive effects on test scores). Similarly, the effects of low levels of schooling (mother's education less than high school) are universally negative, but they are often insignificant and quite small.

The converse is true of occupation levels, which are overall less powerful than education. Having a mother employed in unskilled work is consistently detrimental, but the effects are relatively small (with betas in the range of −.02 to −.03), except for a slightly larger effect when it comes to attending community college. Having a parent in a professional or managerial occupation does not affect outcomes, once other dimensions of family background are considered.

Similarly, income has consistently positive effects, but they are significant only for two of the test scores (math and history) and for high educational aspirations.[5] The other measure related to income—saving for college—affects, as we might expect, dimensions of college-going: the intention to continue education after high school, the completion of an academic program, and the likelihood of attending a four-year college. Otherwise, income is not particularly powerful. Of the various measures conventionally thought to measure overall socioeconomic status, parental education is by far the most important.

One dimension of parental values—aspirations for their children—is almost as powerful as their education. High parental aspirations for their children affect students' aspirations (not surprisingly), as well as their plans to continue education, complete an academic program, and obtain a diploma; these effects are much more powerful than the influences on test scores. Low aspirations, on the other hand, affect the entire range of outcomes, with betas that are sometimes over .10 (or less than −.10). The combination of low aspirations and low education levels, or conversely high aspirations and high education levels, is particularly powerful.

In contrast, another measure of family values sometimes asserted to affect schooling positively—religious affiliation—is usually not significant, and coefficients are generally modest when it is. In results not included in table B.3, religious observance reduces the likelihood of low aspirations for black and Latino students significantly more than for white students, though it also reduces math and reading scores among blacks—so overall there is no strong support for the effects of religion in African American and Latino communities.

Family Structure

Once education and income are considered, living in a female-headed household reduces the accumulation of credits and the likelihood of receiving a diploma. I interpret this as reflecting the relative lack of pressure, support, and encouragement that students receive when their mothers have so many responsibilities without a spouse to share them.

Family instability is, if anything, detrimental to schooling, though its effect is statistically significant only for the likelihood of continuing to a four-year college. However, the measure of family change developed here may not be especially powerful since it largely reflects the effects of divorce and separation and probably fails to capture the truly hideous effects of violence, drugs, and shifting housing on very poor students (see, for example, LeBlanc 2003). However, changing schools is clearly detrimental (as others have found, including Rumberger and Larson 1998). Residential instability does not particularly affect test scores, but it does reduce all measures of progress—credits accumulated, completing an academic program, completing a high school diploma, and going on to a four-year college. The finding that it increases rates of attending community colleges is testament to the second-chance nature of these institutions: students with promise who, because they have changed schools, have not completed enough credits or the academic courses required for a four-year college, or have parents who failed to save for college, can still go to community college and continue up the ladder of educational opportunity.

The potential negative effects of having a mother tongue different from English are not particularly substantial. English-language learners typically have lower reading test scores, not surprisingly, but effects on other tests are insignificant. And the effects on credits accumulated are positive, perhaps reflecting the additional effort that immigrant groups are often said to make in school.

A Summary of the Quantitative Findings

As was true for school resources, the effects of family background are weakened somewhat in specification 2, which includes tenth-grade test scores. Indeed, a few variables that are strongly significant in specification 1—particularly high maternal education—become insignificant in specification 2. The reason, particularly for measures of family background (like maternal education) that are time-invariant, is that the lagged test scores themselves embody strong family background effects. Interestingly, then, the effects of family background measures are much weaker in specification 2 than are the effects of school resources. This finding again casts doubt on the conclusion in older literature that school effects are weaker than those of family background.

As was true for school resources, there is some evidence that—aside from parental education and aspirations, which affect all outcomes (that is, they have *common* effects)—the variables that reflect family influences do not have consistent effects on all outcomes: their effects are *differentiated*. Several variables (like being a member of a female-headed family and changing schools) affect progress through schooling but not test scores or attitudes. Conversely, religious values affect test scores, presumably reflecting discipline and diligence, but not other outcomes. Similarly, some demographic variables differ in their effects on test scores versus progress. Males do better than females in test scores (except for reading), but their progress, completion, and rates of attending four-year colleges are lower. With racial-ethnic effects on test scores much higher in an absolute sense than the effects of race-ethnicity on aspirations or progression through schooling, the current emphasis on test scores overstates racial-ethnic differences; if we were as concerned with progress through high school as with test scores, the racial "gap"—almost always stated in terms of learning measures (see, for example, Jencks and Phillips 1998)—would seem smaller. Physical disability affects test scores negatively, but not progress; this suggests that the benefits of special education, or other supportive treatments of disabled students, emerge in ways that are not well measured by test scores.

Overall, then, the effects of family background come largely through parental education and aspirations for their children, and secondarily through the negative effects of mothers in low-skilled occupations—but not through income. Some of the beta coefficients (in the range of $\pm.05$ to $\pm.11$) are quantitatively more powerful than the beta coefficients for most effects of school resources, with the exception of curriculum tracks. And as was true of school resources, some dimensions of family background—particularly changing schools and living in a female-headed family—influence attitudes and measures of progress more than they influence test scores, exemplifying the value of including a broader range of outcome measures in considering effects on schooling.

QUALITATIVE RESEARCH AS EVIDENCE OF CAUSALITY

Quantitative analysis from data like NELS88 can clarify that various dimensions of family background affect (or fail to affect) schooling outcomes, but they cannot be precise about the causal mechanisms underlying these effects. The qualitative literature is more helpful here, because it can typically describe in much greater detail how different dimensions of family background affect children. Unfortunately, because this literature is vast and comes from many different disciplines and perspectives, summarizing it briefly is almost impossible.[6] Often researchers have been able to find whatever they were looking for: those concerned with particular racial-ethnic minorities have found differences in the treatment of black and Latino students; those more attuned to issues of class have found class effects overriding racial effects; those concerned with language issues have found differences in language acquisition; those concentrating on family structure have found female-headed families—or families with shifting composition or unstable families—to have detrimental effects on their children. But a different interpretation is that the effects of family background—and the effects of such powerful variables as parental education and family stability—are so varied and so pervasive that they influence outcomes in multiple and overlapping ways.

The Many Dimensions of Parental Background

One way to start unpacking family effects is to review what the literature says about the variables I stressed in the previous section. Parental education, for example, underlies a considerable literature about "families as educators" (Leichter 1974)—that is, parents as the first and most comprehensive teachers of their children, whose influences not only prepare children for the start of school but continue as they reinforce school lessons with dinnertime conversations, help children with their homework, provide educative activities and trips, and exert constant pressure to succeed. Well-educated parents can also better inform their children about the paths through a complex schooling system, one that is more transparent to those who have been through it—hence the concern for youth who are "the first in their family to go to college." And the idea that parents of different class backgrounds have varying advantages in preparing their children for school, an old idea in wide circulation at least since the beginning of the nineteenth century, has recently been restated in economic language by Pierre Bourdieu (Bourdieu and Passeron 1977). His notion of "cultural capital" describes a variety of attitudes and values that are helpful in formal schooling and more likely to be passed on by middle-class families.

Another dimension of education comes through language: professional parents (compared to working-class and welfare parents) talk with their children more, use larger vocabularies, use more diverse language, provide more affirmative feedback rather than corrections and discouragements, and are more likely to respond to their children (Hart and Risley 1995).[7] Basil Bernstein (1995) has contrasted the "restricted codes" of working-class families—particularistic and tied to local meanings—with the elaborated codes of middle-class families, which are more universalistic, abstract, and consistent with the language of schools. The ways in which Shirley Heath (1983, ch. 7, epilogue) contrasts the middle-class townspeople, or "mainstreamers," with both black and white working-class populations in Piedmont mill towns also stress language and literacy differences, as well as many other differences related to rhythms of life, views of schooling, and interactions with the wider world. Similarly, Patricia Gándara's (1995) review stresses literacy as the key to school engagement, with differential literacy arising from language differences among families. Much of the qualitative literature on the effects of family background stresses the role of language, and the effects on English tests in table B.3 and on other language-related school competencies are the results.

It is less obvious how family background should affect math performance and subjects related to math, and there has been much less research on math-related activities within families.[8] However, an ethnographic study of two- and four-year-olds by Geoffrey Saxe, Steven Guberman, and Maryl Gearhart (1987) revealed a large number of math-related activities taking place in families, including number-oriented play, counting and grouping, and activities related to telling time and spatial relations. The observers found few and insignificant differences between middle-class and working-class families at age two, but class-related differences emerged by age four, particularly on more complex tasks, suggesting that the development of language in children is associated with the emergence of class differences. (Class was measured for this study by Duncan's index of socioeconomic status.) To some extent, these results are due to differences in parenting that affect many outcomes—for example, middle-class parents are more responsive to their children, more cooperative, more involved in teaching and playing, and less directive and authoritarian, and they use more elaborated language—but specifically for math activities, middle-class mothers structured more complex goals on more difficult problems than did working-class mothers, helping their children achieve more elaborated results than the children could have achieved on their own. The role of middle-class parents in helping their children on complex mathematical activities is likely to continue as their children grow older and encounter increasingly complex math in school (Hess and Holloway 1984).

Still other dimensions of class emphasize the interactions between middle-class parents and their children, which presumably apply to all subjects and many behaviors in formal schooling. Annette Lareau's (2003) concept of "concerted cultivation" describes the efforts of middle-class parents to engage their children in a variety of activities (such as music and dance lessons and sports activities) and to interact with their schools and teachers, much as schools themselves are devoted to concerted cultivation on behalf—ideally, but not necessarily—of all children. In contrast, working-class parents are more likely to leave their children to their own devices, to converse less with their children, and to have less interaction with their schools. In an earlier work, Lareau (2000) stresses the differences between middle-class families interacting with schools—they tend to see schools as complementary to their efforts and therefore try to participate in and collaborate with them—and working-class families viewing the efforts of schools as essentially separate from and independent of what parents do, often being intimidated by schools and educational authority, and therefore engaging much less in influencing the schooling process (on Latino parents, see Romo and Falbo 1996). Lareau's work also reinforces the differences in language patterns among families of different classes, including verbal agility and fluidity, use of abstract concepts, and practice in the "rules of the game," including facility in speaking with adults.

These descriptions of interactions between parents and schools are quite similar to those of Reginald Clark (1983), who describes the varying ability of African American parents—middle-class and working-class, in two-parent and one-parent families—to channel their children's activities. In an interaction between parental and community influences, negative influences such as gangs are more likely to attract black lower-income children and youth who have not been channeled or directed by parents. Clark also notes the ways in which black middle-class parents, in both one- and two-parent families, are more likely to foster "interpersonal competence," including knowledge of how to interact with adults, a skill that serves them well in school. In this work, Clark defines class by parental occupation, though the differences among families are associated more with education than with occupation—and for many families the two coincide.

Overall, the qualitative literature reinforces the importance of parental education in schooling outcomes. But it also clarifies that the causal mechanisms are varied and include the educational consequences of more complex language patterns in well-educated families, the differences in the child-rearing practices and attitudes of middle-class parents (for example, Lareau's "concerted cultivation" and Clark's "interpersonal competence"), and the ways in which middle-class parents interact with social institutions, including schools.

The Importance of Parental Aspirations

In many ways, the finding that aspirations play such an important role runs contrary to much of the qualitative literature. Many authors have taken great pains not to denigrate parents and to stress that all parents want the best for their children and hope that their children will do well in school. As Lareau (2003) expresses this, there are fewer differences in *attitudes* among parents than in *behavior*. But parental behaviors convey expectations in many ways: in the pressures on youth in low-income families to contribute to family income; in the tendency in Latino families to not "let go" of girls and to expect young males to work; in the likelihood that chaotic families will pay less attention to their children's school attendance, behavior, and performance (LeBlanc 2003); in the presence or absence of what some have called "academic press," as important in families as in schools. Students who reported their parents' low expectations of them in the NELS88 data may well have been reacting more to these kinds of behaviors than to attitudes.

The Effects of Parental Occupations

Research that focuses specifically on the effects of parental occupation seems less common, even though occupation is usually often considered a component of class or socioeconomic status. However, Melvin Kohn (Kohn 1977; Kohn and Schooler 1983) has confirmed that parents in professional and managerial occupations are more likely to promote independence in their children, while parents in working-class and routine occupations are more likely to stress conformity, obedience to rules, and conventionally "good behavior"—these values coming in obvious ways from the requirements of their own work. (The importance of independence in Kohn's work is parallel to Lareau's "concerted cultivation" and Clark's "interpersonal competence": all three ideas make the point that middle-class children are more likely to be the active and motivated students whom teachers most enjoy.) Independence is more likely to lead to strong school performance—particularly in classes that emphasize constructivist or balanced pedagogies and student-centered approaches and in high-track rather than low-track classes. Conversely, the patterns of conformity and obedience that working-class parents instill are likely to be more appropriate in middle and lower tracks or in high schools dominated by working-class students.

A very different interpretation of occupation is that individuals in unskilled positions simply do not understand the connection between schooling and employment and thus leave their children unclear about this connection (Rosenbaum, Deil-Amen, and Person 2006; Schneider and Stevenson 1999)—an understanding that is crucial now that schooling has become the dominant route to vocations. Alternatively, working-class parents may not value schooling as a route to upward mobility, preferring to stress instead hard work as the mechanism of the American Dream,[9] while parents in professional occupations are sure to stress education. (See also Shirley Brice Heath's [1983] descriptions of how parents pass on attitudes toward schooling.) Like education, parental occupation affects schooling in several different ways; because parental education and occupation both operate to some extent, it is as difficult to disentangle them with qualitative evidence as with quantitative analysis.

The Role of Family Composition

Many authors have focused on family composition, especially the negative effects of living in a female-headed household—because such households tend to have lower income, less attention from adults, and a lack of male role models. But in a comparison of two- and one-parent black families, Clark (1983) found that "family intactness is not a necessary or sufficient condition for high quality learning in the home" and pointed instead to family interactions and the role of parents in promoting "sponsored independence" rather than engaging in unsponsored or laissez-faire child-rearing. (Lareau's concept of "concerted cultivation" is similar to this finding, though she did not look explicitly at single-parent families.) These conclusions are consistent with my result that, once other aspects of families like parental education and income are considered, living in a female-headed family does not affect learning as measured by test scores. It does, however, reduce progress as measured by credits earned and high school graduation, presumably because single mothers are less able than two-parent families to monitor their children and keep them on track to graduation.

Similarly, language problems have been the focus of enormous amounts of research and advocacy on behalf of children described as "English learners" or "language-minority" students. Revisiting the theme of linguistic facility as it relates to parental education and class, we see that language may operate differently in different communities: while both Latino and Asian students are more likely than others to have a non-English native language,[10] for other reasons Latino and Asian American students succeed quite differently in schools. Thus, the effect of language is less powerful once other dimensions of family background are considered, especially parental education and aspirations.

Family (in)Stability as a Factor

Family instability is surely detrimental to children, though again, there are different ways to conceive of instability. One way is to look at marital instability—parents separating, divorcing, remarrying, and re-creating family constellations that are more or less stressful and supportive of children. While the long-run consequences of divorce are often negative (Wallerstein, Lewis, and Blakelee 2000), the short-run effects can be either positive or negative—perhaps explaining why the effects of family change measured in this way are relatively weak in the NELS88 results.

Physical mobility, a different type of instability, can have greater effects for a student than marital instability by disrupting the curriculum, the accumulation of course credits, and relationships with other students and teachers alike; students moving continuously from one school to another have to make a series of adjustments that cost them effort, time, and continuity. What causes physical mobility is not well researched, but my informal questioning of teachers indicates that housing problems—being evicted, being unable to pay rent, having intolerable arguments with housemates—are more often to blame than the middle-class mobility of parents being transferred to new jobs.

In addition, ethnographic and journalistic accounts describe the farming out of low-income children and youth among relatives and "cousins" when one member has a crisis, is evicted, or is otherwise unable to care for a child (DeParle 2004; LeBlanc 2003). It is easy for students in these situations to escape going to school since no one is really paying attention to their comings and goings. And so the measurable dimensions of instability are pallid compared to the reality of the worst-off families, for whom the confluence of poverty, violence, drugs, and mental health problems creates a perfect storm of debilitating conditions.

THE EFFECTS OF RACE AND ETHNICITY

Another dimension of family background is race and ethnicity—if only because these characteristics are inherited from parents. Family background in the United States is frequently racialized: race is used as a proxy for class, and many more schooling outcomes are measured for racial-ethnic groups than for groups defined by any measures of class. In this section, I examine the effects of race and ethnicity—being white, African American, Latino, Asian American, or American Indian.[11] (I leave the effects of gender and physical disability to chapter 5 on students as resources.) These racial-ethnic variables are conventionally included in almost all analyses of educational outcomes, and in virtually every analysis—qualitative or quantitative—they prove to have substantial effects on most outcomes, even after considering the influence of many other variables. Although this finding is nearly universal and surely unsurprising, it is also undesirable because it leaves the causal mechanisms linking demographic variables to schooling outcomes unclear. For example, finding that Latino and black students perform less well than white and Asian Americans on tests or measures of progress might lead to explanations from heredity, though evidence from twin studies and other sources has ruled out this persistent interpretation (see, for example, Fryer 2006; Fryer and Leavitt 2004, 2005; Nisbett 1998; Saxe, Guberman, and Gearhart 1987). The remaining differences among racial-ethnic groups might be reflected by differences in family background, in student motivation and engagement, and in school resources, in which case the effects of demographic variables should become zero once these other factors are considered.

So continuing to find racial and ethnic effects even after considering a wide array of other explanations—the "racial and ethnic residuals," we might call them[12]—creates puzzles of interpretation. Furthermore, finding racial or ethnic differences (or gender differences) leaves us in a policy quandary. Race-ethnicity and gender cannot be changed, as school resources and some dimensions of family background can be; if racial discrimination is responsible for the results, these social attitudes are also difficult to change and are sometimes beyond the ability of schools to influence. So wrestling with the meaning of the demographic "residuals" is a crucial step to understanding what these variables mean and how their effects can be moderated.

Disentangling the effects of race and ethnicity from all the other factors to which they are related requires some statistical analysis, and as in previous chapters, those readers who are uncomfortable with statistical analysis might skip to the section on "Making Sense of Racial-Ethnic Differences." To examine the magnitude of the racial-ethnic residuals, we can examine equations in which different kinds of independent variables are considered. In table B.4, I present the coefficients of demographic variables from three specifications. The first includes only demographic variables and reflects the overall differences in means among these groups—the simple black-white test score gap, for example, or the gap between whites and Latinos in the probability of graduating from high school. The second specification (which is also specification 1 from tables B.2 through B.4) includes all demographic variables plus school resources, family background measures, and measures of student connectedness to schooling. For some variables, a third specification includes a lagged dependent variable—for example, test scores or educational aspirations in tenth grade.[13] The third specification locates some of the cause of racial and gender effects in prior performance whose effects persist over time, especially for test scores rather than attitudes. Table B.4 also gives the ratio of the beta coefficient in specification 2 or 3 to the beta coefficient in specification 1.[14] The first of these gives the fraction of the overall gap that is explained by school and nonschool resources, while the second gives the fraction explained by these variables plus tenth-grade variables. If we could explain racial differences in education outcomes by class differences and school resources, this fraction would be 100 percent.

Unfortunately, the racial and ethnic effects in table B.4 are all consistent with what others have found, even after controlling for a large number of school resources and family background effects. These are all in the same directions as in previous studies, with black, Latino, and American Indian students consistently doing less well than white and Asian American students. American Indian students perform roughly like black and Latino students, with lower test scores, a lower probability of graduating from high school, and a lower chance of enrolling in a four-year college. Asian American students perform better than whites on math test scores only, confirming a racial stereotype, but they also have higher educational and occupational aspirations and higher measures of progress through high school, including graduation and subsequent movement into four-year colleges. For blacks, Latinos, and Asian American students, the racial-ethnic gaps are much more substantial for test scores than for attitudes and measures of progress—that is, the beta coefficients on racial characteristics are higher in absolute value—indicating that the emphasis on test scores in the accountability movement has exaggerated racial and ethnic differences.

In deciding which of these residuals to use, I focus on specification 2, which controls for many dimensions of family background (or class), for variation in school resources, and for student motivation and engagement.[15]

Once these dimensions have been considered, the racial-ethnic coefficients fall dramatically; for example, the black-white math gap falls to 49 percent of the overall difference, and the Latino-white gap falls to 40 percent.[16] The black-white differential in receiving a high school diploma is only 45 percent of the simple difference, while the Latino-white difference in completing high school becomes statistically insignificant. The advantage that Asian Americans have over white students in aspirations appears only in the simple specification 1; it becomes insignificant in specification 2, as is any advantage in progress through high schools (except for a small advantage in completing an academic program). These differentials remain larger for African Americans than for Latino and American Indian students, though Latino students lag behind black students in occupational aspirations, completing academic programs, and enrolling in four-year colleges. There are no racial-ethnic differences in educational aspirations, but black and American Indian students are less likely to complete diplomas after controlling for the effects of family background and student behavior. Black students are *more* likely than others to attend a four-year college, however, and they shun community colleges—a pattern in the African American community of dedication to going to college and avoiding community colleges as "not real colleges."

Overall, the racial-ethnic coefficients for test scores in specification 2 are higher in an absolute sense than are any coefficients for aspirations or progression, so again, a focus on test scores to the exclusion of other outcomes inflates several of the racial and ethnic differentials. Nonetheless, these residuals need to be explained if we are ever to reduce the racial-ethnic achievement gaps: even though they are markedly lower than the overall differences among racial and ethnic groups, some of these remaining differences are still quite large. Blacks still do worse than whites in all test scores and in earning high school diplomas. Latinos do worse in all subjects, and their higher educational aspirations are not matched by higher rates of completing high school diplomas or moving on to college. American Indians, like blacks, do worse than white students on all test scores, and their rates of high school completion and four-year college enrollment are lower.

Making Sense of Racial-Ethnic Differences: Unmeasured Effects

To summarize the results, differences associated with racial and ethnic differences persist even after controlling for variation in family background, in school resources, and in measures of student commitment to schooling. We still have to make sense of the fact that many demographic "residuals" or racial and ethnic "gaps" exist even after we try to explain away these residuals by variables correlated with race and ethnicity. One strategy for explaining these residuals is to turn again to the qualitative literature about families and schooling, as I did earlier to examine the effects of family background.

One plausible interpretation is that unmeasured dimensions of family background and school resources are partly responsible. For example, the measures of family change in the NELS88 data, which emphasize changes in family composition, fail to consider the extreme instability in some families associated with husbands and boyfriends coming and going, children moving among households, the predatory violence in many low-income communities, the complications of drugs and alcoholism, and the lack of continuity in responsibility for children (DeParle 2004; LeBlanc 2003). These conditions in extreme cases are poorly measured by the family variables available in NELS88, and so some dimensions of family background that are particularly detrimental to school performance are unmeasured.

Similarly, the negative effects of some *communities* as distinct from parents are nowhere measured in the NELS88 data. One example is Geoffrey Canada's (1995) uncomfortable analysis of how older black men pass on practices of resistance, predatory activity, and violence to younger black men. The lack of role models who have achieved success through schooling in some black and Latino communities or on Indian reservations far from mainstream labor markets—an issue that is widely recognized in mentoring programs—is another aspect of community background that is not well measured by any dimension of family life. More recently, some researchers have begun to trace the effects of popular culture; for example, Travis Gosa (2007) has found that hip-hop music became more antischool after 1994, and this effect of popular culture might explain some of the alienation from schooling among black youth (though plenty of white and Latino youth listen to such music too). The point is that even detailed data sets fail to measure the full range of family and community effects.

In addition, the measures of school climate in NELS88, which depend on responses to relatively mild statements like "teaching is good" and "there's real school spirit," fail to describe the hellish conditions in some urban schools (see, for example, Anyon 1997; Kozol 1967, 1992) where almost no one is teaching very much, personal relationships of all kinds are hostile (Payne 1997), students spend a great deal of time roaming the halls, and teachers spend most of their time attempting to maintain order. The instability in some urban schools—with students entering and leaving, teachers with low levels of experience turning over, long-term substitutes being used to fill many vacancies, classes doubling up because of vacancies unfilled, principals and superintendents coming and going, and district policies frequently changing—is more dreadful than anything the NELS88 data can measure. The reality of school resources can be much worse than anything described in quantitative data—and at the same time much better for some upper-middle-class parents who send their children to creative, supportive, exciting schools whose perspectives are consistent with those of parents and students. Because these unmeasured effects of parents, community, and schools are likely to be related to class, race, and ethnicity, they tend to inflate the apparent effects of these demographic variables rather than reflecting the true effects of family background and school conditions.[17]

The Extent of Student Mistreatment

However, another explanation for the racial/demographic residual that is evident from the qualitative literature—as well as from my own experience—is that racial and ethnic mistreatment is common in public schools. This dimension of schooling and school resources is generally ignored in policy-oriented writing. For example, the conventional analysis of achievement gaps (see, for example, Jencks and Phillips 1998) starts with the differences between black and white students in test scores and then goes on to emphasize policies—improvements in school resources like teacher quality and compensatory early childhood programs—that do not address any dimensions of race or ethnicity and that are therefore "color-blind" or race-neutral.

Other writing focused on black and Latino students, however, clarifies how often these groups are mistreated.[18] Mistreatment may be obvious and conscious, as in the physical abuse of students (Anyon 1997), but since overt racism is no longer in style, mistreatment is more likely to be covert and unconscious. One problem is that many students of color feel invisible or marginalized in the classroom—invisible in the sense of being ignored and in having their concerns about race (race in history, race in politics, race in daily interactions) ignored. These students are more likely to be demeaned for their language, whether nonstandard English or foreign; the usual approach to teaching standard English is simply to correct a child's language (Wheeler 2007), but if not carefully carried out, such correction adds to hostility between teachers and students. More generally, some students perceive their schools as trying to replace their home culture with mainstream middle-class norms, rather than add to that culture, in the approach of multiculturalism—an approach that has been labeled "subtractive schooling" by Richard Valenzuela (1999). Racial-minority students are less likely to find adults who can serve as mentors, sponsors, and protectors (Gándara 1995); the frequent complaint among these students that "there's nobody here who looks like us" reflects another dimension of feeling out of place, especially in colleges and universities. Their teachers, who are predominantly white, are likely to be unfamiliar with their family circumstances and to have a range of cultural and racial misconceptions—or simply different cultural styles (Irvine 2000). Minority students are more likely to be the victims of the well-documented problem of lower teacher expectations (Ferguson 1998; Thompson 2004; Weinstein 2002). They suffer from various negative stereotypes and stigmas that white students do not face, and, ironically, these may have become worse since *Brown v. Board of Education* and the end of de jure segregation because many more black students have left segregated schools for integrated ones (Zirkel 2005). These students are more likely to be disciplined and suspended or expelled over infractions that other students are not punished for, particularly under "zero-tolerance" policies borrowed from the adult criminal system.[19] As Ann Ferguson (2000) has expressed this, African American boys in particular are "adultified"—treated not as rambunctious kids who make mistakes but as adults on potentially criminal paths. And all these processes start early: in Ferguson's ethnography, the trajectory of school practices and cultural differences that set students up for failure became most evident in fourth grade—an explanation for the "fourth-grade slump," which I revisit in chapter 6.

The idea that there are cultural differences between schools and some families has a long history (Deschenes, Cuban, and Tyack 2001). The problem is that students from the families that differ most from the culture of schools—those from working- and lower-class families, racial and ethnic minorities, and immigrant families—find themselves in conflict with the "rules of the game" in the classroom, that is, the codes of behavior, language, and relationships and the sense of what is valued (Delpit 1995; hooks 1994; Ladson-Billings 1994). When entire schools are filled with such children, hostile relations between teachers and students—and often among students and among teachers as well—often dominate, creating the kind of hostile environment that precludes any effective reform (Payne 1997; Payne and Kaba 2001).

Many successful African American and Latino individuals remember their own schooling as filled with both subtle and overt mistreatment, and among teachers this can become the basis for discussions about schools and racial equity (Williams 2005).[20] The field of critical race theory is based partly on autobiography and personal anecdotes about mistreatment in schools and other settings; this conceptual approach has insisted on and made extensive use of "voice" (or voices)—the personal and community experiences of people of color (Dixon and Rousseau 2005). Testimony about the steady flow of mistreatment, sometimes labeled "micro-aggression" (Solorzano 2001; Solorzano, Ceja, and Yosso 2000)—the individually small but constant incidents of mistreatment, often unconscious, that cumulatively affect African American, Latino, and other minority groups—often comes from individuals who were able to fend off that abuse or to find other individuals to help them defend against constant belittling, but who, in looking back on their education, have nonetheless seen the persistent harms in such abuse. Individuals who are unable to find other sources of support or to rise out of this misery drop out of school in some way or another; moreover, they often remain permanently fearful of and hostile toward formal schooling and participate very little in their own children's schooling.

The dominant metaphor to describe the lasting effects of these various insults is "scarring," as in James Baldwin's (1955) comment: "I can conceive of no Negro native to this country who has not, by the age of puberty, been irreparably scarred by the conditions of his life. . . . [T]he wonder is not that so many are ruined but that so many survive."

The metaphor of scarring implies that mistreatment has lasting effects and is not simply a series of small events that students can readily overcome; the literature on "micro-aggressions" also intimates that however small individual incidents may seem, their cumulative effects are profound. Similarly, those who have examined potential high school dropouts often describe minority students as having been progressively alienated from school by a series of individually small but cumulatively powerful events related to race and ethnicity. Many describe dropping out of high school as a process of cumulative alienation, not the result of specific events (Fine 1991). In some widely cited (but empirically controversial) analyses, this alienation in turn leads to "resistance" to schooling (Willis 1977) or to a lack of effort in order not to appear to be "acting white" (Fordham and Ogbu 1986). The metaphor of scarring also reminds us, once again, that schooling is a dynamic process: it takes place over a decade or more, and its cumulative effects—whether the steady encouragement and support of middle-class children or the steady disparagement of low-performing black, Latino, and working-class children—are poorly reflected in conventional cross-sectional analysis.

Finally, my own experiences provide ample illustration of the mistreatment of racial and ethnic minority students. Many of my students are preparing to be principals and district officials,[21] and they repeatedly describe the powerful injustices of their own schooling experiences or of the experiences they see in urban schools. Their commitment to improving urban schooling reflects in part their desire to provide more supportive places for black and Latino and other immigrant children. My own observations of classrooms in schools and community colleges confirm the prevalence of various forms of mistreatment. In observations in high schools throughout the 1990s and in more recent research in San Francisco Bay Area schools, I often saw teachers belittling students—for failing to follow directions or answer questions correctly, for making too much noise, for not living up to the teacher's expectations. In one math skills class, for example, an African American instructor criticized his students for being passive learners by first telling them, "A lot of you just want to get in the class and get burped"; then, after he had them read math problems out loud, he commented, "Most of you are choral readers," meaning that they could read well only in unison but could not read individually for meaning. He also commented that they were "making the wrong choices" in not paying attention to their schoolwork and to reading in particular: "There's a certain mannerism you have to have to be successful in school." All true, but his remarks were delivered in a harsh and corrective manner, and he did not take the time to investigate what the appropriate "mannerism" was and why it was appropriate. Later, during a library period ("libraries are all about equity"), the librarian spent much more time creating order than she did encouraging reading. A day of such barbs would surely undermine the confidence of anyone. The fact that a white middle-class observer from a prominent university could observe such incidents indicates that teachers do not think such behavior is something to hide from visitors.[22]

From a number of different but consistent sources, then, I conclude that at least some of the racial, ethnic, and class differences in outcomes are due to mistreatment of various kinds—sometimes indifference, sometimes abuse, sometimes low expectations, sometimes conflicts created by language and behavioral differences, sometimes harsh correctives. Within the framework of the improved school finance, respectful and supportive treatment of students is yet another abstract resource. Embedded in the personal relationships of the school as a whole as well as in the long history of racial, ethnic, and gender relationships, this resource is difficult to identify or measure and even more difficult to know how to enhance. But there are ways to do so: through classroom observations, which can help teachers first identify unconscious but destructive behaviors and then work to moderate them; through the use of contrastive analysis to teach students standard English and "school behavior" in respectful ways that do not demean them (Wheeler 2007); through the "courageous conversations" and discussion about race and ethnicity promoted by some reformers; and through the introduction of practices from the wide array of culturally relevant pedagogy and multicultural education, all of which try in different ways to make schooling more supportive to racial-minority students.[23] When I return to reforms at the school level in chapter 9, such forthright approaches to the issues of race and ethnicity will surface again as ways of responding to the racial and ethnic gaps that often start our discussions of inequitable outcomes.

Overall, then, the qualitative literature can help us understand the causal mechanisms underlying the effects of family background and demographic characteristics. These mechanisms are even more varied and complex in ethnographic and journalistic accounts of families and schools than they are in even the richest qualitative data set. Fortunately, quantitative and qualitative evidence are quite consistent with one another, confirming the crucial role of families in preparing their children for formal schooling. While the rise of schooling as the primary means of access to occupations has changed the mechanisms by which families pass on economic success to their children, it has not changed the basic patterns of inequality in conventional success through schooling.

THE ROLES OF FAMILIES AND SCHOOLS: IMPLICATIONS FOR SCHOOL REFORM AND NON-EDUCATIONAL POLICY

The results discussed in this chapter raise an obvious policy question: what can public policies do to reduce or eliminate the effects of family background on schooling outcomes, since these effects are both highly in-equitable and—from the perspective of the Education Gospel, concerned with cultivating the skills of *all* future workers—inefficient because they fail to develop the capacities of some individuals? Some answers to this question lie within education policy, but these solutions ignore the range of non-school policies necessary to reduce some of the disjunctions between par-ents and schools and thereby equalize educational opportunities. What is necessary is not an either-or policy: either an attempt to improve schools while some families sink deeper into need, isolation, and instability *or* an at-tempt to bring about greater equality among families before the schools can be made more equal. A better approach should be a "both-and" position—both reforming schools so that that they have greater capacity to educate low-performing students *and* trying in every way possible to improve those conditions of family life that affect the ability of students to benefit from the schools. I return to this issue in chapter 12 and outline in more detail the non-educational policies implied by the results in this chapter. It does not much matter whether we frame such approaches as developing a family pol-icy to strengthen the ability of all families to raise their children, as strength-ening the welfare state, or as creating the economic and social foundations for strong and equitable forms of human development (Grubb and Lazerson 2004, chs. 8 and 9). In every instance, social policies would search for the *complementarities* between social policy and educational policy rather than let one wither in favor of the other, as now seems to be happening.

A simple narrative describes this situation: the African parable "It takes a village to raise all children," popularized by Hillary Clinton (1996) and em-bedded in school-based reforms like the Comer schools (Comer 1996) and full-service schools (Dryfoos 1994). What it takes to establish a new narra-tive is partly a recognition of the ways in which older narratives are exagger-ated, outdated, or dysfunctional; the narrative of the private family raising its children independently of other social institutions is surely all of these. The development of new narratives also requires evidence of new and effec-tive practices. Evidence about exemplars among social programs (see, for example, Schorr 1998), school reforms that successfully incorporate par-ents, and forms of parent outreach and education that are not demeaning are all useful in reconstructing a vision or narrative. And a new narrative may also require a new politics, in this case one that is collective rather than self-interested, future-oriented rather than oblivious to future consequences, principled rather than opportunistic, and clear about current realities rather than mendacious.[24] If we are to raise all of our children well, relying on the strengths of schools as well as parents, then we have no choice but to de-velop new visions and public narratives to guide us.

Chapter 5

Students as Resources: The Effects of Connectedness to Schooling

STUDENTS ARE themselves resources for learning, just as various school practices and dimensions of family background are. If students are absent from school, or mentally distracted, or unconvinced about the value of schooling, then even the best instruction and the most supportive school climate may have little influence. The inclusion of student connectedness to schooling in the models developed in chapter 1—particularly in figure 1.2, in which many different resources affect student outcomes—also reflects Magdalene Lampert's (2001) vision of the classroom: the interaction of the teacher, the student, the curriculum, and the larger institutional setting of formal schooling influences the learning that goes on within it. In more conventional terms, student connectedness to schooling encompasses many dimensions of motivation and engagement, which have long been a concern of psychologists worried about the individual preconditions for student success (summarized in National Research Council 2004).

The variables I use to describe student connectedness to schooling encompass some conventional aspects of motivation and engagement, like the amount of homework students do, their absences from school, and their history of getting into trouble for attendance or behavior problems. Other dimensions, like how much they work and the amount of television they watch, reflect distractions from schooling whose potentially negative effects have been well documented. Still others represent peer effects, a phenomenon that has concerned observers of high schools at least since *Middletown*, a classic study of a high school in the 1930s (Lynd and Lynd 1929). The distracting effects of having a baby are obvious, and pregnancy prevention efforts have been a fixture of many high schools. In the first section of this chapter, I present the effects of these variables, which lead to a series of obvious admonitions for students that educators and parents have articulated for at least a century.

While it is possible to see these dimensions of student behavior as innate, the improved school finance and figure 1.2 imply that school resources as well as family background might influence student connection to schooling. The second section of this chapter therefore reports on my efforts, largely disappointing, to identify the causes of variation in student connectedness to schooling—and in particular the effects of school resources.

A somewhat different effect on schooling outcomes may come from student values and perceptions about schooling and learning. In the third section of this chapter, I examine several dimensions of the values that student embrace, including their orientation toward the occupational value of schooling, their interest in affiliating with others, more escapist values, and altruistic attitudes. These prove to have various significant effects on measures of both learning and progress, which show—not surprisingly—that the values students get from their parents, their communities, and the large and powerful culture outside the school influence what happens inside. Once again, a full accounting of the effects of schooling outcomes requires us to consider a broad variety of influences and resources.

Overall, the results in this chapter confirm the value of considering students as resources for their own schooling. (See also table 2.1, specification 4, in which these variables add significantly to the explanatory power of equations for schooling outcomes.) Identifying aspects of student engagement that influence outcomes does not always mean that schools and policies can find solutions to potential problems. For example, students sometimes work because their families need their earnings, and the power of popular culture—which manifests itself in many ways, including its sexualized portrayal of relationships, its consumerist and individualistic ethic, its portrayal of schooling as uncool, and the din of the Education Gospel about the economic value of schooling—is difficult to counter. As with other school resources, the links between funding and efforts to enhance connectedness to schooling are often ambiguous: teenage pregnancy prevention and health centers surely require additional funding, while enhancing motivation and engagement by changing pedagogical approaches requires vision and careful professional development more than money. But at least identifying the power of students' own behavior and beliefs provides ways to understand the multiple resources that affect school outcomes and can clarify the variety of approaches to increasing school effectiveness.

THE EFFECTS OF STUDENT CONNECTEDNESS TO SCHOOLING ON OUTCOMES

The variables that measure student connectedness to schooling encompass some conventional aspects of motivation and engagement that are proxied by amount of time spent on homework, whether a student has gotten into trouble for attendance, and absences during high school, but also by whether a student has gotten into trouble for behavioral problems—often a sign of disengagement from schooling. In addition, two variables measure activities that might compete with schooling for attention: hours of work (an extensive literature shows the negative effects of employment; see, for example, Greenberger and Steinberg 1986; Marsh and Kleitman 2005) and how much television a student watches. Three measures of peer groups are included: one describing whether a student's peers intend to go to college, another describing whether the student's peers are likely to drop out, and a third denoting membership in a gang. Peer effects presumably operate by reinforcing pro-school and anti-school behavior as well as encouraging time-consuming activities that either draw students closer to or push them further away from schooling.

Two measures of extracurricular activities have been included: participation in school-based activities, and participation in outside activities like youth organizations, religious groups, and political groups. Participation in non-academic aspects of school life tends to reinforce a student's identification with school (called, at the postsecondary level, "social integration" by Tinto 1993) and therefore to improve school performance. Conversely, students who are generally resistant to schooling also fail to participate in extracurricular activities (Marsh and Kleitman 2002; Eckert 1989). The effects of activities outside the school are more ambiguous: they may compete with schoolwork and harm academic performance, or they may foster engagement and interests that carry over to improved school performance.

Two variables describe whether students have sought out counselors and whether they have received school help with filling out applications, completing financial aid forms, writing essays for applications, or visiting colleges. Both are compound variables, reflecting an interaction between student initiative and the presence of sufficient services at a high school. A variable describing reading outside school is included, since reading for pleasure surely reinforces the ability to read for instrumental purposes, including schooling.

Finally, having had or expecting a baby by twelfth grade is also included; this is a measure of distraction from schooling, like the variables for employment and television, but in a more extreme form. Furthermore, Joyce Ladner (1995, chs. 5 and 8) has described a kind of "choice" among African American girls—either to do well in school and avoid sexual encounters with a view toward future options, including employment, or to engage in a more active social and sexual life leading to motherhood rather than sustained education and employment. The effects of having a baby may therefore reflect not only the time and emotional demands of being a mother but also a psychological "decision" to take a different route than schooling and employment.

As before, readers unfamiliar with regression analysis might skip to the last paragraph of this section, which summarizes the findings. For others, the results of different dimensions of student connectedness are presented in appendix table B.5. For the results describing test scores I include two specifications, one without and one with tenth-grade test scores. The latter is an effort to make sure that these relationships are appropriately causal rather than explainable by unmeasured variation in prior school achievement.

Almost all of the results are precisely what we might expect. Students who report that they read outside of school do better on test scores except in math (not surprisingly), and some of these effects (for reading and history tests) are particularly strong. Readers also have higher educational aspirations and higher aspirations for continuing past college, though their actual progress, graduation, and college-going are not any higher than for nonreaders. In a result not shown in this table, a higher rate among readers of receiving a GED ($\beta = .055^{***}$) suggests that at least some readers are autodidacts who learn well on their own, a capacity that serves them well in testing and in educational activities that require initiative (like earning a GED) but may not suit them for the rigid structure of high school.

Students who spend more time on homework consistently have improved test scores, while employment and television-watching consistently reduce scores. Doing more homework increases educational aspirations and the expectation of continuing past high school. Contrary to expectations, time spent on homework reduces the total number of credits accumulated (though not the probability of completing an academic program), suggesting that students who do more homework concentrate on those courses necessary for college-going, not on electives with uncertain payoff. Similarly, more time spent on homework appears to reduce the likelihood of high school completion, though it increases the likelihood of attending a four-year college. While these results seem odd, they may describe a situation in which students who are diligent about homework do so to attend a four-year college, while some of those who do not do much homework nonetheless graduate but continue to two-year colleges ($\beta = -.036$), a middling course for students with middling achievement. Time spent watching television also negatively affects all test scores as well as measures of aspirations, confirming that television both distracts students from schoolwork and makes viewers dumber. Attendance problems consistently reduce test scores, as we might expect; behavior problems negatively affect progress measured by credits accumulated, completion of a conventional academic program, and, especially, completion of a high school diploma.

Peer groups have the expected effects. Individuals whose friends are likely to go to college have higher test scores and higher aspirations and expectations of continuing in schooling, and they are more likely to complete an academic program and go to a four-year college. Hanging around with dropouts does not affect test scores, but it does reduce progress through high school and completion. And the effects of being in a gang are consistently negative for a wide range of outcomes, including test scores (except science), occupational aspirations, and two measures of progress through high school (completing an academic program and continuing to a four-year college), though gang membership enhances the likelihood of going to a community college.

Conversely, participating in extracurricular activities has uniformly positive effects, both on test scores (except math) and especially on educational aspirations, progress through high school, and continuing to a four-year college. This replicates the generally positive effects of extracurricular activities in other studies (Feldman and Matjasko 2005; Marsh and Kleitman 2002). It also confirms a pattern, well described in Eckert (1989) and other ethnographies of high school, of some students (variously described as "jocks," "preps," "collegiates," or "socialites") who participate actively in the life of the school, are generally highly successful and well liked—in contrast to "burnouts," "kickers," "hoods," "greasers," "skaters," "potheads," or "punks," who fail to participate in high school life, generally do not learn much, are often defiant of school authority, and in every way exemplify a lack of connectedness to schooling. Similarly, activities outside of school have positive effects on learning, educational aspirations, accumulating credits, completing an academic program, and continuing to a four-year college. The only novelty is that outside activities, reflecting engagement with community, youth, political, and religious organizations, also increase test scores, as if these activities (unlike school-based extracurricular activities) improve either academic diligence or ancillary learning.

Much to my surprise, the effects of seeking out counselors are consistently positive—on test scores, occupational aspirations, the likelihood of continuing in schooling and various measures of progress, including high school graduation and continuing to a four-year college.[1] I interpret this as the compound effect of both the information and the guidance that counselors can provide and of the initiative that students show in going to counselors—since in most high schools the student-counselor ratio is so high that most students do not automatically see counselors (NRC 2004, ch. 6; Schneider and Stevenson 1999). The fact that seeing counselors has consistently significant (if moderate) effects suggests the value to students of being able to consult with adults other than teachers. Conversely, seeking help with schoolwork has consistently negative effects on test scores; while this finding might reflect the fact that students who seek such help have low test scores to begin with, it holds up even with tenth-grade test scores included. More plausibly, seeking help has positive effects on aspirations, credits accumulated, the receipt of a diploma, and continuing to a four-year college—again suggesting that a culture of student support enhances progress through high school, though not necessarily learning and test scores.

Having a baby does not affect most test scores (except for reading), but it reduces the expectation of continuing schooling past high school, credits accumulated, the likelihood of graduating, and the likelihood of going on to either a two- or four-year college; these young women are more likely to receive a GED ($\beta = .073$**), whose value in finding a job and in gaining access to further higher education is limited (Murnane, Willett, and Boudett 1995). Obviously, these effects are stronger for females than for males. The effect of having a baby is particularly powerful in lowering the educational aspirations of black women, reducing the likelihood that black women will complete a high school diploma, and reducing the likelihood that black and Latina women will go to either a two- or four-year college[2]—confirming Ladner's (1995) fear that young minority women are more likely to be derailed from an educational route by having a baby.

Finally, a few variables representing intermediate educational outcomes influence subsequent outcomes. In extensions of the specifications in table B.5, completing an academic program enhances the likelihood of completing a high school diploma ($\beta = .088$***) and entering a four-year college ($\beta = .106$***), but reduces the likelihood of entering a two-year college ($\beta = -.083$***). Similarly, high math scores—which do not influence high school graduation significantly—enhance the likelihood of attending a four-year college ($\beta = .123$***) but decrease the likelihood of attending a community college ($\beta = -.086$***); high reading scores also enhance the likelihood of attending a four-year college ($\beta = .051$***). Finally—no surprise here—higher SAT scores lead to a higher probability of attending a four-year college ($\beta = .192$***) and a lower probability of enrolling in a community college ($\beta = -.196$***).[3] In these results, community colleges act precisely as they are often described—as second-chance institutions: students whose academic work in high school is not especially strong may graduate, but they are more likely to enroll in a community college than a four-year college or university.

The results for specification 2, which include variables describing test scores and aspirations in tenth grade, only confirm the importance of student connection to schooling on outcomes. The coefficients of specification

2 are lower than those of specification 1, but like the results in table B.1 for school resources, those that are significant in specification 1 usually remain significant. Again, this finding strengthens the causal interpretation of these variables; for example, the negative effects of television-watching, or of employment, cannot be due merely to the fact that low-scoring individuals watch more TV and work more. Instead, these measures of student connectedness continue to have substantial effects even when prior school performance is considered.

Finally, in these results, as for school resources, some variables measuring dimensions of student connectedness affect almost all dimensions of schooling: the amount of homework completed, visiting counselors, hours of employment, and participating in extracurricular activities and outside activities. In the terminology I used in chapter 2 and borrowed from Rumberger and Palardy (2005), these have *common* effects on most outcomes. Many others affect different outcomes and therefore have *differential* effects. As for school resources, this leads to the obvious prescription that concentrating on dimensions of student connectedness to schooling with *common* effects might be the most powerful approach to improving outcomes.

These results are precisely what we would expect, and they lead to a series of maxims that all teachers and parents articulate: do your homework; read instead of watching television, which can only rot your mind; don't cut classes; don't get in trouble; run with the right crowd and don't ever join a gang; participate in extracurricular activities (though don't overdo it); participate in activities outside of school, since they foster broader interests and values; seek out help from counselors if you need it; for girls, either stay away from boys, learn how to say no, or learn about contraception; and if you want to go to a four-year college, complete an academic program, learn as much as you can, get good grades, and do well on SATs. For those who do not do well in their studies, community college is always a second-chance option, though it is less likely to lead to a BA degree. None of these conclusions is surprising, but they clarify the extent to which schooling outcomes are affected by obvious forms of student behavior and engagement that have not generally been included in simple production functions.

Furthermore, some of these results offer possibilities for school interventions that might strengthen students' motivation and engagement. Counselors may be particularly effective, perhaps in personalizing schools; after-school programs and extracurricular activities provide alternatives to employment and television; health clinics within high schools may reduce sexual activity and therefore pregnancies. Certain approaches to instruction enhance motivation and engagement, including practices that are more student-centered and constructivist or balanced (NRC 2004, chs. 1–3). Some dimensions of connectedness may be difficult for schools to counter, particularly the student values examined later in the chapter, but these results provide some guidance for high schools to recognize the importance of students as resources.

INFLUENCES ON STUDENT CONNECTEDNESS TO SCHOOLING

The logic of the improved school finance, summarized in figure 1.2, suggests that family background may influence dimensions of student connectedness to schooling, as parents pass on different attitudes toward school and aspirations for schooling and exert varying demands on their children (to earn money, for example, or take on child care responsibilities). In addition, various school practices may influence dimensions of student behavior. For example, the National Research Council's (2004) review indicates that motivation and engagement in high schools are higher when there is close adult-student supervision; when students have some autonomy in selecting tasks; when they can engage in constructing meaning on their own rather than taking the passive role in a teacher-centered classroom; when curricula are well structured with clear purposes; when high schools have a challenging curriculum and a strong emphasis on achievement; when students can take multiple paths to competence; and when programs allow them to develop a clearer understanding of schooling and its relationship to future activities. These approaches to instruction and curriculum are measured in the NELS88 data by such variables as the pupil-teacher ratio (reflecting the possibilities for greater adult-student interaction), innovative approaches to teaching, the curricula students are in (since remedial, vocational, and general tracks are often less challenging), and magnet schools with their attempts to develop more coherent curricula. Student support services, such as access to counseling and tutoring, may also influence engagement, as might a wider variety of support services not included in the NELS88 data (NRC 2004, ch. 6).

As a result of this logic, I estimated a series of equations with measures of student connectedness to schooling as the dependent variables and family background, demographic variables, and school resources as the explanatory variables.[4] The effects of family background fell into readily understandable patterns associated with the same dimensions of class that influence schooling outcomes (see chapter 4). High levels of maternal education increase extracurricular activities and lead to fewer absences and less TV-watching, whereas low parental aspirations for children lead to fewer extracurricular activities, fewer outside activities, and more absences. Income per family member has few effects, though it does reduce hours of working, confirming that youth employment is at least partly a matter of family necessity. Similarly, students who knew their families had saved for college worked less and had fewer absences.

Changing family conditions has several negative effects on student ability to benefit. Changing schools reduces extracurricular activities, and family changes lead to more absences, more problems over attendance and behavior, fewer college-bound peers, and more peers likely to be bound for dropping out. Having a baby reduces outside activities and leads to more absences and more TV-watching. All these effects are quite consistent with effects of such variables on schooling outcomes as well.

Two measures of family background are more powerful in explaining student ability to benefit than in explaining school outcomes directly. Educational materials in the home, measured in the eighth grade, lead to more extracurricular activities, more outside activities, more reading, more homework, better attendance, and less television. This appears to be a measure of the family's orientation toward education, which then continues to influence student behavior. Finally, being in a female-headed family—which had no direct effects on schooling outcomes (see table B.1)—leads to more absences, more trouble with the school over attendance, and more behavior problems in school. This suggests that the relative lack of time for adult supervision in female-headed families leads in turn to student problems in school.

None of these effects is particularly powerful: the beta coefficients range between .03 and .07, with high levels of parent education and low parental aspirations having the strongest effects, as was true for effects on schooling outcomes. However, they indicate that there are two independent mechanisms by which family background affects schooling outcomes: one effect directly on outcomes—as families provide the educational support, aspirations, conditions of stability rather than instability, and sometimes fiscal support important for learning and progress—and another effect via student engagement, motivation, and general ability to benefit from instruction.

In contrast, the effects of school resources on student behavior prove to be sporadic and weak. The only strong results are those for the non-academic curricular tracks (the vocational, general, and remedial programs), which consistently reduce the amount of homework and the number of extracurricular and outside activities, while increasing the amount of TV-watching.[5] Students in these non-academic tracks report fewer college-bound peers and more peers likely to drop out, not surprisingly, since students intent on graduating and going to college are unlikely to enroll in these non-academic tracks.

In addition, a number of school resources affect student absenteeism, which (from table B.5) is one of the most harmful influences on progress through high school: innovative or progressive teaching, greater time devoted to active instruction rather than administration and routine instruction, and greater principal (rather than outside) control of the school all lead to fewer absences. Students who report getting help have fewer problems

with behavior and attendance, attesting to the value of student support services. And having science facilities reduces the amount of absences and television, suggesting that schools with good facilities can lure students back
into school and away from distractions. So the results suggest once again that
general, vocational, and remedial tracks need to be replaced by more demanding alternatives and that there are many ways for high schools to improve attendance.

However, these effects are few and far between, and coefficients are not
particularly high. The explanatory power of these equations is poor, with R-
squareds ranging between .04 and a high of .20 (for having college-bound
peers, a dimension of student connectedness strongly influenced by family
background).[6] Furthermore, some school resources we might expect to influence connectedness—like seeing counselors (which affects many school
outcomes), the adult-student ratio (indicating the potential for more adult
contact), and the school's climate—have no influence on any measures of
student behavior. So, even with a rich data set, it proves impossible to understand very much of the variation in students' connection to schooling.

There are several explanations for these relatively weak results. One
might be that student behavior is too individual and idiosyncratic, too much
influenced by a variety of cultural factors outside schooling, to be explained
statistically. Another is to acknowledge that student connectedness is condi-
tioned by a long trajectory of experiences, extending back to the early
grades, which cannot be measured by twelfth-grade experiences alone. If in
addition the consistency of these experiences, rather than the level of them
in recent years, influences student connectedness, then again capturing the
effects of schooling on motivation and engagement requires much lengthier
data sets. This means that cross-sectional analysis is inadequate to describe
the dynamic complexities of schooling, a subject to which I turn in part 2.

One final possibility is that, while schools do try to enhance motivation
and engagement, the effects of such efforts may be either positive or negative. Some high schools do have counselors and academic support services
like tutoring, but they are likely to be overwhelmed—the average coun-
selor-student ratio in the country is about 500-to-1, for example, though it
varies substantially and may be 1,000-to-1 in low-resource schools, compared to recommendations that it lie between 100-to-1 and 250-to-1
(American Counseling Association 2006). Counselors and tutors often follow approaches that are unlikely to be effective: drills in most tutoring, and
"trait and factor" approaches sometimes belittled as "test 'em and tell 'em"
for guidance.[7] Choice schools may work well sometimes, but some start-up
schools are plagued with fiscal and organizational problems; similarly, the efforts to establish small schools and schools-within-schools—a more recent
development than the NELS88 data can reflect—have faced the difficulties
of creating and sustaining such schools, and these difficulties make it all too

easy to forget the original purposes of more supportive learning environments. As I argue again in chapter 9, the practices that schools adopt in order to motivate and support students—after-school programs, tutoring, and various curricular interventions—are often ineffective; their influence depends on the right combination of vision, planning, staffing, professional development, and resources, including some money.

Gender and Disability

The variables describing individual students' characteristics include gender and a simple measure of disability: the response to a question about whether the student had ever been in a program for the physically handicapped. These are complex variables in the sense that they have multiple interpretations. For example, when we find that girls do worse than boys in math and science but better in reading, we are left with competing explanations from heredity and socialization; the common argument that girls are more diligent in their schoolwork and boys are more interested in other activities should ideally be reflected in the effects of student engagement and motivation, not by a gender coefficient.

The results of gender on outcomes, presented in table B.4, are unsurprising. In these results measured in 1992, males do better than females in math, science, and history but less well in reading. (These results are now badly dated, since more recent results indicate that girls do as well as boys on math tests and presumably in science as well; see Hyde et al. 2008). Males have lower occupational aspirations and are less likely to think they will continue in formal schooling past high school. Measures of progress through high school—credits accumulated, academic programs completed, and (marginally) completion of a high school diploma—are consistently higher for females, who are also more likely to enroll in four-year colleges. However, the gross differences between males and females in reading scores and measures of progress are reduced substantially by introducing other independent variables, especially those that measure connectedness to schooling. Furthermore, the gender differences in math, science, and history tests scores are *increased* in specification 2, when measures of student connectedness are introduced, indicating that male advantages in these subjects are larger once their lower levels of effort and motivation are considered. Finally, many differentials in test scores are substantially reduced in specification 3, in which prior test scores explain a good deal of variation; evidently, "knowledge begets knowledge" for all students, and gender differences (except in math scores) are much smaller once this mechanism is considered.

The patterns of connectedness to schooling explain some of the gender differences. Males are more likely than females to participate in extracurricular activities (though less likely than females to participate in outside activities); the beneficial effects of these activities on progress through high school are noted in chapter 2. But males do less homework and work more hours; have more absences and are more likely to get into trouble for attendance; and are much more likely to join gangs and less likely to have college-going peers. With the exception of participation in extracurricular activities, these attributes indicate that males are less motivated by schooling than are females, a result that has become more widely appreciated with the realization that young women are more likely to complete high school and continue to college.

For students with physical disabilities, test scores are lower than those of nondisabled students, but the overall differences are reduced substantially in specifications 2 and 3, when school and nonschool resources are introduced. These students have slightly *higher* educational aspirations than others, and they are *more* likely to complete academic programs and to complete high school degrees than their peers. Evidently, their test scores are not indicative of their success in moving through high school, perhaps reflecting greater determination on their part.

The Effects of Student Values

Student attitudes toward schooling may also be forged by social attitudes and influences. One of the questions asked of seniors in NELS88—"How important is each of the following to you?"—was followed by fifteen different expressions of values and attitudes. From this I have constructed four different measures: one reflecting the value of schooling as a form of occupational advancement, an obvious result of the Education Gospel; one indicating the value placed on affiliation with others, including family and friends; a third reflecting the importance of entertainment and escapism; and a fourth reflecting altruistic attitudes. While my personal interest lies in the effects of vocational conceptions of schooling, all these values reflect another dimension of students as resources: the attitudes they have toward schooling and life goals may influence how they do in school. The question is whether these attitudes matter, even after all the other effects of family background, a large number of school resources, and other dimensions of motivation and engagement are considered.

The effects of these variables are displayed in table 5.1, which again presents beta coefficients describing the effects of a one-standard-deviation change in the independent variables (the measures of student attitudes) on a standard-deviation change in the dependent variables (schooling outcomes).

These results are quite consistent. Higher levels of vocational orientation *reduce* learning as measured by all four test scores (and SAT scores, for those who took the SAT), but they also *increase* educational aspirations and students' intentions to continue their education past high school. That is, more

Table 5.1   The Effects of Student Conceptions on
             Educational Outcomes

Educational Outcomes	Vocational Orientation	Personal Affiliation	Escapism	Altruism
Math scores	−.041***	−.012	−.022**	−.054***
Science scores	−.044***	−.038***	−.003	−.025**
Reading scores	−.060***	−.037***	−.016	−.007
History scores	−.051***	−.053***	−.009	.005
High educational aspirations (grade 12)	.061***	−.034***	.005	.032***
Continuing past high school	.066***	−.009	0	.011
SAT score	−.076***	−.062***	−.003	−.010
High educational aspirations (age 20)	.044***	−.017	.009	.014
Total credits	.008	.001	.021	−.012
Academic program	−.024	−.007	−.008	−.015
High school diploma	.018	−.016	−.015	−.007
Enrolled in a four-year college	.044*	−.035***	.015	−.009
Enrolled in a two-year college	.005	.016	−.016	.003

Source: Author's computations.
*significant at 10%; **significant at 5%; ***significant at 1%

vocationally oriented students want to continue in school longer, because it is clear from the rhetoric around earnings that more time in school usually leads to higher earnings and occupational status, but they put less effort into learning. This is precisely what John Bishop (1989) argued when he noted that there are powerful incentives to increase the quantity of schooling (years of education and degrees), but weaker incentives to improve the quality of education as measured by learning and test scores.[8] So, paradoxically, the stronger orientation to one's occupational future encouraged by the Education Gospel appears to reduce learning in high school.

Furthermore, despite increased aspirations, high levels of vocational orientation do not lead to higher levels of schooling, as measured by completing high school or entering two- or four-year colleges. (The effect on enrolling in four-year college is only marginally significant.) The reason is that students who are more vocationally oriented have higher aspirations but somewhat lower grades and SAT scores, so the two effects—both of which affect completion and college-going—cancel each other out. Overall, then, students with a vocational orientation do *not* continue longer in schooling *and* they learn less during high school—so the effects of these attitudes are clearly negative.

In contrast, other student attitudes have less consistent effects. Students who stress personal affiliation and relationships perform less well on tests and SATs and have lower educational aspirations (but not lower attainments). Students who want to do good in the world do less well in math and science, perhaps a reflection of a concentration on the humanities and social sciences, which they may see as more beneficial for future work in social advocacy. Escapist attitudes, somewhat surprisingly, have very few significant influences aside from a small negative effect on math scores. Of the different student perceptions of what is important in life, then, vocational perspectives are more powerful than others.

To be sure, these results can tell us only *that* certain values affect student learning and by how much, not *how* they influence learning. For vocational orientation, however, two ethnographic studies provide more insights into causal mechanisms. Denise Pope's (2001) ethnography of a wealthy California suburban school clarifies that most of these relatively privileged students viewed school as a way of getting into good colleges and well-paid careers. Their method of "doing school" placed enormous emphasis on earning high grades, for which they developed various stratagems; engaging with the material or exploring its complexities, by contrast, was not especially important to them. Indeed, as several students complained, the school was not set up to encourage more sophisticated ways of thinking: the press of too many students, the isolation of courses and teachers from one another, the fragmentation of the school day, and the pressure to cover the subjects required for college had all led to a school culture that was hostile to "higher-order thinking." At a different level of the education system, Rebecca Cox's (2004) ethnography of community college students in composition classes reveals the multiple ways in which vocational motivations can affect learning. The vocational intentions of the subjects of her study led to highly instrumental conceptions of learning. Anything that was apparently unrelated to occupational goals—including developmental (or remedial) education as well as general education, and anything that smacked of being "academic" in the negative sense of being unrelated to the real world—was systematically avoided, and students in both college-level and remedial or developmental writing courses consistently voiced impatience with "wasting time" on unnecessary content.

The most obvious problem from both these studies is that many students systematically undermine their own learning by focusing on grades rather than content, on efficiency rather than understanding, and on useful or *relevant* courses rather than those that might amplify their intellectual sophistication. These behaviors help explain the results in table 5.1: paradoxically, the vocational argument about the value of formal schooling undermines performance and directs students away from some of the "higher-order thinking" pushed by advocates of the Education Gospel.

More generally, if we had better information about and measures of other social and cultural distractions and their effects on student values—the antischool bias of hip-hop and Hollywood movies, which portray teachers as dunces; the attractions of violent video games that present no positive social roles; the meretricious elements of Disney culture—we might be able to understand yet other dimensions of students' commitment to schooling (or lack of commitment). Once again, the resources influencing schooling outcomes are considerably more extensive than we usually understand.

POSITIVE APPROACHES TO A RICHER SCHOOL EXPERIENCE

The most powerful results in this chapter are unsurprising. As generations of parents and educators have admonished their students, they need to do their homework, attend school regularly, avoid getting into trouble over attendance or behavior, hang with the right crowd by seeking out those planning to go to college and avoiding potential dropouts, avoid distractions like employment and television, and engage in extracurricular activities and outside activities that have their own educative value and role in enhancing students' attachment to schooling.

Unfortunately for educators, these patterns of student behavior are more a function of family background than of school efforts. The effects of parental education on initiative ("sponsored independence" and "concerted cultivation"), of parents' aspirations for their children, and of parents' orientation as reflected by the educational materials in their homes all reinforce the need for the non-educational policies I examine more carefully in chapter 12. But these results also confirm the value of certain school resources as well. Replacing traditional vocational, general, and remedial tracks with some other curriculum—either a more demanding college-oriented curriculum or the approaches sometimes referred to as "pathways," or theme-based approaches—would benefit student commitment to schooling. Poor attendance, which has negative effects on many measures of learning as well as progress through high school, can be improved by several practices. And conventional or behaviorist teaching not only is less effective in enabling students to learn, as measured by tests, but also reduces attendance (see table B.1 again), creating an indirect negative effect on learning—consistent with the evidence about the pedagogical approaches that enhance motivation and engagement (NRC 2004, chs. 1–3).

Finally, students come to high schools with their own attitudes about schooling and learning—some of them the result of family background, some of them the product of long years of school experiences, and some of them nurtured by the larger society. Sure enough, just as defenders of older traditions in American education would assert, vocationalist and instrumental attitudes reduce learning without any compensating positive effects on, for example, high school completion or college-going. This is partly an example of social influences invading the classroom and affecting how and what students learn. However, it also represents one of many cases in which student perceptions and instructor perceptions are inconsistent with one another. Teachers and schools have opportunities to correct or moderate student attitudes—for example, by presenting the century-old arguments against narrow conceptions of schooling, particularly in a period when rapid change is likely to make narrow training obsolete. Whether high schools can counter some of the other values that are detrimental to learning is less clear, but at least a full accounting of the resources affecting schooling can reveal where the problems lie.

Overall, then, including student commitment to schooling as a resource has opened up several avenues, both for understanding educational outcomes and for clarifying a variety of policy options and educational reforms. When we try to understand the patterns of dynamic inequality in chapter 7, students' commitment will emerge again as a crucial factor influencing inequalities among students over time.

Part II

Dynamic Inequality and the
Effects of School Resources over Time

Chapter 6

Equity and Inequality: From Static to Dynamic Conceptions

THE FIRST FIVE chapters of this book were principally about the effectiveness of school resources, but expanded the conception of resources well past the simple resources that preoccupy most policy discussions. Of course, the results reported in those chapters also shed a great deal of light on inequalities in outcomes, since inequalities in school resources (and nonschool resources like family background)—the inequalities described in table 1.1—create inequalities in educational outcomes as well. As mentioned in the introduction, the test scores for fifteen-year-olds measured in the Program in International Student Achievement (PISA) data are more unequal than in virtually any other developed country, and inequalities in educational attainments—comparing high school dropouts to those with advanced professional and academic degrees—are enormous as well. Figure I.1 revealed that, with a broader measure of learning—the International Adult Literacy Survey (IALS)— inequality in the United States is the highest of all developed countries, as is inequality of earnings. The irony is that concern about unequal educational outcomes should be so high in a country of such high levels of inequality.

Whether inequalities in education are also inequitable is a different question, since equity is a normative issue that cannot be established without conceptions of equity. However, the results in chapter 4 about family background—the finding that outcomes differ systematically by several measures of class—and the effects of race and ethnicity on outcomes generate the suspicion that *inequity* and not just *inequality* is at work in our schools. The black-white test score gap has come to represent basic inequities in this country (see, for example, Jencks and Phillips 1998), and the lower rate at which Latinos and African Americans complete high school represents other crucial outcomes that are inequitably distributed. But in a formal sense, we must establish conceptions of equity before we can make the leap from evidence of inequality to conclusions about equity.

Concerns about inequality and inequity in formal schooling have extended over at least two centuries, back to the charity schools for poor children established in the early nineteenth century so that they could have access to at least basic schooling. Similarly, the movement for common schools in the first half of the nineteenth century—with a common curriculum for all students—was intended to establish public support for grammar schools through grade 8 so that all students might have access to a basic education regardless of family background. Even though schooling did not yet have an important economic or vocational role, Horace Mann's description of public schools as the "great equalizer of the conditions of men" at least introduced the idea that schooling might overcome the differences among children that they brought to school with them. Subsequent efforts to equalize funding—starting with Cubberly's discovery after 1900 of inequalities in district spending and continuing through the long struggles over racial segregation in the 1940s and 1950s, the development of Great Society programs like Title I and Head Start, and the lawsuits after 1970—have also been heirs to the idea that the schools ought to establish greater equity in an inequitable society. The most recent efforts to improve the test scores of low-performing students, in state accountability systems and the No Child Left Behind Act of 2001, constitute part of a continuing series of efforts to establish greater equity through schooling.

However, on closer examination, these different initiatives against inequality have defined equity in different ways. Drawing on the history of equity in this country, as well as on the ideas of the improved school finance, I develop a matrix or "landscape" of equity concepts in the first section of this chapter. One of the problems in achieving equity in this country, then, is not only the fierce political opposition to the policies that might move toward equity, but also the serious disagreements about what equity might mean. Clarifying the varying conceptions of equity may not deter individuals and partisan groups from disagreeing about equity, but it can at least identify the sources of disagreement and the cases in which certain forms of equity cannot lead to other forms.

A further problem is that most of our conceptions of equity and our measures of inequality are cross-sectional. For example, those concerned with test score gaps usually compare the scores of white students with those of African American and Latino students at one moment in time (see, for example, Jencks and Phillips 1998); diatribes against inequalities in funding compare the wretched resources in urban schools with the sylvan conditions in wealthy suburbs (for example, Kozol 1992) or the spending in high-wealth and low-wealth districts; complaints about the allocation of teachers contrast the proportion of inexperienced and uncredentialed teachers in city versus suburb. However, what really counts for many dimensions of adult life is dynamic inequality—the inequality that develops among students over the long years of elementary, secondary, and then postsecondary education. Students start school with initial differences, and at least in this country these differences widen steadily. By twelfth grade, the differences among individuals are enormous: some have dropped out of school altogether and are still reading at an elementary grade level, while others have accumulated many AP credits and are about to enter the best universities in the world. The differences at age thirty are wider still when we compare high school dropouts to individuals with advanced professional degrees.

Since what counts in the end is dynamic inequality—and then its normative counterpart, dynamic equity—I devote the second section of this chapter to conceptualizing dynamic inequality. Part of the purpose is to understand which mechanisms might widen (or narrow) inequality over time; not surprisingly, several of these inequalities involve the same school and nonschool resources I investigated in a static or cross-sectional context in chapters 2 to 5. Furthermore, there is no reason to think that widening inequality develops in smooth and constant patterns: discontinuities or "bursts" of inequality may take place at certain points in the trajectory of schooling—for example, at the transition into high school and perhaps at various other transition points. If so, then the institutional structure of schooling and its many transitions may also influence dynamic inequality, and creating dynamic equity may require modifications in these institutional patterns.

Another purpose of this chapter is to provide the conceptual basis for returning to the NELS88 data to examine empirically how inequality changes over the period between grades 8 and 12 and to test whether the hypothesis of increasing inequality over time is correct. These results, reported in chapter 7, find that divergence among students not only is present but is also associated with familiar racial-ethnic and class characteristics, violating at least some conceptions of equity from this chapter. Having confirmed the power of dynamic inequality, the question is then what schools can do to overcome it. Chapter 8 examines a small sample of schools to see what they are doing for their lowest-performing students—that is, what they are doing to reduce dynamic inequality. While a few schools prove to be quite active, in most cases the approaches are fragmented, incomplete, and ineffective. In light of this troubling discovery, it becomes clear that we need an expanded approach to both effectiveness and equity, the subject of part 3.

Raising questions about dynamic inequality therefore creates a large and difficult agenda for school reform and policy. But without confronting the dynamic nature of schooling and its tendency to reinforce both the strengths and weaknesses of prior levels of preparation, some conceptions of equity—particularly those focused on outcomes—can never be met, and it will be impossible to correct the high level of educational inequality in the United States.

VARYING CONCEPTIONS OF EQUITY: THE LANDSCAPE OF POSSIBILITIES

Conceptions of equity have varied substantially, both among different advocates and over time. The nineteenth-century common school conception was comparatively simple: all students should have access to a common curriculum and should complete the undifferentiated grammar school program (to grade 8). As high schools developed, they were still dominated by a unitary curriculum and a simple conception of equity; as the "Committee of Ten," a group of prominent educators convened to create a uniform high school curriculum for college admissions, declared in 1893, "Every subject which is taught at all in a secondary school should be taught in the same way and to the same extent to every pupil so long as he pursues it, no matter what the probable destination of the pupil may be, or at what point his education is to cease."[1]

But shifts around 1900 associated with the spread of ideas about the vocational purposes of education changed conceptions of equity (Grubb and Lazerson 2004, ch. 7). Once schools came to be seen as preparing boys to become professionals and businessmen, metalworkers and electricians, and girls to become teachers and secretaries, a uniform education was irrelevant and inefficient, and ultimately inequitable as well. As two educators objected to the common school ideal:

> Instead of affording equality of educational opportunity to all, the elementary school by offering but one course of instruction, and this of a literary character, serves the interests of but one type of children and neglects in a measure the taste, capacity, and educational destination of all others, and of those, too, whose needs are imperative and to whom the future holds no further advantage. (Elson and Bachman 1910, 361)

The new conception of *equal opportunity* provided different experiences for students with different occupational goals: the academic track for middle-class students bound for college and then professional and managerial work; industrial education for working-class boys bound for factories; commercial education for working-class girls heading for clerical positions; and home economics for future homemakers. This conception of equal opportunity implicitly provided different forms of schooling geared to the probable future occupations of boys versus girls, middle-class versus working-class students, white versus black students. Such differences—which we would call tracking—do not seem equitable now, but against the rigidity of the common school they did seem equitable a century ago. This form of differentiation was also a legacy of the administrative progressives, to whom such tracking was efficient as well as equitable since it allowed instructors to teach to a narrow range of abilities.

This shift in conceptions of equity took place as the goals of schooling modulated from civic and moral purposes to occupational preparation and as the ideals surrounding schooling shifted from political to economic conceptions. Ideals of equality in the United States have been applied much more to *political* equality—to equality before the law, equality of social and legal stature, and voting rights—than to *economic* equality. The only ideal of economic equality with any real power has been equality of opportunity (Pole [1978]1994). This ideal promises equity in the race for success, not equality in results—and certainly not equality of earnings or income in an economy of high and growing inequality like ours. Consistent with an older Protestant ethic of individual effort, equality of opportunity stresses the need for individuals to take advantage of opportunities offered and to earn their position through diligence and hard work (now especially through schoolwork) and through merit rather than through compensatory efforts like affirmative action.

Varying Conceptions of Equal Opportunity

Several versions of equality of opportunity have developed historically, in addition to others that philosophers have dreamed up.[2] American lexicographer and author Noah Webster eloquently described one conception in 1793:

> Here [in the United States] every man finds employment, and the road is open for the poorest citizen to amass wealth by labor and economy, and by his talent and virtue to raise himself to the highest offices of the State. (Pole [1978]1994, 118)

Outcomes might be unequal, then, because of differences in work, thrift, abilities, and character, but there ought to be no barriers due to family background, race, geographic location, or other artificial factors.

A stronger version of equal opportunity subsequently emerged, one that required more than the elimination of obvious barriers. Andrew Jackson articulated a complaint about variation in what government provided:

When the laws undertake to add to the natural and just advantages [of superior industry, economy, and virtue] artificial distinctions, to grant titles, gratuities and exclusive privileges, to make the rich richer and the potent more powerful, the humble members of the society—the farmers, mechanics and laborers—have a right to complain of the injustice of their Government. . . . If it would confine itself to equal protection, and, as Heaven does its rains, shower its favors alike on the high and the low, the rich and the poor, it would be an unqualified blessing. (Pole [1978]1994, 145)

Therefore, any differences in what government provides to the rich and to the humble should be eliminated. But this in turn leads to two different interpretations: (1) either the elimination of all differences, implying a standard of equalization or equality among all *individuals*; or (2) the elimination of the relationship in which government favors one *group* over another, the high over the low, the rich over the poor—or a reduction to zero of the correlation between any characteristic of interest (race, ethnicity, gender, foreign birth, class, and so forth) and some aspect of education, even if differences *within* categories continue to be substantial.

Neutrality Versus Equality

As an example of the second type of equity, John Coons, William Clune, and Stephen Sugarman (1970) advocated wealth neutrality, in which the relationship (or correlation) between property value per student and spending per student would be eliminated. However, as the *Serrano v. Priest* case unfolded, challenging the unequal distribution of revenues between property-rich and property-poor districts in California, wealth *neutrality* was replaced by *equality* as a standard. Much of the litigation following *Serrano* sought greater equality in spending per students, not simply wealth neutrality that would eliminate the relationship between wealth and spending. Similarly, advocates for equal access to higher education have argued for policies that eliminate the relationship between race or ethnicity and college access, reflecting a neutrality standard; an equality standard would argue that everyone should have access to higher education (the doctrine of College for All). So Jackson's complaint about "artificial distinctions" of government can lead either to a neutrality standard or to an equality standard, the latter being in every way more stringent and difficult than the former—especially if we recognize that there may be differences in "labor and economy, talent and virtue" among individuals.

Adequacy: A Weaker Standard

A recent variant of equalization has been *adequacy*, the idea that each child should be provided an education in which no one falls below a minimum

(Clune 1994; Minorini and Sugarman 1999). Adequacy is a weaker standard of equity than equalization since it calls for guaranteeing only some minimum level, not a common level, and it does not provide for neutrality among groups at all since, if some group of students—for example, English learners or recent immigrants—are brought up to a minimum while native English speakers are beyond the minimum, there will remain substantial differences in outcomes for immigrants and non-immigrants. Adequacy suffers a further ambiguity: the level of adequacy must be defined, and historically the conception of what constitutes an adequate education has varied substantially as resources once considered unnecessary come to be seen as central—guidance counselors, or music and art specialists, or libraries, or smaller classes, or audiovisual equipment, or computers.[3]

The common approaches in litigation over school finance have been to define adequacy as (1) the spending levels of districts or schools with high levels of performance, or Adequacy 1; (2) the spending necessary for specific resources (qualified teachers, certain pupil-teacher ratios, sufficient textbooks, and so forth) that professionals judge to be adequate, the "professional judgment" model, or Adequacy 2; or (3) a level of spending sufficient to bring all students to some adequate level of outcomes, which itself needs to be defined, or Adequacy 3.[4] The first two of these presume that the levels of spending deemed adequate are sufficient to achieve strong outcomes, but that the ways in which adequate budgets are constructed do not link spending to outcomes. The third approach does examine explicitly the relation between inputs and outputs, but empirical work (like Duncombe and Yinger 1999) relies on conventional production functions with low explanatory power and fails to recognize the uncertain connections between spending and outcomes (reviewed in chapter 3). Adequacy has sometimes been viewed as an advance over equalization because of its *potential* to link spending to outcomes, but in practice it rarely does so. It may lead to recommendations for increasing spending over current levels, but unlike the improved school finance, it has never suggested how that spending should be used to be most effective.

Compensatory Efforts

A fourth version of equal opportunity has emerged repeatedly, certainly predating adequacy, since simply equalizing the "gratuities and exclusive privileges" between the rich and the humble might ignore the different levels of preparation that children bring to school. A more active approach has asserted a governmental role in favoring some groups or individuals who have been disadvantaged through no fault of their own (Pole [1978]1994, ch. 11). These "policies of correction," or compensatory efforts, extend back at least to the nineteenth-century charity schools; the current examples,

now in the form of No Child Left Behind, date from the compensatory education programs of the 1960s.

The compensatory version of equal opportunity has assumed that some
children may be unable to take advantage of opportunities because of their
impoverished family background or unfamiliarity with the culture of schooling (Deschenes, Cuban, and Tyack 2001). Unfortunately, policies of correction have often suffered from the suspicion that their targets are deficient in
fundamental ways, leading to deficiency-oriented correctives that may harm
students as much as help them—for example, the constant barrage of corrections about behavior and language that are part of the mistreatment of African
American, Latino, and immigrant students, as noted in chapter 4.

Applications of Equality: From Access to Outcomes

In the shift from the simple equality of the common schools to equality of
opportunity, then, educational opportunity has been conceptualized in several different ways. A second reason for the elusiveness of equal opportunity
is that it has never been clear what aspects of schooling it should address.
Here we can use the insights of the improved school finance to clarify the
different dimensions of schooling that might be subject to equity claims.[5]
Conceptions of equal opportunity might be applied to simple *access* to publicly funded schools, as in the efforts to include black students in all-white
schools and colleges, or disabled students in schools from which they had
been barred. These conceptions might also be applied to the *funding* of
schools, the dominant application in school finance cases. Conceptions of
equity might also apply not to funding but to *resources*, including the simple,
compound, complex, and abstract resources introduced in chapter 1. For
example, the *Williams v. California* case requires adequate textbooks, qualified teachers, and appropriate physical facilities in all schools, shifting from
funding to resources as the target of equity.

Both revenues and resources are inputs; alternatively, conceptions of equity could apply to *outcomes*—test scores, graduation rates, attitudes and values developed, rates of entering postsecondary education. The historical
tendency to rely on equal opportunity as a substitute for equality of outcomes, however, prevents the widespread use of this conception. The goals
in No Child Left Behind of having all students achieve "proficient" levels of
performance on standardized tests is a rare example of equity applied to
outcomes (in this case to adequacy or proficiency of outcomes), as is the requirement in twenty-five states that students pass exit exams to graduate
from high school—again, an adequacy standard.

The differences among access, funding, resources, and outcomes are derived explicitly from the logic of the improved school finance: access requires funding (the problem throughout the nineteenth century and much

of the twentieth), funding may (but often does not) lead to effective school resources, and certain resources in turn affect outcomes (as in figure 1.2). Conversely, as we shall see in examining the equity effects of school finance litigation in chapter 11, equity in funding without understanding the process by which funding can be used to enhance effective resources leads neither to equitable resources nor to equitable outcomes.

As summarized in table 6.1, there are at least five different conceptions of equal opportunity applied to four aspects of schooling. This is what I call the "landscape of equity," and in the table I provide some illustrative policies and court cases for each conception. (Since most forms of equity are not systematically addressed, we might call this the "landscape of *inequity*.") One conclusion from this "landscape" is that we can find school practices, reform efforts, legislation, and litigation in virtually every one of the cells; that is, the different historically derived conceptions of equity really are used in conflicts over education, and the different applications—to access, funding, resources, and outcomes—contribute to lively and ongoing debates.

The Landscape of Equity: Inconsistent and Shifting Concepts

These different concepts of equity, however, are inconsistent with one another. Wealth neutrality has required the elimination of wealth differences among districts as barriers to funding (cell 10), which addresses only some of the variation that equal funding (cell 6) or Adequacy 1 and 2 (cell 14) have sought to eliminate. The efforts to provide compensatory funding or resources (cells 18 and 19), smaller classes for ELL and special education students, or more counselors for Latino students to correct their misperceptions about college-going (Grubb, Lara, and Valdez 2002) often lead to complaints based on the equity criteria of equal funding or resources (cells 6 and 7), since students and parents who are not so favored complain that others have unfair advantages. (I think of this as the "politics of resentment": those not favored resent the advantages that "other people's children" have.) The court in the *Williams* case ordered minimally acceptable levels of textbooks, facilities, and teachers (cell 15) but left the funding up to the legislature; the resulting funding levels have been wholly inadequate, and the principle of equal (and low) funding of students set by *Serrano* (cell 6) may also weaken the *Williams* solution. When the Bush administration set targets in NCLB of minimum levels of proficiency for all students (cell 16), it failed to provide sufficient funding or technical assistance for schools to develop the most effective resources (cells 18 and 19), so low-performing schools face targets that they lack the capacity to meet.

There has often been a dynamic process of shifts among different conceptions of equity. Despite the high hopes for the *Brown v. Board of Education*

Table 6.1   The Landscape of Equity: Applications of Equity Concepts

Conceptions of Equity	Applied to Access	Applied to Funding	Applied to Resources	Applied to Outcomes
Noah Webster: "No barriers"	1. Policies of inclusion: special education, desegregation by race, gender	2. Neutrality-oriented school finance (Coons, Clune and Sugarmen 1970)	3. Policies of inclusion applied to special programs (like AP); language policies for ELL students	4. Affirmative action
Andrew Jackson: "No artificial distinctions" (equality)	5. The common school movement	6. *Serrano;* equality of funding; district efforts to eliminate intraschool inequality	7. Kozol (1992); equal resources for counselors and specialists	8. Radical egalitarians?
Andrew Jackson: "No artificial distinctions" (neutrality)	9. No differences (of gender, race, etc.) in AP or honors courses, in high-status majors	10. Wealth neutrality; income neutrality; racial neutrality in funding	11. Equity in the allocation of qualified teachers	12. No achievement gaps by race or gender; no ethnic variation in high school dropout rates
Adequacy	13. Minimum school standards; accreditation standards in postsecondary education	14. Adequacy 1 and 2; foundation formulas	15. *Williams;* class size reduction; "qualified teachers" in NCLB; state interventions for low-performing schools	16. Adequacy 3; minimum standards in NCLB; state exit exams

Policies of correction	17. Affirmative action for entry into elite public high schools and postsecondary education	18. Compensatory education; weighted student formulas	19. Compensatory education; early childhood programs; allocation of the best teachers to the lowest-performing students	20. Affirmative action for PSE access; Vonnegut, Player Piano[a]; set-asides for minority- and female-owned businesses

Source: Author's compilation.

[a] In *Player Piano* (1952), Kurt Vonnegut describes a world in which individual gifts are countered by social constraints: for example, especially intelligent individuals have their thoughts interrupted by electrical impulses every thirty seconds; especially graceful dancers are weighted down with sandbags. These egalitarian impulses effectively eliminate the effects of the superior "labor and economy, talent and virtue" noted by Webster, rather than getting low-achieving students to perform at higher levels. These are examples, in school finance jargon, of "equalizing down" rather than "equalizing up."

Note: Adequacy 1: the spending levels of districts or schools with high levels of performance. Adequacy 2: the spending necessary for specific resources (qualified teachers, certain pupil-teacher ratios, sufficient textbooks, etc.) that professionals judge to be adequate (the professional judgment method). Adequacy 3: a level of spending sufficient to bring all students to some adequate level of outcomes, which itself needs to be defined.

ELL = English-language learner
AP = advanced placement
NCLB = No Child Left Behind
PSE = postsecondary education

decision, desegregation lawsuits motivated by concerns over access for black students (cell 1) failed to lead to greater equity in resources (cell 3) or outcomes (cell 4), partly because white families resegregated themselves through white flight to the suburbs; indeed, some of the commentary about the *Brown* decision after fifty years seems surprised that greater equity in access did not accomplish more in terms of funding, resources, or outcomes. Lawsuits about school funding, relying on a different legal rationale but also a different conception of equity (cells 6 or 14), became more prevalent starting around 1970 and in effect superseded the earlier interest in integration and access. To prevent charges of favoring middle-class and white students, many districts have moved to a standard of equal funding (cell 6) for all schools, but this has left especially needy students with the same funding as less needy students, prompting shifts to compensatory funding (cell 18) via weighted student formulas that provide additional revenues to low-income students, special education, and English-language learners (ELLs). The problems with equality in *Serrano*-like cases (cell 6) led lawyers to develop adequacy lawsuits, partly on legal grounds and partly in the hope that this strategy might lead to funding based on outcomes (cell 16); similarly, the *Williams* case, focusing on specific school resources (cell 15), arose because of the ineffectiveness of the *Serrano* case based on funding (cell 6). Reformers thereby change the equity conceptions they use as policies based on prior conceptions of equity prove ineffective or as some legal strategies become more attractive or others are eliminated—for example, when the Supreme Court, in cases involving Seattle and Jefferson County, Kentucky, all but eliminated using race as the basis of assigning students to different schools to create desegregated schools, a form of equity in access (cell 1).[6]

It might be possible to come up with rational ways of moving through the "landscape of equity"—starting with access and moving to funding, then resources and outcomes, or worrying about eliminating favoritism (Webster's barriers), then shifting to neutrality, then equality, before arguing for compensatory efforts. Indeed, the logic of the improved school finance all but requires such a process: it starts with desirable outcomes (table 6.1, column 4), then tries to identify the school and nonschool resources that enhance these outcomes (column 3), and finally asks what funding (column 2) *and* other inputs are necessary to enhance these resources. But in practice, advocates have based their arguments for equity on a variety of more opportunistic reasons, depending on which problems seem most pressing and which legal approaches are most available.

A final difficulty is that equality of opportunity presents a never-ending series of evidentiary problems. Equality itself is easy to measure, if hard to achieve. But since opportunity is an abstract quality, it is hard to know when it has been achieved except when outcomes are equal, which is precisely the condition that equality of opportunity does *not* guarantee. It has been easier to know when equal opportunity fails to exist, and so the dominant approach has been to challenge the conditions that clearly preclude educational opportunity. Exclusion has been the most obvious example, and challenges to exclusion—a lack of access—have been prominent in the long struggles over racial segregation, the battles to include students with disabilities, the movements to provide equal access to educational opportunities and non-education programs (like sports) for women, the reforms eliminating tracking, and the debates over language programs for English-language learners.

Another seemingly obvious barrier to equal opportunity has been underprovision of funding, at least if we make the common assumption underlying the myth of money that money is inherently powerful. This has been, of course, the focus of school finance reform and lawsuits, and so column 2 of table 6.1 (equity conceptions applied to funding) is full of school finance litigation and resulting legislative reforms. However, as chapter 3 illustrates and as I argue again in chapter 11 in examining the possibilities of school finance litigation, the focus on funding does not solve most of the real problems. So we find ourselves in a vast landscape of conceptions of equity that are inconsistent with one another, shift over time, have been unevenly applied, and are of unknown efficacy.

CONCEPTIONS OF DYNAMIC INEQUALITY

The conceptions of equity in table 6.1 all measure differences among individuals or groups at one point in time—they are static measures of equity. In contrast, when we consider the overall effects of formal schooling, we need to recognize the dynamic process by which people become educated. Children start formal schooling, say, at kindergarten, with unequal capacities, both cognitive (such as their knowledge of letters and numbers, vocabulary, and sophistication of language) and noncognitive (their ability to get along with others, conceptions of what school is all about, and patterns of interactions with adults).[7] These unequal capacities are the result of the variation in their family backgrounds as well as in earlier forms of schooling, like early childhood programs.

Equalizing these initial differences might be the responsibility of early childhood and family intervention programs like Head Start, Early Head Start, the Child Care and Development Block Grant (CCDBG), and some programs funded under No Child Left Behind. Schools might then narrow these initial differences, maintain them, or cause them to widen. In the United States, however, these differences appear to be magnified over time. For example, as Roland Fryer and Steven Leavitt (2005) show, modest black-white differences at the beginning of kindergarten, largely explained by some simple socioeconomic status variables, increase over the period until the spring of third grade. Meredith Phillips, James Crouse, and John Ralph (1998) estimate that initial black-white differences are roughly doubled by the end of twelfth grade, though the metric by which differences are measured and the data used make a great deal of difference to this kind of conclusion.[8] Similarly, in Charles Hargis's (2006, fig. 1) display of scores on the Peabody Individual Achievement Test (PIAT), the range of scores for the middle 50 percent of students widens steadily over time. Russell Rumberger and Patricia Gándara (2004) have found that English learners are one and a half grade levels behind native English speakers by grade 5, two years behind by grade 8, and four and a half years behind by grade 11, a clear divergence in relative performance. Therefore, the growth patterns of high-, middle-, and low-performing students look something like the solid straight lines from kindergarten through grade 8 in figure 6.1, which diverge steadily between these two grades. Alternatively, since there are obviously many million individual growth trajectories associated with many million students, we can interpret the trajectories in figure 6.1 as the outer bounds of individual growth curves, or—because there are surely some students with extremely divergent trajectories—as the outer bounds containing the middle 90 or 95 percent of students.

Measures of Outcomes

Unfortunately, it is difficult to collect data appropriate to the entire K–12 trajectory. Test scores are one measure of learning outcomes, but tests generally change over K–12 education, so that there are no tests appropriate for the entire period. Some competencies promoted in high school—inferential abilities, the capacity to recognize and solve problems in different fields, the ability to formulate abstract concepts and mental models—are inappropriate for first-graders. In high school, valuable outcomes include measures of progress—like credits accumulated, the passage of key "gatekeeper" courses like algebra 1, the accumulation of the academic courses necessary for college admission, completion of the high school diploma, and subsequent enrollment in postsecondary education—but comparable measures of progress are less obvious in elementary schools. The attitudinal outcomes in high school, like educational and occupational expectations, have no ready counterpart in elementary grades, where being socialized to school-like behavior and learning various socioemotional skills (impulse control, anger management, cooperation) are more important. Many different schooling outcomes are desirable, then, but they change over the years of schooling. In practice, therefore, growth functions like those in figure 6.1 may be estimated only in segments of a few years at a time, though pondering trajectories over longer periods of time may still be conceptually useful.

Another complication is that there are many outcomes to measure (on

Figure 6.1   Potential Growth Trajectories, Kindergarten Through
               Grade Twelve, by Schooling Outcomes

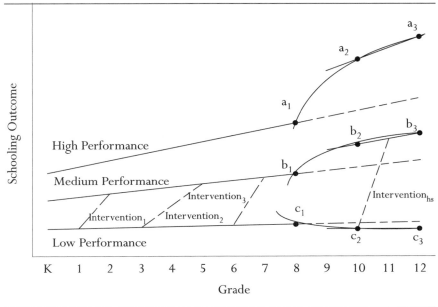

Source: Author's compilation.
Note: Outcomes in this graph conventionally refer to test scores and other measures of learning, but they might also include measures of progress through schooling, measures of connectedness to schooling, and attitudes related to schooling.

the Y-axis) or (in the current vocabulary) many different kinds of achievement gaps. There is no reason to think that trajectories over time for different outcomes look the same. As table B.4 confirms, the racial gaps in test scores are larger in grade 12 than the racial gaps in credits earned or the likelihood of high school graduation. Therefore, the degree of divergence may be smaller or greater for some outcomes compared to others, and perhaps—as I found in chapter 2 in comparing common versus differentiated effects of resources—test scores respond differently over time to some variables while measures of progress are affected by others. A multidimensional version of figure 6.1 might allow us to see the differences in patterns of inequality over time for different outcomes, an analysis I present in chapter 7 in comparing the growth patterns of test scores with those for aspirations.

With multiple outcomes, inequalities in some outcomes might be countered by other outcomes. For example, some students (sometimes called "nerds") might have high levels of cognitive ability but low levels of interpersonal skills, while others ("jocks" or "preps") develop high levels of interpersonal skills and popularity and adequate levels of cognitive ability. Another version of the American Dream, particularly for small-town boys and African Americans, has been to achieve a high level of athletic ability in football or basketball or "cool" musical ability to compensate for lower levels of cognitive accomplishments. A follower of Howard Gardner ([1983]1993) and his seven (now eight) conceptions of "intelligences" or capabilities would want to know about the development of all of them—though schools often ignore all but linguistic and spatial-mathematical competencies. Obviously, compensating inequalities do exist for individuals, but many of them are hard to measure because they require data on multiple kinds of abilities, many of which are not usually collected in school-based surveys. Empirically, most measurable schooling outcomes are positively rather than negatively correlated with one another.[9] Thus, in practice, compensating inequalities are less prevalent than outcomes that reinforce one another; in general, students who tend to do well on one measure do well on others as well. In chapter 7, then, rather than developing a multidimensional map of various outcomes, I simply show that the trajectories for different outcomes vary.

Mechanisms for Explaining Divergence in Relative Performance

Figure 6.1 raises a second obvious question: what causes growth trajectories to diverge rather than converge? One explanation focuses on the psychology of learning, and specifically on the contention (for example, by Resnick 1989) that "knowledge begets knowledge"—individuals with higher initial levels of learning may be able to learn at a faster *rate* than others, possibly because more knowledge gives them the conceptual understanding and ability to develop constructs that facilitate subsequent learning. The diverging trajectories of figure 6.1 reflect the assumption that those with higher initial levels of outcomes progress at a faster rate, with a steeper slope.

Another possibility is that students with low levels of initial outcomes become discouraged or shamed by their low performance, while high-performing students are motivated by their success and further encouraged by parents and teachers. This leads again to low initial levels of performance reducing rates of improvement. A special case of this explanation is the mistreatment of racial-minority students: if black, Latino, and American Indian students are subjected to slights or indifference or "micro-aggressions," they may become discouraged or disconnected from schooling. The difference in this second explanation is that encouragement and discouragement may be visible in measures of student engagement and motivation. In this case, including such measures of student behavior among independent variables explaining growth trajectories would weaken or eliminate the tendency for growth trajectories to diverge.

A different explanation focuses on the continuing effects of family background. If the initial differences among students are due to dimensions of family background—like parental education or aspirations for their children—that continue to reinforce or undermine schooling outcomes, then initial differences will continue to diverge over time since all of them are due to family background. However, if it were possible to measure *all* possible effects of family background and include them among independent variables, then trajectories controlling for family background might remain parallel rather than diverging. A variant of this explanation interprets divergence in terms of summer effects: middle-class students continue to improve their abilities over the summer as a result of continued reading, dinner-table conversations, trips, and other enrichment activities, while working-class students lose some of what they have learned during the school year. Indeed, in some research, summer effects account for *all* of the divergence in test scores over time.[10] The explanation from summer effects absolves schools from responsibility for diverging achievement and places it more clearly on continuing family effects.

Yet another explanation notes that school resources are often allocated according to student performance. For example, the "best" teachers (or at least those with the most experience) are able to choose which students they teach, and they usually choose to teach the "best" students, or the honors and AP classes, or they move to suburban schools with higher-performing students. Conversely, low-performing students are stuck with or assigned the most inexperienced teachers with the least seniority, or they are assigned to low-ability tracks with weaker teachers and lower expectations, or they are assigned in high school to general or vocational tracks with low teacher expectations, weak curricula, and unmotivated peers. There is a substantial literature documenting that teacher expectations and demands—an abstract resource—vary between black and white students (Ferguson 1998) and among other groups of students as well (Weinstein 2002).

In addition, resources are often allocated by family background or race: high-SES students are more likely to live in districts with high spending and well-credentialed teachers, while poor and minority students are more likely to be found in urban districts with lower levels of spending (especially relative to need), uncredentialed teachers, overwhelmed administrators, and incompetent district staff. Stability—of students and teachers, principals and superintendents—is yet another abstract resource that may contribute to divergence, particularly given the contrast between relatively stable suburban schools and the many urban schools that are so unstable that sustained reforms over long periods of time become impossible. This view implies that the unequal allocation of school resources—some of them measurable in the NELS88 data, some unmeasured—is to blame for diverging performance rather than (or in addition to) family background.

Another problem that might contribute to divergence in students' relative performance is the inability of some teachers to keep up with grade-level curriculum norms. In theory, state standards specify the appropriate grade-level materials, and these are one of the mechanisms—along with grade-level textbooks—that might prevent divergence. In practice, however, some teachers fall behind grade-level norms. One specific illustration of variation in teacher demands comes from an exploratory study by Hollingsworth and Ybarra (n.d.), who examined classroom materials like worksheets, quizzes, and assignments in one San Diego elementary school and compared these materials to grade-level norms. The results, described in table 6.2, show that all materials were on grade level in kindergarten and grade 1. But slippage behind grade-level norms began as early as second grade, when 23 percent of math materials and 20 percent of language arts materials were at first-grade level. The slippage became increasingly serious after that: 98 percent of both math and language arts materials were below grade level by fifth grade.[11] This pattern of steadily falling behind grade-level norms might happen if teachers are simply unaware of grade-level norms, in which case efforts to get them to learn and then teach to state standards would be effective. If, however, teachers of low-performing students find themselves slowing down the curriculum to accommodate the students who need more time to master competencies, or if teachers with low-performing students need to reteach earlier material, the patterns in table 6.2 may be due less to teacher ignorance than to ineffective remedial techniques, and then the only solution is a much more complex approach to improving rates of learning. I return to these issues in chapter 8, where I show that the methods used in many (but not all) schools for helping low-performing students are often fragmented and ineffective.

Finally, student connectedness to schooling or ability to benefit from instruction may also contribute to divergence in outcomes. The process of dropping out of high school, for example, has often been described as a dynamic one: the student initially experiences failure, becomes discouraged, fails to exert as much effort as his or her peers, becomes increasingly attracted to distractions like television, games, and street life, suffers more failure, and begins a downward spiral of disengagement that ultimately ends in dropping out (Fine 1991; Alexander, Entwhistle, and Kabbini 2001). Stories of individual students finding a supportive teacher who reverses their poor performance and motivates them to perform well in school are among the staples of the motivational literature. But without such interventions, divergence in students' connectedness to schooling will contribute to diverging outcomes.

Evidently, there are many possible factors that contribute to divergence.

Table 6.2   Curriculum Material Taught by Grade Level

| | Meets Grade Level Standards | | | | | | |
Grade	K	1	2	3	4	5	Average Grade Level
Mathematics							
K	100						K
1		100					1.0
2		23	77				1.8
3			45	55			2.6
4			40	40	20		2.8
5		2	35	59	2	2	2.7
Language arts							
K	100						K
1		100					1.0
2		20	80				1.8
3		2	14	84			2.8
4		2	30	35	33		3.0
5			28	60	10	2	2.9

Source: Hollingsworth and Ybarra (n.d.).
Note: The figures give the proportion of classroom materials in each grade (the row categories) meeting the grade-level standards of the column categories; for example, in second grade, 23 percent of mathematics materials were at first-grade levels and 77 percent were at second-grade level.

Since the solutions to these potential problems vary substantially, it is worth trying to disentangle which of these explanations is responsible. Some of them—the effects of family background, for example—can be quantified; others, like the tendency of teachers to fall behind grade-level norms, are exceedingly difficult to measure, though placement in general, vocational, and remedial tracks is one proxy for this problem. But of course, all of these possible explanations may operate to one degree or another; if all of them—and others that we might think of—operate to some extent *and* reinforce one another, this might explain why growth trajectories diverge so consistently.

Discontinuities or "Bursts" in Trajectories

A different complication is that outcome trajectories might not be smooth and continuous, as they are on the left side of figure 6.1. A good example is the transition from eighth to ninth grade. Some students, especially the lowest-performing students, drop out literally or constructively and fail to make any further progress. Yet other students, presumably those who have fallen relatively far behind but still stay in school, are relegated to a series of remedial courses or even special education classes, which tend to use the weakest forms of instruction—drill and repetition—on subjects that students should have mastered in early grades, meaning that remedial students fail to progress in the content associated with high school. Other low-performing students are relegated to general or vocational tracks in which the curriculum is watered down, teachers have lower expectations of students, and peers have relatively low ambitions. At the upper end, some high-performing students gain access to AP and honors tracks, and their rates of learning accelerate. Many students in the middle follow a middling program, neither honors nor remedial, that prepares them for regional universities or community colleges.

The right-hand side of figure 6.1 illustrates these patterns, which lead to a burst or explosion of inequality from eighth to ninth grades, and then to progressively greater inequality over the high school years. (Of course, *observed* inequality may be less than *actual* inequality because dropouts are no longer included in any data collection; in practice, we usually observe only the top two of the trajectories in the right side of figure 6.1, not all three.) When such a burst takes place, the likelihood of students catching up—on the trajectory labeled "Intervention$_{hs}$" in figure 6.1—seems virtually impossible, because the rate of learning along this trajectory is so much higher than at any other point on any trajectory. In addition, older students are more likely to become unmotivated by then, and adolescents often have things to do—some of them self-destructive—other than remain diligent students, so student ability to benefit from instruction may undermine even careful intervention efforts.

Such bursts of inequality are surely not confined to the transition from middle school to high school. Another such explosion may occur somewhere during the third or fourth grades, when many educators observe that schools shift from teaching basic competencies like reading and math to using these competencies to learn content. This may create widening differences between those who have mastered basic academic skills and those who have failed to do so; students who lack this mastery of basic skills and who may also have failed to learn school-appropriate behavior and "study skills" are sometimes said to suffer from "the fourth-grade slump" (Samuels 2007). The transition to middle school, with a different pattern of teachers and subjects and often formal tracking, may cause another such burst of inequality. While there is not much empirical evidence about such bursts, Phillips and her colleagues (Phillips, Crouse, Ralph 1998, table 7.7) find a particularly high increase in the relative gaps of reading and math scores between white and black students in seventh and eighth grades. Similarly, the variation in Peabody test scores reported by Hargis (2006) seems to increase markedly in grades 3 and 7.[12] In countries where early tracking takes place, as in Switzerland with its four tracks beginning at age twelve, or many European systems with traditions of separating academic and vocational students into different schools around age fifteen, the testing and tracking procedures may cause their own bursts of inequality (Dupriez and Dumay 2005). The transition from secondary to postsecondary education causes an enormous burst of inequality in virtually all countries. In the United States, for example, some students gain access to elite institutions where they work exceedingly hard; other students enroll in a variety of finely differentiated postsecondary institutions (including community colleges and short-term job training), where they progress at different rates; and many students fail to continue their schooling at all.

In many ways, the development of an educational system in this country has tried to create coherent pathways through different levels of schooling— for example, by establishing a graded system with regular progression, by developing a clear transition from the old grammar school to high school, and by creating a uniform high school curriculum so as to simplify the process of applying to college. But system-building has concentrated on *creating* pathways through different levels, not on making them *equitable*. The burden of adjusting to new schools has always fallen on students and their parents, and this has been particularly true where the transitions are the most challenging—in moving from high school to postsecondary education, for example.

If a schooling system is subject to a series of such bursts of inequality, then instead of the smooth and diverging trajectories of the left side of figure 6.1, the discontinuous trajectories of figure 6.2 are more likely, with inequality over time a function not only of the slopes of these trajectories but also of the institutional patterns causing these bursts. If such bursts exist, then growth trajectories will be nonlinear rather than linear; the segments in figure 6.2 suggest trajectories that are convex to the origin. Over shorter segments of time, other nonlinearities may emerge: In figure 6.1, connecting $a_1 - a_3$ and $b_1 - b_3$—representing the NELS88 data for eighth, tenth, and twelfth grades—leads to nonlinear growth paths concave to the X-axis, while dropouts (connecting c_1, c_2, and c_3) may show convex growth paths. But whatever the empirical patterns might be, the possibility of bursts in inequality implies that transitions between grades, patterns of grouping and tracking, and selective dropping out of school are also responsible for inequality over time.

THE CHALLENGES OF DYNAMIC EQUITY

If schooling outcomes diverge, as in figure 6.1 or 6.2, this creates challenges for schools—and districts, states, and the federal government—to prevent such divergence, or indeed to create convergence. These trajectories imply

Figure 6.2   Discontinuous Growth Trajectories, Kindergarten
Through Grade Twelve, by Schooling Outcomes

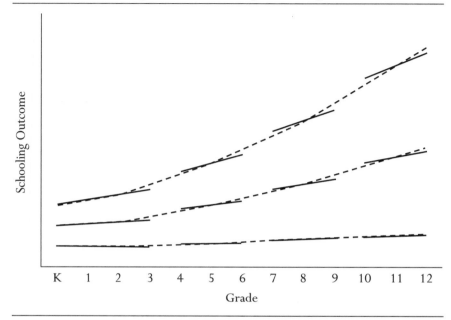

that helping low-performing students catch up with their high-performing
peers is easier early in the school process—for example, between first and
second grades (at Intervention$_1$)—than later, as at sixth grade (Interven-
tion$_3$). This is simply because the slope of intervention efforts, which describes the rate of learning required to catch up, is necessarily greater in
higher grades. This is part of the logic of catching any learning deficits earlier rather than later. In addition, by later grades, and especially by high
school, the many years of low performance may have established behavior
patterns that make accelerated learning even more difficult.

Alternatively, a program of catching up might last over two or three
years, as at Intervention$_2$, which might seem more feasible in the sense that
it would not require such a high rate of learning. However, there are few
mechanisms for coordinating interventions over several years, except perhaps Individual Education Plans (IEPs) for special education or similar student plans sometimes developed for students who are behind. (The method
of intervention called a Learning Center in chapter 8 is one example of a po-

Figure 6.3   Potential Growth Trajectories, Kindergarten Through
Grade Twelve, by Schooling Outcome

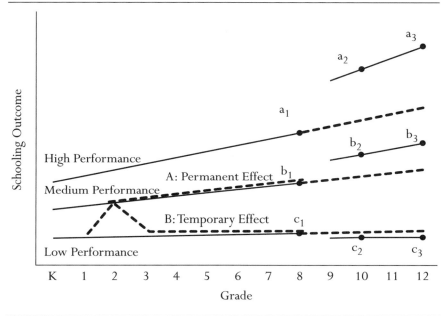

Source: Author's compilation.

tentially multiple-year learning plan.) In any of these cases, finding methods of instruction that accelerate learning well above the normal rate is self-evidently difficult; it may require a relatively expensive intervention like Reading Recovery, using one-on-one instruction with carefully trained specialists (D'Agostino and Murphy 2004).

Yet another issue involves the effects of different reforms and interventions on students' growth trajectories. In figure 6.3, trajectory A represents a reform effort with a permanent effect: students master a particular competence (like reading for meaning, using fractions and decimals, or absorbing conventional conceptions of "school") and then are able to continue performing at satisfactory levels for the rest of their schooling—that is, the effect of the single-year intervention is permanent. The assumption underlying many interventions is that their effects are permanent. For example, the Perry Preschool shows effects lasting to age forty (Schweinhart et al. 2005), and Chicago's Child-Parent Centers had positive effects at age twenty-four. Henry May and Jonathan Supovitz's (2006) study of America's

Choice comprehensive school reforms finds positive effects that accumulate over time. The very name "Reading Recovery" implies a permanent recovery from substandard reading performance. In practice, however, the results for programs in first grade seem to last at least to the end of the second grade, but truly lasting effects have rarely been established, and Reading Recovery researchers urge that schools provide supportive services beyond first or second grade (see also Hiebert and Taylor 2000).

The alternative possibility is depicted in trajectory B: a single-year intervention has a temporary effect only, so that after a period of improvement the student's performance degrades to what it was before the intervention. The difficult conditions of second-chance programs may contribute to interventions having only short-run effects. If trajectory B holds, then interventions must be permanent rather than temporary, and students who enter schooling behind their peers must have constant additional support rather than short-term interventions—that is, "policies of correction" that are permanent. Unfortunately, we know very little from the formal evaluation literature about the long-run effects of educational improvement and intervention; many results show only short-run effects.[13] For the moment, it is sufficient to point out that long-run effects of interventions matter a great deal to inequality over the long run, contrasting trajectories A and B, and that *assumptions* about long-run effects may be incorrect.

Finally, figures 6.1 and 6.2 also clarify that the cross-sectional differences at any point in time—at the end of twelfth grade, for example, or at the end of elementary school—are due not to school resources, family background, and student behavior in that grade alone, as in conventional production functions, but to a series of family resources, school resources, teaching practices, tracking mechanisms, student behavior, and student choices extending back at least to kindergarten. Insofar as possible, therefore, educators and researchers need to consider this entire trajectory of resources in understanding the differential performance of students and what can be done to remedy these inequalities.

What would conceptions of equity look like in a dynamic sense rather than in the static world of table 6.1? One precept emerging from the improved school finance is that dynamic conceptions of equity would focus initially on outcomes and then move backward to implications for resources and then funding. That is, the challenge is to identify the *effective* resources that need to be equalized to achieve any particular conception of dynamic equity.

Then, based on the conceptions of equity in table 6.1, four conceptions of dynamic equity suggest themselves. One measure would follow the logic of equality: that is, all students would have equal rates of learning, and growth trajectories would be parallel rather than diverging, without the bursts of inequality depicted in figures 6.1 and 6.2.[14] Absolute equality is, of course, an impossible standard to meet, since it requires that all individual differences—including all those due to "labor and economy, talent and virtue"—be countered by "policies of correction" or compensatory policies. Alternatively, neutrality would ensure that the average growth trajectories of *groups* of students—groups defined by race-ethnicity, by various measures of class, by gender, by immigrant status, perhaps by region—are parallel rather than diverging. That is, there would be a zero correlation between the slopes of learning trajectories and group characteristics like gender, race and ethnicity, dimensions of family background, and disability status. Working backward from outcomes to the resources and then the funding required for this conception of dynamic equity, equity in this sense surely would require policies of correction or compensatory policies, with students initially at low levels of performances receiving more of the *effective* school resources, and the funding necessary to create these greater school resources, than high-performing students receive, on a sustained basis throughout the elementary and secondary grades. This approach brings with it both educational difficulties—whether school resources are powerful enough to overcome differences in family and student resources—and political difficulties because middle-class parents might not embrace the radical redistribution of resources that dynamic equity might require.

Third, we might develop a dynamic conception of equity based on adequacy: every student upon leaving high school should have mastered certain competencies at levels deemed adequate. The efforts to require passing high school competency exams or exit exams represent one expression of this conception, though with narrow measures of outcomes (usually just math and English scores) and relatively low levels of competence (Achieve Inc. 2004). Other high school reform groups have proposed different measures of minimum competency that are intended to prepare students adequately for both postsecondary schooling *and* employment, but largely through conventional academic outcomes (American Diploma Project 2004). The ideals of preparing students for both successful college enrollment and successful employment upon leaving high school—the "college *and* careers" approach to creating pathways through high school—is another expression, with still broader outcome measures (Oakes and Saunders 2008).

Defining minimally adequate levels of competence at a fixed point in time might lead to desperate last-minute measures to cram for competency exams, as happens in many high schools where students fail early administrations of exit exams. Ideally, however, an adequacy approach would lead to longer-run efforts over four years (or more) to shift low-performing students to a trajectory high enough to meet minimum standards. As illustrated in figure 6.4, this would mean shifting students onto trajectory B early in their schooling rather than attempting the last-minute intervention described by C, which requires an unreasonably high rate of learning. Equity in

Figure 6.4　　Trajectories to Meet Adequate Outcomes

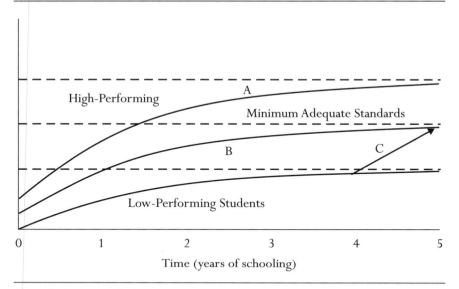

Time (years of schooling)

Source: Author's compilation.

a dynamic sense would then require eliminating low-performing tracks like remedial and general tracks, enhancing the use of innovative and "balanced" approaches to teaching, improving school climate, increasing the experience of teachers in secondary education and in teaching in the field for which they were trained, and following the other recommendations developed to substantially reshape high schools. All of these are precisely the opposite of the isolated interventions using drills and other behaviorist approaches that are common in last-minute cramming efforts. When we return in chapter 8 to the general policies that schools have developed to create dynamic equity—that is, to boost the performance of students who have fallen behind their peers (or "equalizing up")—we will see a similar difference between the desperate efforts to adopt "silver bullet" curricula and the more measured, longer-run efforts to improve the quality of instruction and re-create the climate of schools.

Finally, the strongest measure of equity would incorporate policies of correction, or compensatory approaches, trying to eliminate any initial differences by causing trajectories to converge. This requires, of course, faster rates of growth for low-performing students than for high-performing students. Periodically, for example, some programs claim to accelerate learning or to provide two years of achievement growth in one year; for example, promotional materials claim that "*Language!* accelerates the literacy learning process!"[15] But whether such high rates of learning can be sustained for a number of years or for larger populations of students remains unknown, partly because evaluations of interventions rarely take a dynamic view of outcomes. And so both educational and political difficulties are greater in attempts to achieve dynamic equity through converging trajectories than through equality or neutrality.

A dynamic approach therefore opens up a number of research and reform possibilities. One implication is that we can understand the vast differences among high school students—whether in the NELS88 data or in the PISA and IALS data allowing for comparisons among countries—as the results of a long period of diverging trajectories.[16] Another is that we can see schooling outcomes at any one moment not as the result of resources in that school year alone, but rather as the result of an entire history of schooling, school resources, the support of family and community, and the development of students' own ability to take advantage of school offerings. In turn, that means that greater equity in a dynamic sense probably requires a series of steady improvements over many years of schooling rather than last-minute "cramming" efforts, a subject to which I turn in chapters 8 and 9.

The most important empirical question from a dynamic perspective is determining the causes of diverging trajectories. This is the subject of chapter 7, using the NELS88 data to understand not the cross-sectional patterns of schooling outcomes and effective school resources (as in chapters 2 to 5), but the growth in outcomes between eighth and twelfth grades. These results also confirm the value of new approaches to school and nonschool resources since a variety of compound, complex, and abstract resources, as well as families and students, prove to affect these trajectories.

Chapter 7

Dynamic Inequality:
Schooling Outcomes over Time

THE HYPOTHESIS of dynamic inequality is that schooling outcomes may diverge over time, adding inequalities created during the entire trajectory of formal schooling to those inequalities that students bring with them to school. Only by examining these possibilities empirically can we know whether schools, as well as nonschool resources including family background, lead to divergence, neutrality, or convergence, though the little information we have indicates that divergence is typical. The NELS88 data used in part 1 are well suited to answering this question, since they have three years of comparable data—for grades 8, 10, and 12—allowing estimation of these trajectories, or growth models, over a five-year period. The large amount of information about school and nonschool resources in the NELS88 data also enables us to see whether on the whole these resources contribute to divergence or whether they moderate (or even reverse) its effects. To be sure, it would be preferable to analyze data for more than a five-year period. For example, some districts have collected longitudinal data that describe student test scores over longer periods of time, but such district data do not include the large amount of information in NELS88 about school and nonschool resources.[1] In this chapter, I therefore continue to draw on NELS88 data, including information about resources drawn from previous chapters, to explore patterns of change over time.

Of substantial importance for the results reported here, students were administered tests based on item response theory (IRT) in all three years for math, English, science, and history. IRT models create scales that are well suited for studying change in ways that standardized tests are not (Seltzer,

Choi, and Thum 2003; Seltzer, Frank, and Bryk 1994). Standardized tests, in contrast, typically vary from year to year and therefore must be calibrated to be consistent with one another over time (Dorans, Pommerich, and Holland 2007). Unfortunately, unlike test scores, many other outcome measures used in chapter 2 cannot be readily calculated for each year; for example, high school graduation occurs only once, and the completion of an academic program can be measured only in grade 12. In addition, some variables describing progress cannot be measured reliably for all three years of the NELS88 data, especially in grade 8, when concepts like credits earned are inapplicable. These measures of progress, which proved illuminating in chapter 2, therefore cannot be used in growth models. In addition to test scores, then, only three outcome measures are available for all three years: students' educational aspirations, students' occupational aspirations, and students' assessments of whether they are likely to continue their education past grade 12. Furthermore, some information from teachers, students, parents, and administrators was measured inconsistently in the first three waves of NELS88 and therefore cannot be included in growth models; a full array of resources can be included only for simpler equations describing grade 12 outcomes, like those underlying chapters 2 through 5. There is, then, a trade-off in analyzing outcomes: examining simple cross-sectional results requires less data overall but allows for analysis of more variables at a given time, whereas the study of dynamic inequality requires consistent data over a period of time, with a more limited amount of consistent information about schooling outcomes and resources.

The results in this chapter rely on estimation of linear and nonlinear growth models using the statistical methods of hierarchical modeling. Such methods are more difficult to understand, and the results more complex to explain, than the ordinary least squares methods used in chapters 2 to 5. Therefore, readers unprepared for technical discussions should skip to the final section of this chapter, "Reaching for Dynamic Equity," where I summarize the important conclusions from these statistical results.

EXAMINING CHANGE WITH LINEAR GROWTH MODELS

Growth models, which are conceptually equivalent to estimating small segments of the trajectories in figure 6.1, depict potential growth trajectories at low, medium, and high levels of performance. In this case, the segments describe the period from grade 8 to grade 10 to grade 12. The simplest linear equation to describe a segment from grades 8 to 12 for one individual is:

$$Y_{ist} = \pi_{0is} + \pi_{1is} TIME_t + r_{ist} \tag{7.1}$$

where Y_{ist} is an outcome measure for an individual i in school s at time t. The intercept π_0 represents outcomes for eighth grade, and π_1 describes the effect per year of schooling on outcome measures (since TIME has values of 0, 2, and 4 for grades 8, 10, and 12). Each individual has a unique growth function, but of course NELS88 includes many individuals in many schools, so both the intercept and the slope may vary across individuals and schools. Approximately thirteen thousand students in the NELS88 data can be used to estimate equations like 7.1, so there are about thirteen thousand separate growth equations—a veritable blizzard of segments like those on the right-hand side of figure 6.1. Although these individual growth trajectories would be too numerous to interpret, the average values of the intercept π_{0is} and the slope π_{1is} are of interest.

But we want to include more than time when we try to explain outcome measures such as test scores and aspirations; the full range of school and nonschool resources examined in prior chapters should also explain dynamic outcomes. Some of these resources vary over time. Among school resources, for example, teacher attitudes, pedagogical methods, and school climate vary over time as students change teachers and schools. Student behavior and connectedness to schooling may also vary over time if a student goes into a slump in high school or if a student goes into a slump and then recovers, and changes in these variables may explain changes in outcomes. On the other hand, some measures of family resources are constant over time—for example, parental education, occupation, and language spoken in the home are considered fixed, since they do not vary much over five years, and demographic variables such as gender and race-ethnicity are also fixed or time-invariant.[2] Such models can be estimated by the methods of hierarchical models using the procedure PROC MIXED within STATA (Singer 1998); they generate intercepts like π_{0is}, slopes like π_{1is}, and the effects of resources on both intercepts and slopes.[3]

Starting from equation 7.1, we can see whether individuals with higher intercepts (higher scores in eighth grade) also have higher slopes (higher rates of learning), in which case divergence will occur. We can also analyze which time-invariant variables increase or decrease the intercept and the slope or rate of progress over time. If different independent variables explain the variation in intercepts and slopes—for example, if effective school resources are allocated to high-performing students and thereby increase both intercepts and slopes—then we will be able to detect this both in differences in the slopes and in the individual components of these growth trajectories.[4] So by varying the specifications of these growth functions and including different school and nonschool resources, we can learn more about the divergence in growth functions and what causes them.[5]

With this approach, there are three sets of results to examine: the parameters π_0 and π_1 with different specifications, particularly to see the patterns of these parameters across schools and across individuals; the coefficients of time-invariant variables such as measures of class and race; and the effects of variables that change over time, such as income, the pupil-teacher ratio, school climate, income per dependent, and measures of student connectedness to schooling. Appendix table B.6 presents the first of these describing the parameters π_0 and π_1 with different specifications ranging from simple to all-inclusive. The first specification is a simple model like equation 7.1, including only the effects of time. The second specification includes all independent variables, both time-invariant and time-varying, including school resources, family background, and student ability to benefit.[6] Unlike conventional regression results, the intercepts π_{0is} and the slopes π_{1is} are not constant but vary across schools and across individuals within schools. Their patterns can be described by coefficients of variation (denoted cv) and correlation coefficients (ρ) describing the correlation between intercepts and slopes.[7]

From table B.6, all test scores improve over time on the average, since the coefficients on TIME in row 8 are positive and highly significant. Educational and occupational aspirations (H Ed Asp and H Oc Asp, respectively) also increase over time, though the remaining attitudinal variable—the student's perceived likelihood of remaining in school past graduation (ContEd)—does not increase; indeed, it appears to decrease, at least in this simple specification.

Although these general patterns describe all students, variation among schools is substantial (in rows 1 and 2), and variation among individuals within schools is even greater (in rows 4 and 5), as described by the coefficients of variation of intercepts and slopes. Rates of improvement vary substantially more than intercepts describing starting values for eighth grade (rows 1 and 4), so differences among schools and among individuals in learning *growth* are greater than the differences at grade 8; this shift by itself implies that trajectories diverge over the high school years. In addition, variation among individuals *within* schools (rows 4 and 5) is higher than variation *among* schools (rows 1 and 2)—perhaps because high schools are usually larger and more heterogeneous than elementary and middle schools, so more of the total variation among all students is among the highest- and lowest-performing students within particular schools.

The correlations between slopes and intercepts are of particular interest because they indicate divergence of growth trajectories when positive, convergence when negative, and neutrality or roughly parallel slopes with a correlation insignificantly different from zero. These correlations can be calculated both for variation among schools (table B.6, row 3) and for variation among individuals (row 6). Evidently, the simple growth trajectories diverge for most test scores, so that inequality becomes worse over time. (The only exception is history test scores, for which the school-level covariation is insignificant.) However, when other independent variables are added in speci-fication 2, the correlations fall toward zero and even become negative in a few cases, though not always significantly so. (The individual-level correla-tion for reading is negative and significant, as is the school-level correlation for history.) This suggests that growth trajectories might be neutral or even converge once other independent variables, including school resources and student behavior, are considered. I explore this finding later in the chapter.

In contrast to test scores, educational aspirations, occupational aspira-tions, and the perceived likelihood of continuing education past twelfth grade generally converge. To some extent this seems puzzling: it means that student attitudes toward schooling and occupations are converging even as educa-tional attainments measured by test scores are diverging. But it is also consis-tent with earlier cross-sectional findings for outcomes other than test scores, presented in chapter 2: while some aspects of school resources, family back-ground, and student behavior affect all outcomes, others (particularly those involving the nature of instruction) affect test scores but not other outcomes, while some (particularly those describing high schools as supportive commu-nities) affect progress and attitudes but not test scores. So some outcome measures are relatively independent of others, and schools may be successful in minimizing differences in some of them (like aspirations) even as others (like test scores) continue to diverge. Over the long run, of course, educa-tional progress and attainments matter the most. This finding unfortunately suggests that schools as currently constituted are the most effective in nar-rowing inequalities in the least consequential outcomes.

The Effects of Different Resources on Linear Growth Models

The data in table B.6 lead to another question: Is the reduction in diver-gence, or in some cases the shift to convergence, caused by variables that policy might influence, particularly policy related to school resources? Or do the changes result from the continuing effects of family background and other factors (such as gender, race-ethnicity, native language) generally thought to be beyond the power of schools? To illustrate the effects of differ-ent sets of independent variables, table B.7 presents the critical covariances between slopes and intercepts, again transformed into correlation coeffi-cients, from four specifications:

- Specification 1 includes the effect of time only.

- Specification 2 includes the effects of family background and demo-graphic variables as well as time.

- Specification 3 includes the effects of school resources and student connectedness to schooling as well as time.

- Specification 4 includes all independent variables as well as time.

The differences between specifications 1 and 3, and between 2 and 4, reflect the influences of variables that might be considered controllable, particularly school resources. The differences between specifications 1 and 2, and between 3 and 4, reflect the influences of family background and demographic measures, effects on outcomes that might be influenced by social policies outside of schooling but that cannot always be affected by schools themselves.[8]

The results for test scores in table B.7 are quite consistent. The positive correlation between *school* slopes and intercepts, indicating divergence, is almost wholly explained by demographic and family background measures; once these are introduced, in specification 2 compared to 1, or in specification 4 compared to 3, the divergence among schools vanishes. This proves to be a transfer of explanatory power from random components to demographic and family background variables. In plain English, the overall divergences among school trajectories are explained largely by differences in race-ethnicity, other demographic variables, and the family backgrounds of students—not a particularly surprising finding in a country where so much racial-ethnic and class segregation exists among communities and therefore among high schools. Once these variables are considered, there is a further small reduction in this crucial correlation, in the neighborhood of .055 to .10 for different test scores, due to school resources and student behavior and motivation. This suggests that school policies can moderate the effects of divergence, though the extent of this moderation is small in current practice, and small compared to the effects of family background.

The variation in the crucial covariance among *individuals* within schools follows a somewhat different pattern. Variation among individuals within schools is much larger than variation among schools in both intercepts and slopes. The divergence among individuals (specification 1) is consistently lowered by about .05 by school resources and student behavior (specification 3); it is lowered slightly more, by between .055 and .10, by demographic and family variables (specification 2). So for the largest component of variation in individual growth trajectories—the variation among individuals within schools—"controllable" variables contribute almost as much to reducing the crucial correlation as do "uncontrollable" demographic and family background variables, and the power of "controllable" variables would be even more powerful if NELS88 had a full range of the school resources (especially high school tracks) used in chapter 2.[9] For reading scores, the initial pattern of divergence ($\rho = .046$) becomes insignificant

($\rho = -.001$) once school resources and student behavior are considered, then falls to a significant $-.043$ (indicating slight convergence) once family background and demographic patterns are included. For history scores, both school resource/student behavior variables and demographic/family background variables reduce the initial correlation of .100, to .048 and .024, respectively, and the complete specification indicates neutrality (an insignificant $\rho = -.011$). For math and science scores, however, relatively high levels of divergence (in specification 1) are moderated but not eliminated by other variables, so increasing inequality is larger for these two "technical" subjects. In a world where science, math, and technology are often viewed as the basis for innovation and competitiveness, the greater inequality in these outcomes is especially discouraging.

So schooling makes a difference in another way: school resources, and whatever efforts enhance students' engagement and motivation, not only increase learning but also reduce dynamic inequality, as measured by the covariation between slopes and intercepts of individual growth trajectories. To be sure, our schools are not now set up to maximize this equity effect, because both within and among schools the most powerful resources—the best teachers, the most effective pedagogies, the highest curriculum tracks—go to the highest-performing students. But if these resources were differently allocated—as happens when schools and districts try to allocate more resources to the lowest-performing students, as in some schools profiled in chapter 8 and in the exemplary districts profiled in Springboard Schools (2006)—then the modest effects in reducing divergence that we can see in table B.7 would be more powerful.

The patterns for student attitudes in table B.7 are different from those for test scores, replicating the finding from chapter 2 that different outcome measures respond differently to resources. In general, both educational and occupational aspirations converge over time for individuals (from specification 1), rather than diverging, as test scores do. While the extent of convergence is increased somewhat by other independent variables, this effect is relatively small. So dynamic inequality is a serious problem for test scores, particularly math and science, though a more equitable distribution of school resources might allow neutrality or even convergence. On the other hand, dynamic inequality in aspirations is much less of a concern.

The Effect of Time-Invariant Resources: Family and Demographic Variables

When we examine the effects of time-invariant family background and demographic variables on growth trajectories, the results are unsurprising. The coefficients in table B.8 provide information about the *differences* in the intercepts and slopes between males and females, black and white students, and so on. For math, both the intercept and the slope for males are higher than for females, so that males outscore females in eighth grade, and these differences increase over time; this is also true for science and history. (Some of these patterns are now obsolete, as females now score as well as males on math tests, and possibly on science tests too; see Hyde et al. 2008.) Females do better in reading, however, and again these differences increase over time. Asian Americans, the "model minority," do substantially better than white students both in eighth grade and over time in math, but not in other subjects, tending to confirm stereotypes of Asians doing much better in math but not in language-related subjects. African American, Latino, and Native American students do worse than white students in every subject, and again the differences become larger over time. Students with physical disabilities suffer the same disadvantages. Those whose language is not English have initially lower scores in reading, science, and history, but their relative scores *improve* over time (significantly so for science and history), reflecting, not surprisingly, the advantages of more time spent in an English-language environment.

These results for racial and ethnic groups echo similar results from chapter 4, but they are especially worrisome because they indicate that the racial-ethnic differences in grade 8 become even larger over the high school years. These results measure racial-ethnic differences *after* considering variation in school resources, student connectedness and motivation, and the other effects of family background; they therefore represent the dynamic versions of the racial-ethnic residuals identified in chapter 4. That is, these are differences associated with race and ethnicity that cannot be attributed to changing income, other dimensions of class, student behavior, or lower levels of school resources; they demand some other explanations. As in chapter 4, the inability to measure accurately the debilitating effects of truly dreadful schools and unspeakably unstable families may account for some of this unexplained residual, but again, dimensions of racial-ethnic mistreatment are also plausible explanations—particularly as informal tracking develops in middle school and then high school, as counselors and teachers begin to make both overt and surreptitious decisions about who is "college material," and as discipline problems become more contentious. So once again, there are good reasons to be concerned that "color-blind" policies—changes in the core practices of schooling, including the redistribution of effective resources—may be inadequate to eliminate these racial-ethnic effects over time. When I return to the school practices that might moderate dynamic inequality in chapter 9, I outline a number of measures intended to confront these particular sources of inequality head on.

Shifting to measures associated with class differences, maternal education influences virtually all test scores and slopes: better-educated mothers provide their children with substantial advantages that continue to increase over time, with the differences particularly large in math.[10] The presence of more educational materials in the home, a variable measured only in eighth grade, creates initial advantages, but these do not increase over time (except for science scores). Overall, however, test scores vary with gender, race-ethnicity, and family background in ways that we might (unfortunately) predict: the differences evident in eighth grade become more pronounced over time. Evidently, whatever schools do for students, they allow growth trajectories associated with these common demographic variables to diverge.

One way to see the magnitude of divergence over four years is to calculate the percentage increase in the gap from eighth grade to twelfth grade due to differences in slope coefficients alone. Table B.8 gives these results for test scores only. For example, in the upper-left corner of this table, the difference in the rates of learning math between males and females (the differences in the slope coefficients) accounts for an additional increase of 57 percent over the eighth-grade differential by twelfth grade.[11] For the black-white test score gap in math, differences in rates of learning add an additional 27.7 percent to the already substantial eighth-grade difference. These percentage increases vary widely; some slope coefficients are insignificant and add nothing to differences in outcomes, while others imply a doubling of the gap in test scores from slope coefficients alone (for example, the male-female gap in science scores). The middling effects suggest increases in various gaps between grades 8 and 12 from 15 to 40 percent due to divergence of slopes, which seems practically as well as statistically significant. If such rates of increase were maintained over thirteen years of K–12 education rather than over the five years reflected in these data, they would imply increasing gaps of 45 to 120 percent of initial differences, the latter representing more than a doubling. *Random* variation among schools and among individuals within schools also adds to the overall divergence of growth trajectories (according to table B.6, rows 3 and 6), so altogether, the divergence of growth trajectories is larger even than indicated by the figures in table B.8.

The results in table B.8 for attitudinal measures are quite different, however. Males have lower educational and occupational aspirations than females and report a lower probability of continuing their education, though their occupational aspirations improve over time relative to females—a result that could be interpreted as the differential effects of both overt and covert counseling. Black students have high educational aspirations, and they and Latino students initially indicate a higher likelihood of continuing their education—though the slope coefficient for black students is negative, perhaps as they fall behind through high school and come to see the difficulties of completion. Disabled students also have lower aspirations than others. Those whose native language is not English—first-generation immigrants— have higher aspirations, perhaps because of the effects of migrating to the

United States for a better life. Finally, the effects of family background on educational and occupational aspirations are not as powerful as they are for test scores, though parents with the highest levels of schooling do lead their offspring to have substantially higher aspirations. Overall, however, aspirations are less powerfully affected by these demographic and family background measures than are test scores. It is easier to imagine reform programs improving aspirations and student intentions to continue in formal schooling, even as test scores may be more resistant to change. This implication mirrors the findings from twelfth-grade outcomes measured in chapter 2 and also reflects the conclusion from that chapter that many whole-school reforms have enhanced motivation and engagement without improving learning and test scores.

The Effects of Resources Varying over Time

The final results to explore are the coefficients on the time-varying variables. Unlike the earlier results—for example, the coefficients of table B.1, discussed in chapter 2—these results describe the effects of school resources on *growth* in outcomes for students as they move from grade 8 to grade 12, not on *levels* of outcomes in grade 12. The results in table B.9 mirror almost perfectly, however, the results from simple cross-sectional equations presented in chapter 2.

School Resources

Of the simple resource variables associated with schools themselves, the pupil-teacher ratio proves to affect changes in test scores (except history), as well as educational and occupational aspirations, in the direction that might be expected: having more pupils per teacher reduces these measures. (Remember that this variable, which divides total students by the total number of teachers, might operate by increasing the overall numbers of adults with whom students interact and the personalization of the high school, but it is not a good measure of average class size.) On the other hand, real teacher salaries—which might be a proxy for teacher quality if higher salaries are used in some districts to attract a larger pool of teachers from whom to choose—has little influence except on science test scores. Teacher experience in secondary education has some influence, while the effects of having instructors who teach the subject of their undergraduate major— rather than teaching out-of-field—are positive and substantial.

Few measures of instruction are consistently measured among the three waves of data, but one—labeled "time structure"—describes the use of time for administrative chores, discipline, and other activities unrelated to instruction. A higher value for this measure consistently reduces test scores (though it does not affect student attitudes), confirming the significant negative effect of this particular dimension of instructional focus. A positive school climate leads to better growth rates of learning, as we might expect, whereas negative events such as fighting, drugs, and gang activities reduce the growth in both test scores and aspirations. These effects clarify the importance of school climate, an abstract resource not generally related to spending, to outcomes over time as well as to twelfth-grade results.

Finally, the effects of school size are nonlinear and describe a function that is convex—it reaches a minimum at low levels of enrollment (for example, 158 students for math and 284 for reading)—indicating that test scores generally increase with increasing size. Like the results in chapter 2, however, the effects of size become insignificant when lagged dependent variables are introduced,[12] and size proves to affect outcomes not directly but indirectly, through its effects on teacher innovation, teaching in-field, the likelihood of negative events, teacher experience in the current school, and teacher salaries, assumed to be related to teacher quality.[13] Once these other variables have been controlled, there is little evidence that size itself affects high school performance, and so there is no strong argument in these results for smaller high schools—reinforcing the point made by others that small size itself is ineffective unless it is used to enhance the school resources (including climate and instructional quality) that do make a difference to outcomes.

Family Background

The time-varying measures of family background in table B.8 include income and aspirations for children, both of which are consistently powerful. Indeed, real income per dependent is much more significant in growth models than it is in simple cross-sectional results. Both low aspirations and high aspirations for children affect test scores in expected ways—compared to the cross-sectional results in table B.3, where only low aspirations had significant effects. It is possible, of course, that having a less complete set of family background variables (for example, parental occupation and changing schools are missing) causes the remaining variables to be more significant. Overall, however, family background has effects on *growth*—not just on *levels* of learning—that are powerful and quite consistent.

Student Connectedness to Schooling

The effects of student ability to benefit are all consistent with the results discussed in chapter 5: students who do their homework, avoid television and paid employment, and attend school regularly do better over these five years than students who do not. In addition, students who engage in activities outside of school perform better, a result that may reflect either selection effects or the educative power of nonschool activities. As mentioned in chapter 5, the conventional advice to students about their behavior and engagement proves to be right.

POTENTIAL BURSTS OF INEQUALITY

In chapter 6, I raised the possibility of periodic "bursts" of inequality in educational outcomes, especially at transition points like the move from eighth grade to high school. If such a burst takes place, then increases in inequality would be largest from grade 8 to grade 10 and somewhat smaller from grade 10 to grade 12. Furthermore, as illustrated on the right-hand side of figure 6.1, growth trajectories would not be linear but would instead have some curvature to them, in most cases concave to the X-axis.

The NELS88 data can be used to test these propositions. Table 7.1 presents the test score means, the standard deviations, and the coefficients of variation (the standard deviation divided by the mean) for each grade. All test scores increase, as they should if students are learning more from their coursework (and confirming the effects of TIME in table B.6, specification 1). From figure 6.1, the measure of variation should be in the units in which test scores are described—in this case, points on IRT tests—and therefore the standard deviation is the most appropriate measure of inequality. This measure behaves precisely as my hypothesis about bursts of inequality implies. In the case of math test scores, for example, inequality measured by the standard deviation increases from eighth to tenth to twelfth grade, from 11.73 to 13.58 to 14.10 points. The increase between eighth and tenth grade (1.85 points) is larger than the increase from tenth to twelfth grade (0.52 points), and the same pattern holds for the other three tests.[14] Furthermore, this pattern holds (with very few exceptions) for different gender groups, for different race-ethnic groups, for disabled students, for students whose native language is not English, and for students from families with different levels of maternal education, low and high. This confirms that indeed a burst of inequality exists as students enter high school; levels of inequality increase consistently, but they increase more between eighth and tenth grade, when the dislocations of the transition to high school are first experienced, than between tenth and twelfth grade.

A more sophisticated way of testing for such bursts of inequality is to estimate nonlinear growth trajectories. With information collected in three different years, the NELS88 data are sufficient to exactly identify quadratic growth trajectories for each individual. Formally, this means that equation 7.1 becomes:

$$Y_{ist} = \pi_{0is} + \pi_{1is}\,TIME_t + \pi_{2is}\,TIME_t^2 + r_{ist} \qquad (7.2)$$

Table 7.1   Test Scores and Measures of Variation

	Eighth Grade	Tenth Grade	Twelfth Grade
Mathematics			
Mean	36.67	44.25	48.95
sd	11.73	13.58	14.10
cv	.320	.307	.288
Reading			
Mean	27.41	30.95	33.41
sd	8.53	9.92	9.98
cv	.311	.321	.298
Science			
Mean	19.00	21.85	23.64
sd	4.79	5.94	6.15
cv	.252	.272	.260
History			
Mean	29.77	31.73	35.01
sd	4.50	5.07	5.32
cv	.151	.155	.152

Source: Author's calculations.
sd = standard deviation
cv = coefficient of variation

The parameter π_2 describes the curvature of the growth trajectory: a value insignificantly different from zero implies linearity, while a negative value describes growth trajectories that are concave to the X-axis, as most of the growth trajectories in figure 6.1 are.[15]

Estimating such growth models confirms that average growth trajectories are nonlinear and convex to the X-axis (TIME) for most dependent variables, before the influence of other independent variables is considered.[16] That is, π_1 is consistently positive and significant; π_2 is negative and significant except for history test scores (for which it is positive) and educational aspirations (for which it is insignificant, implying a linear trend). When specifications include a variety of time-varying and time-invariant independent variables in addition to TIME and TIME^2, the average growth trajectories remain concave ($\pi_2 < 0$) for math and history scores, high educational aspirations, and high occupational aspirations, but this coefficient is insignificant for science and reading, and thus these trajectories are linear.

Overall, the measures of inequality in table 7.1 and the experiments with quadratic growth trajectories are largely consistent with the hypothesis of a burst of inequality as *individuals* transition from middle school to high school. Furthermore, the results confirm that average trajectories for all gender, racial-ethnic, and family background groups follow the same pattern, implying a burst of inequality for all *groups* as well. To be sure, these results are somewhat uncertain because there are only three data points in the NELS88 data, and further investigation with other data and more observations over time is appropriate. But the results have confirmed the possibility of bursts of inequality as students progress through their education, of which the transition from middle school to high school is just one. In turn, this suggests that the differences among students increase not only because growth trajectories diverge, but also because of bursts of inequality at significant transition points that further increase differences by race-ethnicity, by measures of family background, by gender, by disability, and by language status. In turn, this implies that policies intended to enhance dynamic equity must counter not only the effects of school resources and family background on learning and aspirations but also the inequitable effects of transition as well.

REACHING FOR DYNAMIC EQUITY: THE COMPLEXITY OF UNEQUAL EDUCATIONAL DEVELOPMENT

The results in this chapter confirm the value of taking a dynamic approach to variation among students. In the first place, test scores do go up over time, as we would hope, as do educational and occupational aspirations. But they certainly do not increase at equal rates, and a major conclusion is that divergence in outcomes predominates, at least over the period from eighth to twelfth grade. Many patterns over time are familiar from cross-sectional results: divergence is associated with racial-ethnic differences, with variation in family background, and (less consistently, especially now) with gender differences. And random components of outcomes—the components that cannot be explained by all the independent variables available in a rich data set like NELS88—also contribute to divergence. The processes that generate the large cross-sectional inequalities in learning among U.S. students, visible in national, state, and district data as well as in international comparisons like table I.1, are dynamic, unfolding over the years of schooling.

Once again, school resources make a great deal of difference, this time to *growth* in outcomes in addition to outcomes at any point in time. In addition to effects of the pupil-teacher ratio, variables describing teachers, their use of time in instruction, and school climate affect the growth in test scores, confirming again the value of considering compound, complex, and abstract resources. Somewhat surprisingly, school resources moderate the divergence among *individuals* within schools to some extent, implying that, if resources were differently distributed, among students, dynamic inequality would be moderated even more. But what schools have been unable to do, at least as they are currently structured, is to overcome the continuing effects of some variables—race-ethnicity, family background, and gender—in causing growth trajectories to diverge, particularly for test scores. Based on these results, convergence in outcomes measures would require a great deal more compensatory or equalizing efforts than our schools have managed to provide.

In contrast, the divergence that we see among *schools* is explained almost entirely by family background and demographic characteristics, including race and ethnicity. That is, the concentration of working-class and racial-minority students in some schools, usually referred to euphemistically as "urban" schools, explains some part of dynamic inequality, rather than differences among schools in resources. One implication is that moderating the class and racial segregation of urban schools—that is, developing more powerful policies related to residential location—would moderate some part of dynamic inequality.

As has been true in earlier cross-sectional results, the dynamic patterns for different schooling outcomes vary—the issue introduced in chapter 6 as that of multiple outcomes (including different "intelligences") diverging and converging in different ways. Math and science test scores diverge more than do scores in English and history—a form of inequality that may prevent more students from gaining access to the jobs associated with new technologies and the "knowledge revolution." While test scores tend to diverge, aspirations for education and occupations tend to converge over time and have different patterns by race and ethnicity. Schools can influence attitudes more readily than learning and test scores, again reinforcing the need to understand the school resources that can change patterns of learning.

Finally, there is at least some evidence that the process of dynamic inequality does not operate smoothly, but that bursts of inequality take place at crucial junctures, particularly (for these data) during the transition from middle to high school. Both the variation in test scores and the estimates of nonlinear growth trajectories confirm that differences in learning increase more sharply in the first years of high school than they do between tenth and twelfth grades. Subject to examining other potential bursts of inequality, the patterns of schooling may well look like those depicted in figure 6.2, with steady divergences among students punctuated by bursts of inequality that cause even larger differences to develop.

While many results about dynamic inequality seem depressingly familiar, there are at least some rays of hope for meeting the dynamic conceptions of equity developed in chapter 6. The effects of school resources in these dynamic results mirror almost precisely the cross-sectional findings in chapter 2, reinforcing the conclusion that school resources broadly understood can strongly influence the *growth* of educational outcomes as well as the *levels* of outcomes. Furthermore, variables that are potentially controllable through education policy—school resources of different kinds as well as the motivation and engagement of students—have some effects in reducing divergence, among both schools and students. To be sure, these effects are small and are in particular much smaller than the disequalizing effects of race-ethnicity and family background. But American schools are not now structured to minimize inequality—indeed, some would argue that they are structured to *reinforce* inequality (see, for example, Bowles and Gintis 1975; Grubb and Lazerson 2004, ch. 8)—so any mitigating effects of these resources at all are somewhat surprising. If some mitigating effects exist, they could be made stronger, though that would require substantial changes in the distribution of educational resources.

These dynamic results raise yet another often-overlooked possibility. If bursts of inequality take place at transition points like the movement into high school, then school, district, and state policies could play important roles in making these transitions smoother. Currently, a few high schools have ninth-grade academies, both to introduce ninth-graders to the expectations of high school and to provide additional instruction for students who are behind their peers; these include the Talent Development model, the approach of First Things First, and other efforts to create special transition-related practices. A few high schools try to coordinate with middle schools to prepare students for the transition—for example, by arranging for middle school students to visit high school campuses. In addition, with the development of state standards, *if* all schools follow them carefully rather than falling behind state norms (see table 6.2), students should be prepared for subsequent grades. Other policies could be borrowed from countries with more egalitarian school practices than the United States—for example, Finland has a particularly coherent approach to students who have fallen behind that uses several levels of intervention (described in Grubb 2007), and Korea makes explicit efforts to narrow variation in the quality of high schools by strengthening the resources in low-performing schools. (Some districts and states are now trying these policies, as I discuss in chapter 10.) But current efforts to improve transitions seem uncommon, fragmented, and poorly conceived, as I illustrate in the next chapter. This suggests a reform agenda focusing more carefully on transitions—an agenda that individual schools are less effective in pursuing than districts, with their responsibility for many levels of schooling.

There are, then, a number of specific school and district policies that could be developed to reduce dynamic inequality by smoothing the transitions among levels of schooling, whether the fourth-grade slump, the transition to middle school, or the transition to high school. But it is also necessary to think of who or what policy body might be responsible for dynamic inequality. One potential response—and the only common practice in this country—is to declare that parents should be responsible for guiding their children through educational opportunities. Unfortunately, the variation among parents in their own education, income, and aspirations for their children is part of the problem. Furthermore, the mobility of students—especially of low-income children—and the instability of families are two of the problems in creating steady trajectories in schooling, since moving and instability are so disruptive to learning and progress. So family responsibility—the basis of choice and other neoliberal approaches examined in chapter 12—cannot be a powerful solution *unless* differences among families are substantially narrowed.

Another answer is to make individual schools responsible for improving their practices in various ways. Individual schools cannot always coordinate with other schools, however, and in particular they tend not to manage the possible bursts of inequality at crucial junctures—like the transition into high school. Districts might be responsible for managing the bursts of inequality at these junctures, because they coordinate schools at all levels. The results discussed in the next chapter, however, suggest that most districts have weak to nonexistent coordination policies among schools, and some have adopted policies actively detrimental to learning, such as scripted curricula and remedial approaches. Of course, states are also responsible, partly because they establish curriculum guidelines and standards that attempt to shape teaching from grade to grade.

So we might envision a rational division of labor, with states providing curriculum guidelines, funding, and an overall vision of equity over time; districts improving the transitions among schools and developing some guidelines for school-level reforms; and individual schools reforming their teaching practices and improving the many abstract resources—climate, trust, coherence, stability, internal accountability, distributed leadership—that contribute to learning. And then it might also be possible to develop nonschool policies—in health, mental health, housing, community development, income support, and other programs of the welfare state—that are complementary to schooling in order to minimize the many effects of family background.

Achieving dynamic equity sounds like a tall agenda, and it is. But the alternative to such a reform is to maintain the highly inegalitarian U.S. schooling system—the most unequal of all developed countries. There are many reasons for these inequalities, of course, but one is that school policies develop in bits and pieces, without any overall vision, without any coherent equity agenda, and without any attention to the dynamic nature of inequality. What conceptual and empirical research on dynamic inequality can contribute is a framework for understanding the complexity of educational inequality and a vision for reforming it.

Chapter 8

Correcting Dynamic Inequality in Practice: Exploring What Schools Do for Low-Performing Students

IN THE PREVIOUS chapter, I confirmed that inequality among students increases over the period from eighth to tenth to twelfth grade, in a pattern I have referred to as dynamic inequality. The increases over time are most strongly related to family background and to demographic variables, including race and ethnicity, though there is some evidence that school resources and improvements in student commitment to schooling can moderate dynamic inequality. Furthermore, dynamic inequality increases not steadily but in bursts—for example, when students move from middle school to high school—so the question of what schools do to moderate dynamic inequality includes the question of how they treat transitions. These patterns and the finding that school resources are now allocated in ways that reduce dynamic inequality only a little raise, first, the descriptive question of what (if anything) schools are doing to break this pattern (especially under the pressure of state accountability and No Child Left Behind) and second, the normative question of what schools could do to achieve dynamic equity.

For elementary and secondary education, the initial question centers on what schools are doing for their lowest-performing students: what are they doing to help low-performing students learn at rates at least equal to other students, and how are they helping with transitions and other potential bursts of inequality? In the language often used in school finance, we should see what schools are doing to "level up" low-performing students, and we certainly would hope not to see schools "leveling down," or narrowing inequalities and achievement gaps by neglecting high-performing students. A substantial literature on interventions tends to focus on specific programs or practices—on the effectiveness, for instance, of such programs as Open Court or Read 180, or of after-school programs or tutoring—rather than on what individual schools do. But students experience the practices that schools adopt. In shifting the focus from particular practices to schools, three colleagues and I have examined an exploratory sample of schools[1]—a sample large enough to enable us to detect patterns, though obviously too small to be widely representative, particularly because our sample is confined to the San Francisco Bay Area. In the next section, I describe the twelve public schools and our methods of collecting information about their practices for students who are behind—practices that could *potentially* minimize dynamic inequality. I concentrate for now on school-level actions, postponing until chapter 10 a discussion of the district, state, and federal policies that might improve dynamic inequality.

I next evaluate some of the practices that schools have adopted to help low-performing students. Many schools incorporate general practices, like after-school programs and tutoring. Others use specific curricula, usually labeled interventions, that target different levels of the K–12 system; these programs emphasize reading and math and are usually self-contained. I review here not only whether these programs are effective but also how schools (and sometimes districts) "choose" among alternatives, often in casual and poorly informed ways.

The concluding section summarizes some implications for the allocation of resources, broadly defined in ways consistent with the improved school finance, and for educational policy. I then return to the different versions of dynamic equity raised in chapter 6 and argue that this conception poses substantial challenges to the existing system of education.

AN EXPLORATORY SAMPLE OF PRACTICES AT TWELVE SCHOOLS

Educational institutions at virtually all levels—at various points in K–12 education, including ninth grade; in community colleges and four-year colleges; even in graduate school—develop special programs for students who are behind their peers or who are behind standards (sometimes ill defined) that establish what students should know. And thankfully so: the alternatives are either more stringent "admissions" requirements to make sure that underprepared students never advance to the next level or "sink or swim" attitudes toward students who lack basic skills and who are thus left to suffer on their own. The ubiquity of remedial or intervention efforts is testimony to a powerful American belief in second chances and in institutional rather than individual responsibility for student progress.

At every level, the practices that educational institutions follow vary considerably. It is often difficult to understand such variation because case studies often focus on apparently exemplary efforts—for example, the analysis of Railside School, which adopts a sophisticated approach to mathematics (Boaler and Staples 2008); the school profiled by Rochelle Gutiérrez (2000); or the effective schools literature profiling practices in supposedly effective schools. The vast number of dreary remedial efforts—a label that usually connotes routine drill-and-practice approaches—are rarely described, partly because they are so familiar and partly because it is difficult to learn much from bad practice. But it is also difficult to know how effective intervention efforts are, or how they can be improved, without knowing more about what now happens.

In this chapter, then, we examine twelve schools, located for convenience in the San Francisco Bay Area. We found these schools through personal contacts and through references from these schools to other similar schools in their districts, sometimes referred to as "snowball" sampling.[2] While such sampling was far from random, it was random with respect to practices at these schools; that is, we did not choose schools because we knew that they had particularly active or lackadaisical approaches to inequality. The final sample includes six elementary schools, an oversampling that is appropriate given that many intervention efforts are concentrated in the early grades; three middle schools; and three high schools, including a continuation high school that was deliberately chosen because continuation high schools are one of the institutional alternatives for students lagging in credits earned.[3] All the schools meet the conventional criteria for "urban" schools, with high proportions of low-income and racial-minority students, and their scores on the state's standardized tests are relatively low. Table 8.1 provides basic information about each of the twelve schools, including their dominant approaches for students who are behind. I refer to schools, districts, and principals throughout this chapter by pseudonyms.

We visited these schools in the spring of 2006. In each, two of us spent one day interviewing the principal and other key individuals like the heads of intervention programs, after-school programs, student learning centers, and tutorial efforts. We also returned to see classes, after-school programs, or Saturday classes not operating the day we were there. In districts where school personnel mentioned some district influence, we interviewed the district superintendent for instruction. In addition, we observed classes devoted to helping students who were behind, including "skills" classes in English and math, classes using off-the-shelf intervention curricula, after-school programs, and any other classes that were important in a school's corrective program, including a Saturday class in one school and a lunchtime

Table 8.1   Characteristics of the Twelve Schools Visited

School/District	Grade Levels, SES[a]	Race-Ethnic Composition[a]	API Scores[b]	Summary of Approaches
Cityscape Charter / Charterhouse	K–8, 400 students, 85% free or reduced lunch 65% ELL	80% Latino 15% African American 5% Pacific Islander	State = 7 Similar Schools = 10	Assessment and correction with direct instruction Finely differentiated assessment Three-part decision structure (academic team, SST, special education)
Hillcrest Elementary / Littlefield USD	K–5, 440 students, 45% free or reduced lunch 30% ELL	40% Latino 25% White 10% Asian 10% multiple response 10% Pacific Islander 5% Filipino 2% African American	State = 7 Similar Schools = 4	Learning Center model (K–2-focused) Differentiated instruction and PD Hero-principal Single-track, year-round school
Wagner Elementary / Grossmont USD	K–5, 340 students, 75% free or reduced lunch 30% ELL	45% Latino 35% African American 10% White 5% Filipino 3% Pacific Islander 1% Asian	State = 3 Similar Schools = 2	District-specified scripted curricula Limited resources for intervention (not all students who qualify are served)
Lakelands Elementary / Littlefield USD	K–5, 300 students, 30% free or reduced lunch 20% ELL	45% White 25% Latino 20% Asian 5% African American 3% Filipino 3% Pacific Islander 1% multiple response	State = 9 Similar Schools = 8	Assessment and correction through booster club (24 students out of 300) Pull-out program taught by special education aide Other "little programs" SST and individualized plans

School/District	Demographics	Race/Ethnicity	Ranking	Interventions
Happy Valley Elementary/ Greenlands ESD	K–5, 435 students, 55% free or reduced lunch, 35% ELL	45% Latino 40% White 10% Asian 5% Filipino 5% African American 2% multiple response 2% Pacific Islander	State = 5 Similar Schools = 2	Multiple disconnected interventions Many "little programs" (mostly following assessment/correction approach) Each teacher identifies four students to target Vision and Learning Center model under development
Travis Academy/ Charterhouse	K–5, 200 students, 85% free or reduced lunch, less than 4% ELL	95% African American 1% Latino 1% Asian	API 690 (statewide ranking of 3 out of 10)	Assessment and correction using READ 180 Many smaller efforts Some looping; stable teachers and students Active principal
Horace Middle School/Taylor USD	6–8, 425 students, 60% free or reduced lunch, 10% ELL	40% African American 25% Latino 15% multiple response 15% White 5% Asian	State = 4 Similar Schools = 7	Improving instructional capacities of teachers through differentiated instruction Resource class in English and math, same teachers Smaller classes for struggling students Zero-period classes Mental health services
David Smith Middle School/ San Sebastian USD	7–8, 820 students, (NA)% free or reduced lunch, 30% ELL	55% Latino 15% African American 10% Asian 10% Filipino 5% White 5% Pacific Islander	State = 4 Similar Schools = 8	In-school math and English interventions instead of electives Saturday Academy run by Kaplan "Families" of 125 students

Table 8.1 *Continued*

School/District	Grade Levels, SES[a]	Race-Ethnic Composition[a]	API Scores[b]	Summary of Approaches
Grossmont Middle School/ Grossmont USD	6–8, 900 students, 60% free or reduced lunch, 15% ELL	40% African American 30% Latino 15% White 10% Filipino 2% Pacific Islander 1% Asian	State = 2 Similar Schools = 1	District-specified intervention (SRA Reach, High Point) Reform coordinator position responsibilities unclear After-school program to compensate for long-term sub
Bellson High School/Bellson USD	9–12, 1635 students, 35% free or reduced lunch, 16% ELL	45% Latino 25% African American 15% White 10% Asian 5% Filipino 2% Pacific Islander	State = 2 Similar Schools = 3	Many "little programs" (includes study center) Summer school, study center contracts for ninth-graders Small learning communities
Taylor High School/Taylor USD	9–12, 340 students, 30% free or reduced lunch, 5% ELL	35% White 30% African American 15% multiple response 10% Latino 7% Asian	State = 7 Similar Schools = 7	Small schools-within-schools Ninth-grade support team After-school intervention coordinator Accelerated reading classes Smaller introductory and intervention classes Ninth-grade grade Life Academy

School/District	Demographics	Racial/ethnic	API	Interventions
West Creekside Continuation High School/Bayside USD	9–12, 185 students, 30% free or reduced lunch, 25% ELL	30% White 25% African American 20% Latino 10% Asian 10% Filipino 2% Pacific Islander 2% American Indian	525 API (no rankings available)	PD on differentiated instruction CAHSEE math and English intervention Intervention coordinator (tenth-grade case manager for at-risk students) RISE (after-school plus services) Smaller classes More interpersonal contacts CAHSEE intervention Interventions held during second period Planning advisory program where adviser tracks progress toward graduation

Source: Author's compilation.

Note: All schools and districts are referred to by pseudonyms.

SST = Student Study Team

PD = Professional development

CAHSEE = California High School Exit Exam

RISE = Responsibility, Integrity, Strength, Empowerment

CST = California Standards Test

[a] School data are taken from the California Department of Education website and have been rounded to the nearest 5% to avoid identifying specific schools.

[b] California's Academic Proficiency Index: Average school scores on the CST are used to rank schools in deciles from 1 (low) to 10 (high). In addition, groups of "similar" schools are developed based on racial-ethnic characteristics and school lunch eligibility, and all schools are again ranked from decile 1 (low) to decile 10 (high) compared to similar schools only.

library period in a school that emphasized that "libraries are all about equity." Of course, two person-days of observation are insufficient to understand any one school deeply or to understand how particular practices interact, and twelve schools are but a tiny fraction of the almost ninety-six thousand public schools in the country. So we stress the exploratory nature of this research. However, we did get to the point described by qualitative researchers as saturation (Glaser and Straus 1967; Straus and Corbin 1990): the point when we ceased seeing new practices or hearing new rationales articulated for these efforts.[4] Schools vary enormously in the specific mix of approaches to students who are behind, and a "census" of practices would make it possible to see how common different approaches to dynamic inequality are. But the basic approaches and their underlying theories of action prove to be more limited.

Who Is "Behind"?

Schools are unanimous about what it means to be "behind": in an era when state and federal standards define who is at grade level ("basic" or "proficient") and who is below grade level ("below basic" or "far below basic"), students who are below basic or proficiency levels as demonstrated on standardized tests in English and math are behind. (In California, the California Standards Tests [CST] determine this, and for high school students the California High School Exit Exam [CAHSEE], administered from tenth grade on, identifies students who might fail this requirement for graduation.) In addition, high school students may be behind because they lack enough credits to graduate. There are, of course, many other conceptions of what it might mean to be behind, but only once did another conception of low performance arise. The principal we call Ms. Yeong from Horace Middle School mentioned that low-income black and Latino parents compare their children's performance at Horace not with grade-level standards but with the performance of low-income black and Latino students in other schools.[5] In addition, one teacher objected to our language of some students being "behind," noting that students might be ahead of or behind others in many different ways and that teachers should not make any assumptions about what students know and can do—implicitly referring to the problem of teacher expectations (Weinstein 2002). However, his view was an isolated one. The notion that teachers should not know what students can do lest they condemn a student with low expectations has been overwhelmed by the idea that teachers should know exactly what students can and cannot do so that schools can intervene appropriately—particularly in the approach we call assessment and correction. And the common practice in accountability systems of labeling students "below basic" or less than "proficient" has made any objection to this disparaging language moot.

One result of defining who is behind by standardized test scores in reading and math is that the curriculum in many schools has collapsed to these two subjects. Many principals and teachers, lamenting the narrowing of the educational landscape, have tried to hold on to courses and activities (including after-school programs) that they describe as "enrichment." But even the common language of "core" and "enrichment" activities is objectionable because it indicates that everything but core subjects can be jettisoned—a narrow and impoverished conception of education. And so, given the wide variety of outcomes possible for any conception of dynamic inequality, an emphasis on reading and math implies that inequality in other outcomes— in other academic subjects, in conceptual abilities, in connectedness and progress through school—are likely to become even more unequal, since schools for low-performing students focus on only two of many possible outcomes.

Variation in Scope

The schools in our sample varied enormously both in what they did and in the intensity of what they did—that is, in the fraction of students who received the benefits of any particular practice. At one end of the spectrum, Horace Middle School had an extensive program of staff development to enable *all* teachers to use differentiated instruction, in addition to a wide variety of specific programs for specific groups of students and subjects. The principal had a clear rationale for a comprehensive approach: "One thing doesn't work for everyone. You start with the basic or core aspects of the school [classroom instruction] and then look for opportunities and pieces and whatever might work for some individual students." Similarly, Hillcrest Elementary had a comprehensive approach it called a Learning Center that reached *all* students in K–2, as well as a roster of additional programs.[6] The Learning Center used an array of assessments to evaluate all students as they entered the school; then the Learning Center team met three times a year to consider the case of every student and develop plans similar to an individualized education plan (IEP) for all students who were below grade level. At Taylor High School, schools-within-schools and learning communities provided more personalized experiences for many but not all students. The three schools with comprehensive plans were all run by hero-principals (Copland 2001) who worked with their faculty in "distributed" ways—with leadership shared among faculty and administrators (Spillane 2006). This observation suggests that only principals with strong visions, high levels of energy, and the personal power to persuade others in a school are likely to establish comprehensive schoolwide plans. Unfortunately, there are not enough hero-principals to staff all schools; lacking hero-principals, the majority of schools are more likely to engage in fragmented efforts.

At the other end of the spectrum, Lakelands placed most of its emphasis on an intervention that treated only twenty-four students out of three hundred in pull-out efforts, and its other interventions were similarly small. Bellson High had a miscellany of small programs, but without any overarching logic. The interventions in these schools were opportunistic and disconnected from one another, reflecting no coherent plan or vision of what to do for students who were behind. Like many schools that carry out a variety of small initiatives—often called "Christmas tree schools," for having a collection of bright lights hanging from rotten branches—these schools lacked any coherence in their approaches (Newman et al. 2001).

In the middle were schools that had developed a number of activities but without a guiding vision. Two schools in our sample were part of a district (Grossmont) that had adopted a districtwide plan of scripted instruction using SRA Reach for all students who were below basic, so these schools were not free to develop their own plans or visions. And a case of its own, with a vision but no activities, was Happy Valley Elementary School, which had planned a nested series of actions for students who were behind (somewhat like the approach in Finland; see Grubb 2007) but had not implemented any of these plans when we visited.

The conclusion that the schools we visited varied enormously in the intensity and coherence of what they did for students who were behind reflects the enormous variability of the U.S. education system. The mechanisms that might have ensured consistent approaches were largely missing. No district in our sample had developed a coherent approach to dynamic inequality applicable to all its schools, although a few districts elsewhere have done so (see chapter 10). The state of California has done nothing to develop coherent approaches, though a few other states have created statewide approaches to capacity-building (also reviewed in chapter 10). Nor has the federal government provided guidance to districts or schools that fall behind in their Annual Yearly Performance (AYP), and indeed the federal efforts that might provide help—the curricula approved by the Reading First program or the practices evaluated in the What Works Clearinghouse—are misleading because they omit some potentially promising practices (again covered in chapter 10). So schools have been largely on their own in devising programs to combat dynamic inequality, a situation that is certain to breed enormous differences in practices.

THEORIES OF ACTION GOVERNING INTERVENTIONS

Despite the enormous variation in what schools do, a relatively small number of theories of action, or conceptions of why a particular action might be effective, govern these efforts. Theories of action, following Argyris and Schön (1978), are conceptions of why specific actions—in this case the interventions a school has adopted, like an after-school program—might have certain effects. A program that has no coherent theory of action, or that operates according to a theory based on incorrect assumptions, can achieve desired outcomes only by chance. Furthermore, while reformers can often articulate their *espoused* theories of action, they often act on the basis of more informal and unconscious *theories in use*, which may not be the same. Six primary theories are described here: (1) intensification, (2) development of instructional capacity, (3) assessment and correction, (4) restructuring, (5) continuity and stability, and (6) noncognitive support services. Specific programs are often developed based on a combination of these theories.

Intensification

One of the most common approaches to helping students who are behind is to spend more time on the same material. This involves reteaching or preteaching; devoting double (or triple) periods to one subject; creating special "skills" classes to reinforce the material in "regular" English or math classes; offering zero-period or Saturday classes or after-school programs; or tutoring, either in small groups or one on one. Intensification usually involves giving students "more of the same" and increasing the amount of time in the kind of teaching that students have in their regular classes; the crucial question is whether additional time by itself is sufficient. Some schools, however, provide "enrichment" classes that are quite different in their teaching approaches from regular classes, or they use specific methods like Reading Recovery, in which specially trained teachers work one on one or in small groups of students.

Supporters of intensification sometimes cite the time-on-task literature, claiming that more time yields more learning, but this is a misreading. The research on time stresses the differences among allocated time, engaged time, and academic learning time; only academic learning time—engaged time focused on specific learning tasks—is strongly related to both achievement and positive attitudes toward schooling (Cotton 1989). Furthermore, instruction becomes engaging only under certain conditions, as I have already summarized in chapter 5: when it is based on forms of learning whose relevance is clear; when it uses a wide array of students' skills and interests; when it poses appropriate challenges to students; when it allows for some student choice and autonomy; when schools develop close relationships between students and adults; when instruction allows students to take an active role in constructing meaning; and when programs are well structured with clear purposes (NRC 2004; Yair 2000). These are all practices associated with more constructivist and student-centered approaches, problem- or project-oriented methods, and different ways of contextualizing instruction or being clear about its importance in other spheres of life. Unfortunately, the dominant instructional methods of drill and practice, "remedial" methods, and now scripted or semiscripted curricula violate virtually all these precepts for motivation and produce low rates of engagement, especially for minority students (Yair 2000, table 1). Since increased time in drill-oriented "skills" classes violates all the precepts for engagement, there is no reason to think that any additional learning will occur. Indeed, even advocates for extended time have admitted that "simply extending the school day will not transform a failing school into a successful one" and note that leadership, improved instruction, a data-driven focus on continuous improvement, and a positive school culture are also necessary (Farbman and Kaplan 2005, 8–9). As a theory that can work only under the right conditions, intensification is another reform that may be necessary but not sufficient (NBNS).

The Development of Instructional Capacity

In an approach quite different from "more of the same," teachers shift to different pedagogical methods—more constructivist approaches, project-based learning, math for understanding and other conceptual or meaning-centered approaches, and differentiated instruction. The idea is that low-performing students will benefit, not from an increased amount of conventional teaching from which they have not learned so far, but possibly from different student-centered approaches that stress conceptual development—as implied by the results in chapters 2 and 7. One example of this theory, practiced in Horace and Cityscape Charter, is differentiated instruction—adjusting instruction to the different understandings of students. The Horace practice of doubling time on reading or math—in math support and reading support classes following constructivist rather than remedial methods—represents a combination of intensification and innovative instruction. Similarly, carefully developed tutoring methods like Reading Recovery combine intensification (in one-on-one or small-group work) with nonstandard teaching methods by highly trained individuals.

In these schools, the effort to develop instructional capacity, though led by the principal, is very much a *schoolwide* responsibility. It requires extensive professional development of the kind described by Judith Warren Little (2006) and involves the cooperation of teachers, the sharing of expertise, minimal use of outside exerts, and a focus on specific elements of good instruction—developing questioning methods, incorporating projects, developing lesson plans, finding ways to meet state standards so that instruction is more consistent from class to class. In schools with active principals, classroom observations by the principal, department heads, or specialized coaches—ranging from quick ten-minute walk-throughs to observations over an entire period—accompanied by feedback, suggestions, and further support, are also crucial elements. But instructional capacity is very much a complex resource: it requires not only some money—sometimes for coaches, sometimes for release time—but also vision, leadership, and cooperation.

Assessment and Correction

The most common approach to helping students who are behind is assessment and correction, sometimes called diagnosis and remediation, or Response to Intervention (Brown-Chidsey 2008; Samuels 2008). The idea is first to assess students to determine who is behind, in which subject or detailed area within a subject (for example, word attack skills, vocabulary, or comprehension), and then to develop ways to correct problems, often with off-the-shelf curricula. The best-known of such interventions is probably Reading Recovery. Sometimes schools develop informal (and unfunded) versions of IEPs for such students that *may* include individual tutoring as well as off-the-shelf intervention. The number of assessment instruments is enormous, as is the number of intervention programs available from publishers and university developers, so in practice the specific approaches to assessment and correction are almost limitless.

The approach of assessment and correction seems obvious and "natural" since state and federal accountability systems identify students who are below grade-level norms and penalize schools if these students are not brought up to basic or proficient levels. However, as natural as they may seem, assessment and correction approaches raise several complex issues, including their deficiency-oriented construction, grouping, the conflation of academic and behavioral problems, bureaucratization, and the inherent limitations of correction.

1. Deficiency-oriented construction. One problem, at least to some educators, is that such approaches are by construction deficiency-oriented: they identify weaknesses on standardized tests that must be corrected, often by using remedial drill-and-practice approaches. Mechanisms of correction can be based on other pedagogical approaches; for example, the principal of Horace described its math skills classes as "basic but not remedial" because they depended on unconventional problem-solving approaches developed by the Mathematics Assessment Collaborative (MAC). But nonremedial approaches to correction require careful attention to teaching methods, and these may not be part of a school's response.

2. Grouping. Assessment and correction require that some students be grouped for correction (or interventions, or skills courses), and such grouping may become a new form of tracking—in a period when tracking has become a dirty word. To combat this, some schools carry out assessments more frequently than once a year, ranging from three times a semester in the Hillcrest Learning Center to once every two weeks in Cityscape Charter.

The idea is to learn instantly when students have mastered particular competencies and to move them quickly out of intervention status. Similarly, in differentiated instruction, students may join a group to learn a particular subskill and then be moved out of that group upon mastery; differentiated instruction requires continuous assessment and reassignment. But this does not always happen. For example, the assistant principal at Grossmont Middle School commented that the scheduling problems associated with moving students at midyear effectively prohibit quick reassignment. In some schools, students stay in intervention classes for an entire year, until "recent" test scores come out in the fall; if the intervention is ineffective, as many are, then the results are negative forms of tracking, with students assigned on the basis of test scores to low-quality teaching that can only put them further behind. Furthermore, since intervention usually takes place in pull-out classes, students in these programs typically miss science and social studies and fall further behind in noncore subjects. In the Grossmont district, for example, the courses planned for 2006–2007 included three periods of SRA Reach for students behind in reading and two for those behind in math. Such students are likely to go through high school having taken little more than English and math courses; they stand little chance of completing the broad requirements for entrance into public universities, and their only access to higher education will be through community colleges. In addition, with a curriculum of stultifying drill, it is likely that more students will become even less committed to school and will drop out.

3. *Mixing academic and behavioral problems.* Assessment and correction seem to be used not only for academic difficulties but also for the behavioral issues that might cause low test scores. For example, Wagner Elementary acknowledged placing some students with behavioral problems in intervention classes, and the math skills teacher at Horace claimed he got the behavior problems no one else wanted. So skills classes may be used as dumping grounds for behavioral problems. The problem then is that students who score poorly because they are disengaged are placed in scripted and semiscripted interventions likely to exacerbate their estrangement from school, and no effort is made to diagnose and correct the causes of their poor motivation.[7]

4. *The bureaucratization of intervention.* In Horace, the Learning Center model of Hillcrest, and the multilevel approach of Finland (Grubb 2007), assessment and correction were relatively quick and fluid: teachers corrected any problem as quickly as possible with minimal disruption to ongoing classes. But assessment and correction in most schools have become subject to new bureaucratic procedures. Some districts use the state's test as their assessment, but these scores are reported only once a year and cannot be used for quick, flexible, skill-specific assignments. Schools that want to assess students more frequently have instituted their own assessment proce-

dures, but these additional assessments are not calibrated to state standards. In Grossmont, four independent assessments were available for use in identifying which students were behind—the California Standards Test, assessments devised by the district given every two months, the curricular assessments every two weeks embedded in off-the-shelf curricula, and the tests associated with SRA Reach—all independent of one another, and only one of them (the CST) linked to state standards. To be useful, all of these assessments required additional teacher training and time to analyze the results—work that further distracted teachers from teaching.

In addition, some schools had set up several committees to examine individual students. Most schools had a Student Study Team (SST), usually composed of administrators, teachers, counselors, and special education teachers; the SST reviewed the progress of students doing poorly and recommended some of them for special education assessment. However, some schools had found the SST process unsuitable for identifying students who were unlikely to qualify for special education but still needed additional support. In Cityscape Charter, for example, teachers identified students who were behind every two weeks; then the Academic Team (AT) identified students having problems in just one area; an SST evaluated students with multiple problems; and students eligible for special education were examined in an eligibility review. The advantage of this complex structure was that students with varying levels and kinds of difficulties could be identified and then individualized plans could be devised for them, but the process of assessment and adjudication via committees was complex and time-consuming. In a large bureaucratic district like Grossmont, these procedures might result in a situation similar to that of special education, with ultra-formalized procedures (Huefner 2000; Martin, Martin, and Terman 1996).

5. *The effectiveness of correction.* The success of assessment and correction can only be as good as the corrective efforts adopted. Even in our limited sample of schools, an enormous variety of school-created and off-the-shelf curricula were being used. Most claimed to be "research-based" or "proven practices," though (as I argue later) the research was usually missing, faulty, or skewed. These schools and districts usually did not have the technical capacity to read and critique evaluations, so they relied on hearsay, publishers' "evaluations" of their own products, and the state's politically motivated list of approved curricula to make decisions. The process by which schools adopted these off-the-shelf interventions was haphazard: the principal of Travis based her decision on hearing about a charter school's experience in Los Angeles; the Grossmont district had heard "good things" about High Point from other nearby districts; and others noted that they had only a few state-approved programs to choose from. David Smith Middle School chose Kaplan to run its Saturday School because Kaplan could accommodate its

schedule, not because of instructional advantages. There were exceptions to these haphazard choices, of course: having developed a set of subject-specific curriculum committees, the Taylor school district chose curricula partly on the basis of consistency with teachers' pedagogical preferences. But otherwise, there is every reason to suspect that the effectiveness of interventions was essentially random: there was not enough systematic evidence about effectiveness, and not enough careful deliberation. The result, once again, was a patchwork of reforms of unknown effectiveness, hurried into place by accountability pressures.

One underlying problem is that federal and state accountability mechanisms exert pressures to adopt reforms quickly, since schools must avoid falling into Program Improvement status for even a year. Long-term investments in the teacher capacities necessary for changing instruction (Little 2006) or long-run efforts to adopt differentiated instruction, as in Horace Middle School, are difficult to adopt in an environment of short-term pressures. So schools end up desperate for something to do, and in this climate many grab at any program that promises improvement.

Embedded in the process of selecting corrections, or interventions, is a pedagogical battle akin to the math wars or the reading wars—what we might call the intervention wars. Some schools—all the schools in Grossmont by district fiat, David Smith Middle School, the high schools adopting test prep programs for the California High School Exit Exam (CAHSEE), and elementary schools such as Wagner and Cityscape—had adopted scripted and semiscripted curricula like SRA Reach, Language!, and Open Court.[8] These are approaches that depend on drill and repetition, information transfer, behaviorist motivation, and textbook-centered rather than student-centered instruction; truly scripted curricula do not even allow for the modifications of a teacher-centered approach. Other schools—Horace with differentiated instruction and problem-based approaches, Hillcrest with more differentiated instruction, and Taylor High School with theme-based schools-within-schools and a district math curriculum chosen on the basis of consistency with the district's pedagogical principles—drew more on constructivist, meaning-oriented, project-based, and student-centered traditions. In the middle were the two charter schools, which relied on direct instruction but had worked with their teachers to develop more flexible forms than the scripted and semiscripted approaches.

The "interventions wars" are part of a much longer debate over pedagogy, of course, and particularly over the pedagogy appropriate for low-performing students, who have often been subjected to the most rigid and disengaging behaviorist approaches.[9] There is no reason to think that this long-running debate can be resolved in the context of intervention efforts. But reformers should at least recognize that this "war" is taking place and that the choices of intervention contribute to the battle.

Restructuring

Yet another theory behind efforts to help low-performing students involves restructuring to ensure that students receive more personal attention. This theory underlay the creation of small, theme-based schools-within-schools at Taylor High School, for example. It is also the rationale for continuation high schools, with small classes and a single teacher who stays with students (as in elementary schools) rather than multiple teachers (as in comprehensive high schools). More personalized environments have the *potential* for allowing teachers to craft alternative forms of learning, including project-based or work-based learning, and to create the conditions for greater motivation and engagement (NRC 2004, ch. 7), but whether schools do in fact develop alternative approaches to instruction in restructured environments is uncertain, and the record in continuation high schools is poor (Castro 2002). In addition, the evidence presented in chapter 2, both from NELS88 data and from the evaluation of whole-school reforms, indicates that dimensions of personalization may improve progress through high school, including graduation, but not performance on tests, which requires more specific attention to enhancing the instructional practices of teachers. Restructuring may therefore achieve only some of the goals of improving school for students who are behind.[10]

Continuity and Stability

Several of the twelve schools had developed mechanisms to improve continuity over time, particularly across school years—a special problem in urban schools with high teacher turnover and student mobility. Both charter schools had adopted looping, the practice of teachers staying with the same students for two or three years; the explicit rationale is to improve stability for students who already have too much instability in their lives. Cityscape Charter had developed a "transfer of knowledge" among teachers at year's end: teachers in feeder schools consulted with teachers who would be working with their students the following year about student progress, strengths, and weaknesses. (Note that this can work effectively only in a school with low teacher turnover.) Bellson High School consulted with eighth-grade teachers in its feeder schools to identify the students likely to have the most trouble in transitioning to high school; it then placed those students in a special learning community to strengthen their basic academic skills as well as their study skills—like the ninth-grade Success Academy of Talent Development High School (Kemple, Herlihy, and Smith 2005).

In another effort to maintain stability, the charter schools in our sample had created the conditions that, according to Richard Ingersoll (2004), reduce teacher turnover: better salaries as well as helpful working conditions, such as administrative support, fewer intrusions, better student discipline, and faculty participation in decisionmaking. Teachers at these schools appeared to be more stable than those in similar public schools.[11] Finally, Hillcrest is a single-track year-round school; this approach is thought to minimize summer effects, especially among low-SES students, who, lacking organized summer activities, are particularly likely to forget what they have learned (Cooper et al. 2003, table 7).

These efforts to maintain continuity are responses to the problems of transition and the potential bursts of inequality identified in chapters 6 and 7. However, they are fragmented and patchy. Only one of the three high schools in our sample focused on the transition from eighth grade, and its efforts were confined to only the most at-risk students. The other points of difficult transition—the transition into middle school, the transition into middle elementary grades around fourth grade—received no attention in any of these schools. None of the districts in which these schools were located attempted to develop districtwide transition mechanisms. Most of the transition efforts in American education seem to be concentrated at the change from early childhood education into kindergarten or the change from high school to college; transitions within the K–12 years, and their potential effects on inequality, have been largely ignored.

Noncognitive Support Services

In addition to attempting to improve instructional conditions, many of the twelve schools had tried to enhance various support services to students who were falling behind, including health and mental health services, sexuality and teenage pregnancy prevention programs, family support services, anger management, and efforts to help students avoid the lure of the streets, like a community-based organization (CBO) program called Street Soldiers. These efforts were based on the assumption that students with other distractions and problems would be unable to concentrate on schoolwork; in effect, these were efforts to enhance connectedness to schooling. Such services have long been proposed as part of Comer schools (Comer 1996), full-service schools (Dryfoos 1994), early childhood programs that follow the Head Start model, Geoffrey Canada's multipronged efforts in the Harlem Children's Zone, and other reforms that provide support services in addition to instructional reforms.

The problem is in finding the resources for such services. Taylor High School's well-regarded health and mental health services were provided by the city; Horace Middle School had similar arrangements; and several schools (including Cityscape Charter) had been able to use CBOs to provide specific services. But these arrangements were patchy and inconsistent, and often they were the result of hero-principals actively recruiting contributions of various kinds—a mixed blessing, since this activity converts principals into professional beggars and distracts them from their instructional responsibilities. Until we as a country can provide support services for schoolchildren routinely (NRC 2004, ch. 6), such efforts are likely to remain idiosyncratic and uneven.

There were, to be sure, many smaller efforts with different theories of action. Some schools cited parent participation as important in creating consistency between school and home as well as parental reinforcement of school lessons. Hillcrest had developed a system of getting parents onto campus as volunteers, but efforts to enhance parental participation elsewhere were patchy. The principal of Horace Middle School embarked on a nutrition program that provided healthy snacks instead of junk food; she had observed that sugar jolts at lunch and snack time disrupted classroom learning. The search for "opportunities and pieces and whatever might work for some individual students," as she described it, was never-ending by the active principals and teachers in our sample schools, who made many small efforts too numerous to catalog. These efforts, however, like most such efforts, were particularly fragmented and patchy; the majority of these efforts in our initial sample fell into the six theories of action discussed in this section.

WHAT IS MISSING? THE EFFECTS OF RACE, CLASS, AND GENDER

It is also worth noting what was missing from the school-level efforts in the twelve sites we explored. The dominant responses for students who had fallen behind were curricular and pedagogical changes—familiar mechanisms of school reform, modifying the "technical core" of schooling.[12] But despite the fact that students who are behind, or below basic, are predominantly African American, Latino, and immigrant, the twelve schools we observed had not explicitly focused on race or ethnicity or on dimensions of family background, aside from some ineffective efforts to enhance parent participation. When schools in our sample did specifically address recent immigrant students, the problem was discussed as a technical one: finding enough time to provide access to English, finding the right instructional approach, or, in California, finding ways around a particularly pernicious limitation on instruction in a student's mother tongue (Prop 227). One exception to this pattern was an ELL teacher at David Smith Middle School who thought it essential to incorporate issues of history, culture, social support, and analysis of social hierarchies into the way he taught his ELL students *and* to address the adjustment issues they faced—but neither the High Point curriculum nor the district supported these possibilities. In addition, Horace Middle School had developed a program for young girls to build social skills and conflict management because fights among these largely African American girls had gotten out of hand. Otherwise, any attention to race, ethnicity, class, gender, or language background was missing.

As I elaborate in chapter 9, teachers and schools elsewhere have taken these dimensions of student differences seriously, and there are many practices intended to moderate the effects of race and ethnicity. To be sure, discussions about race and racism, ethnicity, class, and gender are hard conversations to have in schools, and falling back on the more familiar territory of curriculum and instruction is surely more comfortable. But as long as there is an unavoidably racial or ethnic dimension of various achievement gaps, as I showed in chapters 4 and 7, some part of dynamic inequality will go uncorrected if schools do not confront the enduring problems of racial and ethnic differences.

RESOURCES

A final issue to confront is that of resources, including money as well as all the other school resources incorporated into the improved school finance. Located in a relatively low-spending state—where it is difficult for local districts to increase their own tax rates to enhance spending—many schools in our sample could not include as many students in intervention programs as they would have liked. Particularly expensive programs were unlikely to be used: only one school in our small sample used Reading Recovery, an expensive program with some of the best evaluation evidence. Happy Valley had to get a special grant to support Read 180, and that program will surely end once funding ends. Lakelands exemplified the fiscal problem. As the principal noted about additional resources, "It's really so little." There was no money in the school's budget for interventions and no additional funds for staff development; the school psychologists, who were shared with other schools, spent all their time on special education, and the elementary school counselor split her time among fifteen schools for one-on-one counseling. Lakelands had $26,000 in state school improvement funds and, when we visited, had already spent $20,000 on a physical education aide, surely a low-priority "improvement." The middle-class PTA parents did not want to spend "their" money on low-performing students, and volunteer resources from a local church and a company were both paltry and unsuitable for students with behavior problems. The district had provided no additional help for low-performing students, and the state's efforts were a waste of money (as I document in chapter 9).

In the absence of new funding, several schools had reallocated resources in clever ways.[13] When the principal at Lakelands discovered that a very small number of students (about ten) received all extra resources, she instituted a reallocation process in which the school tried to direct its inadequate resources to students about whom teachers were concerned. Horace had reallocated students so that inexperienced teachers had fewer students and especially needy students were in classrooms with more experienced teachers. Horace and Hillcrest had allocated all their staff development funding to improving instruction. They had also used physical education periods strategically to reduce class sizes: while half the class was at phys ed, the other half was engaged in intensive instruction. All these schools were constantly trying to get volunteer resources, especially for after-school programs and tutoring, though (as we will see) the effectiveness of volunteers is suspect. These were all creative ways to reallocate and to stretch the available resources under conditions of scarcity.

The wish lists of most principals and intervention teachers included specific resources consistent with a particular vision of reform. These included, for example, reading experts, counselors, professional development related to teaching, improved after-school programs, bilingual aides, full-time parent liaisons, more school days per year with fewer breaks, longer periods (as in block scheduling), a longer day for enrichment (so that students would not need to choose between support classes and electives), more involved teachers whom principals would have more time to listen to, and more health and mental health services for specific problems (vision and hearing, asthma, obesity and diabetes). These wish lists were consistent with the direction these schools had already taken, and they focused not on money but on the real resources that educators thought would narrow existing differences in achievement—true to the precepts of the improved school finance.

EVALUATING INTERVENTIONS: WHAT IS WORKING AND WHAT IS NOT?

Many approaches to helping low-performing students, particularly assessment and correction, entail neither fundamental shifts in instruction, as in Horace Middle School, nor fundamental restructuring, as at Taylor High School, but the adoption of specific intervention efforts for specific groups of students. Sometimes, as at Travis Charter School, these interventions are relatively comprehensive and backed up by a well-developed assessment system; in other cases, they are scattered and fragmented and contribute to a lack of coherence. But no form of assessment and correction can work unless the corrective programs are themselves effective.

The issue of how to judge effectiveness has itself become contentious. The U.S. Department of Education and its Institute of Education "Sciences" (IES) has argued that random-assignment evaluations constitute the "gold standard" of evidence, though some other complex quantitative methods are sometimes acceptable. Against this view, many commentators have countered that random-assignment methods are too narrow, and a National Academy of Sciences panel has called for a broader conception of effectiveness (Shavelson and Towne 2002).[14] There is no resolution of this debate on the horizon, and in practice different individuals judge evidence not only by the "gold standard" but also by the preponderance of the evidence, the advertisements of curriculum publishers, and what a friend in a neighboring school claims. Here, I use the preponderance of the evidence, especially as summarized in meta-analysis and research reviews that attempt to be comprehensive in the literature they examine.

Nearly all of the schools we examined had adopted after-school programs, a particular form of intensification. The after-school programs we observed looked similar. They were typically operated by aides with a high school education rather than by teachers. Students spent the first hour doing homework, occasionally asking the aide (or volunteer tutors) for help; they spent the second hour on a variety of "enrichment" activities, including art, music, and games. The programs were poorly connected to regular instruction, though some schools had developed written records to coordinate classes and the after-school program. These voluntary efforts seemed to attract middling students, not the lowest performers who most needed them; the problem of luring this latter type of student had not been resolved.

Unfortunately, the research on out-of-school-time (OST) programs, including before- and after-school programs, has been largely negative (Bodilly and Beckett 2005; Kane 2004). What little evidence it has found indicates that such programs have at best modest positive effects on risky behaviors like drug use and sexual activity, but that school behavior and test scores do not improve, though high school students in one program (Upward Bound) earned increased numbers of credits and improved their graduation rates. A more recent meta-analysis of these programs (Lauer et al. 2006) was somewhat more positive: it concluded that average effects were small but statistically significant. The most effective programs were tutoring programs for reading, especially one-on-one tutoring. Overall, these studies support an emerging consensus about the practices necessary for effective programs: a clear mission, high expectations, a supportive emotional climate, a small total enrollment, trained personnel who remain with the program, appropriate content and pedagogy related to students' needs, integrated family and community partners, and frequent assessments. So the casual after-school programs we observed, which followed almost none of these recommendations, were testimony to the desire to help low-performing students, but they were unlikely to have much effect.

Tutoring is another prevalent practice that is usually included in assessment and correction. One-on-one and small-group tutoring programs have been found to have modest effects on test scores; both college students and trained community volunteers appear to be effective, either individually or in small groups.[15] An earlier review (Wasik and Slavin 1993) confirmed the value of one-on-one tutoring, particularly in programs with the most comprehensive models of reading rather than in those (like phonics) that address only a few components. Again, a rough consensus has emerged about the elements of effective tutoring: a coordinator knowledgeable about reading and writing instruction, structure in tutoring sessions, training for volunteers, and coordination between classroom instruction and volunteers. So, like the after-school programs, the casual tutoring we observed in our sample—where schools solicited volunteers from nearby universities, churches, CBOs, and companies but provided little training, no structure, and no contact with classroom teachers—was unlikely to be particularly effective.

Furthermore, we suspect that the quality of tutoring is likely to become even worse as private tutoring programs contract for $2 billion now available in federal funds. The training of tutors will be unregulated; tutors will be unlikely to coordinate with regular teachers since these private providers will be both physically and philosophically distant from the school; the curriculum and pedagogy will not match those used in regular programs; much of the money will go to companies rather than to tutors; and untrained tutors with little preparation and no guidance will probably fall back on the routinized teaching reflected in most workbooks and textbooks.[16] Several schools within our sample (Happy Valley, Hillcrest, and Cityscape Charter) had elected to provide their own tutoring as a way of monitoring its quality and integrating tutoring with regular instruction, but too many schools across the country are likely to waste their resources on outside tutoring.

In addition to these two common practices, a great deal of intervention uses off-the-shelf curricula developed by textbook publishers, university researchers, and individuals with their own visions of teaching. The twelve schools we observed used too many specific programs for us to review all of them, so we concentrated on SRA Reach, Read 180, Open Court, Language!, and the Diversity in Mathematics Education (DiME) program, developed to teach math to diverse students, including low-performing students.[17] The first problem is that evaluations are elusive. While some programs (especially Read 180) are conscious of the need for evidence, in other cases we had to make many phone calls and do a great deal of Web-sleuthing to find anything that could be called an evaluation. School leaders do not have the time or expertise to conduct this difficult search, particularly when they need programs in several subjects for many grade levels. So the failure of districts and the state to provide technical assistance and the lack of more accessible reviews from the federal What Works Clearinghouse means that school leaders must make decisions on their own. It is no wonder, then, that the decisionmaking process is truncated and that schools often rely on hearsay from other schools.

The common claim that a program is "research-based" is almost always incomplete. The clearest example comes in reading: because the literature indicates that early reading requires phonemic awareness, every program that includes phonemic awareness declares itself to be "research-based." But as the National Research Council review of reading research clarifies, phonemic awareness is necessary but is far from sufficient (Snow, Burns, and Griffin 1998). Many off-the-shelf curricula spend very little time on comprehension, give students few opportunities to read intensively, and do not require them to create their own meanings from reading, so they conform to research on effectiveness on only one of many elements. Furthermore, these curricula ignore research suggesting that phonemic awareness need not take more than twenty hours over a year, or about seven minutes per day, compared to the fifteen to twenty-five minutes spent in this area in most Reading First schools (National Institute for Literacy 2003). The conclusion that the time-on-task literature supports intensification is a similarly incomplete reading of the research. So educators should be skeptical of claims that programs are "research-based," since this phrase is all too often an exaggeration.

A third consistent problem is that the quality of outcome evaluations is usually quite mediocre. The most common method is to examine a single school, or sometimes a district, and then look at pre-tests and post-tests without any outside comparison group; there is rarely any data on the characteristics of students in the program, so it is never clear whether the students chosen were a random group, a high-performing or low-performing group, or some other distorted sample. In studies with control or comparison groups, characteristics of the comparison groups are not usually compared to characteristics of the treatment group, so it is impossible to be sure that they are similar. Even when these tests are normed to grade-level equivalents—as when researchers claim two years' progress in one year (for example, Grossen 2004)—there are many other plausible explanations for improvements: the fact that students who drop out are not included in results; regression to the mean; practice effects; selection effects; and effects due to changes in composition as students enter and leave schools and classrooms. Often studies are collected and reported by curriculum publishers, but we might suspect that only positive studies are included in their promotional material; the arduous search for the studies typical in meta-analysis is not evident. Most studies report means and sometimes standard errors, but the literature rarely uses regression controls, and then for only the simplest variables (like eligibility for school lunch).

In many cases the outcome measures are poorly chosen. For example, the initial evaluation of Open Court used a test of oral word reading rather than any measure of comprehension; students using Open Court and Direct Instruction tested well on phonics but had low levels of reading comprehension (Wilson 2005). In many cases "comprehension" is measured indirectly in ways that have little to do with understanding; for example, the widely used DIBELS measures comprehension by counting the words a child uses while retelling a story. In other cases, as in Read 180, tests designed for the intervention itself are used, so the results are automatically biased in favor of the program. So many evaluations flunk a basic precept of Evaluation 101: outcome measures should be related to desirable outcomes, not to meaningless proxies.

Quite apart from these simple failures in evaluation methods, there are two more fundamental dilemmas in evaluations of these programs. Programs that are relatively self-contained—the curriculum materials of Open Court or Read 180, for example—can be assessed using conventional evaluation techniques. But some approaches to intervention—the DiME program, the program examined by Boaler and Staples (2008) at Railside School, the efforts at Horace to adopt differentiated instruction—are not discrete programs but rather extensive efforts to change teachers' views and practices about instruction, content, and the capacities of students. These efforts cannot be evaluated in conventional ways—for example, by examining test scores before and after the intervention or for experimental and control students—since one of the central questions is whether and how teachers change their approaches and how students change their attitudes. So the conventional practices of evaluation—assessing programs as if they are simple binary events—are themselves biased in favor of simple scripted and semiscripted programs and against more complex approaches to reform.

In addition, intervention programs may be effective because they substitute a modestly coherent curriculum, with some minimum level of professional development, for incoherent teacher-developed practices that fail to meet state standards—that is, they substitute something for nothing. This may be particularly true for Read 180: a number of evaluations report that the comparison group students actually declined in their performance, suggesting either that the comparison group was not comparable or that it was taught in badly structured classes. But this does not imply that the program evaluated would be superior to well-developed conventional instruction following state standards; for that claim, the evaluators would have to make sure that the comparison students are in such classes. As an example, Margaret Moustafa and Robert Land (2002) compared Open Court with classes using what they label "contemporary reading instruction," a balanced approach that includes phonics but also practices from whole language. They found contemporary reading instruction to be more effective than Open Court, an appropriate comparison, even if Open Court might be more effective than "nothing"—that is, more effective than poorly planned instruction following no standards or logic. But when evaluation studies fail to clarify the comparison program, it is unclear what an intervention might be superior to.

Finally, as if evaluation were not difficult enough already, from the perspective of dynamic inequality all existing evaluations ask the wrong question. The question is not whether students in specific interventions, most of them by definition low-performing, improve more than students of unknown comparability in classes of unknown quality. Rather, the important question is whether rates of improvement are comparable to those of middling students (referring to figure 6.1) or are even higher, so that low-performing students can catch up to their middling peers. Without such information, it is impossible to know whether these interventions have any chance of narrowing the divergence in performance typical of American schools.

Overall, then, the evaluation evidence suggests that most interventions are unlikely to be effective. Many of them—after-school programs and tutoring—are being implemented in haphazard ways, ignoring what the research literature has concluded about effective practices. The evaluations of specific curricula are partial and misleading, and many of these programs violate both the conclusions about effective instruction and the precepts for motivation and engagement. Furthermore, many schools are adopting scripted and semiscripted programs—falsely touted as "proven practices"—that have no chance of improving learning beyond the most basic skill levels. The pressures of accountability are stampeding many schools into making changes that are likely to be the least effective.

WHAT WOULD DYNAMIC EQUITY REQUIRE?

Our examination of a small number of schools helps to clarify why educational outcomes in the United States are so unequal, as figure I.1 illustrated. Students start schooling with differences that come in the first instance from their families and communities, though these differences are in turn rooted in the large inequalities in income illustrated in that figure, in many dimensions of family background, in community characteristics, and then in virtually every other condition of a child's life (health, housing, nutrition, and on and on). But the efforts to help students who are behind—now universally defined as behind norms defined by state and federal accountability systems—through a variety of practices that, by construction, are second-chance programs, with all their inherent difficulties, are themselves varied, fragmented, incomplete in their coverage, and largely ineffective. A few schools in the sample—Horace, with differentiated instruction; Taylor High School, with theme-based small schools; Hillcrest, with its Learning Center—had relatively comprehensive plans that addressed large numbers of students. But most other schools provided special efforts for much smaller numbers, particularly through assessment and correction. Reading got by far the most attention, with math a distant second; other subjects—the ones not tested in the state and federal accountability system, including social studies and history, science, art, and music ("enrichment" rather than "core" subjects)—were ignored and even undermined by the tendency to use pull-out classes and skills classes that displaced these subjects. In addition, coverage by grade levels was uneven, with concentrated efforts for students during the early years of elementary school and in ninth grade. Many of the specific interventions used were ineffective if well intentioned, as were the nearly ubiquitous efforts to develop after-school and tutoring programs. There were virtually no efforts to smooth transitions or to prevent bursts of inequality from taking place; remedial efforts rather than prevention were the norm. Consistent attention to divergence, which might be necessary to squeeze together the growth trajectories illustrated in figure 6.1, was simply not present.

These results indicate that one of the possibilities raised in chapter 7—that school resources can reduce dynamic inequality if they focus on effective resources and if they are more equitably distributed—is very far from realization. Even under the intense pressure of state accountability and No Child Left Behind, many schools are trying to narrow inequalities among students with resources that cannot possibly be effective. Furthermore, the differences among schools—necessarily the responsibility of districts, states, and the federal government, not of schools themselves, and largely the product of class and racial-ethnic differences—are yet another dimension of the overall problem that, in this small sample, districts are not addressing. (Some other district effects are reviewed in chapter 10.) So substantial challenges remain in developing more equitable schools—the subject of chapters 9 to 12.

Efforts to help students who are behind inevitably confront restrictions on resources—not only resources in the sense of money but the other school resources, like vision, consistency, collaboration, strong leadership, and stability, that money cannot buy. If educational institutions thought of narrowing achievement gaps as part of the normal operation of schools—as is true in Horace Middle School, which ensures ongoing professional development to enhance differentiated instruction, or in Finland, where it is assumed that multiple layers of intervention and appropriate teacher training will be provided for all schools—then additional resources might not be necessary. But in the United States, the baseline or "normal" allocation of resources—part of the "grammar" of schooling, the ways in which we normally think of public schools (Tyack and Cuban 1995)—is consistent with divergence in educational attainment, and any attempt to narrow these differences requires additional funds. Neither districts nor state governments nor the federal No Child Left Behind policy has provided adequate resources to match the equity targets they pose, and so divergence continues to be the norm.

Finally, the results in this chapter add to the explanation for why the money myth is incomplete and why the relationship between spending and outcomes is weak. The schools we have profiled were spending considerable money—and even more abstract resources, including principal attention, teacher effort, meeting time, and reform energy—providing second chances to students who had fallen behind. But as long as their efforts were fragmented and ineffective, this money was being spent with few effects on outcomes. In addition to the conclusions reached by the end of chapter 3—that many effective resources are compound, complex, or abstract and only weakly related to spending—this chapter provides evidence of how ineffectively most schools are using the resources they already have.

There is nothing inevitable about dynamic inequality and the diverging trajectories that we see in the United States. Just as our unequal economic system and weak welfare state generate high levels of earnings inequality, our system of education creates high levels of educational inequality. These inequalities are social and political choices, developed over long periods of time, rather than the inevitable results of our size, complexity, or heterogeneity. Difficult as it may be politically, inequality in educational outcomes can be reversed. Indeed, if we believe the rhetoric of No Child Left Behind, eliminating various achievement gaps and bringing all students to proficiency is the law of the land. It remains only—only!—to figure out how to do this.

Creating dynamic equity would require first that such a conception of equity be articulated and widely accepted. I articulated four conceptions of dynamic equity in chapter 6: equal rates of learning; neutrality in rates of learning among groups of students; a conception based on adequacy in which all students meet some standards considered adequate; and one based on policies of correction, to narrow differences among students over time. The four conceptions vary in their stringency and in the demands they make on reforms, but implementing any of the four would help narrow the inequalities we now see in schools. Second, it would be necessary to reformulate school practices to prevent students from falling behind and to support low-performing students in catching up with their peers. This in turn would require the reallocation of school resources, broadly understood. Some of these changes must take place at the school and classroom level, but they also need to be supported by district, state, and federal policies—an agenda of consistency among levels of the education system that is not now present. Finally, the development of nonschool policies to overcome the varied and continuing effects of family background would also be necessary, as many other countries have recognized through their more generous welfare states. All of these reforms are the subjects of part 3 of this book.

This sounds like a large agenda, and it is. But it is the only way to make good on the rhetoric we have already expressed about our schools: the pleas from the business community and other advocates of the Education Gospel to develop a "world-class" education system; the pledge by the nation's governors in Goals 2000 to be first in the world in science and technology; the requirement in federal law to "leave no child behind" and to make all students proficient by 2014; the claim that "College for All" is a reasonable goal, even when 20 to 30 percent of each cohort fails to graduate from high school. As a country, either we need to develop a system that educates all students to high standards, requiring reforms at all levels and recognizing the variety of resources this will take, or we need to abandon our lofty rhetoric and admit that an inequitable sorting machine is all we want from our schools.

Part III

Implications for School Practice,
Education Policy, and Litigation

Chapter 9

Making Resources Matter: Implications for School-Level Practice

IN THINKING about how to make education more effective *and* more equitable, I start with the school as the unit of reform. Many of the most effective resources identified in chapters 2 and 7 involve school-level policies, such as decisions to place students in general, traditional vocational, or remedial tracks rather than to create alternatives to conventional tracking; policies that affect school climate, both its positive and negative dimensions; and efforts to increase teacher planning time and staff development, particularly with an emphasis on more balanced instruction. Many measures of effective teaching—teachers' use of time, the prevalence of conventional versus innovative or balanced teaching, a teacher's sense of efficacy and control—require a focus on instructional approaches, but if practices are specific to individual teachers rather than schoolwide, then students lurch between ineffective and effective practices and experience inconsistent teaching. Principals and other school-level leaders can see, particularly through classroom observation, what teachers are doing and how they change their practices, and they can provide corrections when appropriate, but this is nearly impossible to do from the district or state level. There are, to be sure, forms of funding that would support schools as they develop effective resources—particularly school-based budgeting from the district level, the use of weighted student formulas, stability of revenues, and adequacy of funding so that schools have enough slack (or spare time and energy) to be able to improve. But there is no substitute for developing the ability of schools to translate these funding patterns into effective resources.

Furthermore, the complexity of school reform—where money is usually necessary but not sufficient and many resources, especially compound re-sources, require several actions simultaneously—means that *under the right circumstances* schools can develop the ability to coordinate a number of changes, but districts and states cannot do this from afar. This has been illus-trated by "natural experiments" in which a state (California) or a district (Chicago) has dramatically increased funding to schools while simultane-ously requiring that the schools develop plans for spending money. These natural experiments allow us to see how money has been spent under nor-mal conditions, and whether it has been spent for resources that are ar-guably effective. A review of such experiments, in the first section of this chapter, finds enormous variation in how schools use new revenues. Unfor-tunately, such spending increases have not led to greater effectiveness on av-erage, especially in California, where such spending efforts have been more extensive than in other states. Instead, various aspects of the planning and spending process have broken down, providing yet other examples of waste in schools and yet other reasons why money may be necessary for effective school reform but is never sufficient. These dismal results raise the questions of what might be necessary to ensure that additional funds are spent wisely and well, and what might enable schools to respond more effectively to re-form pressures in the future.

The second section recapitulates the findings from earlier chapters, espe-cially from chapter 3 (when money matters) and from chapter 7 (on dy-namic inequality). One conclusion from this review is that, even though sta-tistical methods often cannot detect the effectiveness of interactions among school resources, many effective resources require other supportive re-sources: class size reduction *plus* the maintenance of teacher quality, or the elimination of general and conventional vocational education *plus* their re-placement by stronger approaches. This conclusion emerges from the con-ventional examples of waste first developed in chapter 1, as well as from the California and Chicago examples. But it can also emerge from reforms at the *school* level, particularly when schools focus on a simple reform like a new curriculum, a specific intervention, a literacy coach, or conventional professional development and then discover through "unintended conse-quences" that a more complex reform with compound resources would have been more effective—the failure to recognize the need for compound re-sources having led to yet another form of waste. Another conclusion is that many of the most effective resources are not improvements that individuals can make working alone in schools but rather are *collective* resources that can be improved by teachers and leaders working collectively within a school. This eliminates many proposals for improvements in schools that focus only on individuals, such as the common recommendation that the competencies of individual teachers be enhanced or that only teachers from the top third of college graduates be hired, or the allocation of funds to individual teachers for materials and field trips.[1] All these measures may be useful, but except under the right conditions, they cannot improve collective resources.

The first two sections of this chapter deal with relatively conventional conceptions of how schools might improve, albeit with an expanded conception of resources and with results from the rich NELS88 data. But in addition to identifying effective resources, the NELS88 data also identify another source of inequality, the "racial residual" identified in chapter 4 as well as chapter 7—the specifically racial and ethnic dimensions of the achievement gap that cannot be explained by variations in school resources, family background, or student motivation. This is a subject often overlooked in conventional policy discussions—even in analyses of the narrowing of the achievement gap, usually defined as black-white (or Latino-white) test score differences—except by advocates for African American, Latino, and other racial-minority students. But a variety of practices have been developed and used in a few classrooms to make schools more welcoming, more supportive, less mystifying, and less demeaning places for racial-minority students. Such reforms are also good examples of complex resources: they cannot be easily bought; they must instead be put in place by teachers and leaders working collaboratively. Like the other reforms to make schools more effective, these are largely collective resources, since they should operate at the schoolwide level, and so grappling with race-focused reforms requires first a school with enough internal collegiality and trust to face these difficult issues squarely.

The observation that many effective school resources are collective is consistent with the conception of schools described more fully in the last section. This approach goes by many names—distributed leadership, internal accountability, "organic management"—but it always poses a clear alternative to the common Weberian model of hierarchical management usually described (and usually disparaged) as "top-down." The evidence in favor of this conception is widespread if scattered, and it is difficult to prove that it will lead to greater effectiveness—for example, conventional statistical analysis fails to account for its many interactions. But the evidence against schools that are internally incoherent and whose participants act in the isolated ways of the conventional model is quite strong, especially in underperforming urban schools. There seems to be a precondition for schools to spend additional funds wisely, to respond effectively to external accountability, and to allocate their own resources to be most effective: they must first be reorganized along the lines of distributed leadership or internal accountability to be able to make decisions collectively and collegially. So every effort at reform—for example, state programs to provide additional resources to underperforming schools (as in California), district efforts to redistribute funding through school-based budgeting (described in chapter

10), or litigation that hopes to provide more equal funding to various districts (the subject of chapter 11)—requires a "pre-reform" to be effective, or a reorganization of the school itself. In addition to the ability to recognize and develop the effective school resources identified in earlier chapters, this too is part of what I mean by "capacity-building."

Unfortunately, many reforms of the moment—especially those driven by the state and federal accountability movements—discourage the practices outlined in this chapter, as chapter 8 illustrated. One implication is that greater effectiveness and equity, as well as more powerful use of existing revenues, will need to wait for the current accountability movement to be joined with equally powerful district, state, and even federal efforts to improve the capacities of schools—the subject of chapter 10.

NATURAL EXPERIMENTS: WHAT HAPPENS WHEN SCHOOLS GET NEW FUNDING?

One way to see how schools use money and to examine the proposals of the improved school finance is to examine what schools have done in "natural experiments"—that is, when they have suddenly been given additional money to spend, sometimes on specific resources. One example was the effort in California to reduce pupil-teacher ratios in kindergarten through third grade to twenty-to-one—a simple resource, and an expensive one. Unfortunately, the reform experienced a series of problems that illustrate clearly that, to be effective, *simple* resources are insufficient; the unintended consequences of the change clarified the need for *compound* resources instead. With increasing demand for K–3 teachers, schools (especially in urban districts) had to turn to less qualified and credentialed teachers; there was little professional development, and teachers largely failed to change their instructional approaches for smaller groups. Without funding for facilities, smaller classes were often forced to meet in inappropriate spaces (Stecher and Bohrnstedt 2002). The outcome was that test scores on the average did not improve, though some districts—those that could take advantage of additional funding and had adequate supplies of qualified teachers—benefited at the expense of others, especially urban districts with increased shortages of teachers.

Another natural experiment in California has involved a series of reforms intended to improve student test scores in low-performing schools. The Intermediate Intervention/Underperforming Schools Program (II/USP) enacted in 1999 provided additional funding to 430 schools in the bottom half of the distribution of state test scores. Schools were supposed to volunteer for the program, presumably to ensure that participating schools would be willing to undergo reform; then additional state revenue of $200 per student was to be matched by an additional $200 from the district. Schools had to develop a state plan for spending this money with the help of an external "evaluator" (really a consultant); they then faced various rewards and sanctions depending on changes in their subsequent test scores. In theory, this looked like a rational approach to school improvement, with a number of mutually supporting elements: additional funding *plus* a plan by which to spend money rationally, *plus* outside expertise in case schools lacked the ability to develop such a plan, *plus* additional incentives for high performance and disincentives for failing to improve. Indeed, II/USP looked precisely like a compound resource. For the policy crowd in favor of "getting the incentives right" and then allowing schools to develop their own approaches, II/USP was a model program.

In practice, however, almost everything about this program went wrong.[2] No one in California has described II/USP as a series of mutually supportive elements, as I have; schools treated these elements as a series of independent requirements. Many schools were told by their districts to "volunteer," so their participation was coerced, and these schools were evidently not ready—neither in the sense of being willing to participate nor in the stronger sense of having the internal capacity to plan well. Many schools were deeply unhappy with their consultants, and some consultants produced cookie-cutter plans inconsistent with teachers' wishes and school conditions; many of the plans were not thorough investigations of how additional resources might be spent but instead were little more than tinkering with existing practices. The connections between plans and actual activities were loose to nonexistent in many schools. Districts often found ways of failing to provide the additional $200 per student they were supposed to provide by reducing other funding to targeted schools. And as often happens with such programs, the three-year period of the grant proved too short. Some schools already in the process of reform were able to use these funds to further their efforts, but otherwise this expensive effort—about $1.5 billion per year for three years—generated no visible impact.

II/USP was then replaced by the High Priority Schools Grant Program (HPSGP), which again followed what we might call the "California model" of generous additional funding plus planning requirements.[3] The first round of this program provided $400 per student per year for three (and possibly four) years, to be matched with an additional $200 per student from the district. But the first-year evaluation found many of the same problems as with II/USP. District policies were helpful in only three of the nine districts studied, with four of the districts "a challenge"; some teachers reported that their district had impeded their reform efforts. Several of the districts experienced fiscal or managerial crises—a particularly common event in urban districts—and subsequent breakdowns in the implementation process. School-level participants again expressed dissatisfaction with the quality of external consultants, with only two of sixteen schools reporting any positive experiences. Principal turnover and shortages of credentialed teachers contributed to instability in these schools. The outcome was only trivial increases in test scores, and for only seven of the twelve tests administered (Harr et al. 2006). Another evaluation, based on interviews in fifteen schools divided into improving and non-improving, clarified the different ways in which schools spent their additional money. Some, with an existing school improvement strategy, integrated new funding into ongoing plans, but others without such plans simply funded "wish lists" for immediate needs. The schools using money purposefully tended to be internally coherent, while those with minimal collaboration and planning used money in fragmented and opportunistic ways (Timar and Kim 2008). It is unclear, however, that California policymakers have learned anything from this string of failures, since a recently enacted program—the Quality Education Improvement Act (QEIA)—closely follows the patterns of II/USP and HPSGP.[4] Chapter 10 looks at this serious issue connected with fledgling state efforts to develop capacity: can states, districts, and schools learn from their mistakes, or will they continue, like California, to waste large sums in ineffective efforts over and over and over again?

A similar natural experiment took place in Chicago during the 1990s, as part of the Chicago School Reform Act. Along with substantial additional funding, decisionmaking shifted to the school level; local school councils were charged with developing school improvement plans, including decisions about curriculum and pedagogical approaches. In a sample of fourteen schools, five showed improvement on test scores over the 1990s, three held steady, and six (including three of the four high schools) declined, so overall this experiment was not a success. Several common factors distinguished the schools that did improve: they retained the same principal throughout the period; the principal (rather than the local council) provided instructional leadership; the principal and the site councils were both involved in decisionmaking, rather than the principal having extreme control or the site council intervening excessively; and supporting classroom instruction was emphasized (Hess 1999). Once again, it seems that a sharing of decisionmaking is necessary before schools can develop effective plans, and the abstract resources of principal stability and instructional leadership are important components of improvement.

At one level, the saga of these expensive but ineffective programs is yet more evidence about the political economy of waste, a subject I raised in more conceptual ways in chapter 1. States as well as districts and schools are capable of great waste, and state policymakers are often more interested in appearing to do something than in doing the hard work of figuring out what might be effective. But there are other lessons from these examples. One is that many schools—or at least many low-performing schools—are not structured to make coherent decisions even when they receive windfalls of additional funding. They cannot come up with coherent plans for reform, and even if they do have a plan—or have it handed to them, for example, by outside consultants—they cannot implement it faithfully. (I return to the dimension of school capacity in the next section.) In addition, district constraints on school decisions—ranging from "volunteering" schools that are unready to make changes to placing constraints on how new funds are spent, to making poor choices of "evaluators" or consultants, to substituting away some of the revenue intended for schools—have added their own forms of waste to these initiatives, rather than supporting what schools have been trying to do. When I return to district policies in chapter 10, I discuss what some exemplary districts are now doing that instead supports the efforts of schools to develop their own approaches to effectiveness.

THE COLLECTIVE NATURE OF EFFECTIVE RESOURCES: RECAPITULATING THE NELS88 EVIDENCE

If the natural experiments reviewed in the previous section show us how *not* to reform schools, then what changes *should* schools make to improve student outcomes and equity? The results in earlier chapters, particularly in chapter 2 on twelfth-grade outcomes and in chapter 7 on dynamic outcomes, suggest a complex series of reform strategies, most of them corroborated by other evidence.

The Need for Compound, Complex, and Abstract Resources

One conclusion to remember is that while simple resources like the pupil-teacher ratio, teacher salaries, and teacher experience in secondary education have positive effects on outcomes, these are not among the most powerful school effects. The coefficients of these simple resources tend to be lower than many other school resources; experience in secondary teaching tends to improve test scores but not other outcomes, and the number of pupils per teacher—a measure of (im)personalization—improves progress but not test scores (with the exception of math). Furthermore, a closer examination of these simple resources suggests that they usually operate as part of compound resources. For example, more adults per student may help to personalize a high school, but class size reduction—which is different from simply increasing the aggregate number of teachers per student—may be ineffective unless teacher quality is maintained, teachers teach in new ways in smaller classes, and adequate facilities are provided. My interpretation that high teacher salaries are really a proxy for teacher quality[5]—since a greater flow of money to teachers does not directly benefit students—requires that districts able to pay higher salaries also engage in a selection process to enhance quality; surely higher pay without a careful selection process is ineffective. Similarly, the only effective form of teacher experience in my results is experience in secondary schools, which is really a compound resource. These are among the only school resources that can be readily bought by increasing expenditures, but even they require planning and complementary nonfiscal resources, rather than simply adding to the resources that can be readily bought.

Furthermore, a number of complex resources, particularly those related to improving the quality of instruction, proved to be important in the statistical results in chapters 2 and 7. Among the twelve schools we examined in chapter 8, one (Horace Middle School) emphasized enhancing the instructional capacities of all its teachers; others adopted interventions that followed balanced approaches rather than "more of the same" remedial pedagogies, but pedagogical improvements were largely missing from most of these schools. A number of abstract resources, like a school's climate, make a great deal of difference to outcomes, and many others—including stability, coherence, leadership, and internal accountability—have been found effective in other evidence. But many schools trying to improve overlook these ways of restructuring and miss opportunities to become more effective as well as equitable.

Common Effects, Differentiated Effects, or Both?

A second conclusion from the results discussed earlier is that certain resources influence a wide variety of outcomes, with common effects; other resources, with differentiated effects, affect only some outcomes. One strategy for high schools would be to focus first on school resources that have common effects: placement in general, vocational, or remedial tracks; school climate, with both positive and negative dimensions; and school counselors (and perhaps other unmeasured dimensions of student support).[6] But again, reshaping these resources requires careful attention to the alternatives. Replacing general, vocational, and remedial tracks requires either providing a college-bound track for all students—the alternative of a college-prep curriculum as the default track, or College for All—or providing alternative "pathways" or theme-based programs throughout the high school.[7] Each of these alternatives has its own dangers. The conventional college-prep track lacks most of the attributes necessary for motivation and engagement, while the approach of multiple pathways might, if implemented without a concern for equity, lead back to conventional tracking.

Improving school climate, another resource with common effects, seems conceptually straightforward. Such improvement requires a concerted collective effort on the part of all administrators and teachers, however, working carefully with students and parents to reshape the norms of a school, the behavior of students and teachers toward one another, and the policies (like disciplinary policies) that reflect these norms.[8] Similarly, the NELS88 results indicate that increasing the use of school counselors would enhance many outcomes, but in practice many students (including those most in need of support) do not use counselors, and the approaches to counseling are often old and ineffective. If the positive effect of counselors implies the need to develop student support services, then there are many alternatives to conventional practice, including expanded notions of what counselors do from the Puente program, developmental conceptions of support services from the LifeMap program at Valencia Community College, and the kinds of mentoring embedded in Big Brothers/Big Sisters.[9] So while enhancing school resources with widespread or common effects may be a powerful strategy, the most effective versions of that strategy require changing conventional practice.

A second and less uniformly powerful strategy would be to concentrate on school resources with differentiated effects. From chapter 2, the resources that enhance learning as measured by test scores are, unsurprisingly, related to instruction: teacher salaries (presumably as a proxy for quality), teacher attitudes, instructors who teach in their field of preparation, pedagogical innovation, more constructivist or "balanced" instruction, and increased teacher planning time. As many others have found as well, increasing learning requires specific attention to dimensions of instruction, and no amount of school restructuring—creating small schools, learning communities, or theme-based pathways to enhance student choice or setting up magnet or choice schools—can improve learning unless instructional practices change.[10] Conversely, different kinds of school resources, related to personalization and adult contact, enhance progress through high school, including the accumulation of appropriate credits and finally graduation. Such resources include the adult-pupil ratio, help with academic subjects, and extracurricular activities; smaller school size seems to operate not directly but indirectly by enhancing teacher innovation, the likelihood of in-field teaching, and teacher experience in secondary schools and by reducing the frequency of negative events. For high schools that want to enhance both learning and progress, these results provide a number of different resources that should be enhanced. But the importance of differentiated rather than common resources implies that restructuring and personalization are insufficient to improve learning and that improving the quality of instruction does not itself lead to adequate progress, so efforts to improve both learning and progress must emphasize a larger variety of resources.

Student Connectedness to Schooling: Can Schools Help?

A third issue that must be tackled at the school level—even though it has some nonschool dimensions—is that of student connectedness to school or ability to benefit from schooling. Failure to complete homework, irregular attendance, and a pattern of getting into trouble for both academic and be-havioral reasons are signals of this kind of student "resource." Some have cited a general attachment to schooling that, for individuals who are likely to drop out of high school, seems to begin waning as early as elementary school.[11] There has been, to be sure, a long history of debate over these di-mensions of student behavior, with one camp blaming students them-selves—and their families and communities, particularly since measures of class and family background are some of the only variables that influence di-mensions of student connectedness.[12] Unfortunately, unless student- and family-blaming brings about constructive proposals for alternative non-educational policies, it leads only to educators absolving themselves of responsibility.

But another camp has identified many ways in which school practices themselves affect student behavior. The results in chapter 5 confirmed, once again, the negative effects of traditional vocational, general, and remedial tracks, partly since students in these tracks showed lower levels of connect-edness to schooling. (If vocational education incorporated meaningful intern-ships or apprenticeships, a particular kind of compound resource, this might not be true because then school would be an entry into interesting experi-ences and promising careers.) Similarly, several school resources—conven-tional teaching, the use of class time for administration and discipline, a lack of principal control, the inability or unwillingness of students to get aca-demic help—reduced attendance, presumably as students "voted with their feet" under dreary instructional conditions. More generally, as I have noted previously, the National Research Council (2004) review of high schools in-dicates that motivation and engagement are higher (1) when students have some autonomy in selecting tasks; (2) when they can engage in constructing meaning on their own rather than taking the passive role of teacher-centered classrooms; (3) when there is close adult-student supervision; (4) when cur-ricula are well structured, with clear purposes; (5) when high schools have a challenging curriculum and a strong emphasis on achievement; (6) when stu-dents have multiple paths to competence; and (7) when programs allow them to develop a clearer understanding of schooling and its relationship to future activities. Some of these conditions (particularly the first three) are dimen-sions of pedagogical approaches, consistent with a shift to more construc-tivist or balanced teaching. Some (the last four) are dimensions of schoolwide approaches to curriculum. The last one is a function of paying explicit atten-tion to life after high school and the alternatives students face, an issue often inadequately embedded in conventional guidance and counseling. Fortu-nately, most of these improvements can be included in the approaches I have already mentioned—in the improvements to instruction confirmed as effec-tive in the NELS88 results, in various forms of restructuring high schools, or in innovative approaches to guidance and counseling.

These dimensions of motivation and engagement also imply that the academic or college-prep alternative to general, vocational, and remedial tracks is probably less appropriate than a set of alternative pathways through high school (Oakes and Saunders 2008), some of which may have broad occupational themes (business, health, industrial production) while others have a non-occupational focus (the environment, social justice, communications). Such pathways can provide students with choices, with alternative routes to competence, and with ways of exploring the relationship between schooling and their future options, including further education, subsequent employment, and community participation. So, like the effects of family background, high school reforms related to instruction and restructuring can operate in two ways: by directly improving various school resources, and by enhancing the roles of students as resources to the educational process.

To be sure, schools cannot directly control several dimensions of student engagement, although some have tried. Peer relationships have been a subject of concern at least since the 1950s, with the movie *High School Confidential* (sex and drugs in high schools!), and the 1960s, with James Bryant Conant's (1959) complaint about the "social dynamite" created by cooping up adolescents with one another. But peer relationships are largely part of the process of adolescents choosing identities and friends, though some high schools have promoted extracurricular activities as ways to displace negative peer effects (especially gangs). Schools have no control over the income conditions that increase the likelihood of employment for some students; the class conditions (maternal employment, educational materials in the home) that enhance students' school-oriented behavior; whether students come from single-parent families, which are associated with absences and behavioral problems; the cultural issues that reduce reading and increase TV watching and now video game playing; or the effects of outside activities. When I turn in chapter 12 to a variety of non-educational policies, I will look especially at their influence on students' ability to benefit from school.

OTHER COMPLEX RESOURCES: TACKLING RACIAL AND ETHNIC ISSUES HEAD ON

The reforms proposed in the pervious section—focusing on effective resources and acknowledging the differences between those with common effects and those with differentiated effects—would increase the effectiveness of high schools, and they would also enhance equity because most of these effective resources are unequally distributed (as table 1.2 clarified). However, another dimension of inequality that these results have highlighted (in chapter 4 and again in chapter 7 on patterns of dynamic inequality) are the powerful effects of race and ethnicity that cannot be explained away by class, student behavior, or the levels of school resources.[13] Rather than following the conventional analyses that begin with racial-ethnic differences and then propose a set of "color-blind" policies that will apply equally to all students, my interpretation is that some of these unexplained gaps are due to the mistreatment of racial and ethnic minority students. If we avoid the specifically racial and ethnic dimensions of educational inequality, we as a society will never make progress on these dimensions of inequality. Instead, we need to confront these differences head on.[14]

Fortunately, a number of specific practices have emerged that address various racial and ethnic issues directly, and the schools that have adopted them often combine several of these promising reforms. These practices vary a great deal from one practitioner and advocate to another; they have not yet been standardized, as conventional school subjects have been, for example, and there is as yet virtually no evaluation evidence (Zirkel, forthcoming [b]). But depending on the conditions and student populations in the schools that adopt them, these practices promise to reduce if not eliminate the racial-ethnic residuals.

Same-Race Teachers

One of the most common and least controversial recommendations has been to hire more African American and Latino teachers, on the theory that these teachers are more likely to understand racial-minority students and their challenges in moving into school culture, are more likely to be sympathetic and supportive, and can more readily serve as role models. The methods of increasing the numbers of such teachers include special recruitment efforts, grant and loan forgiveness programs, and recruitment of community college students (who are more likely to be black and Latino) into teacher preparation programs. The evidence indicates that same-race teachers do improve the school performance of students, though the effects on test scores are small;[15] effects on persistence and graduation may be larger, however, because greater numbers of African American and Latino teachers, counselors, and administrators are surely part of personalizing high schools for racial-minority students. There are many other potential benefits of having more Latino and black teachers in schools, including the opportunity to create different school cultures and develop diverse teacher-leaders and principals, and so this common recommendation merits continued effort.

Classroom Observations and Reflection

Many examples of mistreating students in general, but racial-ethnic minority students in particular, appear to be unconscious rather than deliberate: teachers in the press of the moment, an assistant principal overwhelmed with discipline referrals, or any adult facing the sometimes baffling behavior of adolescents may lash out at students without thinking. If so, then changing this kind of adult behavior requires some kind of intervention from others, since individuals may be unable to perceive their own behavior. In this case, the practice of classroom observation—which appears to be increasing, particularly in schools that deliberately re-create themselves as learning communities, as described later in this chapter—can identify many kinds of teacher behavior, both conscious and unconscious. Classroom observation, reflection, and discussion of teaching patterns may then allow some teachers to see where their behavior is inappropriate, demeaning, or neglectful of some students. Implementing such practices may be possible only in schools with high levels of trust and cooperation, since classroom observation is a method that can quickly deteriorate if implemented in a climate of accountability and fear (Grubb 2000).

Careful Attention to Discipline Issues

Discipline policies can lead to one of the most consistent forms of mistreatment as educators and students come to loggerheads over behavior, the interpretation of rules, and the appropriateness of punishments—particularly when discipline is enforced with so-called zero-tolerance policies that prescribe referral or suspension for any infraction of the rules (Ayers, Dohrn, and Ayers 2001). To investigate discipline patterns more carefully, a practice has developed in schools concerned about excessive behavioral referrals to identify which students are involved in discipline cases, an exercise that usually identifies a small number of African American (and sometimes Latino) males as responsible for the majority of discipline cases. But a corollary is that it is often only a few teachers who are responsible for the majority of referrals, so most discipline issues result from some interaction of teacher behavior and student response. Indeed, in one investigation based on classroom observations of such teachers, most discipline problems arose when teachers who had the most rigid instructional approaches faced students who were particularly resistant to such methods.[16] These students could be reassigned to teachers with less rigid approaches, or teachers could be taught alternative methods of instruction; this approach would be more consistent with the engaging practices noted earlier and less likely to create opposition in students.

A different approach to discipline might also be appropriate. Discipline policies usually take the form of adult-developed prohibitions imposed on students without their participation. In an alternative originally created in the 1960s as part of efforts to develop schools as moral communities, schools could be restructured so that students rather than administrators alone have responsibility for formulating and then adjudicating the norms of the school.[17] Such a practice would also be more consistent with conceptions of school as a democratic community rather than a place where students lack any power. If students play a role in discipline, at least two benefits may materialize: formulating norms allows students to see why rules and regulations are necessary, and adjudication takes teachers and administrators out of direct conflicts with students. Such an approach to discipline would benefit all students, but given the frequency with which African American and Latino students are embroiled in disciplinary measures, this approach might diminish the sense of mistreatment by educators for them in particular.

Explicit Instruction in Code-Switching

One common form of correction in schools involves language, particularly nonstandard English, including black vernacular English, or Ebonics. When teachers simply correct students, not only does conflict increase, but students are unlikely to understand why their own language is incorrect compared to standard English. An alternative approach involves analyzing differences in speech and behavior in many settings, particularly at home versus at school ("contrastive analysis"), and then teaching children to code-switch, or to speak and behave differently in different settings (as all adults do too).[18] Not only is this approach more effective for teaching standard English, but it also reduces the amount of conflict in schools. The techniques of code-switching can be applied to behavior as well; norms of behavior appropriate for life in school can be contrasted with behavior outside of school, on the playing field, or in the community.

Culturally Relevant Pedagogy and Multicultural Education

Many approaches to teaching racial-minority students have started from the observation of poor performance in schools, with differences between home cultures and school cultures noted as partly to blame. Then some reformers have decided to change *school* patterns rather than to assume that students must adapt to school cultures. These efforts have often been developed idiosyncratically by individual teachers and through individual programs, and they therefore range enormously. An influential categorization by James Banks and Cherry McGee Banks (2004) includes content integration, or infusing the curriculum with materials from racially diverse groups; knowledge construction, or understanding how cultural norms shape our conceptions of knowledge; prejudice reduction, identifying and eliminating sources of personal bias; equity pedagogies that develop instructional approaches designed to create greater equity among students; and the development of school cultures supportive of all students.[19] Some of these practices have become relatively widespread, particularly the efforts to include literature written by black and Latino (or Latin American) authors, which have resulted in diversified reading lists and anthologies of short stories. More substantial efforts include the use of such literature to examine issues of race, identity, and discrimination. Other practices have taught about different racial, ethnic, and cultural groups, providing a broad introduction to patterns of diversity in this country. Some teachers have tried to help racial-minority students through practices that "bridge" the home and the school by, for example, paying more explicit attention to school-based forms of reading and writing or approaches to mathematics; such practices facilitate another form of code-switching from the culture of the home to the culture of the school. One example of such a bridging mechanism is the family literacy program, which teaches parents about "school" forms of reading and writing so that they can reinforce the literacy practices their children are learning in school. Some practices focus on adopting a variety of communicative styles in the classroom, such as more participatory and interactive styles, call-and-response and "signifying" in the black community, talk-story in native Hawaiian cultures, and overlapping talk among teenage girls. Others focus on getting teachers to understand more clearly the backgrounds of their students to improve relations in the classroom. Some approaches take critical perspectives (especially with older students) and teach about racial oppression, discrimination, and the relationships of power in this country; this strand of culturally relevant pedagogy is related to other efforts to use schools for social critique and reconstruction—for example, in Freirean approaches.

None of these practices have been standardized, the evidence for them is varied and often anecdotal, and many seem to be practiced by individual teachers rather than adopted by schools or districts. But the intention of all of them is to create the schooling conditions in which racial-minority students are treated with greater respect and can find more concern within their schools about the racial issues they confront in daily life. For schools that want to improve the learning of minority students, these practices constitute a substantial portfolio of options.

Race Talk and Courageous Conversations

Some schools are trying to talk more forthrightly about racial issues to clarify not only the problems that students face but also the frustrations that teachers feel. These conversations sometimes follow specific formats—frameworks and protocols for teachers and school leaders that can facilitate conversations about what is, after all, one of the most difficult issues our country faces. Examples include Critical Friends groups, in which individuals who have developed sufficient trust can engage in discussions that are both supportive and critical of others—almost a prerequisite for reflection on the classroom observations described earlier—or the methods of Courageous Conversations about race (Singleton and Linton 2006). Sometimes schools and even districts have discussed books, either fictional or nonfictional treatments of race, ethnicity, and class, in order to stimulate open conversation. Such discussions can lead to better collective understanding of the racial-ethnic dilemmas in a specific school (or district) and then to potential solutions, whether from the range of culturally relevant practices or elsewhere. These discussions can replace the awkward "race talk" that often takes place in schools with greater understanding of the codes and patterns of African American, Latino, and immigrant students and others likely to be mistreated.[20]

Confronting Issues of Identity and Racial Identity

One form of mistreatment of African American and Latino students, especially in high schools, is presenting them with a restricted range of potential identities just at the point of adolescence when they are wrestling with the question of who they are and what they might become. The identities of pro athlete and rap star for black youth are well known (and highly unrealistic), and identities as craft workers and service workers are available for Latinos, but the wider variety of possible pathways and identities are often not presented to either blacks or Latinos (Nasir, Jones, and McLaughlin forthcoming). Conventional guidance and counseling has often and accurately been accused of contributing to narrow conceptions of future identities—for example, when counselors tell students that they are not "college material" or when they direct Latino or black students to lower-level tracks and occupations. But the efforts to eliminate such tracking practices have failed to develop more appropriate practice: when counselors preach "college for all" as a way of avoiding charges of bias (Rosenbaum 2001), they substitute a uniform set of recommendations for the difficult work of helping individual students see the range of their options and pathways. So the antidote to restricted identities—for all students, not just racial-minority students—is a more deliberative process during high school of considering the broad range of post–high school options, something that is possible only with innovative approaches to guidance and counseling (NRC 2004, ch. 6).

A related issue is that of racial identity, which is partly linked to narrow conceptions of occupational identity. One of the challenges for all students in a multiethnic society—though this task is surely more difficult for ethnic and racial-minority students—is to determine for themselves what their own race or ethnic status means and how it is related to that of other individuals. The identities that individuals develop, as a result of many influences both inside and outside of school, can be positive or negative or anything in between, but a number of studies have found that a strong and positive racial identity is positively related to school performance. Informal and formal discussions of race and ethnicity and courses explicitly about diversity and multiculturalism provide some forums for students to explore racial-ethnic identity and to develop capacities like the ability to see different perspectives and make better decisions (Zirkel forthcoming b). So once again, there is a great deal that schools can do to help students accomplish these developmental tasks—and to wrestle with the specifically racial-ethnic dimensions of these tasks—though few schools try to do so.

Nonteaching Support: Counselors and Mentors

A number of programs have tried to provide students with same-race mentors, usually individuals who have themselves been successful in school. Such individuals can serve in several ways: as role models, as sources of information about the hidden codes of schools, as advisers about difficult situations, and in some cases, as advocates for students. When such mentors work within a supportive institutional structure that includes orientation, training, and ongoing supervision, and when they learn certain effective behaviors (consistency, dependability, developing trust before trying to change students' behavior), there is good evidence that they are effective in improving school attendance and performance and in reducing self-destructive behavior in students, such as drug and alcohol use and violence (Sipe 1996). Unfortunately, it has often been difficult to find enough appropriate mentors, and the more usual practice of using untrained volunteers as "buddies" is not likely to be as effective.

The Overall Culture of the School

The many policies I have discussed in this section address forthrightly some sources of racial gaps in schools by focusing explicitly on racial and ethnic issues. They provide a vast portfolio of race-conscious rather than "colorblind" possibilities for schools to consider as they confront inequalities in schooling outcomes. At the same time, many of these policies can be understood as racially specific versions of more general precepts about schools. Some of them, like those involving classroom observations and forms of culturally relevant pedagogy, are extensions of efforts to move away from behaviorist pedagogies and toward more student-centered, caring, and "balanced" pedagogy—specifically by rejecting the practices of behaviorist approaches. Others are efforts to personalize schools and support students, consistent with the conclusions in chapter 2, which found such efforts to be effective in promoting progress through schooling. Similarly, evidence from the National Longitudinal Study of Adolescent Health indicates that students in schools that foster feelings of social connectedness and being cared for by teachers and peers are less likely to experience emotional distress or to engage in self-destructive behavior like using alcohol and drugs, engaging in violent or deviant behavior, or becoming pregnant (Resnick et al. 1997)—behaviors that reflect student connectedness to schooling. So it is important to get not only approaches to instruction right but approaches to the overall culture of the school right as well—that is, to develop practices that promote the ability of students not only to construct meaning in their academic coursework but also to construct and reconstruct their identity, their future, and the role of schooling in their future. Within this general approach, the racially specific practices I have outlined here can be understood as particularly race-conscious versions of more general recommendations applicable to all students.

THE SCHOOL AS A LEARNING COMMUNITY: THE COLLECTIVE NATURE OF SCHOOL RESOURCES

Evidently, as the natural experiments described earlier in this chapter reveal, simple infusions of money are not sufficient to reform low-performing schools. In too many of these programs, schools have simply wasted new resources, sometimes failing to develop coherent or effective plans, sometimes failing to follow the plans they have devised, and sometimes failing to maintain changes over time. In other cases, districts have been barriers to effective spending. But some schools have managed to use new resources to good advantage, so the question becomes: what conditions or "pre-reforms" are necessary if additional funding and other resources are to make a difference to student outcomes?

A great deal of evidence suggests that schools need to be fundamentally reorganized in order to make *any* decisions at all, and that many schools held up as exemplars have changed in roughly the same ways. In the conventional model of organization, whether of businesses or schools, a leader—a CEO or principal—holds control and authority and makes most decisions. Within conventional schools, teachers are relatively isolated in their classrooms and participate little in school decisionmaking. They receive their marching orders from the principal and from district and state (and increasingly federal) standards; in extreme cases of scripted curricula, they simply do what the teacher's manual tells them to do. This top-down approach to schooling, linked to Max Weber's model of bureaucratic rationality, emerged from the administrative "progressives" of the period after 1900; their emphasis on rationality, efficiency, and control has not been explicitly challenged until the last few decades.

Characteristics of the School as Learning Community

An alternative approach goes by different names, though these various ways of describing schools (and businesses) have elements in common. One vision, focusing on the nature of leadership, clarifies that leadership may be distributed in many ways rather than following the conventional top-down model, with decisions tightly controlled by the principal (Spillane 2006; Spillane, Halvorson, and Diamond 2001). When leadership is distributed, administrators share decisionmaking power with many other participants; teachers play active leadership roles as members or heads of committees that make crucial decisions about curriculum, budget, and other policies; parents and students have roles in ongoing decisionmaking as well. Leadership may be distributed in many different ways, with different divisions of labor, parallel performance, and coperformance (including the special case of multiple principals, described by Grubb and Flessa 2006). The alternative to the conventional Weberian hierarchy is not a different fixed approach, but rather one that varies with the conditions of schools and even departments.

A similar vision stresses the nature of relationships within schools. The authors of *The New Accountability* found that schools that were most successful in responding to *external* accountability—standards imposed by state and federal governments—were those that had developed *internal* accountability, defined as individual responsibility among participants; a sense of collective responsibility among teachers, administrators, students, and parents; and rules and incentives that constituted the formal accountability system within the school. The principal is crucial in transforming a school from a conventional approach to one with internal accountability, though at the end of the process decisionmaking and responsibility are widely distributed rather than tightly held by that principal.[21] This approach therefore requires strong leadership, not in the sense of an autocratic principal but in the sense of a leader who can motivate teachers, guide the faculty's collective interpretation of external demands, help departments figure out how to meet the course demands of state standards, and figure out what to do with students at risk of not meeting standards. This approach is also consistent with the importance of trust in schools and with the need to establish better personal relations in place of the hostile relationships often visible particularly in urban schools (Payne 1997; Payne and Kaba 2001). Finally, the complex responsibilities of internal accountability provide an answer to how distributed leadership can work in schools that are often described as "loosely coupled"—that is, they have weak hierarchical controls because many teachers and other adults can do as they like once the classroom door is closed. Instead, schools with internal accountability have given up the false freedom of loose coupling for a set of interrelated responsibilities developed, not through "tight coupling" and hierarchical controls, but through collective responsibilities for students.

Brian Rowan and his colleagues (Rowan 1990; Miller and Rowan 2006) have referred to this vision of schools as "organic management," using the terminology from a broader organizational literature.[22] Still others have called this kind of school a "professional learning community," a term in widespread circulation that stresses collaborative decisionmaking among communities of teachers that are focused on student learning and experimenting when current practices do not work (Dufour, Eaker, and Karhanek 2004; McLaughlin and Talbert 2006). Within the business community, the same basic approach—with greater reliance on the decisions of frontline workers—has been called "high-involvement management" to distinguish it from conventional firms where workers have little involvement in decisions (Lawler 1998). Many schools that have successfully reformed themselves and many schools that have high-poverty students but whose successful outcomes have "beaten the odds" describe decisionmaking processes that are consistent with distributed leadership and internal accountability.[23] Such reorganization can also apply to departments within a school, as in the case of the innovative math department in Railside School (Boaler and Staples 2008) or the math department profiled in Gutierrez (2000).

To be sure, many reform efforts now require that school-site councils make decisions or that decisions be made through equivalent processes that reflect distributed decisionmaking. These include NCLB school plans (and Title I plans before that), the school planning processes developed when districts move to school-site budgeting, and many planning mechanisms for state programs, including the California programs for low-performing schools outlined earlier. But where collective decisionmaking is treated as a requirement to be complied with—or "a document for getting money from the state" (Timar and Kim 2008)—it may not change the top-down decisionmaking of conventional hierarchical schools; this is the familiar case of school committees rubber-stamping the principal's recommendations. So imperatives for reorganization such as a top-down requirement for collective decisionmaking are unlikely to work because the bonds of internal alignment are missing. Instead, more subtle approaches to capacity-building may be necessary.

Finally, there is a funding corollary of the school as the unit of reform. If schools are responsible for effectiveness under state and federal accountability standards, and if schools must have responsibility for determining effective resources, then they clearly need control over funding, as in school-based budgeting described in chapter 10. Schools that cannot control funding and other resources (competent teachers, materials and textbooks, professional development) cannot make the collective decisions that lead to effectiveness.

Why Collective Decisionmaking Works

But *why* should schools as learning communities be more effective than those that follow the top-down model? One answer stems from improved approaches to school resources, which show that effective resources are most often collective. Simple resources need not rely on collective decisions: a principal (or district administrator, or state policymaker) with enough money can decide unilaterally to reduce class size, hire better-credentialed teachers, increase teacher salaries, increase spending on books and materials, or buy new computers. Conversely, districts can unilaterally make decisions to increase or decrease simple resources, to allocate teachers and materials to schools, or to establish salary schedules based on conventional practices.

But compound resources by definition require decisions about two or more resources simultaneously and are therefore likely to require cooperation from several decisionmaking sources: class size reduction (a simple resource relying on district or state decisions) *plus* changes in teaching practices (which require teacher cooperation and professional development); computers *plus* changes in teaching (again, teacher cooperation is necessary) *plus* regular upkeep and maintenance (another simple resource); or a change in tracking practices, including the development of theme-based pathways (which requires the participation of many teachers). Individual teachers can undertake some changes in complex resources in their own classrooms, such as pedagogical improvements, but then approaches to instruction will be inconsistent among classes and the effects will be limited. Developing more consistent pedagogical approaches requires cooperation among teachers (especially what educators call "buy-in" to, or agreement with, the new approach) and in turn "new" forms of staff development that again involve the school as a community of teachers-as-learners rather than bringing in outside speakers (Cohen and Hill 2001; Little 2006).

Similarly, most examples of culturally responsive pedagogy and different approaches to multicultural education seem to have been developed by individual teachers changing their own classrooms, but these race-conscious practices cannot change the culture of the school—especially high schools, where students meet many teachers each day—unless a majority of the teachers undertake them. The various efforts to confront racial and ethnic issues head on, presented in the previous section, are yet other examples of complex and abstract resources that require consistency among teachers to be effective; race talk and courageous conversations cannot be carried out in isolated classrooms, and inconsistent adoption of culturally relevant pedagogies (or adoption only by some African American and Latino teachers) will doom them to marginal status.

Abstract resources almost by definition require a community of practice, since they are often embedded in the web of personal relationships within a school. Improving school climate (including the overall effects of a school's attendance rate and proportion of low-income students) requires school-wide effort, as does developing a culture of college-going. The development of trust, internal alignment, and better personal relationships must by definition involve the majority of teachers and administrators; the coherence of the curriculum stressed in research on Chicago schools, for example, required that teachers and administrators take consistent approaches to curriculum and pedagogy rather than wildly varying approaches in different little programs. The "new" approach to professional development—a practice usually invoked as a necessary corollary of virtually any reform—requires that teachers work together in a community of practice within a school over relatively long periods of time (Cohen and Hill 2001; Little 2006). This is quite different from the "old" approach, in which individual teachers attend workshops and conferences and accumulate academic credits for individual merit pay increases—the "Friday afternoon one-shot," widely regarded as ineffective. And the resource of stability—one that is measured imperfectly in the NELS88 data by the mobility of students, leaving out the instability of teachers, principals, district officials, and policies—requires so many different kinds of coordination that it is difficult to know how to develop this crucial element.

If most resources aside from simple resources are collective, then the old model of top-down management cannot work because it cannot assure teacher cooperation, consistent adoption, or "buy-in," the mantra of most teachers and principals. If complex practices need to be relatively consistent across teachers before they are effective, then the old model of isolated teachers in "egg-crate" classrooms, independent of one another, cannot work effectively because it cannot create consistency and coherence across teachers. Since effective complex resources include innovative and constructivist approaches to teaching, the tactic of having isolated instructors use "teacher-proof" curricula—scripted and semiscripted curricula that any idiot can deliver—cannot work; only collective forms of professional development can move teachers toward the instructional expertise required. If at least some important school resources are abstract, embedded in a web of personal relationships within the school, then again, a model built on isolated teachers and administrators who are independent of and aloof from teachers cannot work. Only a high school with distributed leadership and internal alignment can construct the kinds of collective school resources that prove to be most effective in promoting both learning and progress through high school. So the expanded approach to resources of the improved school finance proves to be consistent with the new approaches to school structure and governance developed in the last decade or two. A prerequisite to making schools more effective—or to using money to make schools more effective—is therefore reorganizing them to be more collegial and democratic.

We now have a more complete conception of what it means to build capacity in a school in order to meet the demands of external accountability or the demands of parents and students for high-quality schooling. Capacity has several elements: an explicit focus on instruction, especially on teacher control and on developing constructivist or balanced approaches to teaching; recognition of and support for the many other compound, complex, and abstract resources that improve student outcomes of several kinds; and the ability to organize schools with distributed leadership and internal accountability, in place of the conventional organization emerging from administrative progressivism. When I turn in the next chapter to examine the district, state, and federal policies that might enhance school effectiveness, I concentrate on the policies that can enhance capacity in this specific sense.

Finally, the importance of collective decisionmaking adds another explanation for why the myth of money so often proves wrong—why large sums of money can be spent (as in the various California programs and in Chicago) without much effect on the average. In schools that are not organized for collective decisionmaking and coherent planning, additional money is likely to be frittered away: plans are either incoherent or not followed, or they fail to mobilize effective resources, or other problems like instability undermine reforms. Those schools that have begun reform and have organized themselves into learning communities may be able to make progress with such infusions of money, but most schools cannot. And so money alone proves not to be a solution for many low-performing schools, despite the best of intentions.

Chapter 10

Supporting the Improved School Finance: District, State, and Federal Roles

IN THE PREVIOUS chapter, I focused on schools as the basic unit of reform, partly because many effective resources must be developed at the school level. But schools exist within districts, districts within states, and states within a federal government increasingly determined to shape education according to its own ideology. To be effective the principles of the improved school finance must extend to district, state, and federal policy as well. Otherwise, schools will all too often find their efforts at capacity-building undermined by district or state fiat, by the instability of teacher and principal turnover they cannot control, or by allocations of funds—necessary, if not sufficient—that are inadequate to building the capacity necessary at the school level. Finally, schools cannot create all the conditions for equity on their own, since many sources of inequality are beyond their control: variation in funding as well as educational needs among schools within districts; the imposition of ineffective curricula in many districts and states; transitions among schools that create bursts of inequality in the trajectory of students' careers; variation in funding (as well as educational needs) among districts within states, the focus of equalization efforts back to the 1930s; variation in the quality of teachers, as teachers move among districts; the variation in funding among states, which is responsible for a large fraction of funding inequality but is totally neglected. For schools to develop the resources necessary for effectiveness and equity, there needs to be a "consistency agenda" of supportive district, state, and federal policies that sustain these school efforts.[1]

In focusing on these other levels of policymaking and influence, several principles from improved approaches to school resources are crucial:

- A shift is necessary from a concern exclusively with money and simple resources to a greater concern with capacity-building. This requires greater attention to the wide variety of compound, complex, and abstract resources that affect multiple outcomes. There is still, of course, a need for funding, and I outline funding approaches that districts and states could take that would support school resource decisions. But coming up with the "right" funding formula is not the heart of the matter since money, always necessary but not sufficient (NBNS), still needs to be translated into effective resources.

- Capacity-building requires support for the reorganization of schools. Distributed leadership and internal accountability seem to be crucial preconditions for developing resources. Furthermore, by extension, reorganization of districts, states, and even the federal government may be necessary to support local schools.

- Dynamic as well as static (or cross-sectional) aspects of inequality require attention, since inequalities among students at any point are the product of influences over all prior grades. For example, efforts by half the states to require high school exit exams as a way to motivate students and schools to improve come much too late, since many of the conditions that lead to failure during high school are set much earlier in a student's trajectory; a more effective state policy would identify *and correct* those policies from the elementary grades on that contribute to diverging performance.

The specific policies generated by these concerns will vary, just as district, state, and federal roles now vary in how they undermine (or support) the potential for school capacity-building. But if a single set of principles drawn from the improved school finance could begin to reshape policy, then the consistency necessary for supporting capacity-building at the school level could emerge from the current fog of concerns driven largely by the "old" school finance.

THE ROLES OF THE DISTRICT: THE VARIETIES OF INFLUENCE

Before 1900, school districts were important because they had taxing authority: they could raise money—the resource that seemed in shortest supply—as public education expanded enormously in its earliest days. But districts emerged from the period after 1900 with a larger set of responsibilities, generally focused on administrative and managerial roles and driven by concerns about efficiency, uniformity, standardization, and the elimination of waste—including the abolition of favoritism and graft.[2] These concerns continued to dominate districts throughout the twentieth century, though they were increasingly eclipsed by the rise of state governments as providers of funding, partly in response to demands to equalize resources among districts and to standardize teacher credentials, graduation requirements, textbook requirements, and other inputs to education. By 1983, when *A Nation at Risk* ushered in the "modern" era of school reform, the locus of policy initiatives had shifted to the states, and the dominant response to this particular "crisis" was a set of *state* responses, like increasing graduation requirements and creating new forms of accountability for students and teachers.

Despite the developing effects of state policy, districts have substantial power to promote *or* impede reforms. New interest has developed in understanding districts that appear successful and in replicating their practices. From the perspective of the improved school finance, four issues in district policy are particularly important: the role of the district in supporting schools rather than wasting resources; the role of districts in capacity-building; the increasing use of school-based budgeting, a particular form of district support for schools; and the potential role of districts in enhancing dynamic equity. Like the reorganization of schools, the reorganization of districts seems to be a prerequisite for capacity-building.

Districts, School Support, and Waste

In the theory of waste developed in chapter 1, several sources of waste arise from conflicts or inconsistencies between schools and districts. Districts often buy books and materials that schools do not use; they are often responsible for traditional but ineffective forms of staff development imposed on schools but not requested by them; and they often begin initiatives for purely symbolic purposes or initiate changes that are not completed because of turnover in superintendents, another reform initiative, or lack of oversight. Much of the waste that emerged in California's effort to help low-performing schools came from conflicts between district decisions and schools when districts "volunteered" schools that were unready for reform; imposed district requirements for curricula, teacher and staff hiring, and the use of consultants; or failed to provide the additional funding required by the state. Some of the lackluster results of Chicago's devolution of funding to the school level was due to the instability of the leadership in many schools, to extreme forms of governance in which either the principal or the site council dominated decisions, and to inattention to improving classroom instruction—all dimensions of school performance that the district might have anticipated and corrected if it had not played such a hands-off role. Indeed, districts often do not know how much they are spending in specific schools and on particular programs, much less how to spend money well (Roza and Hill 2006); if districts do not know about spending and resources, it is difficult to know how principals could learn enough about them to allocate resources more effectively.

Similarly, many districts have done little to help schools promote dynamic equity.[3] The district where Lakelands and Hillcrest are located had required its schools to develop IEPs for students retained in grade, and this stimulated some principals to think about what to do for them over time, but the district provided no financial support, very little staff development, and no technical assistance. In fact, the district created some barriers to the Learning Center in Hillcrest because it required loosening district constraints on special ed teachers who worked with students not adjudicated as special ed, something the district did not allow. The San Sebastian, Littlefield, Bellson, and Bayside Districts were alert to the need for school improvements, but they developed no policies to help their schools. In the extreme case of Grossmont, the district imposed requirements on all schools to use scripted programs in both English and math. Such approaches violate all the precepts for engagement and motivation among students and are contrary to findings about positive effects of innovative teaching and teachers' control of their instruction.

Only a few districts were more helpful. Taylor USD, where Horace Middle School and Taylor High School are located, represented the more active end of the district spectrum. That district was trying to promote differentiated instruction and had supported professional development for this effort, which represented a shift in pedagogical practices for all students, not the adoption of isolated interventions without enhancing teacher capacity. The district had adopted the DiME (Diversity in Mathematics Education) program since it had identified serious problems in algebra, as well as the Mathematics Assessment Collaborative (MAC) program from the Noyce Foundation and Guided Language and Development (GLAD), with some district GLAD training and demonstrations. In fourth and fifth grades, teachers were being released to develop a consistent science curriculum—the only example in our small sample of a district or school trying to improve a subject other than math or English. The district was piloting Read 180 in one middle school and Corrective Reading in another; it had also provided libraries and literacy intervention coaches in every school. In addition, the district had invested in a program called Datawise to enable teachers to keep track of students; all schools had an "assessment wall" depicting every student by grade and by test score so that those who were behind were immediately visible. Finally, the process of selecting interventions had been more democratic than the top-down mandates in most districts. The district had avoided scripted and semiscripted curricula because "teachers wouldn't stand for it." The process of selecting DiME had involved convening all math teachers, and the piloting of alternative middle-school reading programs had also included school participation in the final choice.

In an intermediate case, the Charterhouse EMO (educational management organization) overseeing two schools served the role of a district. It stressed direct instruction (but not in scripted forms), focused on preparation for college for all students, provided a great deal of staff development, created the conditions for stability of teachers and students, and was therefore selected by low-income parents who were particularly concerned abut their children's education. But the EMO provided little specific guidance on helping underperforming students, and individual schools retained the choice of intervention programs and mechanisms of assessment and correction.

In examining effective and high-performing districts, some of these same policies emerge.[4] Three apparently high-performing districts in California (Elk Grove, Oak Grove, and Rowland) developed a balance between centralized policies and decentralized or school control—the district version of distributed leadership, with a role for schools to play in district decisionmaking (as in Taylor USD and in contrast to Grossmont's top-down imposition). They also developed processes that allowed for shared learning among schools. Similarly, in Long Beach, a district with a consistent reputation for innovation, schools received more authority under the last few superintendents, and the district developed a balance between a top-down and a bottom-up approach. The district has engaged in a wider discussion of issues, also an element of distributed leadership, and it developed a series of interventions— a K–3 reading initiative, an eighth-grade initiative, and a high school program for ninth-graders testing below grade level—using a process of piloting changes and consulting with stakeholders, including schools, before enacting reforms. The Long Beach district also brought together all members of the community and its organizations, developing the kind of "civic capacity" in which all community organizations support the public schools.[5] In examining areas outside of California, districts able to respond to state policies depend on their capacity to learn new policy ideas, which in turn depends on relations of trust and collaboration within a district (sometimes described explicitly as a learning community at the district level) and on district willingness to engage in problem-solving rather than controlling power. Similarly, a study of district responses to state accountability found that "enterprising districts" worked more actively with schools, got to know individual schools well enough to understand their strengths and weaknesses, and again served as problem-solvers; "slacking" districts used the same approaches for all schools—the dreaded "one size fits all."[6]

This evidence from districts with strong reputations and evidence of success makes clear the importance of "distributed leadership" at the district level—or a willingness to share decisionmaking with schools rather than have the top-down control derived from administrative progressivism. The hope is that such an approach can actively support schools as they develop their own plans and strategies for enhancing effective resources. This could avoid the conflict and outright waste that often results from troubled relationships between districts and schools.

Reformed Districts and Capacity-Building

Other elements of the improved school finance also emerge from these case studies. The analysis of Elk Grove, Oak Grove, and Rowland uncovered the importance of districts having a coherent strategy for maintaining focus on instructional improvement, not administrative issues; these districts show how district officials as well as principals can be instructional leaders. These districts also emphasize building capacity at the school level, especially through professional development to enhance the capabilities of teachers. All three of these high-performing California districts defined it as a district responsibility to create programs so that interventions would be consistent among schools; these programs were generally focused on developing comprehensive teaching strategies to move more students toward proficiency rather than on adopting drill-oriented curricula off the shelf or on utilizing random and fragmented interventions.

Long Beach has had the advantage of stability in superintendents, an abstract resource important at many levels. That district also followed a practice of rotating principals and administrators among positions every five years or so to enable them to develop a *district*wide perspective—a parallel practice in a way to creating teacher-leaders at the school level who can become school leaders. San Diego also focused on instructional capacity through personnel policies, professional development, the development of instructional leaders in all schools, and a process of shared expertise. The district developed its own balanced literacy approach, avoiding the swings in state policy between phonics and whole language. District leaders were clear that restructuring schools—especially high schools—might help, but that restructuring would not be a substitute for improving instruction. (This policy is consistent with the results for differentiated resources discussed in chapter 2: restructuring may enhance progress, but instructional improvements are necessary to enhance learning.) Interestingly, the schools that were the most bureaucratically organized and offered the fewest opportunities for collaboration had the most difficulty using new resources from the district. This suggests again that reform is more likely when both schools and districts have shifted to less bureaucratic, more collegial, and more distributed forms of interaction. Districts that forgot the limitations of conventional top-down policies did not seem to be as effective: many schools resisted top-down high school reforms, and the district found itself looking for more collaborative approaches. Finally, analyses of other districts outside of California have confirmed many of these findings: successful districts focus on instruction and on developing their own role of guiding and supporting instructional improvements at the school level.[7]

It seems especially important for districts to support schools with certain resources, especially abstract resources. Stability is one such resource: districts sometimes contribute to instability by rotating principals every two years, for example, or by promoting assistant principals into open principal positions (often in the most difficult schools) after a year or two. Teacher assignment policies, like leadership policies, also may contribute to instability if teachers move in search of better working conditions within the district. The incoherence of a school's programs may also be partly due to district policy when districts require schools to develop many little add-on programs without any thought to the coherence of the school as a whole (Newmann et al. 2001); such a "Christmas tree" approach (bright shiny baubles hanging on rotten branches) is surely less effective than using the same money to strengthen basic instructional capacity, leadership abilities, and the reorganization of a school into a more collegial learning community.

Another tactic in a few large urban districts—including Miami, New York, and Charlotte-Mecklenburg—has been to develop "zones," or "districts-within-districts," where consistently low-performing schools are grouped for special treatment. In Miami, these schools receive additional district support, including school observations; additional resources, including a longer day and year; specific interventions aimed at reading and math; additional teacher training; instructional coaches; mentors for inexperienced principals; and a 20 percent pay raise for teachers (Gewertz 2007). The Miami zone approach concentrates on a series of resources that are arguably effective (perhaps with the exception of a longer day and year), given the findings of chapter 2, rather than on some of the conventional practices that are expensive but ineffective, like class size reduction and conventional staff development. In many ways, the Miami zone approach looks similar to the California model of providing additional funding with planning requirements to low-performing schools—except that the Miami approach specifies the capacity-building resources that zone schools must adopt, while the California model and its Chicago variant allowed schools to spend money on a variety of ineffective resources and to focus on goals other than instructional improvement.[8]

Overall, there are many similarities between these apparently successful districts and schools that operate in more distributed ways. These districts focus on improved instruction, emphasize capacity-building for teachers and principals, promote more constructivist or balanced teaching approaches, develop consistent interventions, balance district and school policymaking, and attempt to operate in more collegial ways. To be sure, it has not been "proven" that reorganizing districts will lead to improved decision-making and better use of resources (including better use of any additional funding, as in the Chicago case). But there is substantial evidence that schools and districts organized in ways consistent with distributed leadership, collective decisionmaking, and internal accountability are better able to make decisions and respond to external pressures. Conversely, schools and districts that operate in traditional ways seem to have difficulty with these reforms.

School-Based Budgeting

One specific way in which some districts have supported the development of school policies is by giving schools more responsibility for decisionmaking over the allocation of funds. These efforts, usually known as school-based budgeting (SBB), involve sending a certain fraction of district revenue to schools to spend as they see fit.[9] Such efforts follow the logic that schools themselves must be able to determine how money is spent and what resources are developed if they are to be responsible for improving learning. Many (but not all) districts that have adopted SBB have also used weighted student formulas in allocating funds: schools with higher proportions of low-income students, English learners, and special education students receive more money. Often there are different weights for different levels of education as well, and sometimes for specific programs like vocational education or gifted and talented programs. (The weights vary among districts, and it seems that determining weights is largely a political decision rather than one based on cost or effectiveness data, except perhaps in the case of special education.) One of the main concerns that SBB attempts to address is equity among schools, since conventional teacher allocation policies usually lead to experienced and well-paid teachers being concentrated in schools with more white and middle-class students. Indeed, SBB, especially in conjunction with weighted student formulas, has been shown to improve the equity of funding per student among schools.[10]

School-based budgeting is sometimes conflated with school-based management, a reform whereby control over the educational program is handed over by the district to the school. School-based management may or may not be combined with school-based budgeting and school control of resources. However, if school-based management is not combined with school-based budgeting, schools have discretion over less than 20 percent of their budget, and their ability to make substantial changes is correspondingly limited (Odden and Busch 1998, 224).

From the perspective of the improved school finance, SBB is potentially important not only for its equity effects but also because it provides schools with new incentives to learn how to become more effective. Under conventional budgeting, schools typically receive a number of teachers and staff based on their enrollments, books and materials, services for upkeep and maintenance, and perhaps a small discretionary fund for the principal to use for emergencies, field trips, or other "frills." There is little incentive for principals or school councils to think about the conversion of money into resources because they do not have enough control over either their funding or their resources, and indeed most school-level administrators seem to spend relatively little time worrying about the effectiveness of the resources at their disposal (Boyd and Hartman 1988).

But school-based budgeting gives new responsibilities to principals, and usually to school-site councils, to make resource decisions with more substantial sums of money. Therefore, a new incentive develops among those most involved with a school to think about the resources they might want and how to use their available funds to create those resources. Where principals have more say over their budgets, they become increasingly skilled at responding to incentives. In England, for example, heads of grant-maintained (GM) schools allocate resources subject only to a board of governors and the national curriculum; under these conditions, most heads of GM schools have become adept at making rational resource decisions (Finkelstein and Grubb 2000). From the perspective of the improved school finance, the real promise of SBB is that it might lead principals and other participants in school-level planning to become more expert at diagnosing educational problems, determining effective ways of resolving them, and then—since they have the funding to do so—implementing real solutions.

Because principals are not normally prepared to engage in resource decisions, districts have devoted some effort—though rarely enough, given the magnitude of the task—to supporting them with professional development geared to helping them come up with instructional plans for spending the funds they receive.[11] Typically schools must undergo a planning process before spending these resources; often district-established priorities lead to a set of school-specific activities, which in turn determine how the money is spent. The content of this professional development, however, is unclear. In some districts, it seems to be confined to technical details about how to complete spreadsheets rather than focused on preparing principals and site councils to think more deeply about effective resources and their relationship to money. Other districts have worked harder to get principals and school-site councils to learn about the effectiveness of different resources, treating budgeting as a stimulus to develop the most effective resources rather than as a computer programming activity. Unfortunately, there is not yet much analysis of how planning processes work, though an examination of New York City's Performance Driven Budgeting (PDB) initiative revealed that low-performing schools whose principals and teachers lacked knowledge and experience and suffered from instability due to staff turnover have had limited capacity to implement PDB (Siegel and Fruchter 2002). However, steady improvements in such procedures, technical assistance to principals and school budget committees, and incorporation into educational administration programs could result in school-site educators being better able to make effective resource decisions.

So school-based budgeting, ideally with weighted student formulas, provides a way for funding arrangements to support schools as the unit of reform. But once again, money is not enough: new patterns of funding need to be accompanied by the preparation of principals and school-site councils to use their resources wisely. And then districts need to make sure that they support schools in their instructional and budgetary decisions—rather than impeding decisions by slow implementation, contrary decisions, incompetent administration, or any of the other sources of waste identified in chapter 1. With discretionary funding, increased expertise, and district support, principals and schools could then make better decisions about effective resources.

Smoothing Transitions

Finally, districts as well as schools need to consider the diverging trajectories of students, as illustrated in figure 6.1, particularly because much of this divergence cannot be resolved by schools but must be addressed by schools acting collaboratively—under the guidance of a district, for example. A first problem is to diagnose why learning outcomes tend to diverge. If the problem is, as some researchers have found, differential summer effects, then only year-round schools or serious summer school can correct the problem. If, however, the culprits are unequal resources (and especially the resource of qualified teachers and competent principals, who tend to cluster in high-SES schools), then reallocation of resources—for example, through weighted student formulas—may be the answer. If the reinforcing effects of family background are to blame, then districts may need to explore the variety of overtly compensatory programs—early childhood education, parent education and two-generation literacy programs, carefully constructed after-school and summer programs, and other enrichment activities within schools. So far districts have played little role in encouraging more race-conscious policies like those outlined in chapter 9, though districts with pronounced racial gaps in learning and student progress could support schools both by helping diagnose the role of race and ethnicity and then by supporting potential correctives.

Districts could use any of several ways to help with transitions. Teachers could be prepared to continue teaching basic skills even if they are teaching at higher levels; for example, the "fourth-grade slump" that occurs when some students have not mastered basic reading and arithmetic skills could be addressed with differentiated instruction from upper-elementary teachers who reteach basic skills to students who need them.[12] An alternative, based on the Finland approach, is to use specially trained aides to teach basic skills, working closely with teachers rather than remaining independent of the regular classroom, as in the tutoring and after-school programs described in chapter 8. Other interventions may also be necessary, like the intense instruction of Reading Recovery. Some districts have created Ninth Grade Academies, or "houses," which offer more intensive basic skills instruction along with conventional high school coursework so that ninth-graders can catch up while still making progress in high school. The Talent Development High School, with its ninth-grade Success Academy, has been able to increase attendance and credits earned, though the effects on math scores were slight and the effects on reading scores insignificant (Kemple, Herlihy, and Smith 2005). Other transitional academies or houses might also be created for the middle school, both to provide basic skills instruction for students who need it and to introduce former elementary school students to the different structures of the middle school, with multiple teachers covering distinct subjects and sometimes with electives to consider.

At the most ambitious level, districts could create an overall developmental framework to guide students through the transitions they face during their years in the K–12 system. This idea originated with Valencia Community College in Florida, which devised a five-part LifeMap program ("Life's a trip—you'll need directions!") to confront the problem of students dropping out of the college: (1) transition to college, or the preparation individuals do before they get to Valencia; (2) introduction to college in the first fifteen credit hours, when the college assists students both in curriculum choices, including those related to life goals and career goals, and in bolstering academic skills as needed; (3) progression toward the degree, when students accumulate the credits necessary for the options they have chosen or adjust goals as necessary; (4) graduation transition, as students approach graduation and start making plans for subsequent transfer or employment; and (5) lifelong learning—students learn about the continuing process of evaluating options, setting goals, and upgrading their capacities through various forms of postcollege education.[13] The LifeMap program provides, at a glance, many stages of educational development, a vision of the final goal to motivate students through these stages, and a variety of stage-appropriate support. Finally, the Valencia model integrates both academic components and non-academic student services.

Applied to the high school, this approach might include stages for (1) eighth-grade preparation, including basic skill development as necessary to pass high school diagnostic exams; (2) ninth-grade understanding of high school options and requirements for subsequent education and employment, setting preliminary life and career goals, and catching up on necessary basic skills; (3) tenth- and eleventh-grade monitoring of courses and credits for graduation and post–high school options, plus college activities (trips, SAT preparation) as appropriate; (4) a twelfth-grade stage of thinking about life after high school, applying to college and/or exploring employment options, completing graduation requirements, and assessing options in conjunction with local colleges and universities; (5) preparing for the next activity, whether further education, employment, or some combination of the two, and participating in "bridge" programs as necessary (Grubb 2008d). Similar developmental plans for the transition from elementary school to middle school, and for the transition from the family and early childhood education into elementary school, could help to moderate the bursts of inequality that seem to affect the trajectory through schools.

There are many ways, then, in which districts could support schools in their efforts to follow the improved school finance. To do this, districts need to understand what resources are effective under specific conditions and which are likely to be ineffective. Districts could provide schools with a better understanding of their options since there are (at least for large districts) economies of scale in mastering all the complex and contentious evidence about "what works." Districts may also need to be reorganized in the same way schools are as they shift toward distributed leadership and internal accountability, especially in order to understand the differing needs of schools, to gain their trust, and to develop more tailored ways of supporting schools with different needs.

THE ROLE OF THE STATE: EXPERIMENTS WITH CAPACITY-BUILDING

State influences on education have become increasingly powerful, and not simply because states now contribute so much funding (47 percent) to K–12 schools, compared to 44 percent from local sources. Over time, states have played an increasingly important role in regulating their school systems—through teacher and principal credentialing, the establishment of graduation requirements, the development of state standards for what is to be taught, sometimes textbook requirements, and most recently the development of accountability mechanisms to measure the achievement of individual students and schools. With increased state funding and regulation, states could play an active role in supporting schools—and then districts—that are trying to move toward an improved approach to school resources.

Unfortunately, most state policies are still wedded to the "old" school finance and related forms of regulation. Perhaps the best illustration is the discussion around school funding itself, which is largely about the amounts and distribution of funds to local districts and the complexities of funding formulas, what the lawyers behind the *Serrano* case called the "minutiae" of school reform (Coons, Clune, and Sugarman 1970, 65). Rarely do these discussions move from the narrative of money to the range of effective resources; at best, they focus on simple resources, but even then the presumption is typically that districts will decide how state funding should best be spent, and the state will play little role in these decisions. Similarly, with some important exceptions discussed shortly, the logic of accountability measures has been that states will hold schools and districts accountable for outcomes but will not give any guidance for attaining these outcomes.

Categorical Grants

A partial exception to the single-minded focus on money has been the proliferation of categorical grants, which, unlike general-purpose funding, provide revenues to districts with strings attached—requirements that funds be spent for books, or for computers, or for staff development. Two dangers loom in this situation. The most obvious is that categorical grants usually provide a simple resource, and the compound or complex nature of resources is overlooked. Categorical funds for computers and computer-aided instruction provide one common example: schools get state funding for computers but not for professional development so that teachers can use the equipment, nor for maintenance so the computers will continue working; the result is that all too often this resource goes unused. California's class size reduction effort provides another example: most districts have made no attempt to maintain the quality of instructors, offered no professional development to ensure that teachers will teach differently in smaller classes, and provided no additional classroom space, so this effort has led to little general improvement.

The second problem is that categorical funds make coherent instructional and fiscal planning difficult. The usual tendency is for schools to spend a grant in the way it is earmarked—on books, on computers, on staff development—without considering how the school is already spending other resources. This is often a recipe for waste if the most pressing needs in a school are not for computers, or to reduce class sizes, or to update old forms of staff development. The alternative is to devise a coherent plan for instructional improvement, concentrating on the full range of resources that are most effective, and then direct funding to enhance these resources. With categorical funding, this can be accomplished through a technique sometimes referred to as "one-pot budgeting": all resources are conceptually thrown into one virtual pot, the most highly constrained funds are first used on allowable resources in the instructional plan, and then increasingly less constrained resources are used.

Of course, when funding comes from a complex of categorical grants

(and sometimes from private or foundation grants as well), it may be difficult to juggle all these sources of money, and few principals are trained to
think about budgeting and resource allocation in this way.[14] In addition, one-
pot budgeting requires that all resources be available at the point of the
budgeting process, which is most likely to happen when districts allocate
funds to schools all at once through school-based budgeting. Conversely, rational budgeting is almost impossible when schools receive resources in
dribbles throughout the school year. This happens, for example, when states
are late in developing their budgets, or when districts are late in acquiring
and allocating discretionary or categorical funding. Under these conditions,
schools often face the "use it or lose it" situation of having to spend a categorical grant late in the year, and this pressure almost always leads to ineffective spending. The wastefulness of categorical grants is thus one of the
factors leading at both the federal and state levels to periodic efforts to bun-
dle categorical grants into general-purpose unrestricted grants, on the explicit assumption that this will reduce waste and compliance costs and enhance the flexibility and effectiveness of spending. It is also likely to be the
reason behind the generally negative effects, noted in chapter 3, of a high
proportion of revenues from state and federal sources: despite increases in
spending per pupil, these grants almost always have more limitations than
local revenues.

Even when states try to enhance capacity at the district or school level,
they often do so in ways that amount to another set of categorical programs.
For example, as the result of a lawsuit spanning nearly two decades, New
York State recently announced an increase in funding of $225 million for
857 low-performing schools. However, these Contract for Excellence funds
are restricted to five kinds of spending: class size reduction, longer school
days, improved teacher and principal quality, middle and high school restructuring, and full-day prekindergarten and kindergarten. Funds used for
the first two of these categories might be wasted, since class size reduction
without complementary practices is likely to lead to the same kinds of
teaching in smaller classes. Similarly, additional time allocated to academic
work may not enhance engaged academic learning time, which is what matters for enhanced learning; increasing academic learning time also requires
changes in instructional methods and careful targeting of instruction on a
school's learning objectives (Cotton 1989). Once again, compound resources are necessary rather than the simple resources provided by the Contract for Excellence. The other three forms of spending allowed seem more
clearly related to capacity-building; furthermore, if used in conjunction
with funding for class size reduction and expanded academic time—for example, in professional development to enable teachers to make the greatest
use of smaller classes and expanded time—they might create the compound

resources that would be effective. But overall, the Contract for Excellence continues the pattern of categorical funding that has been so detrimental to spending money wisely.

Other Capacity-Building Efforts

A number of states have shifted to new forms of capacity-building, some of them focused on schools and some on districts. Not surprisingly, these have taken many forms, and they are too new for us to understand their effectiveness. But like the efforts of some exemplary districts, these state policies have the potential to enhance capacity in precisely the ways in which I have defined the term: to enhance ability to invest in effective resources and to change the organization of schools and districts. Six emerging practices in particular seem promising.[15]

1. A few states have established forms of professional development aimed at teachers. These include Kentucky's model of Highly Skilled Educators working with new teachers, as well as its new forms of teacher preparation in teacher academies, and California's Beginning Teacher Support Act (BTSA), which provides individual coaching for new teachers. The effectiveness of such efforts depends on careful implementation, and preliminary results suggest that Kentucky's Highly Skilled Educators model is effective only in conjunction with other reforms—another effort that is necessary but not sufficient (Legislative Research Commission 2006). But such efforts have the potential to enhance the quality of instruction and may encourage shifts to more balanced instruction and control over teaching.

2. Only a few states have provided additional funding for low-performing schools. California is one example with its II/USP program and HPSGP. Kentucky's Commonwealth School Improvement Fund (CSIF) also provides funding to targeted schools "in need of assistance" by supporting teachers and administrators in developing sound ways to improve instruction, replicating successful programs developed elsewhere, and encouraging cooperative instructional and managerial approaches to specific school problems— precisely the kinds of capacity-building that are most necessary. Unlike the largely negative evaluations of the California program, a preliminary evaluation of CSIF indicates that it has, both by itself and in conjunction with other reforms, improved test scores by small increments (Legislative Research Commission 2006, table 4.2).

3. Many states have provided external consultants to low-performing schools. These include Kentucky, with its Highly Skilled Educators; Texas, with its Campus Administrator Mentors Program and technical assistance providers; Tennessee, with the Exemplary Educators Program; and California, with external evaluators (really consultants) for low-performing schools. New Mexico provides technical assistance teams; Vermont similarly

forms action planning teams of five to eight members to examine low-performing schools. These teams collect data and propose "doable strategies with specific timelines and targets" that the school community must then approve. How well the external consultants and teams work is unclear. The results from California are not encouraging; however, careful training of these mentors, as Kentucky provides, and constant evaluation and improvement of these programs could make them more effective over time.

4. A number of states have adopted continuous improvement loops for low-performing schools, including Connecticut, Vermont, Tennessee, Texas, New Mexico, and Maryland. The details of these procedures vary, but as in the Connecticut Accountability for Learning Initiative (CALI), schools use data to analyze areas of concern, work to improve teaching and learning in the areas of greatest need, and evaluate the results as input into another round of analysis and improvement. In Texas, a semi-autonomous School Improvement Resource Center has been established to carry out this process; teams visit low-performing schools, conduct needs assessments, develop Campus Improvement Plans, assist in finding administrator-mentors and technical assistance providers, and continue to monitor schools and provide guidance.

5. Rather than (or in addition to) improvements focused on schools, several states have emphasized capacity-building for districts, including Connecticut, Alabama, Florida, Tennessee, and Massachusetts.[16] CALI, in Connecticut, assumes that "the district must take primary responsibility for monitoring the change process" and directs districts to collect information on three tiers of indicators as the basis for improvement efforts. Tennessee assesses the effectiveness of district offices with the Tennessee Comprehensive Systemwide Planning Process, designed to "build a professional learning community among [district] colleagues focused on improving instruction for all students," particularly since prior research with high-priority schools found "a lack of support and capacity building from the school system's central office to identified schools." Massachusetts has a system for identifying underperforming schools but then places the responsibility for improvement on districts.

6. Many states (like the districts mentioned in the previous section) have adopted a tiered system of identifying schools and districts in need of special attention and support. Again, these include Connecticut, Alabama, Florida, Tennessee, and Massachusetts. The practice of identifying low-performing or high-need schools is common, with the school identified receiving more technical assistance or (in California and Kentucky) substantial sums of additional funding, with various other conditions attached. In addition, six states have won waivers under No Child Left Behind for pilot projects in which they focus resources on schools in the worst shape and tailor solutions to the individual school's problems (Zuckerbrod 2008). Ohio has also

adopted a three-tiered system of identifying the districts in greatest need, and these districts receive more intensive coaching (but little beyond technical assistance). The tiering approach explicitly rejects the assumption that formula funding and equivalent attention to all schools ("one size fits all") is appropriate and instead invests more state efforts and resources for capacity-building in some districts than in others.

These efforts at capacity-building are quite different from the traditional state policies of increasing funding, categorical programs, and requirements.[17] Implicitly, they seem to assume that money does not matter that much. Instead, they focus more on the quality of instruction and, in some cases, on school and district leadership rather than on conventional credentials; they often use the expertise of experienced teachers and administrators to improve practices; and they promote highly rationalist practices—data analysis, reliance on methods shown to be effective, continuous improvement processes—in place of the haphazard and fragmented decisions that many schools and districts have made about capacity-building.

The effectiveness of such capacity-building is not yet clear, since these programs are too new to have been widely and carefully evaluated.[18] When states have little capacity to learn from their errors—as in California, which has ignored the negative results of class size reduction and its multibillion-dollar efforts to help low-performing schools—then state policy has little chance of supporting schools and districts in effective ways and states simply add to waste in the system. But when states evaluate their efforts seriously—as Kentucky has done with its various reforms—and then make adjustments, there is every reason to think that more effective state policies can emerge.[19] States that want to improve both the effectiveness and the equity of schooling have many novel options to consider.

The Continued Role of Funding

Even if there is a shift in some states to capacity-building, this always comes in addition to responsibilities to allocate state revenue to districts. So some guidance for the traditional school finance problem of constructing state formulas is still necessary, now with the additional focus of facilitating the development of school capacities to plan and then to budget. Among the precepts for state revenues are the following:[20]

- In states with high amounts of local revenue, there still needs to be some compensation for differences among districts in property value per pupil, which affects the ability of local districts to raise revenues. Therefore, equalizing mechanisms—most often now foundation formulas providing low-wealth districts with more state revenue—need to continue to be used. But in addition, using weighted pupil approaches, as in school-based budgeting, would help allocate revenues to the schools with the highest need for resources. This addition would enable formulas to consider both the variation in property values that have been at the heart of inter-district differences in funding and the variation in student composition.

- States should avoid the use of categorical funds since they hamper the ability of schools to spend their total funding flexibly. Instead, categorical funds should largely be abolished and revenues transferred to general revenues. There may be some kinds of resources that will not be funded without categorical funding; for example, the consistent shortage of student support services, or of counselors ready to work with students in novel ways, might require continued categorical funding. But categorical funding should be justified by clear evidence that effective resources are missing in schools rather than driven by political considerations, pet projects of state legislators, or the "natural" tendency of categorical programs to proliferate over time.

- Price indices should be developed to account for differences among districts in the various costs of education. This is particularly important to urban districts, which usually face higher costs for facilities, materials, and transportation and may need to pay teachers more to attract a pool of well-qualified instructors.

- States should develop a predictable timetable for allocating funds to districts and schools. The problem in many states of failing to develop budgets on time plays havoc at the school level: schools with uncertain state and district revenues cannot plan well, and late and year-end budgeting almost always results in waste. Similarly, the swings in state revenues that come from boom-and-bust cycles in tax revenues hamper reforms that must take place over several years; sometimes reforms already undertaken must be reversed. So once again, stability is a resource; just as districts and states should look to create as much stability in school conditions as possible, they should develop stability in funding—for example, by shifting to more stable tax bases and developing rainy-day funds.

- States need to provide adequate funding to their schools, even though the definition of "adequate" funding levels is likely to remain elusive and to keep shifting as new demands are placed on schools and new practices develop (once computer and science labs, now library media centers). In part, low-spending schools remain ineffective because teachers are so busy with routine demands and leaders are so overwhelmed that they cannot turn their attention to reform—so "adequacy" requires enough slack resources so that teachers and leaders can turn their attention to improvement rather than merely coping with the flood of daily demands.

So the "minutiae" of school funding continue to matter a great deal. However, decisions about these details should be driven not only by the traditional concerns of inter-district equity and levels of spending but also by the need to create supportive conditions for schools as they decide how to spend revenues more effectively.

FEDERAL POLICY: SCHIZOPHRENIC EFFECTS

The major federal education programs since the 1960s have focused on low-income students, special education, and bilingual education programs; with these targets, the complex of federal efforts should have had some effect on inequality of educational outcomes. This is not the place to review all these efforts, though the effectiveness of Title I—the 1965 act to improve the academic achievement of the disadvantaged—has always been contentious, as has also been the case with programs for English learners.[21] Special education, like No Child Left Behind, has created enormous funding problems by requiring more of districts and schools than it provides funds for—the hideous condition of "unfunded mandates." But even worse, special education has often been used as a dumping ground for the most "difficult" and disruptive students, who are often lower-income students and students of color; relegated to weak programs with the least qualified teachers and underequipped classrooms, these students "experience inadequate services, low-quality curriculum and instruction, and unnecessary isolation from their non-disabled peers" (Losen and Orfield 2002). There is no question that federal funding has supported some effective local programs, but between the fact that federal spending has been only 8 percent of K–12 spending and the fact that federal practices have often promoted ineffective efforts (like pull-out programs and special education), it remains unclear whether federal efforts on the whole have narrowed inequalities, despite the commitment of all major federal legislation to equity. This uncertainty continues in No Child Left Behind, particularly since the rhetoric of federal efforts has not been matched by the funding or other resources necessary to enhance school capacity.

No Child Left Behind

The current version of such schizophrenic efforts is the Elementary and Secondary Education Act, or No Child Left Behind, the 2001 revision of

Title I. The crucial question being hotly debated as reauthorization of NCLB looms is whether it has helped or hindered equity, in any sense of the term.[22] Most obviously, as for state accountability systems, the pressures of NCLB—and especially the need to make Annual Yearly Progress toward the goal of having all groups of students score at the "proficient" level by 2014—have made educators acutely aware of the need to improve the schooling of low-performing students. Most schools are highly aware of their status under NCLB and are trying frantically to improve test scores; the efforts of districts and states, varied though they may be, have also been driven by NCLB requirements.

For some advocates, NCLB's articulation of uniform standards for all students is enough to buy allegiance to it.[23] But the equitable intentions of NCLB are not matched by the detail of its requirements, and it has worked in complex and (perhaps) unintended ways. The act has increased the pressure on schools to increase students' performance quickly, and that pressure for immediate results has driven many schools—those in our sample included—to adopt off-the-shelf programs that are of doubtful value and represent quick fixes in place of the longer-run process of enhancing teacher capacity and restructuring schools. NCLB has narrowed the focus to English and math, and within these subjects to those elements that are readily tested—word recognition rather than comprehension, mastery of arithmetic procedures rather than mathematical reasoning. In all too many schools, NCLB has led to narrow efforts to teach to the test, to triage focusing on the "bubble kids" who are on the cusp of proficiency, and sometimes to cheating (Anagnostopoulos 2003; Benton and Hacker 2004; Diamond and Spillane 2004; Kannapel et al. 1996; Woody et al. 2004). Politicians, including George Bush, have been quick to call on schools to prepare students for "a constantly changing world that is demanding increasingly complex skills from its workforce," and many commissions and employers have called on schools to increase rigor and standards.[24] But low-performing students in basic skills interventions prompted by NCLB are likely to be well prepared for neither the demands of the future workforce nor for responsible citizenship, but only for yet more low-level tests—which have little to do with other meaningful goals.

The central question, from the perspective of the improved school finance, is whether NCLB has matched its demands for performance with resources to improve capacity. On this question, the level of revenues in NCLB has been the subject of vociferous debate. On the one hand, the Bush administration claimed that FY2004 spending requests would increase federal spending by 48 percent.[25] However, in the first year of federal funding after NCLB was signed, FY2003, nominal Title I revenues increased by only 13 percent, from $10.35 billion to $11.7 billion; these amounts further increased to $12.3 billion in FY2004 and $12.7 billion in FY2005 and have stayed steady since then—for a total increase of about 23 percent over five years. Many states, using different methods, have complained that NCLB would require them to increase spending by much more than this—by amounts ranging from 31 percent in Indiana to 45 percent in Nebraska, to 81 percent in New York, to between 34 and 80 percent in Montana, depending on location and level of need. Another estimate suggests that the much-ballyhooed "flexibility" procedures of NCLB allow districts to shift around only 4.3 percent of their federal funds (Mathis 2003). And overall levels of spending are misleading because the costs of testing and reporting have been high and because NCLB earmarks funds: for example, 20 percent of district funding must be reserved for the tutoring of students in low-performing schools, and so other funds must be used to send students from low-performing schools to other schools. In practice, then, the additional discretionary funding from NCLB has been inadequate to meet the enhanced demands of the legislation.[26]

To be sure, federal guidelines set aside 4 percent of funding for school improvement activities, and these might well be useful in enhancing the capacity of local schools. However, this set-aside works out to about $500 million—95 percent to schools and districts and 5 percent to state efforts (Archer 2006)—or about $56,000 for each of the 8,446 schools identified in need of improvement. In an era when developing a plan can cost $50,000 (according to California practices), that does not leave anything for continuous staff development, teacher release time, increased teacher salaries to reduce turnover, professional development for principals, external coaches, efforts to improve school climate, elimination of negative distractions (crime, drugs, fighting), or enhanced student support services. Like states, the federal government has set high new standards for schools that few educators disagree with, but it has utterly failed to deliver the resources necessary to enhance the capacities of schools.

The What Works Clearinghouse

The federal government has also established the What Works Clearinghouse, which in theory provides districts and schools with information about effective programs and interventions. A review of the variety of studies that the clearinghouse has accumulated makes it clear that there is little evidence about some programs. For example, only one evaluation study is posted for the highly promoted PLATO program, a computer-based approach to math drill, and that evaluation fails to meet evidence standards. The listing of many programs with no evidence that meets the clearinghouse criteria may serve as a warning to the schools that might adopt them. There is relatively little information about most areas of the curriculum; there are listings for only five elementary math and seven middle-school math programs and no listings at all for high school curricula; only for beginning reading is there information on a substantial number of programs (twenty-five).[27] In comparison to a National Research Council (2004) report about evaluating curricula, the What Works Clearinghouse uses a narrow conception of evidence, accepting only random-assignment methods or elaborate statistical evidence, neglecting all qualitative evidence, and using an odd counting procedure to aggregate evidence across studies (Confrey 2006). Reports in the clearinghouse are written for researchers rather than for principals and teachers unfamiliar with the language of research. Finally, there have been serious allegations that the clearinghouse has limited discussion of the issues underlying research, thereby slanting the materials included.[28] So, while the provision of information about effective practices would be a useful role for the federal government, schools trying to use the clearinghouse to select programs face severely limited information.

Partisanship in Federal Programs

Finally, the federal government has taken a partisan stance in its own activities. The first such activity was establishment of the National Reading Panel, formed in 1998 by the National Institute for Child Health and Development (NICHD). Researchers on the panel all had the same view of the reading process—as decoding followed by fluency and comprehension. This view did not take account of the much greater variety of reading-related competencies emphasized in a balanced approach (incorporated in the review by Snow, Burns, and Griffin 1998). The final report was put together by staff and ideologically motivated consultants, omitted any studies outside this view, had not been carefully scrutinized by even its own members, lacked outside reviewers, and covered only a limited number of topics (Yatvin 2002). It has been widely interpreted as promoting phonics as a "research-based" approach to reading instruction, when more complete research reviews by the National Academy of Science—a non-ideological and evidence-based group—concluded that such instruction requires much more.

The Department of Education also was exposed bribing journalists to promote NCLB in radio, television, and print commentaries. More recently, the Department of Education was caught manipulating grants for Reading First and funding cronies and ideological friends rather than a broader array of promising approaches (Office of the Inspector General 2006)—and Senator Tom Harkin (D-Iowa) has charged Secretary of Education Margaret Spellings with knowing about these manipulations while she was in the White House.[29] So rather than helping schools make sense of the overwhelming amount of literature and off-the-shelf programs about academic subjects, the federal department has distorted the research record and skewed its own grant-making.

The Potential for Future Federal Contributions

Overall, the well-intentioned history of Title I does not support much faith in federal efforts to improve schools. Even though few educators would be willing to lose federal funding, these efforts provide yet another illustration of how additional money does not matter that much. The shift to No Child Left Behind only continues that checkered history: the small amounts of additional funding are inadequate to the additional demands placed on schools and districts, and the ways in which districts and schools spend their revenues are further distorted, as the evidence in chapter 8 indicates. The overall ineffectiveness of Title I efforts continues in NCLB: the evidence so far indicates that NCLB has made no difference in school improvement (Fuller et al. 2007), and while Reading First has increased the amount of time spent on reading, it has failed to increase reading comprehension (NCEERA 2008).

To create a balance of accountability and capacity-building—of sticks and carrots—will require that federal policy develop a more coherent approach to capacity-building. At a minimum, this could take the form of providing funding sufficient to match the increased demands on states, districts, and schools. Even if money is not always necessary for school improvement, many of the changes required to carry out the demands of NCLB cannot be made without additional resources, including funding. In addition, the timetable of reform should be more seriously considered in revisions of federal policy. Any provisions that drive schools away from capacity-building, as I have defined it, and toward the adoption of desperate remedial forms of intervention are counterproductive.

Moving away from the conventional patterns of federal policy—emphasizing requirements and simple funding, the legacies of administrative progressivism—and toward the resource use and capacity-building of the improved school finance will require a very different approach. Indeed, the federal government is so far from schools, both bureaucratically and conceptually, that it is hard to imagine how it could provide the kind of subtle support required of new approaches to resources—especially under ideologically driven administrations like the Bush administration. For the moment, then, it may be necessary to leave federal policy to the provision of information, research, and additional funding for equity purposes and to leave support for capacity-building to states and districts.

THE CHALLENGES OF THE CONSISTENCY AGENDA

In considering whether approaches to school resources are improving overall, we can only be ambivalent. On the one hand, many districts continue to operate in ways that do not support schools, creating enormous waste through their policies and doing little to improve school-level capacity. States have only begun to experiment with new ways to support schools, and some of their efforts have been wasteful on a grand scale. And current federal policy, with its laudable goals for all children but its detrimental effects on practice, continues the pattern of well-intentioned but ineffective practices begun in the 1960s, especially when measured against the conception of capacity-building developed here.

On the other hand, there are many hopeful signs. Some districts are taking their responsibility for capacity-building seriously. Some are moving away from top-down decisionmaking to more collaborative organizations. Some are now strongly emphasizing instruction over previous concerns with efficiency and administration, and various developing practices—among them school-based budgeting and tiering (the identification of some schools for special attention)—are promising as well. Although state efforts may seem preliminary and sporadic, here too a number of practices are emerging that could, with consistent development and improvement, provide support of the right sort to both schools and districts.

District, state, and federal efforts are so ambiguous precisely because we can see two sets of policies being applied simultaneously. The policies put in place by administrative progressivism persist, particularly hierarchical organization, reliance on simple funding and categorical programs, and outcome-based policies and accountability measures. But as districts and states have realized that such traditional efforts will not lead to improvement, new approaches have emerged. I have labeled these practices—and the policies that encourage them—complex and constructivist approaches, and I return to this distinction in the final chapter. For the moment, it is sufficient to recognize that policies may be in transition, with the current confusion coming from the mixture of different approaches.

In moving forward, the ideas of the improved school finance can provide guidance for district and state policies as well as for school practices. What counts in the end is finding a variety of effective school resources, including the compound, complex, and abstract resources usually ignored in policy discussions, and keeping the focus on both the instructional improvement necessary for enhanced learning and the supportive environments critical for student progress. If schools need to be reorganized to develop these largely collective resources, then shifting to more distributed and collective practices for decisionmaking is important as well. District and state policies can be evaluated as to whether they enhance school capacity defined in this way, and then we can distinguish the promising policies described in this chapter from older practices.

Chapter 11

The Implications for Litigation of the Improved School Finance

IN THE PURSUIT of educational equity, litigation has played an enormous role in a variety of areas—in racial desegregation, culminating in the *Brown v. Board of Education* decision and various efforts to enforce it; in the establishment of linguistic rights for English learners, starting with the *Lau v. Nichols* case; in a variety of cases related to gender equity; and in special education, with its complex apparatus of adjudicating disputes between districts and parents acting on behalf of their children.[1] The cases of greatest interest for this book are the lawsuits intended to advance equity in school finance, starting in the last three decades with the *Serrano* case in California and followed by a succession of lawsuits in other states and, more recently, by cases based on claims of adequacy—claims that state constitutions implicitly guarantee that all students should have an adequate education, defined in various ways (Guthrie 2004; Guthrie and Rothstein 2004; Minorini and Sugarman 1999). Indeed, the "landscape of equity" presented in chapter 6 contains many references to lawsuits, since these have been so important in challenging inequalities of various kinds—particularly inequalities of access and of funding.

However, the emergence of litigation as a principal strategy is itself worrisome because it indicates that conventional political and legislative solutions to inequality have failed. Robert Mnookin (1985) has argued that, under our current legislative system, litigation has several advantages over legislation in cases involving children and students: litigation provides greater access to a change process, the opportunity to argue on the basis of principle rather than political expedience, and fewer political problems. This is not surprising: political debates over principled values have usually neglected equity because many Americans (and especially the Bush and other Republican administrations) remain unconcerned about inequality. Under these conditions, the principles about equity embedded in state and federal constitutions are among the few resources that advocates for equity can use.

At a deeper level, democratic politics as currently practiced in the United States—with interest groups of varying influence battling each other for the spoils of government (Macpherson 1977)—has no effective way of articulating a public good (such as equality of educational opportunity), since all that can be achieved is the domination of some interest groups over others (Truman 1951). Furthermore, redistribution within interest-group politics is exceedingly difficult to achieve because those with more resources generally have greater power—that is, a greater coherence and voice for their interest groups, not to mention money in an era of high-spending politics—than those with less; this situation effectively blocks redistribution from haves to have-nots (Lowi 1969). This is the central problem in school finance litigation: the wealthy districts that stand to lose funding and control have been able to block redistribution to poor districts. But when conventional legislative solutions fail consistently, then advocates and lawyers are driven to litigation, often arguing that the egalitarian principles embedded in state or federal constitutions—in the equal protection clause of the Fourteenth Amendment, for example, or in state equal protection clauses, or in state constitutions guaranteeing something like a "thorough and efficient education"—require more equitable treatment of students. The very existence of so much litigation in education is a measure of desperation, an admission that advocates for equity cannot achieve their goals in any other ways.

When political deliberation as a route to reform gives way to litigation, the more subtle actions that legislation could *potentially* foster—in particular, enhancing the capacities of schools to achieve equity, which is certainly possible but (as the prior chapter showed) a difficult feat under the best of circumstances—are replaced by the cruder mechanisms of litigation. Courts normally can prohibit certain practices—for example, the first *Serrano* case declared the state's system of financing unconstitutional—but they cannot construct more effective alternatives, which they usually leave to legislatures. So litigation may work when those activities that should be equalized are relatively simple and when a simple prohibition is a sufficient remedy—prohibiting segregation by requiring access to schools and colleges that have been racially segregated, for example, or prohibiting practices that deny women access to various programs. But as we shift to more complex dimensions of education—resources rather than money, for example, or judgments about what resources are most effective, or outcomes rather than money—litigation becomes increasingly ineffective as a mechanism of reform since the construction of remedies becomes so complex. Indeed, the history of repeated school finance litigation in many states—seven cases in Arizona, three versions of the *Serrano* case in California, three cases in Iowa, six in New Hampshire, and a record ten in New Jersey (Yinger 2004, app. A)—reveals a process of trial and error: courts rule a practice unconstitutional, legislatures respond inadequately, litigation challenges the reform, and on and on. And so, while the simplest measures of inequity (access and funding) may, under the right conditions, be redressed through litigation, more problematic dimensions of resources and outcomes are much more difficult to equalize. The challenge in rethinking the litigation strategies of the past three decades is also to rethink the potential remedies in school equity cases.

In this chapter, I demonstrate why the focus on the funding of conventional school finance litigation has been relatively ineffective.[2] To do this, I draw both on the results of litigation over the past thirty years and on the empirical results, from chapter 2 in particular, showing what kinds of resources are most effective—and showing how weak the connection is between funding and these resources. The implication, as various commentators have argued, is that equalizing funding is an adequate way to address inequities in education. If students are to have more equal opportunities, it becomes necessary to shift to equity conceptions defined in terms of *resources* rather than *funding*. A few promising lawsuits do this—particularly the *Williams* case in California, the *Campaign for Fiscal Equity* case in New York (at least in its early stages), and the *Abbott* case in New Jersey. However, shifting the process of litigation will require that litigators and school reformers collaborate more closely in devising remedies that are both enforceable and more likely to equalize educational outcomes.

THE DISAPPOINTMENTS OF LITIGATION: THE INEFFECTIVENESS OF REVENUE-BASED APPROACHES TO EQUITY

Some of the most powerful examples of litigation have in the end proved disappointing. The case of *Brown v. Board of Education*, which ended de jure racial segregation in schools, is perhaps the highest-profile school-related lawsuit of the twentieth century and is deservedly famous both for establishing a basic principle of equity—public schools should not deny access to racial-minority students—and for supporting decades of litigation against discriminatory practices. The hopes for this decision in 1954 were enormous:

At the time of Brown, nearly all observers—liberals and conservatives, blacks and whites—saw the decision as far-reaching and as something that would fundamentally alter the schools themselves and the way the different races would be taught in them. Once and for all, or so it seemed, black students would get their fair share of care and resources from the public school enterprise. (O'Brien 2007, 1875)

But after the case was settled, the decision still needed to be enforced since, with few exceptions, court cases do not implement themselves. Resistance in the South in particular, the failure of public officials to enforce desegregation laws, white flight, and residential segregation throughout the country continued to undermine the intent of desegregation. The Supreme Court could outlaw overt segregation, but it could not force integration because it could not control the various patterns of mobility and flight to private schools that followed. Probably the greatest boost to the *Brown* decision came in subsequent legislation, the 1964 Civil Rights Act, which granted the U.S. attorney general the right to bring lawsuits and the Department of Education the authority to collect data and provide grants for desegregation (O'Brien 2007); these actions led to many local desegregation orders. Still, such efforts were not enough to stem the effects of mobility, and by 2003 black students were more racially isolated than they had been in 1968 (Frankenberg and Lee 2002); they were still in schools with inadequate resources, including uncredentialed teachers, high teacher turnover, and inadequate materials, computers, and science labs, and inadequate physical facilities, including the wretched bathrooms that have been a leitmotif of complaints since the nineteenth century (Carroll et al. 2004). Many battles had been won, but the war seemed lost. And then the tide of desegregation efforts turned in the 1990s and 2000s, when courts increasingly declared that *Brown* calls not for desegregation, which requires attention to the racial composition of schools, but for "color-blindness," which prohibits such attention.

The fiftieth anniversary of the *Brown* decision in 2004 was therefore an ambiguous celebration. Not only had desegregation failed to mix black and white students, but it was clear that most African American students still attended schools that lacked a "fair share of care and resources." The size of the black-white test score gap and its intractability indicated that *Brown* had not lived up to its earlier expectations. But here we have to ask whether these expectations were reasonable. *Brown*, after all, remedied barriers to access (cell 1 in table 6.1), but it did not do anything about equity in funding or in resources. Even in the absence of resegregation, black students still suffer the resource problems associated with lower tracks, the allocation of the least-experienced and least-credentialed teachers to lower tracks, more conventional and behaviorist teaching, and the kind of mistreatment and stigma I documented in chapter 4 (Zirkel 2005). In retrospect, hoping that desegregation would by itself equalize effective resources was overly optimistic, once we recognize the complex inner workings of schools as well as the powerful impulses to resegregate schools. In the end, intervening events undermined even a case as celebrated as *Brown*, and even its successes depended more on subsequent legislation (the Civil Rights Act) than on the power of the courts.

An analogous example in the arena of school finance is probably the *Serrano* case in California, which was based on a careful legal and empirical strategy (Coons, Clune, and Sugarman 1970). The victory of *Serrano*, with its clear mandate to establish a considerably narrower distribution of spending per pupil, led to great hopes in California. The original idea was that *Serrano* would force the state to "level up"—to make average spending higher while also narrowing the variation in spending. But Proposition 13 in 1978 ended that vision. Limits on property taxation in California and a shift to state revenues caused the state to "level down," and average revenues in real terms began a steady slide; although revenues after Prop 13 showed significant convergence, no similar convergence in student performance occurred (Downes 1992). Subsequent propositions, fiscal instability with an eroded tax base, an increased use of categorical grants rather than the more equalizing general grants, indifferent governors, and an incompetent legislature (as the result of term limits) all undermined the quality of schooling in California. By the 2000s, state test scores on the National Assessment of Educational Progress were among the lowest in the country. *Serrano* was only one of many major influences on schooling over these three decades, and its hope of equalization with increased levels of performance could not be sustained through all these other changes.

Although the early promise of *Serrano* gave way to other events, its early success set off a wave of school finance lawsuits in other states (Yinger 2004, app. A). Virtually all of these lawsuits have sought greater equality, or equity in the sense of adequacy, in revenues or expenditures per pupil among districts within states. The effects of these lawsuits, however, have been distinctly mixed. When we consider the causal chain from lawsuits to legislation equalizing revenues to the distribution of *effective* resources, we can see why using lawsuits to equalize funding does not equalize resources, let alone outcomes.

The first problem is that lawsuits do not by themselves lead to greater equity in revenues or expenditures per student. Existing school finance systems can be outlawed, but if any corrections are to occur, litigation must also lead to legislation that reallocates funding or increases funding to low-spending districts. The resulting legislation is sometimes inadequate, and cases must be relitigated to enforce the original decisions—the problem behind multiple lawsuits in many states. The result is a seesawing back and forth between the courts pressing for equity based on constitutional interpretations and legislatures resisting equity based on conventional interest-group politics—confirming the weakness of conventional legislation as an instrument of equity.

A number of studies have analyzed the effects of litigation on patterns of school funding. For example, Sheila Murray and her colleagues (1998) examined funding within states between 1971 and 1998. They concluded that simple measures of inequality within states did not decrease at all during this period of intense litigation. With a weakly specified model considering some other influences, they concluded that court-ordered finance reform reduced within-state inequality by 19 to 34 percent.[3] However, these results failed to consider differences among states in court decisions. When Alan Hickrod and his colleagues (1997) divided states into six categories reflecting the relative power of litigation in them, they found that only the eight states in category 1—plaintiffs clearly prevailed—saw spending differences decrease, by about 22 percent. The six states in category 2—plaintiffs won but had to file subsequent litigation for enforcement—saw inequality decrease by only 7.5 percent. In the four remaining categories, inequality *increased* in states where litigation lost, and in states with no litigation—an imprecise control group—inequality decreased by 5.7 percent, not much less than in category 2. So only the eight states in category 1 saw substantial decreases in inequality. Similarly, David Thompson and Faith Crampton (2002) examined the burgeoning literature on litigation effects as well as detailed results in four specific states. Overall, the empirical work did not support any hope that litigation would lead to higher levels of funding or to a more equitable distribution, though these authors hedged their bets by acknowledging that litigation might have effects not well described in spending figures—for example, by increasing the visibility of the equity cause, litigation might lead in the long run to conventional legislative efforts.

Most of these investigations have asked whether the relationship between property values and spending—the pattern at issue in virtually all school finance lawsuits—had been weakened through litigation and subsequent legislation. Instead of focusing on property value, the U.S. General Accounting Office (GAO) (1997) shifted to a concept of *income* neutrality, asking whether district spending was correlated with income per pupil. It found that patterns in thirty-seven states favored higher-income districts; only eight states had fiscal neutrality scores that were insignificantly different from zero, and only two—Alaska and Nevada—implicitly followed "policies of correction" by favoring lower-income districts. These results clarify that litigation in many states has not been especially effective: relatively few states (only the eight where litigants clearly prevailed) have had substantial reductions in the variation of spending among districts, and the links to income, one measure of the influence of family background, remain strong in the vast majority of states.

My purpose is not to cast doubt on the value of school finance litigation, although this is a credible argument.[4] There are, after all, symbolic reasons for pressing equity lawsuits, even if the results are weak and inconsistent, and perhaps the threat of litigation causes legislatures to act when they otherwise might not. There is always the hope that lawsuits will trigger more complex state legislative responses—as in Kentucky, for example, where the case of *Rose v. Council for Better Education* led to the comprehensive Kentucky Education Reform Act (KERA) of 1990. But stating equity claims and measuring litigation effects in terms of revenues or expenditures is the wrong strategy, since equalized *funding* does not necessarily lead to equalization of effective *resources* that might affect school *outcomes*. Indeed, as chapter 3 clarified, additional expenditures can at best equalize a few simple resources—the pupil-teacher ratio, teacher salaries, and teacher experience in secondary education (really a compound resource). More money has smaller effects on teacher planning time, the use of counseling, and a reduction in the likelihood of conventional teaching in math. Increasing expenditures rarely affects most of the compound, complex, and abstract resources that enhance learning and progress through high school—at least not as they are usually spent.

Consistent with this argument, there is evidence that, even in those few states where litigation has led to effective legislation, schooling *outcomes* have not been equalized at all. John Yinger (2004) has collected case studies of five states—Kansas, Kentucky, Michigan, Texas,[5] and Vermont—where particularly effective lawsuits have led to significant equalization in spending per student in response to legislation. Indeed, both Kentucky and Michigan passed multiple reforms as the result of litigation, illustrating how lawsuits can lead to more substantial changes than simply finance reform.

The effects of these lawsuits were generally disappointing, despite the fact that all of these states successfully redistributed spending. In Kansas, outcomes measured by dropout rates, reading exams, and math exams were *more* unequal in 1999 than in 1992, the year of the litigation. In Kentucky, inequality in spending went down, but despite this improvement and the other reforms of KERA, inequality in the state's standardized test scores was essentially unchanged; if anything, it increased. As in the *Brown* and *Serrano* cases, the great hopes for systematic reform through *Rose* and KERA were effectively limited, in this case by insufficient attention to implementation, the complexity of initiating multiple contradictory reforms, the inadequate preparation of teachers (perhaps the most crucial dimension of capacity), and inattention to the role of districts (Adams 2000; Goe 2002). In Michigan, where cities in particular benefited from the passage of Proposal A, designed to equalize funding among districts and enhance accountability, there was no evidence that increased funding led to improved student outcomes (such as a higher fourth-grade passing rate), yet another demonstration of how little difference spending makes.[6] The variation among districts in the percentage of students who passed math exams and the percentage with a satisfactory score went down between 1991 and 2000, but this appears to have been due to ceiling effects in the tests rather than to spending patterns. Proposal A also expanded school choice by creating public school academies (or charter schools) and by allowing students to attend schools outside their districts; the number of students taking part, mostly in the Detroit area, more than quadrupled between 1997 and 2001. Over time, this choice may affect inequality among districts and schools in other ways, though, as I argue in chapter 12, this neoliberal approach to schooling is likely to increase inequalities in important school resources.

The Vermont study was the only one to provide any evidence on school resources as distinct from revenues or expenditures. The variation among districts in students per teacher actually increased slightly in the years after the finance reform act, as did variation in average teacher salaries and students per computer. The variation in various test score measures increased slightly for some and decreased for others, but the largest decrease in inequality—for fourth-grade math tests—had started three years before the reform act and therefore could not be attributed to litigation and its consequences.

Overall, then, while inequalities in funding have decreased in a *select* group of states with particularly active litigation efforts—particularly in the category 1 states, which had especially clear litigation outcomes—neither school resources nor schooling outcomes have become more equal as a result. In essence, the distance between litigation and improved outcomes, in these cases based on the "old" school finance, is too great. The intermediate steps—from litigation to legislation equalizing funding, from more equitable funding to revenues spent on effective resources, from improved resources to outcomes—are too numerous, and each step has its own problems. Each is susceptible to undermining by forces ranging from political resistance to legislation, to the structural conditions in districts promoting different forms of waste, to failure to consider which resources (like teacher experience and class size) really require compound resources, to a consideration of too restricted a range of resources.[7] In addition, the demographic and economic conditions in school districts are moving targets over which schools themselves have no control, and—as in California—other aspects of state education policy can swamp the effects of litigation. Overall, the situation that has prevailed over the past three decades has made it exceedingly difficult for litigation focused on equitable revenues to generate more equitable resources or outcomes.

In many ways, there is little to show for three decades of efforts to equalize school finance. To be sure, the distribution of revenues across districts in some states is more equal than it would have been in the absence of state aid policies; furthermore, the symbolic power of equity litigation should not be dismissed, and perhaps the threat of litigation prevents states from allowing spending differences to become too great. But the effects of litigation on the distribution of school resources—those goods and services, including well-prepared teachers and principals, that money might be able to buy and that might be effective in enhancing school outcomes—has been negligible, and the effects on schooling outcomes are completely absent. Therefore, during another period of litigation and legislation, we need to shift our goals from more equal *funding* to more equal *resources*. Unfortunately, it is precisely this shift for which litigation is ill suited, and the challenge is therefore to devise remedies that courts can promote but that also affect the more subtle dimensions of schooling.

IMPROVED APPROACHES TO LITIGATION: ATTENTION TO RESOURCES

If the past three decades of school finance litigation and reform have done little to equalize either school resources or educational outcomes, the obvious implication is that, except for symbolic reasons, it is almost pointless to continue bringing these kinds of lawsuits. The recent trend toward adequacy cases is also ineffective since at the end of the day they simply calculate sums of money that are then allocated to districts.[8] These lawsuits may involve a different level and distribution of revenues than earlier lawsuits, but they still follow the principles of the "old" school finance. A new approach to litigation is necessary, and fortunately there are at least three cases that offer more promising examples.

Most obviously, lawsuits need to promote equity in resources—especially *effective* resources—rather than equity in funding. One recent example is a lawsuit in California, *Williams v. State of California*, initially litigated in 2000 and settled in 2004. It focused not on the inequality or the inadequacy of dollars but rather on real resources in schools and classrooms—fully credentialed teachers teaching in their field of study, up-to-date textbooks in adequate numbers for the students enrolled, and appropriate physical facilities. These are arguably resources with positive effects on various outcomes, and the complaint cited considerable evidence of the effects on learning of these three resources (summarized in Oakes 2004). Furthermore, the lawsuit focused on schools rather than on districts as the unit of concern and remedy; it required that teachers, textbooks, and facilities be adequate in all schools rather than allocating revenues to districts and hoping that the distribution of funds or resources to schools would result in adequate resources (Grubb, Goe, and Huerta 2004).

The settlement of the case in 2004 by the state of California included an $800 million emergency repair program for emergency repairs in low-performing schools, plus additional funds for instructional materials.[9] In addition, the settlement established a procedure following the Uniform Complaint Procedures (UCP): students, parents, and teachers at the school level can file a complaint if books or the condition of school facilities are inadequate or if the school does not have a permanent teacher qualified to teach a subject. (Notices about this procedure must be posted in all classrooms, though there is evidence that many teachers and parents are unaware of these notices.) The principal must investigate and fix the problem within thirty days or forward the complaint to the district if he or she cannot fix the problem. The district must then find a solution within thirty days; those initiating the procedure can file an appeal to the state superintendent if the complaint is not resolved. In addition, county superintendents must visit low-performing schools to determine whether textbooks and materials are adequate and facilities are safe and in good repair. Finally, multitrack year-round schools are being phased out, an unambiguous benefit given that these schools provide instruction under chaotic conditions for only 163 days (instead of 180).

After two years of implementation, several benefits of *Williams* have emerged.[10] One is that the settlement is self-enforcing: no lawsuits have to be relitigated if terms are not met, and the UCP in effect creates a community of advocates around schools who identify and then press for solutions to inadequacies in resources. The proportion of schools with inadequate textbooks has declined; the number of schools needing emergency facility repairs has declined; repairs are carried out more quickly; the fraction of low-performing schools with teacher misassignments has fallen, though only from 49 to 43 percent; and administrators report that improvements are helping them attract and retain qualified teachers. While it is unclear what role county offices of education have played, their oversight responsibilities provide one additional source of both pressure and technical assistance to improve resources.

To be sure, the results of the *Williams* case are not everything that advocates for equity could want. The amount of money appropriated for facilities is wholly inadequate to the problem—many older areas have seriously dilapidated schools—but after three decades of declining revenues and weak political leadership in California, it is difficult to know if a better fiscal settlement could have been achieved without a revolution in the state's politics and governance. The conception of qualified teachers—fully credentialed and teaching in their field of study—does not address the many other instructional conditions necessary to improved learning, especially the need to move toward constructivist or "balanced" instruction. The lawsuit itself and the Uniform Complaint Procedures were restricted to only the three resources identified in the lawsuit and did not extend to a much broader range of effective resources. But the settlement did at least set forth a presumption that districts and the state must provide adequate levels of certain basic resources, a clear procedure for identifying problems, and new requirements for districts and county superintendents to follow in order to remedy those problems.

A second promising case is *Campaign for Fiscal Equity (CFE) v. State of New York*. The decision by the state Supreme Court requires the state to ensure that every school has the resources necessary to provide a "sound basic education," including the capacity for necessary instructional conditions. As Luis Huerta (2006) argues, the *CFE* case could revise the distribution of resources rather than merely funding. The decision mandates an accountability system to measure whether reforms provide a "sound basic education" and commissions the New York Adequacy Study to accomplish this; the results of this study will ascertain practices within schools and classrooms that enhance learning and then allocate revenues to those practices (CFE 2004)— a process that reflects the logic underlying the improved school finance. One result of the case has been a series of Making the Money Matter meetings to involve all stakeholders in ensuring that new revenues are spent well and result in improved achievement—a positive sign that the case might promote effective resources and not just more spending.

Whether the potential of the *CFE* case will be realized, however, is still unclear. The state appropriated $490 million, most of it ($317 million) for New York City, and identified fifty-six districts that are to receive increases in state aid of 10 percent or more. Following the conventional state practice of imposing categorical requirements on how money is spent, districts must develop Contracts for Excellence restricted to five kinds of resources: class size reduction, increased student time on task, teacher and principal quality, middle school and high school restructuring, and full-day kindergarten or prekindergarten. In the initial contracts, about half of the funds were spent on class size reduction and another one-quarter on increasing time on task, usually by lengthening the school day or year; only one-sixth was targeted at improving teacher and principal quality, and less than 10 percent went to restructuring. Each of these permitted reforms is a popular way of spending money, and two of them—enhancing teacher and principal quality and possibly restructuring—can improve the capacity of schools (though both reforms have been allocated relatively little funding). Enhancing teacher and principal quality depends on whether the effort addresses the instructional approaches that their schools take; restructuring to create more personalized environments might enhance progress through schooling but not learning; and other forms of restructuring might not lead to personalization. Moreover, reducing class sizes and increasing students' time on task need to be considered as efforts to enhance compound resources, and so the state's constraints on how funds are spent may undermine their effectiveness.

Furthermore, nothing in the descriptions of the Contracts for Excellence would enhance the capacity of schools to make well-considered internal decisions about additional funding; the state has not made the reorganization of districts or schools a priority. The Campaign for Fiscal Equity complained that much of the money allocated to New York would go to high-performing rather than to low-performing schools, and it objected to the lack of detail about how money would be spent within each of the five categories.[11] So in the CFE case, litigators set in motion a number of ways to target funding on the lowest-performing schools and on the most effective resources, but whether these efforts can survive conventional interest-group politics and the power of the old school finance remains to be seen.

A third promising case is *Abbott v. Burke* in New Jersey, where—after a number of lawsuits—the court in 1998 required the Commissioner of Education to change the allocation of funding. Currently Abbott districts—low-income, with high proportions of students of color—spend about 31 percent more than non-Abbott districts. The court also ordered a set of specific programs and reforms, including preschool programs; intensive early literacy programs in the elementary grades; smaller class sizes for high-poverty students; social and health services; new facilities; and a series of required supplemental programs like full-day kindergarten, health and social service referral, alternative education and dropout prevention, violence prevention, early math instruction, and school-to-work and college transition programs (Abbott Indicators Project 2006). The changes have come more easily in elementary schools than in middle schools or high schools, not surprisingly given the resistance of high schools in particular to reform; however, there are plans in high schools to increase academic rigor and personalization through the development of small learning communities. A series of reports on the individual districts of Camden, Trenton, and Newark provide an enormous amount of detail about practices in these four cities, including much more information than can be found in virtually any other treatise on school finance about funding for early childhood programs, small learning communities, intervention efforts like after-school programs, the prevalence of AP classes, and literacy tutors. One enormous benefit of the *Abbott* case, then, is that the discussion has moved to school resources rather than stalling at discussions about money.

Not surprisingly, enforcement of the decision has encountered many difficulties, including insufficient funding, proposed changes in funding formulas, and—consistent with evidence in chapter 10 about the weak effects of the California efforts to enhance capacity—inadequate staffing, training, input from outside stakeholders, and consistent decisionmaking in the state Department of Education.[12] Improvements for Abbott districts seem consistently threatened by the usual problems at the state level, including inadequate funding and debate over finance formulas—again illustrating "reforming zeal dissipated in confrontation with minutiae." But the judgment has wrestled with the details of some specific resources—the quality of early childhood teachers, early literacy programs, an enormous variety of supplemental programs, small learning communities and restructuring in high schools—as well as with the reallocation of funding. Although the results may still be moderated by the usual political and legislative battles, *Abbott* seems more promising as a starting point than the lawsuits that create remedies focused on revenues alone.

Approaches for Success

The three cases discussed in this section suggest that lawsuits can be more successful if they focus on equity in resources rather than (or in addition to) equity in revenues and that they can under the right conditions lead to enhanced capacity, not just purchasing power in the districts and schools where high-need students live. The challenge in such lawsuits is to identify resources that are effective, to search for inequities and inadequacies in these resources, and then to use them as the focus of litigation. Furthermore, a focus on the school level, as in the *Williams* case, can direct resources to the highest need, even if districts resist change.

These promising lawsuits have all engaged larger communities in the remedies—*Williams* through the widespread reach of the Uniform Complaint Procedures; *CFE* by creating citizen forums in which different stakeholders discuss how funds should be spent; and *Abbott* through its suggestions about and monitoring of how funds are being spent. As a result, there have been broad deliberations not only about the level and distribution of funding but also about how the money is spent. To be sure, levels of funding and the volatility of state revenues are still problems; redistributing revenues among districts remains challenging, as it will always be in interest-group politics; and substantial pressures remain to spend funds in the conventional patterns associated with the old school finance. But these three lawsuits have taken a different direction in that they are concerned as much with effective resources as with money, more aware of the complexities of translating revenues into educational outcomes, and capable of making the distribution of school resources more effective as well as more equitable.

Finally, it is crucial to recognize that the effectiveness of litigation usually comes back to legislation, not only in these three lawsuits but in many more conventional lawsuits (and in *Brown* as well). Even if lawsuits are attempts to bypass the inequities and rigidities of the legislative process, legislative and political deliberations always influence the outcomes in the end. Thus, educators must be ready to participate in these deliberations with clear ideas about the effective practices they want to see implemented in their schools and districts. This is where the improved school finance can provide guidance with its expanded conceptions of resources.

Chapter 12

The Implications for Reform: Conceptions of Schooling and the Role of the Welfare State

BY NOW, we can see more clearly why the money myth—the belief that "the question of sufficient revenue lies back of almost every other problem," and the faith that more money might solve a variety of educational problems—is often wrong, or at best incomplete. A great deal of money is wasted, for a variety of reasons I first examined in chapter 1, and money is especially likely to be wasted in urban schools, with their instability, often antagonistic relationships, and conflicts over basic purposes and pedagogy. Many effective practices turn out to require compound rather than simple resources; many more are complex or abstract resources that may require small sums of money but depend more on vision, leadership, planning, collaboration, and other characteristics that cannot be bought.

At the school level, waste often results from the lack of capacity to plan collectively and implement reforms consistently, so that infusions of money in low-performing schools have very few overall effects even as some schools may benefit, as the evidence in chapter 9 indicated. In addition to a lack of capacity in this sense, schools and school leaders often lack the expertise to decide which resources are effective and which are not, and most districts and states—as well as the federal government with its limited What Works Clearinghouse and its pedagogical conservatism—have not been helpful in providing that expertise. The efforts of low-performing schools on their own to address dynamic inequality, described in chapter 8, are usually fragmented and incomplete, and districts and states are only starting to support low-performing schools appropriately. The inherent difficulty of second-chance efforts cannot be underestimated, and all too many interventions are poorly designed, instructionally inappropriate, and otherwise ineffective. The efforts to force equity through litigation have had largely symbolic and weak effects; even where litigation has equalized funding, it has been unable to guarantee that funding is appropriately translated into more effective resources.

The problems associated with education resources and equity, however, are not simply a series of errors that could be easily corrected once educators and policymakers recognize the limitations of the money myth. At this juncture in American public education, we face several battles—not always well recognized, not always clearly debated—over both the direction of schooling and the social and economic policies within which public education is situated. It may seem a leap from the puzzle that started this book—how to understand the myth of money and the relatively weak role that spending plays in educational outcomes—to a grand consideration of fundamentally different approaches to what both school and nonschool policies should be. Formulating and then implementing a clear alternative to the old school finance, however, proves to require many interrelated changes.

One of these battles involves the nature of schooling itself. Despite the pitfalls and inaccuracies of taxonomies, we can identify at least three relatively distinct approaches to schooling; they overlap, to be sure, but they are still useful in helping us discern substantial differences in assumptions, goals, and policies. The first and dominant approach is the legacy of the administrative progressives, who worked after 1900 to create a more efficient, bureaucratic, and differentiated system of education.[1] A second approach—considered by some to be novel, progressive, and entrepreneurial rather than reactionary and conservative—encompasses choice-based, quasi-market, or neoliberal methods and is exemplified by efforts to create choice mechanisms, charter schools, and *systems* of charter schools like KIPP (Knowledge Is Power Program) academies and Edison schools (now defunct). The third approach, developed throughout this book, focuses especially on the nature of instruction and relies on constructivist or "balanced" pedagogical practices, including greater attention to a variety of effective resources and to the participatory and distributed forms of decisionmaking that might create them, ideally supported by school, district, and even state and federal policies. While each of these approaches to schooling shares some features with the other approaches—especially the conventional approach and the neoliberal approach—each differs in substantial ways. Recognizing these differences among the approaches, especially in how they handle issues of effectiveness and equity, is crucial to understanding developments in this country. At the moment, all three approaches coexist and policies developed by one often affect practices from another, so no consistency or consensus has yet emerged.

The other battle, the subject of the second section of this chapter, involves the nonschool policies within which schools are embedded. I have alluded to such policies throughout this book, particularly in discussing the effects of family background in chapters 4 and 7 and in analyzing student commitment to schooling in chapter 5. Having raised these as important resources for schooling, it would be irresponsible not to outline the noneducational policies that might enhance these resources. I concentrate on policies in the areas of health and housing, neighborhood economic development efforts, the spatial distribution of the population, and income support that are complementary to schooling and that could improve educational outcomes.

The implicit "decisions" to continue using traditional approaches to schooling that neglect many effective school resources and to allow the policies of the traditional welfare state to wither are social and political choices, not just accidents or thoughtlessness. They reflect the historical approaches to schooling that emerged from the nineteenth century and from administrative progressives. They are also the product of our political system, which, rather than following the principles articulated in state and federal constitutions, encourages interest groups to battle among themselves for the benefits handed out by government. Within such a system, it is not surprising to find middle-class parents and their children "winning" in the battle for school resources over working-class and low-income and urban parents and children. Indeed, a different kind of politics may be necessary before the battles over approaches to schooling and over nonschool policies can be resolved. But stopping short of such fundamental reforms, we as a nation should at least realize that the lofty goals we hold for public schooling cannot be realized unless we confront both of these battles.

THE CHANGING BATTLES OVER SCHOOLING

I began this volume with Horace Mann and other advocates for the common schools complaining about "hide-bound conservatism and niggardly parsimony" and with Ellwood Cubberly's declaration that "the question of sufficient revenue lies back of almost every other problem." In the nineteenth and early twentieth centuries, these were indeed serious concerns, since the rapid expansion of public schooling, the growing school-age population, the substantial expansion of high schools after 1900, and the desire to upgrade facilities and professionalize teachers made additional funding a constant challenge. When Cubberly described the inequalities in funding among districts, he was among the first to see that public funding, while more equitable than the private funding that had preceded the common schools, might still be highly inequitable owing to variation in tax bases and incomes. Concerns with funding inequalities have dominated school finance for the past century.

Nevertheless, the Progressive Era and the administrative progressives left more than the myth of money as their legacy. The progressives introduced the administrative and bureaucratic mechanisms, the dominant purposes, and the conventional practices that David Tyack and Larry Cuban (1995) have called the "grammar of schooling" and that I have sometimes referred to as the "default" approach. The structure of time, the construction of grade levels and courses, the methods of testing and accountability, the purposes of basic instruction and vocational preparation with a weakened overlay of civic preparation, the persistence of conventional teaching (Cuban 1993)— all these are so familiar that we often fail to think about their particulars. The administrative progressives were concerned with management and efficiency, with top-down hierarchies running from district superintendents through principals as middle managers to teachers at the bottom, where they had little obvious voice in running schools.

The administrative progressive approach typically incorporates the following ideas:

- *Efficiency and cost-cutting are priorities.* The concern with efficiency— not efficiency in the sense of efficacy or even in the benefit-cost sense—has led to cost-cutting.[2] Thus, urban schools have been constantly exhorted to produce more with less, to search for low-cost solutions to truly challenging conditions.

- *Decisions are driven by accountability and data.* The concern with efficiency after 1900 began a process of counting and measuring. The administrative progressives also collected a great deal of data to make their administrative decisions; in many ways the current accountability movements—with their seemingly precise measurements of learning, their clear incentives and disincentives—and the current penchant for "data-driven reform" represent another legacy. No one wants decisions driven by ignorance, of course, but this approach is objectionable when data are limited (to quantitative forms, for example, or to narrow conceptions of learning), inaccurate, or misleading.

- *Student differentiation proliferates.* The administrative progressives found a particular "solution" to the increasing diversity of students around 1900: rather than place all students in the same schools with the same curricula, they began differentiating—by ability, by vocational aspiration, by race and class, by different forms of disability. The administrative progressive approach to lower-class and African American and immigrant students was to fall back on individual differences and individual rather than institutional explanations for lower performance. The school's challenge was to help working-class and black students adjust to middle-class norms—increasingly for vocational rather than civic purposes—and to Americanize immigrants. We now see some of these ways of differentiating as inequitable, because rather than providing more resources to low-performing students, they invariably ended up with fewer effective resources. The result was a highly inegalitarian schooling system, particularly compared to the other developed countries we like to compare ourselves to. Those inequalities are visually depicted in figure I.1.

The Neoliberal Approach to Schooling

A challenge to the conventional model of schooling has emerged in the past few years, one based on marketlike principles, neoliberal values, and choice mechanisms.[3] Of course, it is difficult to characterize this sector, since almost by definition it encompasses the widest possible variety of approaches. Still, many trends in the neoliberal sector are disturbing, and it is worth identifying its particular characteristics.

The rise of charter schools, choice schools, and voucher mechanisms over the past twenty years has been slow but steady, and a sector or system has now emerged with some distinctive contours. Such schools appear to compete predominantly in urban areas, not in suburban areas, where public schools operate relatively well and most parents are satisfied. As a result, a disproportionate number of students in these schools are minority. In Michigan, for example, black students make up 51 percent of charter school enrollment, compared to 20 percent of total school enrollment. They are often organized into chains of schools operated by charter management organizations (CMOs) and educational management organizations (EMOs) such as Green Dot Schools, KIPP (Knowledge is Power Program), Edison Schools (before it went out of business), and White Hat Management.

As in all markets, the neoliberal educational sector supports enormous variety. Like the car market, which offers tinny Yugos up to Ferrari and Rolls-Royces, this sector includes some idiosyncratic schools with innovative pedagogy, Afrocentric or ethnocentric schools with special curricula, and even "nonschools" like home schooling or the Big Picture Company, which initially tried to have all learning take place in internships. Everyone can find something to support in the mix; with so many variations, it is usually difficult to make sweeping claims about the neoliberal sector. However, a great deal of the neoliberal rhetoric and the pressure to take this approach appears to come not from idiosyncratic and innovative schools, but from

EMOs and CMOs, which have the capital, private backing, and institutional resources to operate chains of schools and which have been most insistent in promoting the virtues of choice and competition. These relatively large organizations now include about one-quarter of all students in charter schools, though the numbers are elusive because many of these private organizations will not provide data, even though they receive public money (Molnar et al. 2007). As we shift our attention to these chains of schools, the distinctive features of this sector become clearer:

- *The work of principals is largely managerial and entrepreneurial rather than instructional.* These principals are responsible for getting new schools chartered, finding additional funding, hiring teachers, and making sure teachers implement conventional programs. In this market-oriented sector, principals are not expected to be instructional leaders, to help teachers develop their instructional competencies, or to work with teachers in collegial and distributed patterns.

- *Teachers appear to be expendable in the process of production.* With the long work hours in the models of Teach for America and KIPP schools, teacher turnover is high, so teachers do not spend enough time in the "profession" to develop expertise in the innovative approaches required in a developmental approach to teacher preparation. Some EMO-run schools, like White Hat Management, use prepackaged curricula; they require some teacher training in the use of these materials but no real professional development.

- *Outcomes are measured by conventional standardized test scores rather than by a broad variety of assessments.* Curricula are usually standardized and focused on tests, subjects are quite conventional, and pedagogy relies on conventional behaviorist approaches and variants like "direct instruction."

- *The climate is regimented and disciplined.* Dress codes and strict norms of behavior are an improvement, to be sure, on the chaotic conditions of some urban schools, but they hardly provide the kind of educationally supportive climate that can enhance outcomes for low-performing students.

- *The benefits of competition appear to be modest.* Advocates of neoliberalism in every area constantly trumpet the virtues of competition. In education, competition does seem to improve the quality of education, at least as measured narrowly by test scores, but many estimates of benefits (one-third to two-thirds) are statistically insignificant, the distributive effects are unclear, and the costs—of regulation and monitoring, for example—are still unknown (Belfield and Levin 2002). In addition, there are public-sector ways of developing forms of choice without the detrimental effects of competition, as many districts have done with small schools, charters, schools-within-schools, and pathways through high school.

These charter and choice schools now have a large structure of support. Some urban districts—Philadelphia, Hartford, Baltimore—have turned some of their schools over to EMOs to manage. The No Child Left Behind legislation calls for failing schools to be converted into charter schools under certain conditions, and this might enhance the growth of the sector in the future. Business organizations—the Business Roundtable, the Business Coalition for Education, the Business Education Task Force, the Council for Economic Development—have periodically issued reports that criticize public schools and call for greater use of managerial practices from business; such groups usually complain that schools do not serve the employment needs of business well, though they never offer to participate in strengthening public education directly. A network of neoliberal foundations—the Broad Foundation, the New School Venture Fund, the Fordham Foundation, the Walton Family Foundation, the Fisher Family Foundation—has provided funding, legitimacy, and visibility to this sector, at the same time denigrating the public schools and conventional teacher and principal preparation.

The ideology of the neoliberal sector is corporate, with its emphasis on efficiency, competition, consumer choice, managerial expertise, expansion through franchising, and profit. It is sometimes difficult to see where the opportunities for profit in education lie. While there may be some economies of scale from larger size (Molnar et al. 2007; Nelson et al. 2001), several other factors seem more important. The neoliberal sector has been uniformly hostile to teacher unions, and some of these chains pay low salaries—particularly considering the amount of effort required of teachers. With high teacher turnover, CMOs and EMOs pay the low salaries of beginning teachers, not the higher salaries of experienced teachers. So the opportunities for profit seem to come largely from teachers, who, as in the usual corporate practice, are seen as workers to be exploited, not as professionals whose development is crucial to the educational enterprise. In addition, EMO-managed schools tend to have fewer special education students and fewer low-income students than the surrounding district schools (Nelson et al. 2001), suggesting that they make some effort to keep out high-cost students. In the end, the opportunities for profit arise from a conventional corporate strategy—keeping worker salaries low and excluding high-cost students.

The "solution" of the neoliberal sector to student diversity is a form of creaming—the traditional method of private education. Charter and choice schools require application, and so they are likely to attract the parents who are most actively engaged in the education of their children. These schools can also dismiss students more easily; as one teacher said, "We have ways of asking people not to come back. We really operate like a private school" (Fischer 2002, cited in Scott 2008). Thus, disruptive or troublesome or low-performing students are more likely to be eliminated.

In addition, the mantra of choice becomes a substitute for conceptions of equity. In a market system, consumers and parents are responsible for making wise choices. If there are inequities in the ability to make choices or inequities in purchasing power, these are beyond the responsibility of suppliers: no one worries that the distribution of Maseratis and mink coats is not equitable. As long as there are no artificial barriers to application—for example, procedures that discourage low-income or special ed students from applying—then the quasi-market presumably takes care of equity. This conception of equity focuses only on eliminating barriers to access, one of the weakest conceptions of equity (see table 6.1). But imposing stronger conceptions of equity on the neoliberal sector would be difficult without weakening the consumer choice and marketlike mechanisms that underlie neoliberalism.

The neoliberal sector represents a distinctive approach to schooling that draws on some strands of administrative progressivism (like managerialism and efficiency) while updating such practices with the language of competition and choice. But neoliberal and quasi-market approaches provide a false choice—between conventional urban schools plagued by waste, inefficiency, and the ineffective use of resources and charter schools driven by quasi-market principles.[4] Both of these alternatives are impoverished in various ways. Neither focuses much on the quality of instruction. Neither moves much beyond conventional tests as measures of outcomes or beyond a narrow range of academic subjects. Neither spends much energy developing the capacities of teachers or principals; neither provides any alternative to top-down management or support for distributed leadership in which teachers would have a greater voice. Neither devotes much attention to civic concerns and critical perspectives—public schools because these purposes have moved off their agenda (in part pushed by the Education Gospel and vocational purposes), and neoliberal schools because their ideology and sponsors will not allow critical perspectives. Neither has addressed the racial and ethnic dimensions of inequality forthrightly. And it is hard to imagine the most wonderful schools in this country—the ones with inspired teaching and rapt students and committed parents, those profiled in Mike Rose's *Possible Lives* (2006) and Karen Chenoweth's *"It's Being Done"* (2007)—following these principles.

The Complex/Constructivist Approach to Schooling

The real choice is not between conventional schools and charter schools; it is between these two limited visions of schooling, on the one hand, and the alternative that I have described throughout this book, on the other. To give it a name, I call this a complex/constructivist approach to schooling—"complex" because it calls for complex learning environments with more varied pedagogies, more innovation, and more student-centered methods in place of traditional teaching methods; and "constructivist" because of the greater use of constructivist or balanced pedagogies and because individuals in these schools and districts need to work collaboratively, both to construct their roles in different ways and to construct the compound, complex, and abstract resources that prove to be so important.[5] This conception also requires different policies from districts, as well as from state and federal governments, that provide greater help to schools in building capacity, as chapter 10 clarified. To be sure, complex/constructivist schools can appear in the neoliberal sector as individuals with unique visions develop charter schools or small choice schools. But this is not the dominant direction of the neoliberal sector, especially of the corporate forms operated by CMOs and EMOs. Such reforms take time, whereas schools and districts stampeded into reforms by high-stakes exams and the need for instant improvement are unlikely to turn to reforms that require such significant changes.

Many elements of the complex/constructivist approach are consistent with one another:

- *The emphasis is on instruction.* The most effective school resources include the quality of instruction (especially with shifts to more innovative and constructivist instruction), supportive professional development, and teachers' control over their own teaching. Principals are instructional leaders, and the districts supporting such schools put instruction first and foremost. While this precept may seem obvious and banal, it represents a clear challenge to the managerial concerns that dominated administrative progressivism and the fanatical attention to efficiency that reigned after 1900.[6]

- *"Making money matter" is a concern.* The myth of money has frayed, and improving schools simply by infusing new revenues has proved impossible. A new emphasis on "what works," even though it is politically embattled, at least points in the direction of effective resources. The concern for making money matter acknowledges that money alone is usually not sufficient to improve outcomes. In this transformation, the role of the improved school finance is to provide a new narrative with a broader conception of resources, including the compound, complex, and abstract resources that must be constructed rather than bought and that are, if anything, *more* unequally distributed than are money and simple resources (from table 1.1).

- *Student attachment to schooling and the behavior that promotes or hampers success in school are powerful resources.* While families and communities influence students' attachment to school and their behavior, the schools they attend also have potential effects, especially through pedagogical and school practices that can enhance motivation and engagement (National Research Council 2004). Such effects are now evident where small schools, schools-within-schools, and other more personalized learning environments have been created, but such practices could be extended much more widely.

- *A battle continues over curricula and purposes.* The academic curriculum established by 1900 continues to dominate, reinforced by accountability systems applied to reading and math only, but many educators—the heirs in many ways of "progressive" or child-centered education—have continued to insist on the importance of a broader curriculum, sometimes described as "well-rounded," "focused on the whole child," "wholistic," or "enriched." The rejection of a narrow curriculum is consistent with a broader focus on many outcomes in addition to basic test scores. This position is important in part because of evidence that it is possible to improve conventional test scores without enhancing more complex measures of learning or other outcomes like progress through schooling.

- *Restructuring schools involves distributed leadership and internal accountability, or professional learning communities.* In these alternatives to conventional top-down management, school leaders, teachers, and parents share leadership and decisionmaking. Such restructuring is consistent with evidence that schools need a different organization before they can use resources effectively or make other decisions wisely (as when they respond to external accountability systems). Distributed leadership and internal accountability also reflect the conclusion that many effective school resources must be constructed collectively rather than developed classroom by classroom or bought off the shelf. As a result, capacity-building within this third conception of schooling requires the reorganization of schools as well as a focus on instructional improvement and effective resources from all participants.

- *The diversity of students remains a primary concern.* The impulse of administrative progressives was to differentiate among students by providing second-class education and fewer school resources to low-performing students so as to prepare them for their "likely" or "realistic" futures, or "evident and probable destinies."[7] By contrast, the complex/constructivist approach differentiates students to provide low-performing students with *additional* resources. Precisely which resources are most effective and need to be increased remains highly debated, of course; schools trying to narrow inequalities have taken different paths of varying effectiveness, as described in chapter 8. But the intention of the complex/constructivist approach in differentiating students is quite different from the practices emerging from administrative progressives.

- *More educators realize the need to confront the racial and ethnic dimensions of inequality in education head on.* The growth of interest in such practices as culturally relevant pedagogy, the vast array of multicultural practices, the development of Afrocentric and ethnocentric schools, and reform efforts that use culturally specific materials, like Puente and Umoja (a program targeted at African American males), are all testimony to the conclusion that "color-blind" policies are inadequate. Even if current efforts still seem to be confined to individual classrooms and unique schools, at least some schools and districts are trying to develop widespread reforms to create more supportive school cultures.

- *More educators recognize that issues of dynamic inequality require attention.* The administrative progressives established a system of schooling in which students progress year by year from one grade to another, and then through standard courses and exams (now the SAT) they progress into college. They relied on a uniform course of study, embedded in textbooks and in teacher training, to maintain continuity among grades. That practice continues today: state standards define what happens grade by grade, and professional development in teaching adheres to these standards. However, aside from creating a structure for continuous advancement, the administrative progressives did not worry too much about the equity of advancement, and in the end the problem of diverging inequality was "resolved" through differentiation in middle school and high school. Now, with greater concerns over equity and over high school dropouts in particular, dynamic perspectives have emerged in questions about whether test score gaps widen or narrow over time, in language about student "trajectories" through schooling, and in recognition of a fourth-grade "slump" and problems with the ninth-grade transition. Although NCLB and state accountability mechanisms have often stampeded districts and schools into ineffective practices, at least they have focused more attention on students who have fallen behind grade-level norms. A view of inequality and equity from a dynamic perspective allows us to pose the right questions about why students so often diverge in their performance.

- *Funding is still a concern.* Obviously, public schools need to get their funding from some source other than cookie sales and car washing; money may not matter that much if it is poorly spent, but it is still potentially important. I outlined approaches to funding and revenue formulas in chapter 10: states could allocate funds to districts using weighted pupil formulas, price indices, and general rather than categorical funding, and they should worry about the stability of funding. In turn, districts could allocate funds to schools according to school-based budgeting, weighted pupil formulas, and how prepared school communities are to make their own resource decisions; then districts should support rather than impede what schools decide. But the detailed revisions of funding formulas—the "minutiae" of school reform—matter less than the cascade of efforts on the state, district, and school levels to spend money and other resources wisely and to focus on effective resources rather than replicating the old patterns of administrative progressives.

In sum, the constructivist and complex approach has given rise to a variety of practices and concerns that are consistent with each other and quite different from both the traditional approach of the administrative progressives and from neoliberal practices. At the moment, all three approaches coexist uncomfortably. Some districts and states are supporting charter and choice schools as well as trying to move conventional schools toward balanced practice. State policies continue the accountability mentality of the administrative progressives even though these mechanisms have thwarted the efforts of some schools to develop innovative instruction and broader curricula. The federal government is wedded to the control mechanisms of the administrative progressives and to neoliberal solutions if these fail, and NCLB has led to the further differentiation of students at the same time that it purports to care about "what works" and to champion proficiency for all students.

So existing policies are a mishmash drawn from all three approaches. The challenge is to align capacity-building in schools, as I have defined it, in complex and constructivist ways and with district, state, and federal policies that support such capacity-building. Just as classrooms can work smoothly only when their components—teacher practices, student expectations, curricular materials, and institutional requirements—are in equilibrium, so too schools trying to operate in complex and constructivist ways can do so comfortably only when district, state, and federal policies support their efforts to do so.

NONSCHOOL POLICIES AND THE DETERIORATING WELFARE STATE

Schools exist not only within a system of district, state, and federal policies but also within a social and economic system, and non-educational policies stemming from this larger system affect them in many ways. When we recognize that families and students are resources to schooling, improving the effectiveness and equity of schooling also requires non-educational policies—not instead of but in addition to reforming schools. And when we identify racial and ethnic disparities in schooling outcomes that cannot be explained by other dimensions of school resources, family background (including class dimensions), and student connectedness, then we must at least ask whether racial and ethnic dimensions of existing school *and* nonschool policies might be to blame. Even though attention to nonschool policies often seems an afterthought or detour in the analysis of education issues, it would be irresponsible to ignore them just because changing them seems politically unattainable.

Many others have attempted to wrestle with the appropriate role of school reform versus more general reform. When George Counts asked *Dare the Schools Build a New Social Order?* in 1932, he went on to tackle what he called the most profound social issue of the day—the "control of the machine," the requirement for public ownership of capital in a democracy. Similarly, W. E. B. DuBois wrote in 1935 (quoted in Tyack 1974, 229) that "race prejudice in the United States today is such that most Negroes cannot receive proper education in white institutions" and that even in school systems "where Negroes are tolerated they are not educated; they are crucified"— implying that racial prejudice needed to be moderated before school reforms were possible. In *City Schools and the American Dream*, Pedro Noguera (2003, 142) concluded that "it will not be possible to improve urban public schools until our society is willing to address the issues and problems confronting the children and families in the communities where schools are located"—problems that include poverty, urban decay and instability, and unemployment.

At the other extreme, most school reformers have said little about the non-educational policies required to support reform. Teacher unions— aside from a very small number of social justice unions (Peterson 1999)— have paid little attention to policies outside of education. The structure of state and federal governments, with education in departments separate from those responsible for health, housing, and welfare, makes it difficult to coordinate across policy areas, resulting in the problems that schools have in finding support services for their students.

In the middle, commentators from various political perspectives have called for "both-and" policies, implicitly remembering John Dewey's warning against "either-or" statements and false dichotomies. Samuel Bowles and Herbert Gintis (1975), among the most prominent Marxist critics of education, called for a distinctive American socialism as well as a different educational system. Harold Howe (1993, 31), Commissioner of Education under Lyndon Johnson, declared that rather than concentrate on fixing schools *or* directly attacking poverty, "the only possible response to this question is that both policies must be followed at the same time." In a widely cited volume,

Richard Rothstein (2004) has clarified the effects of class on schools, much as I did in chapter 4, calling for greater income equality, better health care, and stable housing as well as education reforms like early childhood, after-school, and summer programs. David Berliner's (2005) careful review of the many negative effects of poverty ends by calling for "two-way systems of accountability"—of educators to their communities and of communities to schools. Finally, antipoverty warriors almost always include several ed-ucation policies (particularly early childhood programs and anti-dropout efforts) among their recommendations for transfer programs and labor market reforms, a "both-and" policy for inequality rather than a focus on ed-ucation only.[8]

But these "both-and" policies have been difficult for educators to pro-mote, for at least three reasons. One problem stems from the rhetoric about "leaving no child behind" and the responsibility of educators to believe in the ability of all children to learn. Any educator who suggests that family effects or the wretched conditions of low-income communities are partly to blame for the educational difficulties of some children is criticized for making ex-cuses, for continuing to believe in the "myths and perceptions of who can learn and who can't," for not assuming the responsibilities for improvement. George Bush's famous rebuke of educators—blaming them for "another form of bias: the soft bigotry of low expectations"—has made it difficult for educators to point to the poor social and economic conditions of many chil-dren.[9] The Education Trust, a liberal advocacy group that has been especially ferocious in defending the goals of No Child Left Behind, attacked educators for "giving up" on poor and black children: "How should schools respond to racism and poverty? The fact is that too many educators—including some educators of color—have simply surrendered to these forces, and in so doing are surrendering our children's future" (Wilkins et al. 2006). The position that educators have too often blamed family backgrounds for school failures has great truth to it, but in its extreme form this criticism accuses anyone raising the serious problems of race and poverty—anyone promot-ing a "both-and" solution—of "surrendering our children's future," which are harsh words indeed.

The second problem is that the steady decline of the welfare state has left many children without the support for their well-being that makes learning possible. The welfare state in this country has always been relatively weak and market-oriented, with few policies challenging labor markets in any way (Esping-Andersen 1990). Consistent assaults have come from free-mar-keteers and neoliberals, who are ever eager to sweep away any limits on markets; from corporations, which are eager for schools to provide them with workers but unwilling to pay for either the direct costs of schooling or the indirect costs necessary to make schooling more equitable; and from Re-publicans, who veil their attacks on the welfare state with free-market rhetoric and the mantle of fiscal conservatism while passing tax reductions for the rich, subsidies for corporations, and enormous levels of spending for the military and its unfounded wars (Krugman 2007).

Stepped-up efforts to diminish the welfare state began with the Reagan administration, which relentlessly cut programs for children, income support programs, food programs (including school lunch and breakfast), and antidiscrimination programs. Reagan obscured the effects of these cuts with his genial untruths—like the promise that government cuts would be "equitable, with no one group singled out to pay a higher price"—and the mantra of limited government even after deficits increased spectacularly because of tax cuts and military spending.[10] The attacks continued with a vengeance under a Republican Congress in the 1990s. Bill Clinton capitulated to their pressure and approved welfare "reform" in 1996, ending welfare as an entitlement and replacing income support with Work First, the pressure to go to work rather than remain on welfare.[11] George Bush has continued these assaults, imposing tougher work requirements on recipients of Temporary Assistance for Needy Families (TANF) as well as enacting programs like faith-based initiatives and abstinence-only family planning programs on the assumption that cultural norms are responsible for poverty (Allard 2007). The administration's attack on Section 8 housing vouchers (Verrilli 2004) and Bush's two vetoes of the State Children's Health Insurance Program (S-CHIP) were widely criticized as a betrayal of his earlier promise of "compassionate conservatism." For those who believe in the welfare state as a safety net for low-income children and families—a low level of barely adequate support—the past three decades have been disastrous, and anyone who promotes increases in transfer programs for the poor—even in support of education—is swimming against the tide.

A third problem involves a transformation of attitudes about the relationship between the welfare state and education policies. Increasingly, education policies—particularly reforms that focus schooling on occupational preparation, the emphasis of the Education Gospel—have been promoted as a *substitute* for a strong welfare state rather than a complement, allowing opponents of the welfare state to point to education as the only solution to inequality. Examples are legion:

- Advocates have consistently promoted early childhood programs as a way to moderate the differences among children attributable to their families and communities—rather than investing directly in families through income support programs or more pervasive family policies.

- Promoters of more obviously vocationalized education have characterized it not only as a response to the need for higher skill levels but also as a cure for low incomes.

- Early twentieth-century advocates for African Americans, like Booker T. Washington and W. E. B. DuBois, all believed (despite their differences) that education was critical to the future of their race. This argument continues to be renewed in many agendas for racial and ethnic minorities that stress education rather than (not in addition to) eliminating employment discrimination, facilitating union organizing, or improving the low-skilled labor market and public employment.

- The "war on poverty" of the 1960s was founded largely on educational remedies, not on community development or labor market initiatives. As Lyndon Johnson declared in announcing the Elementary and Secondary Education Act of 1965, "It will help five million children of poor families to overcome their greatest barrier to progress—poverty"— even while it neglected other obvious causes of poverty (Lazerson 1987, 163–66). Similarly, short-term job training has been consistently promoted as a way to reduce unemployment and poverty, starting with the programs of the Great Depression and continuing to the Workforce Investment Act, despite continued evidence of their ineffectiveness and political expedience (Lafer 2002; Grubb 1996)—in place of efforts to reconstruct labor markets through minimum wage legislation, enforcement of antidiscrimination legislation, the defense of worker rights and the promotion of unions, and the development of public employment.

Most recently, when George Bush was asked about the widening gap between rich and poor, he responded with platitudes about education: "The No Child Left Behind Act is really a jobs act when you think about it."[12] Former Federal Reserve chairman Alan Greenspan, a consistent protector of corporate prerogatives and the architect of anti-inflation policies that tend to keep unemployment high, similarly promoted a better-skilled workforce as the solution to trade imbalances and the outsourcing of jobs to India and China—rather than limitations on corporate practices.[13] Several other narratives related to equity have collapsed. We no longer hear anything about a "family policy" to support families, a common proposal in the 1970s (Grubb and Lazerson [1982] 1988, ch. 9). The idea of public employment embedded in the 1973 Comprehensive Employment and Training Act (CETA), which provided the unemployed with both training and employment while meeting social needs such as public housing, has been dead ever since Reagan eliminated public-service employment in 1981. The notion of urban renewal, popular in the 1960s even if badly implemented, at least recognized a responsibility to improve the conditions of cities. Every narrative related to equity has been systematically snuffed out by antigovernment warriors in the last thirty years, leaving only equality of educational opportunity—a particularly abstract, difficult, and contested conception of equity, and one that cannot by itself produce equity even in educational outcomes, never mind in economic, political, and social outcomes.

Current social policy involves a kind of twist: turning to schooling to produce greater equity in a subsequent generation, particularly through NCLB, a program that imposes new requirements without providing low-performing schools the capacities and resources to improve. Meanwhile, programs of the welfare state have been weakened and the policies that might support equity among parents undermined. The tendency to see school policies as substitutes for non-educational policies rather than as complements represents a further narrowing of the already weak welfare state in this country. The result is a vicious circle of interactions between nonschool policies and school policies, each contributing to the greater inequality in the other. In the end, these practices result in extreme positions of inequality in the United States for both the distribution of earnings and the distribution of schooling and learning, as shown in figure I.1.

Given the prolonged attack on the welfare state, the idea of the "foundational state" might provide another way to frame the issues underlying non-educational policies (Grubb and Lazerson 2004, ch. 8). Free-marketeers are quite wrong about the state: rather than interfering with the operations of markets, a set of strong public policies and a great deal of social energy are necessary to maintain nominally private markets in working order. These include monetary and fiscal policies; regulatory policies, including oversight of financial markets to prevent them from cratering periodically; international trade policies; the legal system; regulation of the political system; defense policy; and a system of policing and social order. Such policies provide the foundations for markets to work well; when they are weakened, markets fail in one way or another. Countries that abandon public supports for markets may descend into gangster capitalism (as in Russia), totalitarian regimes (as in many African countries), or the anarchy of a failed state (like Haiti or Somalia). In the United States the weakness of regulation has led to periodic thievery, which the country experienced during the 1980s with the savings and loans and defense industries; during the early 2000s with the collapse of Enron, WorldCom, and other corporations; again in 2007 with the collapse of the housing market as a result of predatory lending practices in the subprime mortgage market; and throughout the years of the Iraq War by the thievery of defense contractors and mercenaries (Glanz 2008). So a strong state and a set of foundational policies are prerequisites for what we call "private" markets to work well. Similarly, the quasi-markets created by neoliberal practices in schooling also fail when consumers are poorly informed, when providers are inept or committed more to profits than to education, or when market-clearing mechanisms fail to operate.[14] Various public policies are essential to create the foundations for economic, political, and educational institutions to work well. These are not intrusions into markets but necessary supports or foundations for well-ordered markets and institutions.

If we believe the rhetoric of the Education Gospel and its faith in the development of a broadly skilled workforce, then the foundational state should create the policies that provide the foundation for a uniformly strong and equitable system of human development. In addition to reforms in schooling, this approach requires social policies that are complementary to schooling and that make the tasks of educators easier rather than harder. In particular, such an approach would require the following:

- *Efforts to counter family-based inequalities.* Early childhood policies, family literacy programs to orient parents and children to literacy practices associated with schooling (Askov et al. 2003), and certain forms of parent education, including those that emerge in outreach efforts like Puente, could moderate the effects of parental education, the most powerful family influence.[15] Such efforts could also offset some differences due to parental occupations and aspirations for children.

- *Housing policies to minimize the mobility of low-income students whose parents have problems finding stable housing.* Since mobility is detrimental to progress through schooling, housing subsidies and public housing should aim to maximize stability.

- *Income support policies to help offset the effects of low income on learning and college-going.* Specific ways to enhance incomes vary and include minimum wage legislation, tax and transfer policies like the earned income tax credit (EITC), and food stamps and other nutrition policies. The list of proposals varies among advocates, but a long list of antipoverty mechanisms exists to choose from.

- *Labor market policies to counter the hideous growth in inequality in this country.* This might include more powerful minimum wage laws, real enforcement of antidiscrimination laws, efforts to make labor organizations easier to organize, and better accountability of highly paid managers to stockholders and regulatory agencies.

- *A full range of health services so that poor health does not compromise a student's education.* Indeed, reforming health care could be one of the most important equity policies for a wide range of citizens (Krugman 2007, ch. 11).

- *Mental health and social services so that low-income children have access to the programs that middle-income parents seek when their children are depressed, angry, antisocial, attracted to drugs or alcohol, or otherwise unable to participate in normal developmental stages.* Such services might enhance connectedness to schooling, which can be undermined by mental health conditions

(NRC 2004, ch. 6) as well as by dimensions of family background and school practices.

- *Nutrition programs that follow the well-accepted practices of school lunch and breakfast programs.*

- *Urban development policies so that no student is surrounded by decay and violence.* These policies in turn need to be complemented by locational policies that operate against the creation of ghettos, including regulation of housing loans and redlining, careful attention to exclusionary zoning, the development of mixed-income housing and mixed-use development, and the careful location of public amenities.

- *Family support and child welfare programs to reduce violence against and neglect of children.*

Some of these services can be provided at school sites; for example, "full-service" schools provide a wide array of social programs to their students (see, for example, Comer 1996; Dryfoos 1994; U.S. GAO 1997). But many foundational policies—urban development, housing policies, income support—are far larger in scope than individual schools or districts can manage; the approach of full-service schools is attractive, but necessarily incomplete.

Requiring the foundational state or a resurrection of the welfare state to compensate for differences in family resources, as well as fostering equality of educational opportunity in the sense of enhanced resources, is an example of a "both-and" policy.[16] It reflects John Dewey's warning against "either-or" statements and false dichotomies, as well as Harold Howe's (1993) declaration that "both policies"—both fixing schools and directly attacking the inequalities that contribute to unequal schooling—"must be followed at the same time." Developing complementary policies is certainly difficult because of the politics of health and housing, urban development, and income support, and because governments are not structured to coordinate their programs. But we should not kid ourselves with rhetoric from the Education Gospel about the "devastating waste of human potential and severe economic costs to our country" of failing to educate poor children if we do not correct the social and economic conditions that make it impossible for some students to benefit from educational opportunities.

FULFILLING OUR HOPES FOR SCHOOLING

The prescriptions in this chapter for a thoroughly different approach to schooling and for a foundational state are a long way, both conceptually and politically, from where I started, with attempts to understand the role of money, school resources, the limitations of the old school finance, and the promise of new approaches. But that is the point: basic approaches to schooling are embedded in a large matrix of social, economic, historical, and political conditions. The narrative of money is a legacy of the period when the rapidly expanding public school system created persistent shortages of funds; that narrative is also a natural extension of a system in which efficiency and economy in spending have been crucial and a legacy of the administrative progressives and their concern with differentiation. The top-down management that has been part of the traditional model of both schools and districts is based on the conventional bureaucratic principles that also dominate business organizations (another legacy of administrative progressives). The simple input-output models that have been used to think about schools follow an industrial model of schooling in which simple inputs lead to increased outputs, within a "production process" that remains a black box. Even as teachers wrestle with differences among students in their motivation and engagement, students are not recognized as resources or seen as active participants in their own education, but rather are viewed as "raw materials" to be processed into finished products—or, in the era of No Child Left Behind, processed into individuals who are proficient on basic skills tests of English and math and no more. The neglect of the racial and ethnic dimensions of schooling, despite persistent concerns with equity (especially in funding), is consistent with the tendency to focus on individual differences and to blame individual students rather than viewing racial and class differences as in part school-based problems (Deschenes, Cuban, and Tyack 2001).

The vision of a complex/constructivist approach to public schooling that I outlined in the first section of this chapter is quite different in its treatment of all these issues. It replaces the myth of money with improved approaches to school resources. To construct collective resources—compound, complex, and abstract—it shifts from the top-down management of the conventional school organization to one characterized by distributed leadership and internal alignment. Rather than seeing students as "raw materials," as in behaviorist and teacher-centered approaches to instruction, these schools are concerned with turning passive (or even resistant) students into active participants in their own education and enhancing students' motivation and engagement with both instructional practices and school structures. The development of policies that confront racial-ethnic and class-related mistreatment is a result not only of taking more student-centered approaches but also of recognizing that achievement gaps will never be closed until we confront such differences forthrightly. Finally, conventional approaches to schooling—both those following the era of the administrative progressives and now those of the emerging neoliberal sector—have treated schools as free-standing institutions, and "school reform" has meant changing the practices of schools only. But of course this is nonsense: not only are schools financially dependent on a system of public taxation, but the success of many students is dependent on the preparation and reinforcement they receive in their families and communities. So school reform is incomplete without complementary nonschool policies in the foundational state or a reconstructed welfare state.

It seems likely that revised approaches to school resources, to dynamic equity, and to a reconstructed welfare state will require a new politics. New approaches certainly require a shift away from interest-group politics, which is based on the self-interest of organized groups, toward a politics based more on principle.[17] They may require a different role for parents since the "politics of resentment," based on battling for one's own children and against the interests of "other people's children," is always and everywhere detrimental to equity. In the realm of schooling, it requires unions that will abandon the politics of industrial unions, with their combative views of teacher-administrator relationships, in favor of professional unionism (Kerchner and Caufman 1993), with teachers joining with school and district leaders to improve instructional conditions, and also in favor of social justice unions, with their commitment to equity outside of schools. Whether we as a nation can achieve such a substantial shift in politics is unclear, though some observers think that the 2008 elections may be a referendum on a new politics. But without at least a moderation of current political alignments, complex and constructivist approaches to schooling and reforms of non-educational policies may be impossible to achieve.

The tendency in this country—indeed, in many countries—has been to invest more and more of our hopes in schooling. Schooling has become the principal mechanism of individual advancement and the mechanism of the American Dream (Hochschild and Scovronick 2003), and in the rhetoric of the Education Gospel, schools and universities are widely viewed as the solution to international competitiveness and growth. Schooling has become one of the principal mechanisms of equity and a substitute for the welfare state; early childhood education is the dominant antidote suggested for the variation among students due to family backgrounds. In a society that often seems hopelessly fragmented and divided, the old hope of the common school—to provide a common foundation of civic and moral understanding for all citizens—seems more necessary than ever before. Turning to schooling seems more attractive and more feasible than many of the alternatives, like turning back to families, with their enormous variation; or reconstructing the welfare state, with its many dismal associations; or relying on corporations, with their relentless and self-serving drive for profit; or turning to churches, community-based organizations, and other institutions of civil society, with their uneven distribution and allegiances.

But we hold these hopes for schooling at the same time that we impose accountability systems without providing schools—especially low-performing schools—with the capacity to meet the demands of these systems. We demand better teaching and equitable outcomes without understanding the approaches to teaching and learning that might make it possible to meet these goals. We continue to create schools in the conventional ways established in the nineteenth century, complaining about industrial-era institutions in the twenty-first century but doing little, especially at the state and federal levels, to encourage schools to develop in different ways. We demand equity without providing either the school resources or the foundational economic and social conditions that might enhance equity. Our demands and our actions are impossibly contradictory, and schools are caught in the middle.

One "solution" might be to moderate our demands on schools—to lower the volume of the Education Gospel, to be more realistic about goals like achieving proficiency among all students by 2014, to confess that we are hopelessly divided as a country about equity, immigration, racial and ethnic injustice, and responsibility for class effects. But lowering our expectations seems precisely the wrong way to go; indeed, the one good result from the accountability movement and from No Child Left Behind is that they have made effectiveness and equity such prominent goals. The only alternative, then, is to work over time to understand a different approach to schooling, to implement the many interconnected elements necessary for a complex and constructivist approach, and to provide both the complex array of school resources and the non-educational policies necessary to realize this vision.

Appendix A

Technical Issues and Variable Definitions

THESE RESULTS are based on the restricted-use sample of NELS88. Three complications arise in estimating equations with NELS88 data. One is the problem of missing data for individual questions. One potential solution—deleting every observation with missing data—would both bias the sample and result in a much smaller sample. In these results, I give each individual with missing data for a particular variable the mean value from the rest of the sample and construct a dummy variable equal to one for those with missing data; this approach exhausts the information available. An alternative, multiple imputation, involves estimating equations for each of the variables for which there are missing data and using these estimated equations to interpolate values (Rubin 1987), but in addition to this method's complexity, there is no causal logic underlying the estimated equations.

A second complication is that NELS88, like every longitudinal data set, lost students over time. NELS88 began with 24,599 individuals in eighth grade; that sample dwindled to 16,489 with complete data for the first three waves and 13,120 for those with the first four waves of data, including students in both public and private schools. The results in this volume, for outcomes as of twelfth grade, start from the second of these samples, though missing data for various dependent variables means that the sample sizes for particular specifications vary from this (see the numbers in table B.2). In addition, the dependent variables for high school graduation and for entry into two- and four-year colleges were drawn from transcript data and the third follow-up, respectively, so these sample sizes are smaller still. Because attrition was nonrandom, the data set includes weights to compensate for attrition so that the sample when weighted can mimic a nationally representative sample. Most results for second follow-up (F2) outcomes in this paper are weighted by F2PNLWT, and for results based on third follow-up (F3) outcomes with F3PNLWT. The use of weights makes a substantial difference to parameter estimates, so software without the capacity to incorporate weights was rejected.

In addition, NELS collected data with a two-stage sampling procedure: schools were randomly sampled, and then students within schools were randomly sampled. Because the students within particular schools are not as varied as students in the entire population—since schools are segregated by family background, including income, parental education, and race—the variation in such a sample is smaller than in the population, and the standard errors of estimated parameters are also smaller than those from a random sample. There are various approaches to correcting standard errors; the results presented here have been estimated by STATA, which uses a Taylor series approach to calculating standard errors.

In the results presented here, all variables are taken from the second follow-up, senior year, unless noted. P refers to the parent questionnaire, S to the student questionnaire, A to the administrator questionnaire, and T to the teacher questionnaire; these provide information about sources of information. "Adj." refers to adjustment for cross-sectional cost differences by Chambers's (1998) measures plus the consumer price index (CPI) for time-series variation, since the CPI is as effective as more complicated indices of inflation (Chambers 1997).

Dependent Variables: Schooling Outcomes

MATHTS	Math test score, scaled	F22XMIRR
SCITS	Science test score, scaled	F22XSIRR
READTS	Reading test score, scaled	F22XRIRR
HISTTS	History test score, scaled	F22XHIRR
CLSRNK	Class rank (percentile)	F2RRANK
HEDASP	High educational aspirations	S43
HOCASP	High occupational aspirations	S64
CONTED	Plans to continue education past high school	S56
TOTCRED	Total credits earned	F2RNWB2A
ACPRO	Completed standard academic program	F2RNWB3A
DIPLOM	High school diploma (transcript-reported)	F2RTROUT
ENR4YR	Enrolled in four-year college (third follow-up)	PSEFIRTY
ENT2YR	Enrolled in two-year college(third follow-up)	PSEFIRTY

Independent Variables
School Resources: Simple Resources

P/TRTIO (—)	Pupil-teacher ratio	A1, A29
LOWTCHSAL	Lowest teacher salary	A37, adj.
HITCHSAL	Highest teacher salary	A37, adj.

Compound Resources

TCHEXP	Average years taught in secondary school	T4.4b
INFIELDTCH	Teaching in field	T4.9, T4.10
PLANTIME	Teacher planning time	A38
STDEV	Staff development time	T4.17
GENED	Student in the general track	S12a
VOCED	Student in the vocational track	S23a
REMED	Student in remedial courses	S13a, b, f, h

Complex Resources

TIMEUSE	Percentage of time on order, tests, administration	T2.12d, e, f
CONVTCH	Conventional teaching approach	T2.13a, c, e, h
INNOVTCH	Innovative teaching approach	T2.13b, d, f, g, i
TCHCONT	Teacher control over practice	T3.2, a–f
TCHEFF	Teacher sense of efficacy	T3.2, a–f
DEPTINNOV	Department innovation	T3.5a, b, k
CONMTHTCH	Math teaching conventional	S19Ba, b, c; S20b
INNMTHTCH	Math teaching innovative	S19Bd, e, g, h, i, j, k, l; S20a, c, d, e
CONSCITCH	Science teaching conventional	S15Ba, b, c; S16b
INNSCITCH	Science teaching innovative	S15Be, f, g, h, i, j, k, l; S36a, c, d, e

Abstract Resources

POSCLIM	Positive school climate	A56b, d, f, g, h, l
NEGEV	Negative events at school	S8
COLPRES	College pressure in the school	A12, A13
INTCONT	Internal school control	A52 (1–3)

PRINCONTR	Principal control	A52 (1)
SCHATT	School attendance rate	A21
SCHSTAB	School stability	A53
%SCHLNCH	Percentage of students receiving free or reduced lunch	A25
SCHPROB	School problems (like tardiness, absenteeism, fighting, theft, gang activities)	A57

Exogenous School Structure and Policy

PRIREL	Private religious schools	A4
PRIVNREL	Private nonreligious school	A4
MAGNET	Public magnet school	A4b
CHOICE	Public school of choice	A4c
ADA	School size: log of school ADA	A1
STEXIT	State exit exam	A42, A43, A44
DISTEXIT	District exit exam	A42, A43, A44
COMPTEST	Competency tests	A42, A43, A44

Family Background

MED<HS	Mother's education less than high school	F1PARED
MEDSC	Mother's education some college	F1PARED
MEDCOL	Mother's education BA degree or higher	F1PARED
MPOCCLO	Mother's occupation low-skilled	P1a, b
MOCCHI	Mother's occupation high-skilled	P1a, b
INC/DED(a)	Family income per dependent (adj.)	P74, P6
COLLSAVE	Money saved for college	P81
PARASPLO	Parental aspirations: some college or less	S42
PARASPHI	Parental aspirations: graduate school	S42
FHH	Female-headed family	P1, P4
FAMCHNG	Family changes	S96
CHNGSCH	Changed school from F1 to F2	P33
LANGNENG	Native language not English	P1, P4
RELIG	Religious observance	P50e, S105, S106
MATER	Learning materials in the home	S35a–h, m (BY)

Student Ability to Benefit

HMWRK	Total hours per week on homework	S25f
READ	Reading outside of school	S32
COUNS	Student use of counseling	S53, S54, S58a
ACHHELP	School academic help	S57
ATTPROB	Ever in trouble for attendance	S9
DAYSABS	Total days absent over four years	RAB88–91
BEHPROB	Behavior problems	P35
WRKHRS	Hours per week working	S88
EXTRACURR	Student time on extracurricular activities	S31
OUTACT	Student activities outside of school	S39
TV	Hours of television per week	S35
COLLPEERS	Peers in favor of college	S69d, e
DROPPEERS	Peers in favor of dropping out	S69a
GANG	Gang involvement	S70, S71
BABY	Had a child or expecting	S76
VOCVAL	Vocational orientation	S40a, c, e, n
AFFVAL	Affiliation with others	S40b, d, g, h, k
ESCAPVAL	Escapist values	S40i, m
ALTVAL	Altruistic orientation	S40f, j

Demographic Variables

MALE	Male	
BLACK	Black	
LATINO	Latino	
ASIAN-AM	Asian American	
AMERIND	American Indian	
HAND	Physical handicap	S13g

Appendix B

Table B.1   Effects of School Resources on Schooling Outcomes

Independent Variable	MATHTS Spec. 1	MATHTS Spec. 2	SCITS Spec. 1	SCITS Spec. 2	READTS Spec. 1	READTS Spec. 2	HISTTS Spec. 1	HISTTS Spec. 2
Simple resources								
Pupil-teacher ratio	−.025**	−.21**	−.011	−.007	−.005	−.004	−.001	.004
Low teacher salary	.025*	.028**	.018	.017	−0.003	−.004	0.015	.013
High teacher salary	.03**	.011	.016	.014	.030*	.020	.041**	.027
Compound resources								
Teacher experience in secondary school	.044***	.031***	.046***	.037***	.031***	.021**	.045***	.034**
Teaching in field of preparation	.023***	.014**	.016*	.009	.018**	.010	.026***	.018**
Planning time	.022**	.012	.034***	.030***	.019	.024**	.018	.024***
Staff development time	.014	.012	−.007	−.008	.007	.004	.008	.006
General education track	−.124***	−.078***	−.114***	.007***	−.091***	−.049***	−.112***	−.072***
Vocational education track	−.110***	−.067***	−.100**	−.066***	−.102***	−.059***	−.116***	−.078***
Remedial education enrollment	−.208***	−.161***	−.138***	−.104***	−.167***	−.126***	−.147***	−.111***
Complex resources								
Teacher use of time	−.031***	−.027***	−.026**	−.023***	−.021*	−.019	−.016	−.013
Conventional teaching	−.022**	−.017**	−.018*	−.013**	−.028**	−.025**	−.013	−.011
Innovative teaching	.007	.005	.008	.005	.014	.013	−.005	−.005
Teacher control	.033***	.028***	.017*	.016*	.020**	.020**	.017	.017
Teacher sense of efficacy	−.019*	−.013	.002	.005	−.004	.001	−.007	−.004
Department supports innovation	.006	−.002	.007	−.002	−.002	−.010	.002	−.007
Conventional math teaching	−.018*	−.011	−.022**	−.019**	−.021**	−.017	−.022**	−.019**
Innovative math teaching	.058***	.049***	.034***	.030***	.035***	.029***	.032***	.028***

	HEASP		HOCASP		LOCASP		CONTED	
	Spec. 1	Spec. 2	Spec. 1	Spec. 2	Spec. 1	Spec. 2	Spec. 1	Spec. 2
Abstract resources								
Positive school climate	.037***	.026***	.046***	.036***	.055***	.040***	.027**	.021*
Negative events at school	−.031***	−.017*	.006	.004	−.042***	−.025**	−.024**	−.009
College pressure	−.006	−.005	−.010	−.010	−.007	−.006	−.017	−.014
Internal school control	.001	−.005	.005	−.001	.002	−.005	−.001	−.005
Principal control	−.012	−.005	−.016	−.009	.000	−.008	−.010	−.004
School attendance rate	.034**	.026***	.040***	.032***	.042***	.035***	.036***	.029***
Percent receiving school lunch	−.032**	−.016	−.036***	−.022**	−.016	−.007	−.046***	−.034***
School problems (administration-reported)	−.005	.012	−.001	.005	.006	.007	−.023	−.014*
Exogenous school structure and policy								
Private religious school	.012	.013	−.028**	−.009	.022*	.014	.014	.019
Private nonreligious school	.005	.008	−.040*	−.029*	−.001	.003	−.025	−.017
Magnet school	−.006	−.007	−.013	−.012	−.012	−.015*	−.014	−.015
Choice school	.013	.015	.005	.004	.005	.006	.018	.019*
ADA	−.466***	−.398***	−.311**	−.287**	−.283*	−.221*	−.370**	−.319**
ADA-squared	.487***	.411***	.329***	.302**	.326**	.254*	.396**	.338**
State exit exam	−.001	.012	−.012	.001	−.026	.010	−.016	−.007
District exit exam	.012	.008	−.005	−.007	−.017	−.021*	−.003	−.004
Competency tests	−.025	−.022	.008	.016	.018	−.016	.013	.022
Observations	12,021	12,021	11,943	11,943	12,020	12,020	11,887	11,887
R-squared	.53	.58	.45	.48	.43	.47	.41	.44

Independent Variable	HEASP		HOCASP		CONTED	
	Spec. 1	Spec. 2	Spec. 1	Spec. 2	Spec. 1	Spec. 2
Simple resources						
Pupil-teacher ratio	−.009	−.008	−.012	−.009	−.012	−.010
Low teacher salary	.022*	.019	.011	.008	−.025*	−.026*
High teacher salary	−.015	−.012	.035**	.033**	.033**	.037**

Table B.1 Continued

Independent Variable	HEASP		HOCASP		CONTED	
	Spec. 1	Spec. 2	Spec. 1	Spec. 2	Spec. 1	Spec. 2
Compound resources						
Teacher experience in secondary schools	.010	.009	.002	.001	-.021*	-.021**
Teaching in field of preparation	.002	.001	.024**	.022*	.014*	.014*
Planning time	-.008	-.008	-.031**	-.033**	-.003	-.003
Staff development time	.009	.009	.024*	.023**	.016	.017
General education track	-.057***	-.042***	-.056***	-.041***	-.012	.001
Vocational education track	-.044***	-.034***	-.097***	-.081***	-.040***	-.028**
Remedial education enrollment	-.049***	-.042***	-.053***	-.045***	-.045***	-.036***
Complex resources						
Teacher use of time	.002	-.001	.021*	.019*	.001	.001
Conventional teaching	-.008	-.009	.014	.014	-.018*	-.016
Innovative teaching	-.010	-.008	-.029**	-.027**	.003	.002
Teacher control	.010	.011	.018	.019	-.012	.012
Teacher sense of efficacy	-.001	.000	-.003	-.002	-.005	-.006
Department supports innovation	-.002	.001	-.011	-.013	-.010	-.009
Conventional math teaching	.005	.004	-.002	.001	.023**	.023**
Innovative math teaching	.024***	.027***	.036***	.022**	.010	.008
Abstract resources						
Positive school climate	-.004	-.002	.033**	.035***	.028**	.032**
Negative events at school	-.029***	-.030***	-.034***	-.029***	-.016	-.014
College pressure	.004	.004	-.023**	-.023**	-.026**	-.024**
Internal school control	.002	-.000	-.021	-.022	-.004	-.007
Principal control	-.005	-.004	-.011	-.009	.007	.009
School attendance rate	.009	.010	-.009	-.010	.017	.018
Percent receiving school lunch	-.001	-.005	-.047***	-.041***	-.025**	-.029**
Frequency of school problems	-.018	-.019	-.001	-.002	.007	.005

Independent Variable	TOTCRED[a]	ACPRO[a]	DIPLOM[a]	ENR4YR[a]	ENR2YR[a]
Exogenous school structure and policy					
Private religious school	.011	.005	.046***	.022**	.016
Private nonreligious school	−.026	−.036	−.025	−.028	−.028
Magnet school	−.010	−.010	−.010	−.014	−.014
School of choice	.011	.011	.007	.005	.006
Average daily attendance	−.032	−.060	.111	.155	.173
ADA-squared	.075	.098	−.085	−.093	−.125
State exit exam	−.009	−.006	−.013	.027	.027
District exit exam	.000	−.002	−.009	.017	.014
Competency tests	.027	.023	.017	−.022	−.023
Observations	13,623	13,623	12,538	14,401	14,401
R-squared	.44	.45	.21	.22	.23
Simple resources					
Pupil-teacher ratio	.012	−.039*	.050***	−.067***	.080***
Low teacher salary	.089**	.006	.015	.013	.008
High teacher salary	−.011	.016	−.007	.013	−.017
Compound resources					
Teacher experience in secondary schools	.016	.001	.001	.020*	−.011
Teaching in field of preparation	.026	.006	−.018	.007	.008
Planning time	.051	−.048**	.016	.001	−.003
Staff development time	−.027	−.032**	−.006	−.015	.028**
General education track	−.059***	−.161***	−.011	−.114***	.051***
Vocational education track	.017	−.136***	.010	−.115***	.008
Remedial education enrollment	−.041**	−.092***	−.049***	−.093***	.021

Table B.1   *Continued*

Independent Variable	TOTCRED[a]	ACPRO[a]	DIPLOM[a]	ENR4YR[a]	ENR2YR[a]
Complex resources					
Teacher use of time	.015	−.009	−.010	−.017	.033**
Conventional teaching	−.044**	−.024*	−.018	−.018	.025
Innovative teaching	.021	.005	.026	.023	−.058***
Teacher control	.047***	.013	.027	.020*	−.006
Teacher sense of efficacy	.028	.015	−.043***	.003	.002
Department supports innovation	−.037**	.027	−.001	−.004	−.005
Conventional math teaching	−.027*	−.023*	.000	.003	.010
Innovative math teaching	.005	.053***	.032*	.025**	−.022
Abstract resources					
Positive school climate	−.006	−.001	.004	−.009	−.022
Negative events at school	−.019	−.030**	.017	−.018*	−.007
College pressure	.016	.031*	−.011	.002	−.010
Internal school control	−.044	.008	−.007	.001	−.004
Principal control	.037*	−.030	.038*	−.028*	.007
School attendance rate	.004	.005	−.010	.000	.007
Percent receiving school lunch	−.034	−.027	−.067***	.011	−.049***
Frequency of school problems	−.007	−.022	−.033	−.014	−.008

Exogenous school structure and policy					
Private religious school	.084****	.074****	-.041**	.043**	-.019
Private nonreligious school	-.122****	-.084****	-.014	.001	.010
Magnet school	.023	.020	-.030	-.016	-.011
School of choice	-.004	-.013	-.037*	-.005	.009
Average daily attendance	-.573	.529***	.033	-.045	-.166
ADA-squared	.460	-.485***	-.077	.084	.145
State exit exam	-.011	.066**	-.022	-.009	-.051
District exit exam	.027	.000	.037	-.022	.031
Competency tests	.010	-.008	-.014	-.052*	.125***
Observations	13,133	13,133	12,927	11,155	11,155
R-squared	.31	.30	.28	.36	.07

Source: Author's calculations.

[a]These results are for specification 1 only.

Normalized beta coefficients: * significant at 10%; ** significant at 5%; *** significant at 1%

Table B.2   The Effects of Fiscal Variables on Effective School Resources

Dependent Variables	Current Expenditures per Pupil	Percent Instructional Expenditures	Percent State Revenue	Percent Federal Revenue	Parent Contribution per Pupil	R-Squared	Number of Observations
Simple resources							
Pupil-teacher ratio	−.234**	−.035	.022	−.014	0	.29	11,325
Low teacher salary	.382***	.059**	−.087**	−.114***	.038	.42	10,230
High teacher salary	.472***	.073***	−.101***	−.195***	−.037*	.62	10,144
Compound resources							
Teacher experience in secondary schools	.120***	.055**	−.018	−.077***	.005	.16	6,681
Teaching in field of preparation	.011	.028	−.049*	.048*	−.041*	.07	6,666
Planning time	.087**	.023	−.063	.074*	−.078***	.12	11,574
Staff development time	−.027	−.052***	−.021	−.026	.023	.08	11,574
Student counseling	.042***	.022*	−.006	.045**	−.002	.10	11,209
Extracurricular activities	.032*	−.015	.017*	−.022	−.031***	.14	11,333
General track	−.003	−.034**	−.004	−.029	−.033**	.10	10,945
Vocational track	.038**	.043**	−.006	.050**	.034**	.15	10,945
Remedial education	.003	−.011	−.021	.008	.015	.15	11,109

Complex resources						
Teacher collaboration	−.092***	−.011	−.063**	−.035	.050**	.25	6,570
Conventional teaching	−.056**	−.025	.031	.014	.003	.04	11,574
Innovative teaching	−.052**	.044	.010	.002	.007	.07	11,574
Teacher control	.048*	.088***	.010	.019	−.093***	.22	7,180
Teacher efficacy	.026	.009	−.052*	.019	−.033	.16	6,655
School and department support innovation	.006	.028	−.090***	.0	.026	.24	6,588
Math teaching conventional	−.035	.033*	−.022	.024	−.010	.05	11,574
Math teaching innovative	−.035	.025	−.029	.008	−.035**	.08	11,574
Abstract resources						
School attendance rate	−.100**	.040	−.071*	−.029	−.113	.21	10,794
Positive school climate	.033*	.015	−.041**	−.007	−.022	.15	11,453
Negative events	−.017	−.029**	−.004	−.006	.009	.20	11,450

Source: Author's calculations.

Beta coefficients: *significant at 10%; ** significant at 5%; *** significant at 1%

Table B.3   The Effects of Family Background on Schooling Outcomes

Independent Variables	MATH		SCI		READ		HIST	
	Spec. 1	Spec. 2	Spec. 1	Spec. 2	Spec. 1	Spec. 2	Spec. 1	Spec. 2
Mother's education less than high school	-.025**	-.010	-.031***	-.020**	-0.008	.005	-0.008	-.001
Mother's education some college	0.021*	-.010	.026*	-.003	0.019*	-.009	0.021*	-.007
Mother's education BA or higher	.105***	.006	.099***	.004	.097***	-.001	.111***	.011
Mother's occupation unskilled	.021**	-.011	-.024**	-.011	-.029***	-.015	-.021	-.012
Mother's occupation professional or managerial	-.007	-.010	-.010	-.010	.001	-.001	.004	.002
Income per dependent (adj.)	.023**	.002	.015	.002	.014	-.003	.023**	.010
College savings	.008	-.001	.011	.001	-.005	-.011	.003	-.003
Parent aspirations low	-.088***	-.068***	-.063***	-.068***	-.075***	-.056***	-.060***	-.045***
Parent aspirations high	.009	-.009	.011	-.009	.017	.001	.020	.002
Female head of household	-.002	.000	-.003	.000	.008	.007	-.015	-.016
Family changes	-.005	-.030	-.017	-.003	-.016	-.015	-.014	-.013
Changed school	-.025**	-.017	-.011	-.005	.002	.005	.002	.004
Language not English	.010	.010	-.022	-.013	-.043***	-.033**	-.011	-.006
Religious	.002	.004	.010	.011	.020*	.018*	.015	.016

Independent Variables	HEDASP		HOCASP		CONTED	
	Spec. 1	Spec. 2	Spec. 1	Spec. 2	Spec. 1	Spec. 2
Mother's education less than high school	-0.011	-.008	0.022	.017	-0.008	-.003
Mother's education some college	-0.010	-.014	0.016	.006	.037**	.026*
Mother's education BA or higher	.054***	.032**	.059***	.036**	.042***	.028*
Mother's occupation unskilled	0.008	.008	-0.015	-.016	-.023*	-.020*

Independent Variables						
Mother's occupation professional or managerial	.005	.000	.011	.005	−.019	−.018
Income per dependent	.031***	.022*	.006	−.001	−.014	−.021*
College savings	.000	−.004	−.001	−.003	.023*	.019*
Parent aspirations low	.019**	.022**	−.161***	−.151***	−.118***	−.106**
Parent aspirations high	.522***	.494***	.050***	.043***	−.034***	−.044***
Female head of household	−.005	−.011	−.010	−.013	−.023	−.023*
Family changes	−.012	.008	.000	.004	.009	.001
Changed school	.004	.003	−.023*	−.024*	−.007	−.003
Language not English	.000	−.006	−.007	−.008	−.024	−.030*
Religious	.019*	.019*	.024**	.022**	−.006	−.002

Independent Variables	TOTCRED	ACPRO	DIPLOM	ENR4YR	ENR2YR
Mother's education less than high school	−.018	.024	−.031	.012	−.012
Mother's education some college	.068***	.021	−.004	.032**	.026
Mother's education BA or higher	.104***	.088***	.012	.145***	−.032
Mother's occupation unskilled	−.032	−.019	−.002	−.004	−.041***
Mother's occupation professional or managerial	−.022	−.011	.019	.004	−.019
Income per dependent	−.028	.020	−.018	.019	.000
College savings	.002	.033**	.008	.053***	−.040***
Parent aspirations low	−.020	−.053***	−.023	−.111***	.000
Parent aspirations high	−.008	.030*	.028	.030***	−.023
Female head of household	−.066***	−.006	−.049***	.021**	−.016
Family changes	−.021	−.015	−.004	−.035***	.004
Changed school	−.082***	−.027**	−.058***	−.041***	.044**
Language not English	.069**	.002	.028	.021	.021
Religious	−.002	−.020*	.010	.016	−.015

Source: Author's calculations.
Coefficients are beta coefficients: * significant at 10%; ** significant at 5%; *** significant at 1%

Table B.4   The Effects of Demographic Variables

				Dependent Variables			
Independent Variables	MATHTS	SCITS	READTS	HISTTS	HED ASP	HOC ASP	CONTED
Male							
Spec. 1	.038***	.147***	-.117***	.072***	-.060***	-.193***	-.098***
Spec. 2	.090***	.196***	-.050***	.138***	-.007	-.154***	-.060***
Spec. 3	.068***	.115***	-.014	.082***	-.001	-.110***	-.050
Coef. 2/Coef. 1	2.36	1.33	.45	1.92	.117	.800	.61
Coef. 3/Coef. 1	1.78	.79	.12	1.14	.020	.57	.51
Black							
Spec. 1	-.228***	-.267***	-.197***	-.182***	.021	-.027	-.022
Spec. 2	-.111***	-.164***	-.099***	-.082***	.024	.020	.024*
Spec. 3	-.035***	-.081***	-.036***	-.032***	-.002	.013	.004
Coef. 2/Coef. 1	.49	.61	.50	.45	1.14	n.a.	n.a.
Coef. 3/Coef. 1	.15	.30	.18	.18	n.a.	n.a.	n.a.
Latino							
Spec. 1	-.171***	-.193***	-.153***	-.153***	-.014	-.031**	.009
Spec. 2	-.068***	-.074***	-.041***	-.038***	.002	.014	.062***
Spec. 3	-.024**	-.029**	-.009	-.009	-.001	.012	.047***
Coef. 2/Coef. 1	.40	.38	.27	.250	.12	.45	10.33
Coef. 3/Coef. 1	.14	.15	.06	.06	.29	.39	5.22
Asian							
Spec. 1	.053***	-.003	.015	.019	.075***	.044***	.048***
Spec. 2	.020*	-.011	.009	.001	.006	.013	.035***
Spec. 3	.009	-.002	.021***	.003	.005	.005	.023***
Coef. 2/Coef. 1	.38	3.67	.60	.05	.08	.30	.73
Coef. 3/Coef. 1	.17	.67	1.40	.16	.07	.11	.48

Independent Variables							
American Indian							
Spec. 1	-.080***	-.081***	-.083***	-.081***	.001	-.010	-.024
Spec. 2	-.039***	-.042***	-.047***	-.045***	.001	.005	-.006
Spec. 3	-.011	-.022	-.019	-.024	-.001	.006	-.008
Coef. 2/Coef. 1	.490	.52	.56	.56	1.00	.50	.25
Coef. 3/Coef. 1	.14	.27	.23	.30	n.a.	n.a.	.33
Disabled							
Spec. 1	-.069**	-.089**	-.093**	-.074***	.030	.003	-.019
Spec. 2	-.027**	-.056**	-.051**	-.038**	.023*	.012	.010
Spec. 3	-.023	-.052**	-.046**	-.035**	.024**	.010	.010
Coef. 2/Coef. 1	.30	.62	.55	.51	.78	4.00	n.a.
Coef. 3/Coef. 1	.33	.58	.49	.47	.80	3.33	n.a.

Dependent Variables

Independent Variables	TOT CRED	ACPRO	DIPLOM	ENR4YR	ENR2YR
Male					
Spec. 1	-.079***	-.069***	-.064***	-.063***	-.008
Spec. 2	-.041**	-.042***	-.025*	-.030***	-.021
Coef. 2/Coef. 1	.520	.610	.390	.48	2.63
Black					
Spec. 1	-.095***	-.049***	-.132***	-.046***	-.026**
Spec. 2	-.033	-.012	-.059***	.027**	-.033**
Coef. 2/Coef. 1	.35	.24	.45	.59	1.26
Latino					
Spec. 1	-.052	-.089***	-.094***	-.093***	.042**
Spec. 2	-.018	-.035***	-.019	-.011	.015
Coef. 2/Coef. 1	.35	.39	.20	.12	.36

Table B.4   *Continued*

| | | Dependent Variables | | | | |
	TOT CRED	ACPRO	DIPLOM	ENR4YR	ENR2YR
Asian					
Spec. 1	.077***	.057***	.024**	.046***	.010
Spec. 2	.025	.028**	.015	.001	-.001
Coef. 2/Coef. 1	.32	.49	.63	.03	n.a.
American Indian					
Spec. 1	-.036	-.015	-.065***	-.048***	-.001
Spec. 2	-.029	.001	-.034**	-.017*	-.006
Coef. 2/Coef. 1	.81	.07	.52	.35	6.00
Disabled					
Spec. 1	.013	.033	.009	-.046**	.026
Spec. 2	.022	.042**	.017*	-.020	.025
Coef. 2/Coef. 1	1.69	1.27	1.89	.43	.96

Source: Author's calculations.
Specification 1: Demographic variables only.
Specification 2: Demographic variables plus all school and nonschool resource variables.
Specification 3: Specification 2 plus lagged dependent variable (if available)
n.a. = not applicable because of sign reversal.

Table B.5   The Effects of Student Connectedness to Schooling

| | | Dependent Variables | | | | | | |
| | MATHTS | | SCITS | | READTS | | HISTTS | |
Independent Variables	Spec. 1	Spec. 2	Spec. 1	Spec. 2	Spec. 1	Spec. 2	Spec. 1	Spec. 2
HMWRK	.061***	.038***	.042***	.025***	.026***	.008	.015	.003
READ	.010	-.001	.059***	.032***	.117***	.080***	.111***	.079***
COUNS	.029***	.024**	.025**	.022**	.032***	.027***	.035***	.031***
ACHELP	-.029***	-.034***	-.041***	-.045***	-.046***	-.050***	-.025**	-.030***
ATTPROB	-.017	-.007	-.034***	-.023**	-.018*	-.009	-.026**	-.013
ABSENT12	-.018**	-.008	-.004	.001	.004	.007	-.016	-.012
BEHPROB	-.016	-.005	-.008	-.001	-.004	.004	-.014	-.006
WRKHRS	-.027***	-.025***	-.026***	-.023**	-.028***	-.024***	-.019	-.017
EXTRACUR	.014	-.005	-.018	-.029**	-.034***	-.042***	-.026***	-.035***
OUTACT	.092***	.063***	.092***	.068***	.071***	.045***	.095***	.023***
TV	.067***	-.040***	-.060***	-.035***	-.043***	-.022**	-.033***	-.018
COLLPEERS	.035***	.014	.020*	.004	.033***	.015	.039***	.023**
DROPPEERS	-.006	.001	-.023*	-.016	-.022**	-.012	-.015	-.007
GANG	-.018	-.012	-.034***	-.027***	-.032***	-.024***	-.049***	-.040***
BABY	-.010	.002	-.009	.001	-.024***	-.011	-.006	.004
VOCVAL	-.041***	-.030***	-.044***	-.035***	-.060***	-.047***	-.051***	-.040***
AFFILVAL	-.012	-.013	-.038***	-.036***	-.037***	-.035***	-.053***	-.050***
ESCAPVAL	-.022**	-.020***	-.003	.000	-.016*	-.013	-.009	-.006
ALTRVAL	-.054***	-.043***	-.025**	-.019**	.007	-.000	.005	.011

Table B.5   *Continued*

Independent Variables	HEASP		HOCASP		CONTED	
	Spec. 1	Spec. 2	Spec. 1	Spec. 2	Spec. 1	Spec. 2
HMWRK	.047***	.038***	.020	.021	.022**	.019**
READ	.021**	.013	.002	−.001	.028**	.030**
COUNS	.019*	.015	.028**	.026**	.052***	.050***
ACHELP	.026**	.020**	.034***	.033***	.146***	.139***
ATTPROB	−.012	−.009	.056***	.058***	.001	.006
ABSENT12	−.001	−.001	.006	.005	−.006	−.006
BEHPROB	.018	.016	.005	.009	−.008	−.007
WRKHRS	−.007	−.010	−.018	−.014	.006	.003
EXTRACURR	.033***	.024***	.022	.014	.025**	.015
OUTACT	.050***	.043***	.018	.014	−.023***	−.027***
TV	−.026***	−.024***	−.025**	−.025**	−.032***	−.033***
COLLPEERS	.063***	.058***	.048***	.043***	.096***	.085***
DROPPEERS	.006	.005	.013	.014	−.029*	−.026**
GANG	−.005	−.004	−.037***	−.035***	−.005	−.022
BABY	−.012	−.009	−.024	−.021	−.041**	−.037*

Independent Variables	Total Credits[a]	Academic Program[a]	High School Diploma[a]	Enrolled in Four-Year College[a]	Enrolled in Two-Year College[a]
HMWRK	.040**	.001	.074***	.022**	−.036***
READ	.005	−.0098	−.016	−.022**	.024**
COUNS	.050***	.022*	.054***	.024**	.016
ACHELP	.073***	.009	.061***	.083***	.010
ATTPROB	−.096***	−.026**	−.108***	−.016	−.006
ABSENT12	−.018	−.030***	−.062***	−.025***	−.017
BEHPROB	−.101***	−.017**	−.103***	−.038***	−.021
WRKHRS	−.031**	−.029***	.028	−.050***	.013
EXTRACURR	.055***	.047***	.025*	.043***	−.015
OUTACT	.031**	.025**	.012	.060***	−.047***
TV	−.030*	−.007	−.019	−.024**	−.013
COLLPEERS	.004	.037***	.027*	.066***	.004
DROPPEERS	−.064***	.000	−.041***	.002	.002
GANG	−.002	−.035***	−.002	−.038***	.036**
BABY	−.050***	−.014**	−.056***	−.033***	−.032***

Source: Author's calculations.

Note: Specification 2 includes a lagged dependent variable.

[a] Results are for specification 1 only.

Beta coefficients: ***significant at 1%; ** significant at 5%; * significant at 10%

Table B.6   The Parameters of Linear Growth Models

	Math		Reading		Science	
	Spec. 1	Spec. 2	Spec. 1	Spec. 2	Spec. 1	Spec. 2
cv (sch int)	.159	.089	.127	.052	.113	.063
cv (sch slope)	.206	.217	.273	.249	.270	.294
ρ (int, slope)	.333	−.113	.267	−.102	.549	−.08
(Z value)	(6.27)	(−1.76)	(4.06)	(−1.14)	(9.09)	(−.91)
cv (ind int)	.267	.243	.259	.209	.196	.188
cv (ind slope)	.477	.552	.800	.792	.639	.892
ρ (int, slope)	.211	.095	.046	−.043	.234	.093
(Z value)	(15.79)	(6.91)	(2.89)	(−2.6)	(13.59)	(4.84)
cv (r_{is})	.085	.083	.120	.119	.114	.114
TIME (standard	3.06	2.57	1.47	1.45	1.118	.763
error)	(.028)	(.091)	(.021)	(.082)	(.015)	(.052)
Number of observations	40,693	40,693	40,703	40,703	40,526	40,526
−2 res LL	286,840	281,954	274,757	270,788	235,372	230,736

Table B.6   *Continued*

	History		Educational Aspirations		Occupational Aspirations		Continuing Education	
	Spec. 1	Spec. 2	Spec. 1	Spec. 2	Spec. 1	Spec. 2	Spec. 1	Spec. 2
	.069	.042	.385	.452	.156	.28	.062	.027
	.238	.217	.707	.707	.385	.333	−.791	.782
	.021	−.379	.071	−.894	−.4	−.671	.577	.414
	(.37)	(−5.22)	(.49)	(−2.72)	(−1.38)	(−1.33)	(1.72)	(.83)
	.119	.112	1.088	2.857	.563	2.073	.178	.144
	.472	.478	3.873	3.162	3.846	3.162	−7.906	4.518
	.100	−.011	−.456	−.474	−.555	−.636	−.100	−.224
	(5.71)	(−.64)	(−16.65)	(−15.44)	(−24.81)	(−26.14)	(−2.31)	(−6.82)
	.068	.067	1.042	1.042	.456	.44	.299	.277
	1.25	1.22	.020	.022	.026	.029	−.004	.007
	(.014)	(.047)	(.001)	(.005)	(.001)	(.007)	(.001)	(.004)
	40,355	40,355	43,126	43,126	34,313	34,313	43,578	43,578
	224,993	220,755	54,957	43,969	46,134	43,195	31,031	25,869

Source: Author's calculations.
Specification 1: Variation within individuals and within schools, with TIME only.
Specification 2: Variation within individuals and within schools, with TIME and all time-varying and time-invariant independent variables.

Table B.7   The Correlation Coefficients Between Slopes and Intercepts

	Spec. 1	Spec. 2	Spec. 3	Spec. 4
Math				
Among schools	.333	−.073	.293	−.113
	(6.27)	(1.16)	(5.61)	(−1.76)
Among individuals	.211	.140	.163	.095
	(15.79)	(10.31)	(12.21)	(6.91)
Reading				
Among schools	.267	−.044	.236	−.102
	(4.06)	(6.49)	(3.50)	(−1.14)
Among individuals	.046	−.005	−.001	−.043
	(2.89)	(0.33)	(0.09)	(−2.6)
Science				
Among schools	.549	0	.484	−.08
	(9.09)	(0.01)	(8.13)	(−.91)
Among individuals	.234	.137	.187	.093
	(13.59)	(7.44)	(10.76)	(4.84)
History				
Among schools	.021	−.351	.010	−.379
	(.37)	(5.35)	(0.19)	(−5.22)
Among individuals	.100	.024	.048	−.011
	(5.71)	(12.30)	(2.65)	(−.64)
Educational aspirations				
Among schools	.071	−.671	−.079	−.894
	(.49)	(2.32)	(0.26)	(−2.72)
Among individuals	−.456	−.480	−.456	−.474
	(−16.65)	(14.58)	(18.16)	(−15.44)
Occupational aspirations				
Among schools	−.400	−.447	−.707	−.671
	(−1.38)	(0.88)	(2.14)	(−1.33)
Among individuals	−.555	−.699	−.669	−.636
	(−24.81)	(25.35)	(25.35)	(−26.14)
Continuing education				
Among schools	.577	.250	.365	.414
	(1.72)	(0.35)	(2.01)	(.83)
Among individuals	−.100	−.224	−.209	−.224
	(−2.31)	(5.97)	(4.40)	(−6.82)

Source: Author's calculations.
Note: Z-values are in parentheses.
Specification 1: TIME only.
Specification 2: TIME plus family background and demographic variables.
Specification 3: TIME plus school resources and student ability to benefit.
Specification 4: TIME plus all independent variables included.

Table B.8   The Coefficients of Time-Invariant Variables

Independent Variables	Math		Reading		Science	
	Intercept	Slope	Intercept	Slope	Intercept	Slope
Male	.644***	.253*** 57.1%	−1.487***	−.057* 15.3%	1.088***	.277*** 101.8%
Black	−6.205***	−.430*** 27.7%	−3.725***	−.291*** 16.4%	−2.591***	−.450*** 69.5%
Latino	−3.616***	−.144** 15.9%	−1.856***	−.075 16.2%	−1.358***	−.215*** 63.3%
Asian American	2.551***	.238*** 37.3%	−.030	.203** 160.7%	.193	.005 n.s.
American Indian	−5.058***	−.487** 38.5%	−3.297***	−.276 33.1%	−1.741***	−.334*** 76.0%
Disabled	−6.182***	−.756*** 62.7%	−4.214***	−.661*** 62.7%	−1.820***	−.483*** 106.0%
Language not English	0.088	.114 n.s.	−1.028***	.106 n.s.	−.503***	.126*** #
Mother's education low	−1.443***	−.297*** n.s.	−1.165***	−.113 161.0%	−.406**	−.163*** 161.2%
Mother's education middle	1.807***	.223***	1.326***	.059	.707***	.063**
Mother's education high	6.779***	.527*** 31.1%	4.545***	.219*** 19.3%	2.276***	.233*** 40.9%
Materials	3.419***	.098 n.s.	2.563***	−.095 49.0%	1.302***	.159*** 49.1%

Table B.8   Continued

	History		Educational Aspirations		Occupational Aspirations		Continuing Education	
Intercept	Slope		Intercept	Slope	Intercept	Slope	Intercept	Slope
.767***	.074*** 38.6%		−.040***	.001	−.160***	.006**	−.021***	−.004**
−1.738***	−.145*** 33.4%		.033***	.002	.020	−.003	.057***	−.009***
−.959***	−.041 17.1%		.015	−.001	−.001	−.002	.035***	.0004
.250	.079 n.s.		.049***	−.001	.021	−.002	.028**	.003
−1.677***	−.079 n.s.		−.050*	.009	−.039	−.009	−.012	−.011
−1.644***	−.293** 71.2%		−.074**	.038***	−.098*	.008	−.089***	.010
−.339**	.151*** ##		.040***	−.003	.053***	−.008	.039***	−.008**
−.577***	−.032 n.s.		.009	−.012	−.030	.016**	−.041***	.003
.685***	.043**		.026***	−.001	.046***	.002	.047***	.0004
2.232***	.174*** 31.0%		.124***	−.0005	.138***	−.006	.064***	−.0003
1.375***	−.023 n.s.		.167***	−.016***	.127***	−.013	.129***	−.003

Source: Author's calculations.
*** significant at 1%; ** significant at 5%; * significant at 10%; n.s. = not significant
# eliminates a gap of −.503 points
reverses a gap of −.339 points to +.265 points

Table B.9   The Coefficients of Time-Varying School and Nonschool Resources

Independent Variables	Reading Test	Math Test	Science Test	History Test	Educational Aspirations	Occupational Aspirations	Continuing Education
School resources							
Simple							
Low teacher salary	−.022	.018	.023***	.006	.0002	.001	.001
Pupil/teacher ratio	−.026***	−.047**	−.021***	.005	−.001**	−.001**	.001***
Compound							
Experience of first teacher	.001	.003	.004**	.006**	.0002	.0001	.0004**
Experience of second teacher	−.006	.001	−.002	.003	.0001	.0002	−.0001
First teacher teaching in-field	.285**	.152	.187***	.011	.021**	.055**	.005
Second teacher teaching in-field	.364***	.567***	.253***	.119	.001	.019*	−.012**
Complex							
TimeStruc	−1.543***	−2.297***	−1.078***	−.733***	−.029	−.049	−.020
Abstract							
School climate	3.387***	2.487***	2.151***	1.473***	.172***	.096***	.121***
Negative events	−1.726***	−1.174***	−.726***	−.640***	−.040***	−.099***	−.004

Table B.9 *Continued*

Family background							
Parent aspirations low	-.992***	-.781***	-.586***	-.570***	-.045***	-.166***	-.147***
Parent aspirations high	.386***	.128*	.312***	.349***	.424***	.062***	-.001
Income per dependent	.014***	.012***	.009***	.009***	.001***	.001***	.0004***
Student connectedness to schooling							
Outside activities	.614***	.894***	.541***	.063	.127***	.042***	.074***
TV	-.183***	-.192***	-.111***	-.028**	-.005***	-.006***	-.004***
Homework	.035***	.047***	.025***	.024***			
Work hours	-.009***	-.008***	-.004**	.002			
Attendance trouble	-5.810***	-4.247***	-3.166***	-3.736***	-.071***	.057	-.347***
Total absences	-.011**	-.037***	-.012***	-.008**	-.001***	-.0001	.0003
Exogenous							
ADA	-2.239***	-2.209***	-.739*	-.208	-.081**	.071	-.083***
ADA-squared	.198***	.218***	.075**	.001	.007**	-.003	.006***

Source: Author's compilation.

NOTES

INTRODUCTION

1. See Kaestle (1983), chapters 6 and 7, and Cremin and Borrowman (1956), especially Mann's "Tenth Report to the Massachusetts Legislature."

2. The term "administrative progressives" is somewhat awkward, since the practices that emerged during the Progressive Era (roughly 1890 to 1920) are no longer viewed as particularly progressive. In particular, progressive education, defined as the more Deweyan and constructivist pedagogical approaches, and the bureaucratic and efficiency-oriented reforms of the administrative progressives were quite antithetical to one another. The best source on the "administrative progressives" remains Tyack (1974); see also Callahan (1967).

3. Policy in many countries is driven by narratives, or widely accepted "stories," about why certain programs are worthwhile. The creation of such narratives typically takes a considerable period of time and many participants. Once widely accepted, policy narratives—like the "Education Gospel" or human capital, the fight against communism or now the war on terrorism—are resistant to change, and subtle empirical evidence (the results that research can generate) is not usually enough to shake the hold of a policy narrative. See, for example, Roe (1994). Policy narratives are similar to the stories that outstanding leaders create (Gardner 1995), except that policy narratives are usually developed collectively rather than by individuals.

4. The rhetoric of the Education Gospel is also dominant in many other countries and international agencies, such as the European Union (EU) and the Organization for Economic Cooperation and Development (OECD); see Grubb and Lazerson (2006).

5. In the landscape of equity discussed in chapter 6, the Coleman Report's conception belongs in table 6.1, cell 11, where school resources are equal among groups defined by race, ethnicity, class, or income but not necessarily among individuals.

6. See Hanushek (1989, 1997) for the U.S. literature and Fuller and Clarke (1994) for the international literature. The effects of family background have been summarized by Sirin (2005), who finds income, parental education, and occupation to have similar-size effects. Unlike my discussion in chapter 4, her review is unconcerned with the causal mechanisms underlying these statistical findings.

7. One technical challenge to Hanushek's discouraging findings has been that a formal meta-analysis (rather than the counting exercise used by Hanushek) is more appropriate. Larry Hedges, Richard Laine, and Rob Greenwald (1994) found more positive results for expenditures per pupil and teacher experience, though the average effect sizes—.0014 and .07, respectively—are still distressingly small. Another challenge has been to come up with "one more study" and to rely on those few studies that do confirm a relation between resources and outcomes—many reviewed in Verstegen (1998) and many drawing on Project STAR in Tennessee. Unfortunately, the tactic of "one more study"—unless the study is quite different from prior studies, which is the tactic of this book—leaves the uncertainty associated with older studies intact. For example, the frequent citations of the Tennessee experiments usually fail to mention an earlier random-assignment experiment in Toronto that had a greater range of class sizes, a more transparent randomization procedure, a richer variety of outcome measures, and a more lucid explanation of the results, but that failed to find effects of resources on five of six test scores (Shapson et al. 1980). The reason, according to researchers who observed classrooms, was that teachers failed to change their practices. The "battle of the experiments" is at best a draw, but at least it clarifies that understanding the effects of class size reduction requires entering the classroom to see what teachers do.

8. For some of the older studies, see Edmonds (1979) and Clark, Lotto, and Astuto (1984). This approach remains attractive; some newer studies include Education Trust (Wilkins et al. 2006), American Institutes for Research (2006), and Timar and Kim (2008). The critiques of the effective schools approach include Purkey and Smith (1983), Rowan, Bossert, and Dwyer (1983), Cuban (1984), Cohen (1983). For a rebuttal of the Education Trust study, see Harris (2006).

9. On the test score gap, see Jencks and Phillips (1998). I take this issue up in chapter 4.

10. On variation in the PISA reading scale, see Kirsch et al. (2002), tables 4.1 and 4.15. On the mathematical literacy scale, see Organization for Economic Cooperation and Development (OECD 2001), table 3.1. For IALS data, see OECD (2000), table 2.2. The data in figure I.1 come from IALS data on reading and math inequality and from the Luxembourg Income Study (LIS) for earnings inequality; see also Nickell (2004), especially table 9.

11. There has been no analysis whatsoever of the interactions between education policy and other social and economic policies, even by European welfare state theorists like Gøsta Esping-Anderson (1990), who admits that education should be considered part of the welfare state. It is not difficult to generate an interactive model in which an unequal schooling system creates more unemployable individuals, who in turn create more potential problems of poverty and dependence for the welfare state. In turn, higher demands on the welfare state in a political system averse to "welfare" create low levels of spending on various non-educational programs, in turn reinforcing inequality in schooling outcomes. That is, the correlation evident in figure I.1 is surely causal, in both directions. However, confirming such a model with country data is considerably more difficult.

12. NELS88 also has data for two years after high school, collected in 1994, and for eight years after high school, collected in 2000. In this book, I make no use of these data except for measures of whether students go on to college after high school, which are taken from the third follow-up in 1994.

13. Regional universities are the less-selective universities serving regional rather than national pools of students, with enrollments predominantly in occupational or professional programs. The private sector also has elite national and non-elite regional universities. Most regional universities are members of the American Association of State Colleges and Universities; for a history, see Dunham (1969).

14. For some of these reports, see Olson (2005); for a brief history of high school critiques, see Grubb (2008c); the most recent is "Reshaping High Schools," a special issue of *Educational Leadership* (8, May 2008).

15. Throughout this volume, I contrast approaches to pedagogy that are variously called behaviorist, teacher-centered, skills-oriented, part-to-whole, and fact transmission with those that are constructivist, student-centered, whole-to-part, and concerned more with conceptual capacities. However, the most judicious conclusion is that instructors should be able to use both of these approaches as appropriate, an

approach often called "balanced." See the discussion of pedagogical issues in chapter 2 and a series of reports by the National Research Council reviewing the enormous literature on approaches to instruction in Snow, Burns, and Griffin (1998), Donovan and Bransford (2005), and National Research Council (2004).

16. See especially Oakes and Saunders (2008), including my own contribution on "weak" and "strong" versions of pathways (Grubb 2008c).

17. My conceptualization of the instruments of education policy is drawn largely from McDonnell and Elmore (1987), with their categories of mandates, inducements, capacity-building, and system-changing efforts. System-changing policies include the encouragement of choice mechanisms and neoliberal approaches, examined in chapter 12.

CHAPTER 1

1. I used to call this the "new" school finance, but this description has been used by Alan Odden (2001) to emphasize adequacy approaches rather than the use of resources within classrooms and schools. The improved school finance is not simply a version of adequacy, as some reviewers have mistakenly stated: it introduces a much richer set of resources than anything in the adequacy literature and identifies which resources can be bought with adequate funding and which cannot. See Grubb, Huerta, and Goe (2006).

2. See especially the articles in Berne and Picus (1994); several articles in Monk and Underwood (1988), especially Gamoran (1988) and Brown (1988); the articles in Odden (1992); and Barro (1989); Cohen, Raudenbush, and Ball (2003); King and MacPhail-Wilcox (1994); MacPhail-Wilcox (1986); Monk (1994); and Odden and Busch (1998).

3. For the American results, see Hanushek (1989, 1997), and for international findings, see Fuller and Clarke (1994).

4. This section has benefited from observations in schools and from exercises in which students in the Principal Leadership Institute (PLI) at the University of California at Berkeley identify waste in their schools and districts.

5. Resource allocation is treated quite briefly in most education administration textbooks. In a random sample, Hughes (1999) has only two pages on funding. Speck (1999) has nothing at all. Seyfarth (1999) and Drake and Roe (1999) each allow a single chapter near the end of their

texts, and both treat resources as budgeting issues rather than as educational decisions. In a small sample of individuals who graduated from Bay Area principal preparation programs, only 10 percent of those in programs other than the Principal Leadership Institute reported being well prepared for budgeting and resources issues, compared to 42 percent of PLI students. For two efforts to clarify the broader funding issues for administrators, see Monk and Plecki (1999) and Miles and Frank (2008).

6.   On the general inattention of principals to budget issues, see Boyd and Hartman (1988); on the lack of information among districts about where resources go, see Roza and Hill (2006); on the inattention to budget issues in educational administration textbooks, see note 5. In addition, the PLI students mentioned in note 4 have tried (often unsuccessfully) to find out about budget procedures in their own schools and discovered the appalling extent of principal ignorance and indifference.

7.   The language of an "equilibrium" comes from Harkin and Davis (1996) and is similar to the idea of coordinating instruction in Cohen, Raudenbush, and Ball (2003). See especially the model of the classroom in Lampert (2001, ch. 3). The lack of pedagogical alignment is at the heart of the conflicts in high schools described by Denise Pope (2001) and in community college classrooms as described by Rebecca Cox (2004) and Grubb and Associates (1999, especially chs. 2 and 6).

8.   Of course, there is substantial variation among these averages; see Jacob (2007, table 1).

9.   On industrial unionism versus professional unions, see Kerchner and Caufman (1993).

10.   See also the discussion by Cohen, Raudenbush, and Ball (2003) of student-centered teaching "regimes," which are ways of adjusting teaching to the interests and capacities of individual students. This idea is similar to the point of Brown and Saks (1975) that teachers may allocate resources differently among students within classrooms.

11.   This is true almost by definition since the variance of a weighted sum is generally greater than the variance of either component, unless the covariance between the two is negative.

12.   More precisely, the final estimating equation is

$$SO_{is} = \pi_0 + \sum_j \pi_j SR_{isj} + \sum_k \pi_k FB_{ik} + \sum_l \pi_l SA_{il}$$
$$+ \sum_m \pi_m EX_{sm} + \sum_n \pi_n D_i + r_{is}$$

where i indexes individuals; s indexes schools; j, k, l, m, and n index the different independent variables; and r_{is} is random variation among students, varying both among individuals and among schools. For selected variables, a second specification includes a term for the lagged dependent variable ß SO^*_{t-1}. The parameters π are estimated with ordinary least squares, while the parameters on lagged dependent variables ß are estimated with an instrumental variables method. I also provide some results with hierarchical linear modeling in Grubb (2008b). Finally, I also broke the sample into subsamples for males and females, different racial groups, and students with low and high parental education. Most coefficients were remarkably stable across these groups, so there is no consistent support for the hypothesis that school resources have more powerful effects for some groups than others.

13.   Family effects could be considered endogenous if schools have active programs designed to enhance parental expectations, including expectations about school attainment, to inform parents about college costs and benefits, or otherwise to influence parental resources. However, there is little information in NELS88 about such programs aimed at parents.

14.   Goldhaber and Brewer (1997) have included a lagged test score measure (eighth-grade scores), but if there is a serial correlation in error terms for test scores—as there proves to be—the coefficient will be biased upward and all other coefficients will be biased downward. They have therefore undercorrected for school resources, and doing so only strengthens their conclusion.

15.   One potential method is to use instrumented values of school resources in place of actual values, eliminating the error correlations that generate simultaneous equations bias. This method is ineffective, however, because such equations explain so little of the variation in resources (Grubb 2006a). That is, there is too little information to identify separate effects of resources on outcomes and also outcomes on resources.

16.   Technically, examining the resource use of schools with strong outcomes requires selecting schools with large positive residuals from equation 1.6, the reduced-form equation from 1.3, 1.4, and 1.5. These are schools that have unexpectedly high levels of effective school resources for their levels of spending per student (high error terms e), unexpectedly high levels of student engagement (high v), or unexpectedly high levels of outcomes given school resources and family backgrounds (high u). Case studies of exemplary schools could then

search for evidence about which of these different characteristics seems important, integrating questions about revenues into the analysis of resource use. But see the warnings about the effective schools literature in the introduction, note 7.

CHAPTER 2

1. High school completion is measured by information on high school transcripts. There is also a self-reported measure of completion in the third follow-up, but self-reported attainment is more likely to be measured with bias than is transcript-based attainment (Grubb 1992, table 3).

2. See the extensive validity studies of the NELS88 tests in Nussbaum, Hamilton, and Snow (1997) and Kupermintz and Snow (1997).

3. The outcome measures not discussed here include measures of optimism about the future, locus of control, and self-conception; student attitude variables measuring vocational orientation, value of affiliation with others, preferences for escapism, and altruistic values, treated as dependent variables; low educational and occupational aspirations; class rank; SAT scores, available for only a subsample of students; passing algebra 1, a gatekeeper course; measures of civic and political engagement; receipt of a GED; and educational aspirations from the third follow-up. Most of the results for these other outcomes are consistent with the results for the twelve included here.

4. Specifically, the correlations among the four test scores are about .75; correlations between test scores and measures of progress are about .20 to .25; the correlations between test scores and aspirations range between .20 and .43, with low aspirations in particular negatively correlated with test scores; correlations between measures of progress and aspirations are about .10 to .20.

5. There are several different ways of thinking about teacher quality. Probably the most common defines quality in terms of credentials and experience; see, for example, the *Future of Children* (2007) special issue on teacher quality, "Excellence in the Classroom." Four other ways of describing teacher quality focus on the practices they follow in the classroom, the approach in my analysis; their knowledge (for example, the categorization of content knowledge, general pedagogical knowledge, and pedagogical content knowledge formulated by Shulman [1987]); their interactions with students, including dimensions like caring (Noddings 1992); and their effects on outcomes, for example,

by examining the value-added associated with individual teachers. The last of these cannot identify high-quality teachers ex ante, only ex post, and is therefore useless for making hiring or policy decisions.

6. Information is available for many more than ten dimensions—NELS88 provides, for example, an enormous amount of information about language issues—but I have eliminated family background measures that failed to have any explanatory power.

7. See chapter 1, note 12, for the final estimating equation. I present the results for different groups of variables in different chapters: school resources in this chapter, family background and demographic variables in chapter 4, and student connection to schooling in chapter 5. For the dependent variables describing test scores and attitudes, a second specification includes a term for the lagged dependent variable $\beta\,SO_{t-1}$. It would be wrong to estimate the second specification with ordinary least squares (OLS) because the residuals $r_{is,t}$ and $r_{is,t-1}$ are correlated; therefore, SO_{t-1} is correlated with the independent variables, and an OLS estimate of its coefficient would be biased. The most straightforward solution is to estimate an equation for SO_{t-1} as a function of tenth-grade variables and then to use the predicted or instrumented values of SO_{t-1}, SO^*_{t-1}, eliminating the correlation between $r_{is,t}$ and SO^*_{t-1}. The coefficients on the lagged dependent variables vary between .829 and .645 when OLS estimation is used, but drop to between .568 and .519 with the instrumental variables technique. The coefficients for lagged aspirations are much lower, between .143 and .253, for instrumented variables, indicating that past test scores have more powerful continuing effects than past aspirations. For more detail about dynamic specifications, see Grubb (2006b, 2006c); for another attempt to estimate equations with lagged test scores but using OLS, see Henry et al. (2008).

8. In many cases, answers from several questions or components of a larger question have been combined, often by counting up positive (or negative) responses and standardizing the resulting variables to range between zero and one. This procedure weights all components of a multipart variable equally. The alternative is to use an estimation method that calculates the weights for different components, like factor analysis, Karl Joreskog and Dag Sorbom's (1979) analysis of covariance structures, or generalized linear modeling (GLM). However, these methods often result in composite variables that are difficult to interpret. In addition, software programs are not available for advanced estimation methods that also allow for weighting and nonrandom sampling.

9. Because I want to include a specification with a lagged dependent variable, only those outcomes with consistent values for dependent variables in tenth and twelfth grades are included.

10. Some of the dependent variables—high educational and occupational aspirations, the intention to continue education, completion of an academic program, the earning of a high school diploma, enrollment in a two- or four-year college—are binary variables. OLS estimates, or linear probability models, are inelegant because they allow probabilities over one and under zero; they also suffer from heteroskedasticity and are therefore inefficient, though this is not a problem with over twelve thousand observations. The results from logistic regressions are precisely the same as those from OLS; I report linear probability models because of the ease of comparison across dependent variables.

11. In specification 2, for those variables for which a lagged dependent variable can be created, the effects of school resources are slightly lower, but those that are significant in specification 1 are almost always significant in specification 2. This provides some reassurance that the causal assumption of school resources affecting outcomes, rather than the other way around, is correct; for example, the effects of experience and teaching in-field are still significant in specification 2, so this positive effect is not due to experienced teachers being able to teach high-scoring students. In addition, the explanatory power of specification 2 is consistently and significantly higher than for equation 1.1, as we might expect. What it means to have an increase in R-squared is that the instrumented lagged dependent variable SO^*_{t-1} reflects not just dimensions of school and nonschool resources; were this the case, then the coefficients on school and nonschool resources would fall and the coefficient β would be significant, but R-squared would remain about the same. Instead, SO^*_{t-1} brings new information into the analysis, reflecting unmeasured dimensions of school and nonschool resources and stable elements of individual error: students who do better or worse than we might expect, given their other characteristics.

12. Unfortunately, there is virtually no evidence about the effects of class size at the high school level; see Robinson (1990) and a recent summary of the class size literature by Ready (2008).

13. Rice does not relate the use of time to outcomes, as I do in the results in table B.1. TimeUse reflects the use of time for administrative tasks, whole-group instruction, and discipline rather than small-group work and projects, and these practices have a consistently negative effect on test scores—providing an indirect mechanism by which class size may affect outcomes.

14. In these data, 37 percent of seniors report themselves to be in the general track, and 12 percent say they are in a vocational track.

15. See also Gamoran et al. (1997), who find that performance in the general track is lower than in college prep, but that "transition" courses designed to get low-performing students up to college level fall in between. The remedial courses in the NELS88 data are therefore lower-level and presumably use more conventional pedagogies than these transition courses.

16. On lower levels of content, see Claus (1990) and Oakes et al. (1992); for the effects on high school graduation, see Reubens 1974. On the effects on employment, an outcome of high school that is not included in this research, see Meyer (1981), Grasso and Shea (1979), and Daymont and Rumberger (1982). Only Daymont and Rumberger find any positive effects on earnings, and these are for those few individuals who find a job related to their vocational field of study—largely young women in secretarial fields.

17. In sociology there has been a ferocious debate about specific ways in which to measure being in a vocational or general track, but all of them find negative effects of the general track; see, for example, Gamoran et al. (1997).

18. For a more benign view of high school tracking than these results indicate, see Jencks et al. (1972, 106–9), based partly on Heyns (1971). There has been an extensive recent debate about the effects of tracking, set off in part by Jeannie Oakes (1985); on the "tracking wars" and for more positive assessments of tracking, see Loveless (1999). However, much of this debate involves the effects of ability grouping in elementary and middle grades, not the common forms of tracking in high schools, and it often examines the effect of tracking on average scores for some group rather than looking at the effects on individuals, as I do.

19. The different ways in which teachers and students perceive schooling can be seen in ethnographic research; for a wealthy suburban high school, see Pope (2001), and for students in a community college, see Cox (2004).

20. Specifications with a lagged dependent variable explain the quasi-difference in test scores $SO_t - \beta\, SO_{t-1}$, comparable to Lee and Smith (1997), not the simple or first-order difference $SO_t - SO_{t-1}$. Explaining the first-order difference would be incorrect since β is not in fact 1 but considerably less—closer to .55 for test scores and to .22 for aspirations. I have left the complexities of specifications using difference equations to another paper (Grubb 2006d).

21. These results are taken from regressions for school resources as a function of funding, exogenous school conditions, family background, and measures of student behavior in Grubb (2006b).

22. The lack of any effect for state exit exams replicates a finding of Warren and Edwards (2005), though these results may reflect the crude measurement of exit exams by a binary variable.

23. The explanatory power of these equations is about the same as those of Elliott (1998), using the same data set but a different sample, and of Ferguson and Ladd (1996), an article widely cited as challenging Hanushek (1989). Goldhaber and Brewer (1997), also using NELS88 data for the tenth grade, find R-squareds on the order of .75. In my results, when lagged dependent variables are included, properly instrumented as indicated in note 7, the R-squared increases slightly to .58 for math scores and to .44 for history scores. When the lagged values are not instrumented, then the R-squared increases substantially, for example, to .85 for math scores and to .63 for history scores.

24. The logic of the improved school finance, with effects that are necessary but not sufficient, implies that modeling outcomes with random effects (the effects of both family background and school resources are allowed to be a function of other school resources) would be appropriate. I did test a number of random effects, but most were statistically insignificant, and none added substantially to explanatory power; see Grubb (2008b) for these results.

25. This result is surprising given that most high school counseling and guidance services are remarkably weak, both because student-counselor ratios are high and because most counselors are absorbed in paperwork, administrative trivia, special education placements, and graduation requirements and use antiquated methods dating from the early twentieth century; see NRC (2004, ch. 6).

26. From question 7 in the student questionnaire, six of the twelve questions are about academic dimensions of school climate (for example, "teaching is good"), while the remaining six are non-academic (for example, "there's real school spirit" and "the school is safe").

27. For a similar conclusion, see also Quint's (2006) summary of three MDRC studies.

28. This also means that the current infatuation with random-assignment experiments, led by the Department of Education's Institute of Educational Sciences, is seriously misleading. Random-assignment methods can evaluate only discrete and bounded practices by assigning schools

(or teachers or students) to engage in a specific practice or to experience its absence (in the control group). If many practices contribute to outcomes, then any one practice can make only a small difference to outcomes, and this difference may be dwarfed by other sources of variation. Such a model is consistent with the common finding of no effects in experimental evaluation, whereas other ways of evaluating practices—for example, with the "preponderance of evidence" standard suggested by the National Research Council (2004)—are more likely to uncover promising effects *and* to explain the conditions under which they are likely to work.

29. College for All, which takes the position that all students should be prepared to enter college, usually reinforces the conventional college-prep curriculum; see Rosenbaum (2001) and Boesel and Fredland (1999).

30. On pathways, see Oakes and Saunders (2008), including my own contribution (Grubb 2008c).

CHAPTER 3

1. Remember that all expenditure measures are corrected for cross-sectional cost differences and for inflation over time (see appendix A). One problem is that revenues and expenditures are measured for districts rather than for schools, since the "Common Core of Data" describes districts. To the extent that spending varies among schools within districts, revenues and expenditures are unavoidably measured with error, and the coefficients on these variables are biased toward zero. One implication is that statistical significance at 10 percent rather than the usual 5 percent might be considered sufficient.

2. Figure 1.2 is a better guide to the final estimating equation used for the coefficients in table B.2. The independent variables include the various measures of expenditures and revenue patterns; the various measures of family background explained in chapter 4, including demographic variables; other exogenous policies; and measures of student commitment to schooling, since schools may respond to their students in deciding what resources to invest in. In this particular case, I include among the exogenous policy variables several measures of school governance, reflecting the hypothesis (developed in Miller and Rowan 2006, as well as in chapter 9) that distributed leadership, internal alignment, or "organic management" influences effective school resources.

3. The result that higher expenditures per pupil reduce overall school attendance rates is surely due to a different causal pattern. Schools with lower average daily attendance (ADA) have higher expenditures per pupil in ADA than schools with similar enrollments and higher ADA. Therefore low ADA, for schools of similar expenditures and enrollment, raises spending per ADA.

4. A common finding from the effective schools literature is that effective schools usually have strong principals; see, for example, Edmonds (1979) and Clark, Lotto, and Astuto (1984). See Grubb and Flessa (2006) on the value of having dual principals, which tends to cost only a small amount more than having a conventional principal. On the importance of leadership to schools with strong internal relationships, see Lemons, Luschel, and Siskin (2003).

5. These results are somewhat more promising than those of Robert Miller and Brian Rowan (2006), who also use NELS88 to test the model of organic management. They conclude that such measures as administrative support, teacher control, staff cooperation, and common planning time have no significant effect on math and reading outcomes. However, there is no reason to think that school organization influences outcomes directly rather than indirectly through effects on resources; Miller and Rowan do not separately estimate the effect of measures of organic management on effective resources, as I do. They also have relatively fewer variables describing school resources. The inability of many schools to make their own spending decisions, given district and state constraints, may also explain why organic management or internal alignment does not affect resource use, as discussed later in the chapter.

6. Of course, these may be overly crude measures of the underlying practices. A dummy variable for a magnet school cannot reflect, for example, whether the school adheres to its central vision consistently, and the presence of an exit exam may have both positive effects on resources—by increasing the attention to teaching—and negative effects, for example, by increasing the rigidity of teaching (as state exit exams do, $\beta = .137^{**}$).

7. This is consistent with the argument of Marguerite Roza and Paul Hill (2006) that most districts do not know how money is spent, much less whether it is spent for effective resources.

8. These characteristics include those that describe school organization and decisionmaking, explaining once again the weak findings of Miller and Rowan (2006).

9. See the website and materials available from DiME: www.wcer.wisc
   .edu/dime.

CHAPTER 4

1. See generally chapter 3 of Kaestle (1983), "Socioeconomic Influences
   on Schooling, 1800 to 1850." On Americanization, see part 4, section
   4, of Tyack (2004).

2. Selcuk Sirin's (2005) recent meta-analysis of the relationship between
   socioeconomic status (SES) and achievement clarifies that SES has
   been measured in many different ways. There has been little agreement on the "correct" measure, but also relatively little discussion
   about the different causal mechanisms of different measures. Sirin's review measures effects by correlation coefficients between SES measures and achievement measures, and these correlations average almost the same for education, occupation, and income (.30, .28, and
   .29, respectively). However, the point of examining regression coefficients with NELS88 data rather than correlation coefficients is to control for other variables, including other dimensions of SES, so different measures of family background may have different influences in a
   regression context even if their effects are similar when measured by
   correlation coefficients.

3. See also Phillips, Crouse, and Ralph (1998), a paper in which a wide
   array of family background variables are constructed from the National Longitudinal Survey of Youth (NLSY) data and the Infant Health
   and Development Program (IHDP).

4. The highest correlation coefficient is .38 between college saving and
   income per dependent. The correlation of high parental education
   with college saving and with materials in the home is .31. Between low
   parental education and materials it is −.28, and between low parent
   education and non-English language it is .28. Otherwise, the correlations are modest and the coefficients are robust in different specifications.

5. However, income has significant positive effects for African American
   students, for science and history scores, and for enrollment in four-
   year colleges. Within particular communities, then, income may be
   more powerful than it is for the population as a whole.

6. For summaries from three recent decades, see Leichter (1974), Hess
   and Holloway (1984), Clark (1983, ch. 1), Scott-Jones (1984), Gándara (1995, ch. 2), and Lareau (2000, ch. 1). See Slaughter and Epps

(1987) for a review of family effects on African American children specifically, with results similar to reviews for all children.

7. Betty Hart and Tod Risley (1995) illustrate a dilemma of qualitative research: their measure of SES is based on occupation, and though in practice they distinguish professional, working-class, and welfare families, occupation, income, and parental education are so correlated in this small sample that it is impossible to disentangle them.

8. Alan Schoenfeld, personal communication, 2007; see also the review by Robert Hess and Susan Holloway (1984), who have many fewer citations for math. Hess and Holloway cite some nonconclusive evidence that family effects are lower for math than for other outcomes, but my NELS88 results in appendix table B.1 suggest that the effects on math are comparable to effects on other subjects.

9. In support of this, the correlation between low-skilled work and low aspirations for students in the NELS88 data is .15.

10. The correlation coefficients are .456 for Latinos and .262 for Asian Americans.

11. In addition to the specifications in table B.4, I also tried more detailed dummy variables for gender by race-ethnicity: black males, black females, and so on. However, the more detailed specifications did not improve explanatory power at all, did not significantly influence any other coefficients, and provided no additional insights about the effects of gender, race, and ethnicity.

12. This kind of problem comes up in other areas of quantitative research. In examinations of earnings, for example, black men on average earn less than white men, even after controlling for as many other variables as possible; this residual has usually been interpreted as a measure of racial discrimination. In growth modeling, equations that describe growth rates among countries invariably find a negative "Africa coefficient," indicating that even after considering a wide variety of factors, African countries have had lower growth rates than non-African countries. From a policy perspective, this is unsatisfactory because it provides no guidance for foreign aid, health measures, government reform, or other growth policies; therefore, empirical growth economists have worked hard to reduce the Africa coefficient by devising other causal variables.

13. Remember that an instrumental variables estimate of the lagged dependent variable is used; see chapter 2, note 7. When the lagged dependent variable itself is included, incorrectly, its coefficient is higher,

and the coefficients of the demographic variables are reduced even more toward zero. It is possible, then, to depress artificially the effects of demographic variables toward zero by using inappropriate statistical methods. For example, value-added models that use $TS_t - TS_{t-1}$ as the dependent variable implicitly assume that the coefficient on the lagged dependent variable is one, depressing the effects of all other variables, including demographic variables, toward zero.

14.   These comparisons can be carried out with unadjusted coefficients as well, but the results are virtually identical.

15.   The differentials in outcomes are further reduced in specification 3, in which prior test scores explain a good deal of variation. However, this specification includes a lagged dependent variable that itself contains a substantial racial-ethnic differential, so it is inappropriate to use the third specification to measure the racial-ethnic residuals.

16.   Charles Clotfelter, Helen Ladd, and Jacob Vigdor (2006) have carried out a similar analysis, comparing raw score differences by race and ethnic groups over grades 3 to 8 with score differences controlling for some measures of class (subsidized lunch and parental education), district type, and region—much more parsimonious controls than I have used. In their results, the black-white math gap is cut to about 62 percent of the raw difference with the addition of these controls, but the white-Latino gap is cut to only about 13 percent of the original difference. Thus, the magnitude of these racial-ethnic residuals depends on the data that are used and the variables that are available as controls, but these residuals still persist.

17.   In technical terms, the problem is one of independent variables measured with error. Then the coefficients on these variables are biased toward zero. If the error is nonrandom—for example, it is correlated with racial-ethnic measures—this increases the coefficients of the racial-ethnic variables. Better measurement would therefore increase the coefficients of family background and school resources measures and reduce the racial-ethnic coefficients, but it is hard to imagine creating a much more comprehensive data set than NELS88.

18.   In addition to the citations in this section, see also those in chapter 9, particularly those on autobiographical approaches and critical race theory. Shelly Zirkel (2005, forthcoming a, forthcoming b) summarizes hundreds of citations about racial and ethnic issues in schools.

19.   On issues related to discipline, see Ayers, Dohrn, and Ayers 2001; Fenning and Rose 2007; Ferguson 2000; Nichols 2004; Skiba et al. 2002; Townsend 2000.

20. See, for example, the personal stories throughout Thompson (2004).

21. These are students in the Principal Leadership Institute (PLI), which prepares school-level leaders, and the Leadership for Equity in Education Program (LEEP), which prepares district leaders. We ask our students to complete an "educational autobiography" in which they reflect on their own trajectory through the educational system, and many of these essays are sources of information about racial and ethnic abuse.

22. Similarly, in a large study of 257 community college classrooms (Grubb and Associates 1999), my associates and I kept a running list of RBTs (Really Bad Teachers) whose classes often "collapsed," leading to either active hostility from students or nonparticipation. Most RBTs were not simply disorganized or ignorant about subject matter; they were abusive to students or they belittled students' class participation—a particularly destructive response to community college students, who often enter unsure of their academic abilities.

23. See especially Wheeler (2007) on the explicit teaching of contrastive analysis and then code-switching; Pollok (2004) on race talk in schools; and the enormous amount of writing on culturally relevant pedagogy and multicultural education summarized in Gay (2000) and Banks and Banks (2004).

24. I refer in this sentence not only to the systematically inegalitarian policies of the Bush administration and of previous Republican administrations but also to the more general inability of interest-group liberalism to develop any vision of the common good, to plan, or to redistribute; see Truman (1951) and Lowi (1969). I have offered another vision—that of the "foundational state"—in Grubb and Lazerson (2004, chs. 8 and 9), briefly recapitulated in chapter 12.

CHAPTER 5

1. See chapter 2, note 25.

2. These results are taken from regressions that were differentiated by race and gender and are not reproduced in appendix B.

3. SAT scores are available only for a biased subsample of students and reduce the sample size from 11,155 to 3,606.

4. I estimated three different specifications: twelfth-grade measures of student ability to benefit as a function of family background, demographic variables, and twelfth-grade school resources; the first specification substituting tenth-grade resources for twelfth-grade resources

to eliminate the potential least-squares bias of the first specification; and the second specification adding tenth-grade test scores and attitudes. The differences among these specifications were small, and all specifications had low explanatory power.

5. Remember that these results hold even when controlling for tenth-grade test scores as well as many dimensions of family background, so that these findings reflect the additional influence of tracking above and beyond academic performance levels and family effects.

6. R-squared gives the proportion of variation in the dependent variable explained by the independent variables and is therefore a simple measure of explanatory power ranging from 0 to 100 percent.

7. On guidance and counseling, see Grubb and Watson (2002). On tutoring, see the brief review in chapter 8.

8. Bishop's (1989) solution was to try to improve the returns to quality of learning by making such information more available to employers.

CHAPTER 6

1. On the Committee of Ten, see Krug (1969, ch. 3). The quotation is from NEA (1994, 17).

2. Amy Gutmann (1987) presents three persistent philosophical conceptions: maximization of life chances; equalization so that the life chances between the least and the most disadvantaged children are narrowed as much as possible; and a meritocratic conception in which the state distributes resources in proportion to a child's ability and willingness to learn. She then proposes a "democratic standard," a Rawlsian approach in which inequalities can be justified only if no child is deprived of the ability to participate effectively in the democratic process. We can sometimes see these philosophical conceptions embedded in school practices—particularly the meritocratic conception, which is reflected in many tracking mechanisms, AP classes, and honors programs, though tracking is usually justified by efficiency rather than equity. But by and large, these philosophical conceptions have been the construction of academics and intellectuals and have not affected legislative battles or litigation. In particular, the Rawlsian arguments that have been so popular among egalitarians have never, as far as I can determine, been articulated on behalf of specific education policies, though I identify a possible exception in chapter 8 at note 7.

3. See especially Grubb and Lazerson (1982), a paper that Marvin Lazer-

son and I wrote for a project of the U.S. Department of Education in which we attempted to define adequacy. We rejected the possibility of developing a coherent conception of adequacy because of the historical swings in the conception of what is considered adequate in education. Adequacy lawsuits have become popular because many state constitutions have phrases describing the support of education that can be interpreted as a call for adequacy—for example, the requirement that the state's children be provided a "thorough and efficient education." But given that adequacy has always been a moving target, one danger of operationalizing adequacy in any way is that it will be quickly outdated, with some districts or schools reestablishing their superiority over others.

4. These three ways of operationalizing adequacy are similar to those in Augenblick et al. (2004).

5. The conceptions of equity developed here are all within what Marion Young (1990) calls the "distributive paradigm," or conceptions of what must be distributed to whom. An alternative that she develops pays more attention to social relations and processes and uses conceptions of domination and oppression as the starting point for conceptions of social justice. This is to say that there are many approaches to equity, none of which is comprehensive. My approach here focuses on policies, litigation, and the historical concepts of equity that have been used in school practices.

6. The decision was handed down on June 28, 2007, in the cases of *Parents Involved in Community Schools Inc. v. Seattle School District and Meredith v. Jefferson County (Ky.) Board of Education.*

7. For documentation on the differences at school entrance, see Farkas (2003), including recent work with the Early Childhood Longitudinal Study Kindergarten Cohort (ECLS-K) data, and "School Readiness: Closing Racial and Ethnic Gaps," a special issue of *The Future of Children* 15(1, Spring 2005).

8. More specifically, they estimate that 56 percent of the twelfth-grade math gap can be attributable to initial differences, with 44 percent attributable to other school and nonschool effects (including family background); the corresponding figures for reading scores are 43 percent and 57 percent. However, by another measure—years behind in vocabulary—the gap is multiplied fourfold over the twelve years. When we turn to outcomes of schooling other than test scores, there is again no reason why differences over time in learning outcomes should be the same for all outcomes and all metrics.

9. For example, among the twenty-nine outcome measures I have derived from NELS88, various test scores are correlated at about .75; test scores are correlated with educational and occupational aspirations at .20 to .30 and with measures of progress (like accumulating credits and receiving a diploma) at .20 to .40; various measures of progress are correlated with each other at .10 to .60 (for the correlation between credits earned and receiving a diploma).

10. See the analysis by Karl Alexander and his colleagues (2001) of Baltimore data, Barbara Heyns's (1978) research on Atlanta, and Daniel O'Brien's (1998) research on a Texas district. In the analysis of kindergarten and first grade by Douglas Downey, Paul von Hippel, and Beckett Broh (2004), schooling tends to reduce inequality (except for black-white differences), but not by enough to offset differences over the summer.

11. The firm that produced this research, DataWORKS Educational Research, appears to specialize in helping schools calibrate the level of material and teaching to prevent falling behind grade-level norms; see its website, www.dataworks-ed.com/home/index.php.

12. On potential problems at grade 4, in the transition to middle school, and in the transition to high school, see also "Early Intervention at Every Age," a special issue of *Educational Leadership* 65(2, October 2007).

13. Evaluations need to be extended over many years to determine short-run versus long-run effects, and long-run follow-ups are rare. The evaluations of the Manpower Demonstration Research Corporation (MDRC) often try to follow up experiments over longer periods of time to determine long-run effects, and the effects are mixed. For example, the Opening Doors Demonstration, which examined enhanced student services in two community colleges, showed that positive effects were short-lived (Scrivener and Au 2007), while the effects of special financial aid in two New Orleans colleges were permanent (Tom Brock, personal communication, 2007). Short-term job training programs like those of the Job Training Partnership Act have only short-run effects on earnings (Friedlander and Burtless 1995). In general, then, the potential long-run effects depicted in figure 6.3 require more information than is usually available.

14. Some districts seem to have accomplished this; see, for example, Springboard Schools (2006), with trajectories for three districts that are parallel rather than diverging.

15. See the website of Sopris West Educational Services, store.cambium-

learning.com/ProgramPage.aspx?parentId=074003926&func
tionID=009000008&pID=&site=sw.

16. Applying figure 6.1 to data for different countries implies that variation at any point in time—for example, PISA test score differences at
age fifteen—is a function of (1) variation in starting points at age five
or six, (2) the practices within countries that lead to differential slopes
of these trajectories, and (3) the structuring of a country's education
system, including the existence of points where testing and tracking
send students on very different trajectories.

CHAPTER 7

1. See, for example, May and Supovitz (2006), analyzing eleven years of
data from Rochester but with only a few demographic variables describing students: gender, race-ethnicity, free lunch eligibility, English
learner status, and special education status.

2. A number of compromises are imposed by the NELS88 data. The
time-invariant independent variables X pose no problems, but the
time-varying variables Z need to be measured for all three years. In
many cases, such measurements are impossible; for example, high
school students are assigned to academic, vocational, general, and remedial tracks, but middle school students are not; many teaching practices described consistently in waves 2 and 3 were not included in the
base-year questionnaire; and families were interviewed in the first and
third waves but not in the second. In some cases, values could be estimated or interpolated for missing data. For example, I interpolated a
value for tenth-grade family income, and I assumed values when students were in tenth grade for maternal occupation based on occupation when students were in eighth and twelfth grade; in addition, I
made assumptions about a student's placement in a female-headed
family, attendance problems, and changing schools based on the consistency of values in eighth and twelfth grades. Errors are therefore
more common in measurements of these time-varying variables than
in other variables, and their coefficients may be biased toward zero. In
other cases, interpolation was impossible, and potentially useful variables could not be included.

3. If we allow the parameters π_0 and π_1 to be random instead of fixed,
and a function of both time-varying independent variables Z (like
school resources and family income) and time-invariant variables X
(like gender, race, and maternal education), then equation 7.1 (the
first-level equation) is

$$Y_{ist} = \pi_{0is} + \pi_{1is} \, TIME_t$$
$$+ \sum_j \pi_{isj} \, Z_{istj} + r_{ist}$$

and the random effects are

$$\pi_{0s} = \beta_{00} + \sum_k \beta_{0k} \, X_k + u_{0i} + u_{0s}$$
$$\pi_{1s} = \beta_{10} + \sum_k \beta_{1k} \, X_k + u_{1i} + u_{1s}$$

yielding a combined model that is an absolute blizzard of potential coefficients:

$$Y_{ist} = [\beta_{00} + \sum_k \beta_{0k} \, X_k + \sum_j \pi_{ij} \, Z_{itj}] + [\,(\beta_{10} + \sum_k \beta_{1k} \, X_k \,) \, TIME_t \,]$$
$$+ [u_{0i} + u_{0s} + u_{1i} \, TIME_t + u_{1s} \, TIME_t + r_{ist}]$$

This includes fixed effects that are functions of both the X_k and the Z_{jt}, slope coefficients that are functions of TIME and the time-invariant X_k, and a random component that varies with TIME. It is possible to make this much more complicated, for example, by making the coefficients π_i of the time-varying independent variables random instead of fixed. However, aside from the practical difficulty that such specifications often fail to converge, they generate too many coefficients to interpret. The final specifications focus instead on the crucial intercepts and slopes of growth trajectories. The results give not only the various parameters but also the variation and the covariation of the random terms.

4.   That is, the *random* components may show no divergence, and the co-variation between u_{0i} and u_{1i} will be zero rather than positive.

5.   Another unavoidable problem is caused by students dropping out after the eighth grade. The developers of NELS88 have constructed a series of weights designed to compensate for nonrandom attrition, in effect weighting more heavily those students who are similar to those who have dropped out. The results presented here are therefore weighted by F2PNLWT, a weight to compensate for attrition between the base year and the second follow-up, when students were seniors. However, there are sure to be unmeasured differences between dropouts and similar students who stay through their senior year, like differences in motivation, in connectedness to schooling, in family support, and in individual problems (drug and alcohol abuse or mental health issues) that are not well measured in NELS88. Therefore, a few of the results are probably affected by self-selection, since students doing poorly—

presumably those with low and declining test scores—drop out, leaving the remaining sample with higher scores than would have been true for the initial sample.

6. Because many independent variables are not available for all three years, it might be reasonable to think that the differences between the first and second specifications would be even greater with a fuller set of resource variables.

7. For example, the standard deviation of the within-school slope divided by the average within-school slope is a coefficient of variation, and the covariance between slope and intercept divided by the standard errors of the slope and intercept is a correlation coefficient; see Seltzer, Choi, and Thum (2003). In addition, the residual variance, or var (r_{is}), can be converted into a coefficient of variation by dividing by the average of the dependent variable Y^*_{ist}, or $cv(r_{is}) = var(r_{ist})^{1/2}/Y^*_{ist}$.

8. One of the two comparisons does not include the other set of variables while the second one does, and the comparisons may differ depending on the covariation between the set of "controllable" variables and the family/demographic variables.

9. Remember that one of the costs of moving from cross-sectional analysis to dynamic analysis is that the variables available for all three years are more limited than those available for twelfth grade. Specifically, the school resource variables in table B.9 are more limited than those used in table B.1.

10. Recall the discussion in chapter 4 about the effects of family background on math, relying on Saxe, Guberman, and Gearhart (1987).

11. For example, the increase in the male-female differential in math scores over these four years is $4 \times .253 = 1.012$ points, which is an increase of $1.012/.644 = 1.571 = 57.1$ percent over the eighth-grade differential of .644 points.

12. Lagged dependent variables cannot be introduced into these growth models because that would require test scores in grade 6, which are not available. The alternative would be to use just two years to estimate these growth functions, but that seems inadvisable since it would mean that growth trajectories are exactly identified and parameters are less efficient.

13. This is contrary to the notion from Lee and Smith (1997) that test score *gains* reach a maximum at moderate levels of enrollment, with both larger and smaller schools having lower test scores. The difference between my results and those of Lee and Smith is due to specifi-

cation differences: they do not include a range of school resources and student measures, all of which reduce the effects of size, and when a lagged test score is introduced—so that independent variables predict *changes* in test scores, similar to their specification—school size becomes insignificant.

14. A relative measure of variation, the coefficient of variation—which is a pure number rather than being measured in test score points—does not behave this way. For three of the four tests (all except math), relative inequality increases between eighth and tenth grade and then falls slightly between tenth and twelfth grade. This may reflect a burst of inequality between eighth and tenth grade and then a reduction in inequality as the lowest-scoring students drop out.

15. These quadratic functional forms are just-identified with three years of data, though with about thirteen thousand students, the parameters should be efficient. In addition to testing the growth trajectories in figure 6.2 by examining the coefficients π_{2is}, we can also observe the covariances in the growth parameters, since in the trajectories depicted in figure 6.1, cov $(\pi_0, \pi_1) > 0$, cov $(\pi_0, \pi_2) < 0$, and cov $(\pi_1, \pi_2) < 0$. However, covariances sometimes differ from these expectations, indicating that certain growth trajectories depart from the regular patterns depicted in figure 6.1. These complex results are no doubt exacerbated by the fact that the parameters π are just-identified t. These results are available from the author on request.

16. The effects of time-invariant variables are also nonlinear, since the fourth equation of note 3 now has terms in $TIME^2$ as well as $TIME$.

17. See the references in chapter 2, as well as summaries of material on ninth-grade transitions like National High School Center (n.d.).

CHAPTER 8

1. This work was carried out with Heather Kinlaw, Linn Posey, and Kathryn Young of the School of Education at the University of California at Berkeley. A much longer version of this work is available from the author on request (Grubb, Kinlaw, Young, and Posey 2006).

2. I am the faculty coordinator of a program for aspiring principals, the Principal Leadership Institute (PLI), and I also teach in a program for aspiring district officials, the Leadership for Educational Equity Program (LEEP). Students in both of these programs volunteered to have their schools participate, and we sought out other schools in the same district or with the same conditions for purposes of comparison.

3. Continuation high schools are one form of alternative education in California. Students are usually sent to continuation high schools when they fall behind in credits earned, when their behavior is unacceptable, or when they need a more personalized learning environment. While the term "interventions" usually refers to specific curricula for students who are behind, a variety of second-chance *institutions* also exist as alternative programs for these students, including special education, independent study, continuation high schools, and schools within the juvenile justice system.

4. More precisely, we reached "empirical saturation," not the "theoretical saturation" stressed in grounded theory.

5. Given the comparison to similar students in other schools, the conventional comparisons among white, black, and Latino students were apparently not the appropriate comparisons for these parents. This also resulted in a rare example of an equitable outcome in a Rawlsian sense: Ms. Yeong asserted that differentiated instruction benefited high-achieving students more than low-achieving students, thereby widening the achievement gap, but this was still equitable because the greater overall inequality improved the performance of the lowest-performing students.

6. The Learning Center model—a carefully designed version of what we call assessment and correction—seems to have emerged from special education as a way of providing additional support for students not adjudicated special education but still needing additional instruction. Among other goals, these centers try to prevent students from falling into special education. In the Hillcrest case, special ed teachers spent some of their time in the Learning Center working with students who were not receiving special education services.

7. Commingling the effects of learning with behavior has also been a long-standing problem in special education; see Artiles and Trent (1994) and Varenne and McDermott (1998).

8. Open Court can be used in many ways, including efforts to develop balanced instruction by using supplemental materials. However, with stringent pacing guides, pressures for coverage, and district administrators who observe classes to make sure teachers are following the curriculum (known in my area as the "Open Court Police"), it turns into a highly scripted approach.

9. See, for example, National Research Council (2004, ch. 3), which describes approaches in math and English that enhance motivation and engagement. See also Knapp and Associates (1995), an extended argu-

ment against the conventional wisdom in instruction (and in favor of "teaching for meaning") with low-income students.

10. See also Grubb (2008c) on "weak" approaches to developing pathways through high schools, confined to restructuring, versus "strong" approaches that also focus on instructional improvement.

11. However, this conclusion is not backed up by any turnover data, and in fact for 2008–2009, half of the teachers in Cityscape Charter will be new to the school.

12. For an argument similar to this, see Oakes, Rogers, and Lipton (2006, 13–16).

13. This is consistent with the practice, described in Miles (1995), of reallocating existing funding to accomplish reform.

14. For opposition to the IES's "gold standard," see Slavin (2003), Schoenfeld (2006), National Research Council (2004), and Confrey (2006).

15. The gains correspond to an effect size of .40 (Elbaum et al. 2000).

16. See Farkas and Durham (2007) and their assessment of tutoring under NCLB, as well as Trelease ([2005]2007).

17. I summarize our conclusions here; a longer version detailing the evaluations of specific curricula is available from the author.

CHAPTER 9

1. See the New Commission's (National Center on Education and the Economy 2007) call for drawing teachers from the top third of college graduates.

2. The state's formal evaluation is O'Day and Bitter (2003). See also Laura Goe's (2003) comparison of three II/USP schools with two low-performing schools that did not receive this grant, and her 2003 analysis of the lack of any II/USP effects on test scores. In addition, Katherine McKnight and Lee Sechrest (2001) describe the low quality of many evaluation plans.

3. Among the states reviewed in chapter 10, only California and Kentucky, with its Commonwealth School Improvement Fund (CSIF) that gives money to targeted schools "in need of assistance," have such spending programs.

4. The Quality Education Improvement Act is supported with funds resulting from litigation against the state. As with previous programs,

QEIA allocates substantial sums of money ($2.9 billion over seven years), with amounts per student ranging from $500 for K–3 to $1,000 for high schools; it limits spending to instructional improvement, improved teacher training, class size reduction, and additional counselors—some of which are potentially effective resources. But without any effort by the state to figure out its errors in the previous two programs and thereby improve the third time around, it seems likely that many schools will (with potential interference by districts) have little of value to show for this funding.

5. Remember that teacher experience in secondary schools is included in these equations, so high pay presumably does not operate by reducing turnover.

6. See NRC (2004, ch. 6) for more detailed evaluations of alternative student services.

7. I have written extensively about such approaches in Grubb (1995) on the integration of academic and vocational education; in NRC (2004, ch. 7) on theme-based approaches to high schools; and in a more recent paper on pathways (Grubb 2008c). While the terminology describing these alternatives has shifted over the last decade, the underlying idea of creating small schools-within-schools with some focus or theme, and with instruction integrated across subjects, is constant.

8. For a behaviorist approach to improving school climate, stressing the importance of schoolwide changes, see Sprague (2004). Christopher Wagner (2006) stresses collaboration and collegiality as two dimensions of school culture.

9. Most of these are reviewed in NRC (2004, ch. 6). On Puente counselors, see Grubb, Lara, and Valdez (2002); on LifeMap, see the web page at the Valencia Community College website, www.valenciacc .edu/lifemap, and Grubb (2008d) for an application to high schools; on the potential power of mentors, see Sipe (1996).

10. For other arguments, both conceptual and empirical, about the importance of improving instruction, see Darling-Hammond et al. (2005) and many other works by Darling-Hammond (see, for example, Darling-Hammond and Baratz-Snowden 2005) and the series of NRC volumes cited in note 15 of the introduction. I note that there are at least four ways of describing good teachers: by discussing how teachers teach, the approach I have taken in the NELS88 data; by describing the credentials that teachers have, the conventional discussion; by understanding the different kinds of knowledge that teachers have, as in Lee Shulman's (1967) analysis of content knowledge, ped-

agogical knowledge, and pedagogical content knowledge; and by identifying effective teachers in statistical models with value-added approaches, which can identify good teachers only after the fact. These four approaches are not necessarily consistent with one another, and only the first one can identify what it is that effective teachers do differently.

11. For some of the literature on connectedness to schooling, see Nasir, Jones, and McLaughlin (forthcoming).

12. See Deschenes, Cuban, and Tyack (2001) on the historically persistent explanations of variation in student performance.

13. Analogous sections are possible on gender issues, class-related issues, and the issues faced by students with disabilities. While the kind of argument I present here would apply to these groups as well, I concentrate on the racial-ethnic issues because they have been so prominent and—unlike the improvements in educational outcomes for girls, for example—so resistant to change.

14. The argument that schools need to face racial and ethnic issues squarely has now been cast as the question of whether schools should be color-blind or not. See "Schools Can't Be Color-Blind" (editorial), *Los Angeles Times*, September 16, 2007; see also Oakes, Rogers, and Lipton (2006), Valenzuela (1999), and Anyon (2005). The enormous literature on culturally relevant pedagogy and multicultural education, including that cited in note 19, also assumes the importance of facing racial-ethnic differences squarely.

15. See especially Dee (2004). In my NELS88 analysis, I included variables for same-race teachers for black and Latino students, but these were consistently insignificant.

16. See Mukerjee (2006). While many schools examine which students and which teachers generate disciplinary referrals, the final stage of analysis—observing what happens within these teachers' classes—is much less common.

17. See Power (1985), based on Lawrence Kohlberg's (1981) conception of moral development. A famous high school—Central Park East, featured in Meier (1995)—developed such a student-run disciplinary system, portrayed in Frederick Wiseman's film *High School II*, but when I visited the school in 1999, this system had fallen apart because the responsible faculty member had left. Like all nonstandard practices, this approach to discipline requires consistent attention to prevent a collapse back into standard practice.

18. See Wheeler (2007) on contrastive analysis and code-switching, and Gutiérrez, Baquedano-López, and Tejada (1999) on repertoires of language practices.

19. For an introduction to this vast literature, see Ladson-Billings (1994), Gay (2000), and Banks and Banks (2004). There are also guides for schools, such as Lindsey, Robins, and Terrell (2004), Bowers and Flinders (1991), Hollins and Oliver (1999), and Cartledge and Lo (2006). See also "Race, Culture, and Identity," the special issue of *Principal Leadership* 8(1, September 2007). Finally, for readers who need hundreds of citations to be convinced, see Zirkel (2005, forthcoming a, and forthcoming b).

20. There are many presenters and workshops around the country that help schools discuss racial issues, and it is impossible to describe here the variety of practices they represent. On the awkward conversations that often take place in schools, see Pollock (2004).

21. See Carnoy, Elmore, and Siskin (2003); on the role of principals in such schools, see Lemons, Luschel, and Siskin (2003).

22. See chapter 3, note 5, giving some reasons why their efforts to test the effects of organic management on reading and math scores were unsuccessful.

23. See, for example, the "beat the odds" schools, described in Chenoweth (2007), where principals share leadership with teachers and teachers are given time to plan and work collectively and to observe one another. See also the descriptions in Rose (2006) of democratic schools with collaborative relations among teachers as well as more respectful and egalitarian relations between teachers and students. The improving schools in California's High Priority School Grant Program are also examples of schools with internal coherence and distributed leadership (Timar and Kim 2008).

CHAPTER 10

1. For a study of California that comes to the same conclusion about consistency, see Cohen and Hill (2001).

2. On the roles of administrators, see Cuban (1988); on administrative progressivism, see Tyack (1974).

3. See also Kannapel and Clements (2005), who concluded in their effective-schools study of eight elementary schools that district support was highly varied.

4. The effective-districts literature suffers from one of the flaws of the effective schools literature: uncertainty about whether the districts chosen for analysis are indeed exemplary rather than well known for reforms that make no difference. On district issues, see Springboard Schools (2006), Austin et al. (2006), Darling-Hammond et al. (2005), and Rumberger and Connell (2007), relying extensively on Fruchter (2007) and Supovitz (2006).

5. On the importance of civic capacity—the cooperation of all civic groups within a district in helping the schools be successful—see Stone (2001).

6. See especially Spillane and Thompson (1997), Snipes, Doolittle, and Herlihy (2002), McLaughlin and Talbert (2006), Murphy and Hallinger (1993), and Hightower et al. (2002).

7. See the citations in note 4.

8. I caution that the effectiveness of the zone approach has not yet been evaluated, and the Miami plan is quite contentious, as illustrated by even a brief consultation of Internet references.

9. On school-based budgeting, Alison Cole (2005) has pulled together the practices in numerous districts; see also Goertz and Odden (1999).

10. For an examination of the effects of SBB on the equity of intra-district resource distribution, see the series of publications available from the Annenburg Institute for School Reform; see also Odden (1999), Miles and Roza (2004) Roza and Miles (2002), and Miles, Ware, and Roza (2003).

11. On the cursory treatment of resources in most educational administration textbooks, see chapter 1, note 5.

12. It is not clear that teachers can master differentiated instruction without considerable pre-service education or professional development. Note that the Finland approach relies heavily on an extensive pre-service teacher education that lasts four and a half years and incorporates several internships under the supervision of master teachers, including one devoted solely to teaching heterogeneous groups of students.

13. On the five stages of LifeMap, see www.valenciacc.edu/lifemap/stages_ps.asp.

14. See again the references in chapter 1, note 5.

15. The most useful compilation of state practices is Calkins et al. (2007),

which I have augmented by examining reports from a number of other states. See also Redding and Walberg (2007), which documents the NCLB requirements for developing statewide systems of support. However, it is difficult to tell from this volume what states are doing.

16. See also Rumberger and Connell (2007) on the potential role of states in developing district capacity.

17. It is difficult to know how frequent these practices are, but in a sample of ten states that we examined intensively, all had developed a tiering system; almost all (eight of ten) provided technical assistance to low-performing schools; five of the ten supported districts, and five had helped schools use data. Only one of the ten, plus California, provided additional funding.

18. See also Calkins et al. (2007), which summarizes the efforts of ten states as "mostly tentative steps, and more frustration than success."

19. See also the highly critical evaluation of Tennessee's efforts, *State Approaches to Improving Tennessee's High Priority Schools* (Offices of Research and Education Accountability 2006).

20. Many of these ideas were proposed by the Finance and Facilities Working Group, K–12 Education of the California Joint Committee to Develop a Master Plan for Education, of which I was a member; see the *Final Report* (March 2000) for much more detail.

21. See Vinovskis (1999), Farkas and Hall (2000), and Puma et al. (1997). On programs for English learners, see Minow (1997), Hakuta and Cancino (1977), and Arroyo and Ziegler (1993).

22. The NCLB was not reauthorized before the 2008 presidential elections, and most observers think that reauthorization will not take place until 2010. The fact that there has been so much controversy about the effects of NCLB is testimony to the uncertainty about the legislation and what it has accomplished.

23. See, for example, the testimony of Kati Haycock of the Education Trust (2005): "This law strengthens the hands of those who are working to improve overall achievement and close the achievement gaps," and, "We are on the right path"—despite pointed criticism of NCLB's implementation. See Education Trust, "Closing the Achievement Gap in America's Public Schools," at www2.edtrust.org/edtrust/press+room/haycock+testimony+9.29.05.htm.

24. Quoted from George Bush's introduction to NCLB, available at: www .whitehouse.gov/news/reports/no-child-left-behind.html (accessed

November 16, 2006). On the movement for rigor and standards, which is long on rhetoric about the importance of higher standards but short on ways to achieve them, see Grubb and Oakes (2007).

25. See U.S. Department of Education, "Introduction: No Child Left Behind," available at: www.ed.gov/nclb/overview/intro/index.html (accessed November 16, 2006).

26. See also Welner and Weitzman (2005) on the "soft bigotry of low expenditures" in NCLB.

27. See www.whatworks.ed.gov (accessed on February 26, 2008). The What Works Clearinghouse promises to update its listings, though its topics now exclude many of those that schools would want to know about.

28. See the discussion in *Educational Researcher* 36(2, March 2006): 3–23.

29. *Congressional Record*, September 29, 2006; Hoff (2006).

CHAPTER 11

1. See Yudoff et al. (2002) for an overview of litigation in education, much of which has to do with equity.

2. For another critique of litigation, specifically of adequacy lawsuits, see Hanushek (2006), which presents substantial evidence of spending without any associated improvements in outcomes; see especially Evers and Clopton (2006) and the argument from Roza and Hill (2006) that districts do not generally know how to spend money well. Unfortunately, the book provides no guidance about what schools should do, unlike my efforts to find evidence about effective school resources, and its pedagogical conservatism flies in the face of considerable evidence about balanced instruction.

3. Murray, Evans, and Schwab (1998) also noted that only one-third of total variation among districts in the country is within-state inequality; the other two-thirds is due to among-state inequality, which is untouched by state-level litigation—suggesting that state-level litigation fails to address the majority of even revenue inequality.

4. See, for example, Lindseth (2007), who notes that adequacy lawsuits failed to yield any substantial victories between 2005 and 2007. Several of his explanations are similar to mine, including the reluctance of courts in many states to take on issues that they see as the responsibility of state legislatures; the conclusion that increasing spending is not

the answer; and the sense that court remedies have not been effective in enhancing student achievement. However, since Lindseth is a lawyer who defends states against school finance cases, his own analysis of the reasons for legal outcomes may be biased.

5. Although there is some weak evidence that inequality in expenditures per pupil did decrease in Texas, there is no evidence about other resources or outcomes, so I do not further discuss the Texas case.

6. Total expenditures per pupil appear to increase the change in the fourth-grade pass rate, but when pass rates lagged one year are introduced, there is no significant effect of spending (Cullen and Loeb 2004). The difference equations presented in chapter 2 in the second specification clarify that the coefficient on the lagged dependent variable must be estimated with an instrumental variables technique, rather than being assumed to be one.

7. This argument is similar to that in Pressman and Wildavsky (1979), the original analysis of implementation problems: if there are multiple steps in implementing a program, and possibilities for veto at each step, the likelihood of successful implementation is low.

8. See chapter 6 on the three definitions of adequacy; the most common approach—the "professional judgment" model—depends on conventional norms of adequate resources rather than on any evidence of effectiveness. Ironically, I argued back in 1982 that there could be no stable conception of adequacy because the concept had varied so much over time and across regions; see Grubb and Lazerson (1982).

9. It is worth noting that the result of the lawsuit was a settlement with the state of California rather than the usual judgment declaring a finance system unconstitutional and forcing the legislature to respond. The settlement avoided a protracted legislative battle and arguably allowed a more subtle remedy—including various oversight mechanisms—than the usual lawsuit.

10. For an evaluation of the effects of *Williams*—carried out by the two organizations that brought the lawsuit, so the document's interpretation of the effects may be somewhat rosy—see ACLU Foundation of Southern California and Public Advocates Inc. (2007).

11. See McNeil (2007) on the efforts to link spending to achievement; see also CFE, "Where Will the Money Go?," available at www.cfequity.org: CFE_PublicComment_On_DOE_Proposed_Contract_for_Excellence_8-15-08_Final.pdf.

12. See the various news releases from the Education Law Center, avail-

able at www.edlawcenter.org; the "Top Stories" read like a series of constant threats to the letter and spirit of the *Abbott* case.

CHAPTER 12

1. The term "administrative progressive" is somewhat awkward, and the practices that emerged during the Progressive Era (roughly 1890 to 1920) are no longer viewed as particularly progressive in the conventional sense. In particular, progressive education defined as a more Deweyan and constructivist pedagogical approach was antithetical to the bureaucratic and efficiency-oriented reforms of the administrative "progressives." The best source on the administrative "progressives" remains Tyack (1974); see also Callahan (1967).

2. Economists worry about many conceptions of efficiency, most of them incomprehensible with the technical apparatus of economic theory. "X-efficiency" corresponds to getting the most possible out of inputs, and the failure to do so can often be construed as waste. Programs can be efficient in a benefit-cost sense even if their costs are high—for example, the Perry Preschool program with its high costs but high benefit-cost ratios. There are many interpretations of efficiency, and the low-cost interpretation is only one among many.

3. Following the advice of David Stern, I use the terms "quasi-market" or "marketlike" because true markets cannot exist in education: the "commodity" is too different from the conventional products bought and sold in markets, there are usually no market prices, the incentives of producers and consumers are more complex, and the market-making mechanisms found in conventional markets for goods and services—the wholesale and retail trade sector, the FIRE (finance, insurance, and real estate) sector—are almost totally missing in education. For critiques of neoliberal practices in other countries, see Finkelstein and Grubb (2000) for English developments and Fiske and Ladd (2000) for New Zealand; see also Cuban (2004). This section on recent developments in the United States is based on Scott (2008), House (1998), Tyack (2004), and Emery and Heineman (2004).

4. Note that, unavoidably, the efforts to determine whether charter schools are more effective compare "regular" schools—most of which follow the traditional approach—with charter schools; see, for example, Carnoy, Elmore, and Siskin (2003) and Charter School Evaluation Publications from the Evaluation Center at Western Michigan University, available at www.wmich.edu/evalctr/charter, especially Miron, Coryn, and Mack-

ery (2007). The right approach would be to compare charter schools and regular schools with complex/constructivist schools.

5. This is explicit in the conception of the constructivist leader: the principal works in less authoritarian and more collaborative ways with his or her "pupils," the teachers (Lambert 2002).

6. See Cuban (1988) on the mix of managerial, instructional, and political concerns among leaders. He uses "political" in the sense of the many small value-laden decisions required in schools—for example, over which students and which subjects are to be favored—but its meaning also extends to the conventional political concerns of interest groups that districts and states face.

7. This famous phrase comes from Charles Eliot, the president of Harvard, in an explicit argument that schools should be sorting mechanisms; see Lazerson and Grubb (1974, document 13, 136).

8. See, for example, Center for American Progress Task Force on Poverty (2007), which makes five recommendations for transfer programs, three for labor market interventions, and three for education reforms: increasing early childhood education, connecting disadvantaged youth with schooling opportunities, and expanding Pell grants. Other examples include Cauthen (2007), Bernstein (2007), and "The Next Generation of Antipoverty Policies," a special issue of *The Future of Children* 17(2, Fall 2007).

9. Bush has repeated this statement as a mantra many times since he first made it in a speech to the NAACP on July 10, 2000, available at: http://www.washingtonpost.com/wp-srv/onpolitics/elections/bushtext071000.htm. In the same speech, Bush also declared that "strong civil rights enforcement will be the cornerstone of my administration"—an obviously empty promise.

10. See Grubb and Lazerson ([1982] 1988), especially the postscript titled "Let Them Eat Ketchup: The Plight of Children in the 1980s." On the constant lying during the Reagan administration, see Green et al. (1983).

11. For an argument that welfare bureaucracies have badly managed the transformation to Work First, see DeParle (2004). The effects of the 1996 reform are still being debated; they appear to be more moderate than either proponents or opponents predicted, but it also appears that the worst-off families with the least ability to work have indeed suffered.

12. See Commission on Presidential Debates, "The Third Bush-Kerry

Presidential Debate," October 13, 2004, available at: www.debates
.org/pages/trans2004d.html.

13. See Federal Reserve Board, "Testimony of Chairman Alan Greenspan
     Before the U.S. House of Representatives Committee on Education
     and the Workforce," March 11, 2004, available at: www.federal
     reserve.gov/boarddocs/testimony/2004/20040311/default.htm.
     For evidence that Greenspan prevented early attention to predatory
     lending and the subprime mortgage debacle, see Andrews (2007).

14. See the analysis of "strong" versus "weak" markets in education in
     Grubb and Lazerson (2004, chs. 8 and 9).

15. Only certain forms should be considered because the history of parent
     education is also full of paternalistic efforts that have not been partic-
     ularly successful (Grubb and Lazerson [1982] 1988, ch. 8; Schlossman
     1976).

16. See Esping-Andersen (1990) for an expansive conception of the wel-
     fare state. See also the volume of essays *Why We Need a New Welfare State*
     (Esping-Andersen et al. 2002).

17. See especially Macpherson (1977), who outlines four stages of democ-
     racy, including one succeeding interest-group liberalism that he bases
     on the Port Huron Statement.

REFERENCES

Abbott Indicators Project. 2006. *The Abbott Districts in 2005–2006*. Newark, N.J.: Education Law Center (spring).

Achieve Inc. 2004. *Do Graduation Tests Measure Up? A Closer Look at State High School Exit Exams*. Available at: www.achieve.org.

ACLU Foundation of Southern California and Public Advocates Inc. 2007. *Williams v. California: The Statewide Impact of Two Years of Implementation*. Los Angeles: ACLU Foundation of Southern California.

Adams, Jacob. 2000. "Resource Equity and Educational Adequacy." In *All Children Can Learn: Lessons from the Kentucky Reform Experience*, edited by Roger S. Pankatz and Joseph M. Petrosko. San Francisco: Jossey-Bass.

Alexander, Karl, Doris Entwhistle, and Nader Kabbini. 2001. "The Dropout Process in Life Course Perspective: Early Risk Factors at Home and School." *Teachers College Record* 103: 760–882.

Alexander, Karl L., Doris R., and L.S. Olson. 2001. "Schools, Achievement, and Inequality: A Seasonal Perspective." *Educational Evaluation and Policy Analysis* 23(2): 171–91.

Alexander, Nicola A. 2003. "Considering Equity and Adequacy: An Examination of Student Class Time in New York State Public Secondary Programs, 1975–1995." *Journal of Education Finance* 28(winter): 357–82.

Allard, Scott. 2007. "The Changing Face of Welfare During the Bush Administration." *Publius: The Journal of Federalism* 37(3): 304–32.

American Counseling Association (ACA). 2006. "The Effectiveness of Counseling." Available at: www.counseling.org.

American Diploma Project. 2004. *Ready or Not: Creating a High School Diploma That Counts*. Washington: American Diploma Project.

American Institutes for Research (AIR). 1999. *An Educators' Guide to Schoolwide Reform*. Arlington, Va.: Educational Research Service.

———. 2006. *Comprehensive School Reform Quality Center Report on Middle and High School Reform Models*. Washington: AIR.

Anagnostopoulos, Dorothea. 2003. "The New Accountability, Student Failure, and Teachers' Work in Urban High Schools." *Educational Policy* 17(3): 291–316.

Andrews, Edmund. 2007. "Fed and Regulators Shrugged as the Subprime Crisis Spread." *New York Times*, December 18, p. 1, 28.

Anyon, Jean. 1997. *Ghetto Schooling: A Political Economy of Urban Educational Reform*. New York: Teachers College Press.

———. 2005. *Radical Possibilities: Public Policy, Urban Education, and a New Social Movement*. New York: Routledge.

Archer, Jeff. 2006. "Building Capacity." *Education Week*, September 13, S3–12.

Argyris, Chris, and Donald Schön. 1978. *Organizational Learning: A Theory of Action Perspective*. Reading, Mass.: Addison-Wesley.

Arroyo, Carmen, and Edward Zigler. 1993. "America's Chapter I/Chapter I Programs: Why Has the Promise Not Been Met?" In *From Head Start and Beyond: A National Plan for Extended Childhood Intervention*, edited by Edward Zigler and Sharon Styfco. New Haven, Conn.: Yale University Press.

Artiles, Alfredo J., and Stanley C. Trent. 1994. "Overrepresentation of Minority Students in Special Education: A Continuing Debate." *Journal of Special Education* 27(4): 410–37.

Askov, Eunice N., C. Kassab, E.L. Grinder, L.M. Semali, D. Weirauch, Eugenio Longoria Saenz, B. Van Horn. 2003. "Filling in the 'Black Box' of Family Literacy: Implications of Research for Practice and Policy." Paper presented to the twentieth annual meeting of the Rutgers Invitational Symposium on Education (October). Pennsylvania State University, Goodling Institute for Research in Family Literacy.

Augenblick, John, Jennifer Sharp, Justin Silverstein, and Robert Palaich. 2004. "Politics and the Meaning of Adequacy: States Work to Integrate the Conception into K-to-12 School Finance." In *Money, Politics, and Law: Intersections and Conflicts in the Provision of Educational Opportunity*, edited by Karen DeMoss and Kenneth K. Wong. Larchmont, N.Y.: Eye on Education.

Austin, James E., Robert B. Schwartz, Jennifer M. Suesse, and Allen Grossman. 2006. "Managing at Scale in the Long Beach Unified School District." Cambridge, Mass.: Harvard University, Public Education Leadership Project (August 24). Available at: www.hbsp.harvard.edu.

Ayers, William, Bernardine Dohrn, and Rick Ayers. 2001. *Zero Tolerance: Resisting the Drive for Punishment in Our Schools*. New York: New Press.

Baldwin, James. 1955. *Notes of a Native Son*. Boston: Beacon Press.

Ballou, Dale. 1998. "The Condition of Urban School Finance: Efficient Resource Allocation in Urban Schools." In *Selected Papers in School Finance, 1996*, edited by William J. Fowler Jr. Washington: National Center for Education Statistics.

Banks, James, and Cherry McGee Banks, eds. 2004. *Handbook of Research on Multicultural Education*. San Francisco: Jossey-Bass.

Barro, Stephen. 1989. "Fund Distribution Issues in School Finance: Priorities for the Next Round of Research." *Educational Evaluation and Policy Analysis* 11(1): 17–30.

Barthe, Patte, Kati Haycock, H. Jackson, K. Mora, P. Ruiz, S. Robinson, and A. Wilkins. *Dispelling the Myth: High Poverty Schools Exceed Expectations*. ERIC ED445140. Washington, D.C.: Education Trust.

Belfield, Clive R., and Henry M. Levin. 2002. "The Effects of Competition Between Schools on Educational Outcomes: A Review for the United States." *Review of Educational Research* 72(2): 279–341.

Benton, Joshua, and Holly Hacker. 2004. "Poor Schools' TAKS Surge Raises Cheating Questions." *Dallas Morning News*, December 19.

Berliner, David C. 2005. "Our Impoverished View of Educational Reform." *Teachers College Record* 108(6): 949–95.

Berne, Robert, and Lawrence O. Picus, eds. 1994. *Outcome Equity in Education*. Thousand Oaks, Calif.: Corwin Press.

Bernstein, Basil. 1995. *Class, Codes, and Control*. New York: Schocken.

Bernstein, Jared. 2007. "Work, Work Supports, and Safety Nets: Reducing the Burden of Low Incomes in America." Briefing paper 200. Economic Policy Institute (October 2). Available at: www.sharedprosperity.org/bp200.html.

Betts, Julian R., Lorien A. Rice, Andrew C. Zau, Y. Emily Tang, Cory R. Koedel. 2006. *Does Student Choice Work? Effects on Student Integration and Achievement*. San Francisco: Public Policy Institute of California.

Bishop, John. 1989. "Why the Apathy in American High Schools?" *Educational Researcher* 18(1): 6–10.

Boaler, Jo, and Megan Staples. 2008. "Creating Mathematical Futures Through an Equitable Teaching Approach: The Case of Railside School." *Teachers College Record* 110(3): 608–45.

Bodilly, Susan, and Megan Beckett. 2005. *Making Out-of-School Time Matter: Evidence for Action Agenda*. Santa Monica, Calif.: Rand Corporation.

Boesel, David, and Eric Fredland. 1999. *College for All: Is There Too Much Emphasis on Getting a Four-Year College Degree?* Washington: U.S. Department of Education.

Bourdieu, Pierre, and Jean-Claude Passeron. 1977. *Reproduction in Education, Society, and Culture*. Beverly Hills, Calif.: Sage Publications.

Bowers, C. A., and David Flinders. 1991. *Culturally Responsive Teaching and Supervision: A Handbook for Staff Development*. New York: Teachers College Press.

Bowles, Samuel, and Herbert Gintis. 1975. *Schooling in Capitalist America*. New York: Basic Books.

Boyd, William L., and William T. Hartman. 1988. "The Politics of Educational Productivity." In *Microlevel School Finance: Issues and Implications for*

Policy, edited by David H. Monk and Julia Underwood. Cambridge, Mass.: Ballinger.

Brown, Bryan W. 1988. "The Microeconomics of Learning: Students, Teachers, and Classrooms." In *Microlevel School Finance: Issues and Implications for Policy*, edited by David H. Monk and Julie Underwood. Cambridge, Mass.: Ballinger.

Brown, Bryan W., and Daniel H. Saks. 1975. "The Production and Distribution of Cognitive Skills Within Schools." *Journal of Political Economy* 83(3): 571–93.

Brown-Chidsey, Rachel. 2008. "No More 'Waiting to Fail.'" *Educational Leadership* 65(2): 40–47.

Bryk, Anthony, and Barbara Schneider. 2002. *Trust in Schools: A Core Resource for Improvement*. New York: Russell Sage Foundation.

Calkins, Andrew, William Guenther, Grace Belfiore, and Dave Lash. 2007. *The Turnaround Challenge: Supplement to the Main Report*. Boston: Insight Education and Research Institute.

Callahan, Raymond. 1967. *Education and the Cult of Efficiency*. Chicago: University of Chicago Press.

Campaign for Fiscal Equity (CFE). 2004. *The New York Adequacy Study: Determining the Costs of Providing All Children in New York an Adequate Education*. Final report. New York: American Institutes for Research/Management Analysis and Planning Inc.

Canada, Geoffrey. 1995. *Fist Stick Knife Gun: A Personal History of Violence in America*. Boston: Beacon Press.

Carnoy, Martin, Rebecca Jacobsen, Lawrence Mishel, and Richard Rothstein. 2005. *The Charter School Dust-Up: Examining the Evidence on Enrollment and Achievement*. New York: Teachers College Press.

Carnoy, Martin, Richard Elmore, and Leslie Santee Siskin, eds. 2003. *The New Accountability: High Schools and High-Stakes Testing*. New York: Routledge.

Carroll, Thomas, Kathleen Fulton, Kane Abercrombie, and Irene Yoon. 2004. *Fifty Years After* Brown v. Board of Education: *A Two-Tiered Educational System*. Washington: National Commission on Teaching and America's Future.

Cartledge, Gwendolyn, and Ya-yu Lo. 2006. *Teaching Urban Learners: Culturally Responsive Strategies for Developing Academic and Behavioral Competence*. Champaign, Ill.: Research Press.

Castro, Alysse. 2002. "Six Impossible Things to Do Before Lunch." Master's thesis, University of California at Berkeley, School of Education.

Cauthen, Nancy. 2007. "Improving Work Supports." Economic Policy Institute briefing paper 198. Washington, D.C.: Economic Policy Institute.

Center for American Progress. Task Force on Poverty. 2007. *From Poverty to Prosperity: A National Strategy to Cut Poverty in Half*. Washington: Center for

American Progress (April 25). Available at: http://www.american progress.org/issues/2007/04/poverty_report.html.

Chambers, Jay. 1997. "Measuring Inflation in Public School Costs." Working paper 97-43. Washington: American Institutes for Research (AIR) for U.S. Department of Education, National Center for Education Statistics (NCES).

———. 1998. "Geographic Variation in Public School Costs." Working paper 98-04. Washington: National Center for Education Statistics (NCES).

Chenoweth, Karin. 2007. *"It's Being Done": Academic Success in Unexpected Schools*. Cambridge, Mass.: Harvard Education Press.

Clark, Donald L., Linda S. Lotto, and Terry A. Astuto. 1984. "Effective Schools and School Improvement: A Comparative Analysis of Two Lines of Inquiry." *Educational Administration Quarterly* 20(3): 41–68.

Clark, Reginald. 1983. *Family Life and School Achievement: Why Poor Black Children Succeed or Fail*. Chicago: University of Chicago Press.

Claus, Jeffrey. 1990. "Opportunity or Inequality in Vocational Education? A Qualitative Investigation." *Curriculum Inquiry* 20: 7–39.

Clinton, Hillary. 1996. *It Takes a Village, and Other Lessons Children Teach Us*. New York: Simon & Schuster.

Clotfelter, Charles T., Helen F. Ladd, and Jacob L. Vigdor. 2006. "The Academic Achievement Gap in Grades 3 to 8." Working paper 12207. Cambridge, Mass.: National Bureau of Economic Research (May). Available at: www.nber.org/papers/w12207.

Clune, William H. 1994. "The Shift from Equity to Adequacy in School Finance." *Educational Policy* 8(4): 376–94.

Cohen, David, and Heather Hill. 2001. *Learning Policy: When State Education Reform Works*. New Haven, Conn.: Yale University Press.

Cohen, David, Stephen Raudenbush, and Deborah Ball. 2003. "Resources, Instruction, and Research." *Educational Evaluation and Policy Analysis* 25(2): 119–42.

Cohen, Michael. 1983. "Instructional, Management, and Social Conditions on Effective Schools." In *School Finance and School Improvement: Linkages for the 1980s*, edited by Allan Odden and L. Dean Webb. Cambridge, Mass.: Ballinger.

Cole, Alison. 2005. "Schools Gaining Greater Control over Their Resources: Recent Budgetary Reforms in School Districts in the United States and Canada." Unpublished paper, University of California at Berkeley.

Coleman, James S., E. Q. Campbell, C. J. Hobson, J. McPartland, A. M. Mead, F. D. Weinfield, and R. L. York. 1966. *Equality of Educational Opportunity*. Washington: U.S. Department of Health, Education, and Welfare.

Comer, James. 1996. *Rallying the Whole Village: The Comer Process for Reforming Education*. New York: Teachers College Press.

Conant, James Bryant. 1959. *The American High School Today: A First Report to Interested Citizens*. New York: McGraw-Hill.

Confrey, John. 2006. "Comparing and Contrasting the National Research Council Report on Evaluating Curricular Effectiveness with the What Works Clearinghouse Approach." *Educational Evaluation and Policy Analysis* 28(3): 195–214.

Cook, Thomas. 2000. "Randomized Experiments in Education: Why Are They So Rare?" *Educational Evaluation and Policy Analysis* 24(3): 175–200.

Coons, John E., William H. Clune III, and Stephen D. Sugarman. 1970. *Private Wealth and Public Education*. Cambridge, Mass.: Harvard University Press.

Cooper, Harris, Jeffrey C. Valentine, K. Charlton, and A. Melson. 2003. "The Effects of Modified School Calendars on Student Achievement and on School and Community Attitudes." *Review of Educational Research* 73(1): 1–52.

Copland, Michael. 2001. "The Myth of the Superprincipal." *Phi Delta Kappan* 82(7): 528–33.

Corley, Robert. 2002. "The Condition of California School Facilities and Policies Related to Those Conditions." Available at: www.justschools.gseis.ucla.edu/research/index.html.

Cotton, Kathleen. 1989. "Educational Time Factors." School Improvement Research Series 8. Portland, Oreg.: Northwest Regional Educational Laboratory (November). Available at: www.nwrel.org/scpd/sirs/4/cu8.html.

Counts, George. 1978. *Dare the School Build a New Social Order?* Carbondale, Ill.: Southern Illinois University Press. (Orig. pub. in 1932.)

Cox, Rebecca. 2004. "Navigating Community College Demands: Contradictory Goals, Expectations, and Outcomes in Composition." Ph.D. diss., University of California at Berkeley, School of Education.

Cremin, Lawrence A. 1961. *The Transformation of the School: Progressivism in American Education 1876–1957*. New York: Knopf.

Cremin, Lawrence A., and Merle Borrowman. 1956. *Public Schools in Our Democracy*. New York: Macmillan.

Cuban, Larry. 1984. "Transforming the Frog into a Prince: Effective Schools Research, Policy, and Practice at the District Level." *Harvard Educational Review* 54(2): 129–51.

———. 1988. *The Managerial Imperative and the Practice of Leadership in School*. Albany: State University of New York Press.

———. 1990. "Reforming Again, Again, and Again." *Educational Researcher* 19(1): 3–13.

———. 1993. *How Teachers Taught: Constancy and Change in American Classrooms, 1880–1990*, 2d ed. New York: Teachers College Press.

———. 2004. *The Blackboard and the Bottom Line: Why Schools Can't Be Businesses*. Cambridge, Mass.: Harvard University Press.

Cubberly, Ellwood. 1905. *School Funds and Their Apportionment*. New York: Teachers College.

Cullen, Julie Berry, and Susanna Loeb. 2004. "School Finance Reform in Michigan: Evaluating Proposal A." In *Helping Children Left Behind: State Aid and the Pursuit of Educational Equity*, edited by John Yinger. Cambridge, Mass.: MIT Press.

D'Agostino, Jerome, and Judith Murphy. 2004. "A Meta-Analysis of Reading Recovery in United States Schools." *Educational Evaluation and Policy Analysis* 26(1): 23–38.

Darling-Hammond, Linda, and Joan Baratz-Snowden, eds. 2005. *A Good Teacher in Every Classroom: Preparing the Highly Qualified Teachers Our Children Deserve*. San Francisco: Jossey-Bass.

Darling-Hammond, Linda, Amy Hightower, Jennifer Husbands, Jeanette Lafors, Viki Young, and Carl Christopher. 2005. *Instructional Leadership for Systemic Change: The Story of San Diego's Reform*. Lanham, Md.: Scarecrow Education.

Daymont, Thomas, and Russell Rumberger. 1982. "The Impact of High School Curriculum on the Earnings and Employability of Youth." In *Job Training for Youth*, edited by Robert Taylor, Howard Rosen, and Frank Pratzner. Columbus, Ohio: National Center for Research in Vocational Education.

Dee, Thomas. 2004. "Teachers, Race, and Student Achievement in a Randomized Experiment." *Review of Economics and Statistics* 86(1): 195–210.

Delpit, Lisa. 1995. *Other People's Children: Cultural Conflict in the Classroom*. New York: New Press.

DeParle, Jason. 2004. American Dream: Three Women, Ten Kids, and a Nation's Drive to End Welfare. New York: Viking.

Deschenes, Sarah, Larry Cuban, and David Tyack. 2001. "Mismatch: Historical Perspectives on Schools and Students Who Don't Fit Them." *Teachers College Record* 103(4): 525–47.

Dewey, John. 1938. *Experience and Education*. New York: Macmillan.

Diamond, John, and James Spillane. 2004. "High-Stakes Accountability in Urban Elementary Schools: Challenging or Reproducing Inequality?" *Teachers College Record* 106(6): 1145–76.

Digest of Educational Statistics 2006. 2007. Washington: National Center for Educational Statistics, U.S. Department of Education. Available at nces.ed.gov/pubSearch/pubsinfo.asp?pubid=2007017.

Dixon, Adrienne, and Celia Rousseau. 2005. "'And We Are Still Not Saved': Critical Race Theory in Education Ten Years Later." *Race Ethnicity and Education* 8(1): 7–27.

Donovan, M. Suzanne, and John D. Bransford, eds. 2005. *How Students Learn: Mathematics in the Classroom*. Washington: National Academies Press.

Dorans, Neil, Michael Pommerich, and Paul Holland. 2007. *Linking and Aligning Scores and Scales*. New York: Springer Verlag.

Downes, Thomas A. 1992. "Evaluating the Impact of School Finance Reform on the Provision of Public Education: The California Case." *National Tax Journal* 45(4): 405–19.

Downey, Douglas B., Paul von Hippel, and Beckett Broh. 2004. "Are Schools the Great Equalizer? Cognitive Inequality During the Summer Months and the School Year." *American Sociological Review* 69: 613–35.

Drake, Thelbert L., and William H. Roe. 1999. *The Principalship*, 5th ed. Upper Saddle River, N.J.: Prentice-Hall.

Dryfoos, Joy. 1994. *Full-Service Schools: A Revolution in Health and Social Services for Children, Youth, and Families*. San Francisco: Jossey-Bass.

Dufour, Rebecca, Robert Eaker, and Gayle Karhanek. 2004. *Whatever It Takes: How Professional Learning Communities Respond When Kids Don't Learn*. Bloomington, Ind.: National Education Service.

Duncombe, William D., and John M. Yinger. 1999. "Performance Standards and Educational Cost Indexes: You Can't Have One Without the Other." In *Equity and Adequacy in Education Finance: Issues and Perspectives*, edited by Helen F. Ladd, Rosemary Chalk, and Janet S. Hansen. Washington: National Academies Press.

Dunham, E. Alden. 1969. *Colleges of the Forgotten Americans: A Profile of State Colleges and Regional Universities*. New York: McGraw-Hill/Carnegie Commission on Higher Education.

Dupriez, Vincent, and Xavier Dumay. 2005. "L'inégalité des chances à l'école: Analyse d'un effet spécifique de la structure scolaire" (The Inequality of Chances at School: An Analysis of the Specific Effect of School Structure). *Revue Française de Pédagogie* 150: 5–17.

Eckert, Penelope. 1989. *Jocks and Burnouts: Social Categories and Identity in the High School*. New York: Teachers College Press.

Edmonds, Ronald R. 1979. "Effective Schools for the Urban Poor." *Educational Leadership* 37(1): 15–24.

Elbaum, Batya, Sharon Vaughn, Marie T. Hughes, and Sally W. Moody. 2000. "How Effective Are One-to-One Tutoring Programs in Reading for Elementary Students at Risk for Reading Failure? A Meta-analysis of the Intervention Research." *Journal of Educational Psychology* 92(4): 605–19.

Elliott, Marta. 1998. "School Finance and Opportunity to Learn: Does Money Well Spent Enhance Students' Achievement?" *Sociology of Education* 71(3): 223–45.

Elson, William, and Frank Bachman. 1910. "Different Courses for Elementary Schools." *Educational Review* 39: 359–62.

Emery, Kathy, and Susan Heineman. 2004. *Why Is Corporate America Bashing Our Public Schools?* Portsmouth, N.H.: Heinemann.

Esping-Andersen, Gøsta. 1990. *The Three Worlds of Welfare Capitalism*. Princeton, N.J.: Princeton University Press.

Esping-Andersen, Gøsta, Duncan Gallie, Anton Hemerijck, and John Myles. 2002. *Why We Need a New Welfare State*. Oxford: Oxford University Press.

Evers, Williamson M., and Paul Clopton. 2006. "High-Spending, Low-Performing School Districts." In *Courting Failure: How School Finance Lawsuits Exploit Judges' Good Intentions and Harm Our Children*, edited by Eric Hanushek. Palo Alto, Calif.: Hoover Press.

Farbman, David, and Claire Kaplan. 2005. *Time for a Change: The Promise of Extended-Time Schools for Promoting Student Achievement*. Boston: Massachusetts 2020.

Farkas, George. 2003. "Racial Disparities and Discrimination in Education: What Do We Know, How Do We Know It, and What Do We Need to Know?" *Teachers College Record* 105(6): 1119–46.

———, and Rachel Durham. 2007. "The Role of Tutoring in Standards-Based Reform." In *Standards-Based Reform and the Poverty Gap: Lessons for No Child Left Behind*, edited by Adam Gamoran. Washington, D.C.: Brookings Institution Press.

Farkas, George, and L. Shane Hall. 2000. "Can Title I Achieve Its Goal?" In *Brookings Papers on Education Policy 2000*, edited by Diane Ravitch. Washington: Brookings Institution Press.

Feldman, Amy, and Jennifer Matjasko. 2005. "The Role of School-Based Extracurricular Activities in Adolescent Development: A Comprehensive Review and Future Directions." *Review of Educational Research* 75(2): 150–210.

Fenning, Pamela, and Jennifer Rose. 2007. "The Overrepresentation of African American Students in Exclusionary Discipline: The Role of School Policy." *Urban Education* 42(6): 536–59.

Ferguson, Ann A. 2000. *Bad Boys: Public Schools in the Making of Black Masculinity*. Ann Arbor: University of Michigan Press.

Ferguson, Ronald. 1991. "Paying for Public Education: New Evidence on How and Why Money Matters." *Harvard Journal on Legislation* 28(summer): 465–97.

———. 1998. "Teachers' Perceptions and Expectations and the Black-White Test Score Gap." In *The Black-White Test Score Gap*, edited by Christopher Jencks and Meredith Phillips. Washington, D.C.: Brookings Institution Press.

Ferguson, Ronald, and Helen F. Ladd. 1996. "How and Why Money Matters: An Analysis of Alabama Schools." In *Holding Schools Accountable: Performance-Based Reform in Education*, edited by Helen F. Ladd. Washington, D.C.: Brookings Institution Press.

Fine, Michelle. 1991. *Framing Dropouts: Notes on the Politics of an Urban Public High School*. Albany: State University of New York Press.

Finkelstein, Neil, and W. Norton Grubb. 2000. "Making Sense of Education and Training Markets: Lessons from England." *American Educational Research Journal* 37(3): 601–32.

Finn, Jeremy D., Gina Pannozzo, and Charles Achilles. 2003. "The 'Whys' of Class Size: Student Behavior in Small Classes." *Review of Educational Research* 73(3): 321–68.

Fischer, Kent. 2002. "Public School Inc." *St. Petersburg Times*, 15 September 2002. Available at: www.sptimes.com/2002/09/15/State/Public_School_Inc.shtml.

Fiske, Edward, and Helen Ladd. 2000. *When Schools Compete: A Cautionary Tale*. Washington: Brookings Institution Press.

Flessa, Joseph. 2003. "What's Urban in the Urban School Principalship: Case Studies of Middle School Principals." Ph.D. diss., University of California at Berkeley, School of Education.

Fordham, Cynthia, and John Ogbu. 1986. "Coping with the Burden of 'Acting White.'" *Urban Review* 18(3): 176–206.

Frankenberg, Erika, and Chungmei Lee. 2002. "Race in American Public Schools: Rapidly Resegregating School Districts." Cambridge, Mass.: Harvard Civil Rights Project.

Friedlander, Daniel, and Gary Burtless. 1995. *Five Years After: The Long-Term Effects of Welfare-to-Work Programs*. New York: Russell Sage Foundation.

Fruchter, Norm. 2007. *Urban Schools, Public Will: Making Education Work for All Our Children*. New York: Teachers College Press.

Fryer, Roland. 2006. "Testing for Racial Differences in the Mental Ability of Young Children." Unpublished paper. Available at: post.economics.harvard.edu/faculty/fryer/papers.html.

Fryer, Roland, and Steven Leavitt. 2004. "Understanding the Black-White Test Score Gap in the First Two Years of Schooling." *Review of Economics and Statistics* 86(2): 447–64.

———. 2005. "The Black-White Test Score Gap Through Third Grade." Working paper 11049. Cambridge, Mass.: National Bureau of Economic Research.

Fuller, Bruce, and Patricia Clarke. 1994. "Raising School Effects While Ignoring Culture? Local Conditions and the Influence of Classroom Tools, Rules, and Pedagogy." *Review of Educational Research* 64(1): 119–57.

Fuller, Bruce, Joseph Wright, Karen Gesicki, and Erin Kang. 2007. "Gauging Growth: How to Judge No Child Left Behind?" *Educational Researcher* 36(5): 268–78.

Galbraith, John Kenneth. 1958. *The Affluent Society*. London: Hamish Hamilton Books.

Gamoran, Adam. 1988. "Resource Allocation and the Effects of Schooling: A Sociological Perspective." In *Microlevel School Finance: Issues and Implica-*

tions for Policy, edited by David H. Monk and Julie Underwood. Cambridge, Mass.: Ballinger.

Gamoran, Adam, Andrew Porter, John Smithson, and Paula White. 1997. "Upgrading High School Mathematics Instruction: Improving Learning Opportunities for Low-Achieving, Low-Income Youth." *Educational Evaluation and Policy Analysis* 19(4): 325–28.

Gándara, Patricia, Marie Mejorado, Dianna Gutierrez, and Miguel Molina. 1998. *Final Report of the Evaluation of High School Puente, 1994–1998*. Oakland: University of California, Office of the President (December).

Gándara, Patricia. 1995. *Over the Ivy Walls: The Educational Mobility of Low-Income Chicanos*. Albany: State University of New York Press.

Gardner, Howard. 1993. *Frames of Mind: The Theory of Multiple Intelligences*, rev. ed. New York: Basic Books. (Orig. pub. in 1983.)

Gardner, Howard. 1995. *Leading Minds: An Anatomy of Leadership*. New York: BasicBooks.

Gay, Geneva. 2000. *Culturally Responsive Teaching: Theory, Research, and Practice*. New York: Teachers College Press.

Gewertz, Catherine. 2007. "Miami 'Zone' Gives Schools Intensive Help." *Education Week*, 17 October, 24–27.

Glanz, James. 2008. "Iraq Spending Ignored Rules, Pentagon Says." *New York Times*, 23 May, A1, A14.

Glaser, Barney, and Anselm Straus. 1967. *The Discovery of Grounded Theory*. Chicago: Aldine.

Goe, Laura. 2001. "Implementation of California's Immediate Intervention/Underperforming School Program: Preliminary Findings." Paper presented to the annual meeting of the American Educational Research Association (AERA). University of California at Berkeley, Graduate School of Education (April).

———. 2002. "Winning the Battle but Not the War: What Happened to Kentucky's School Reform Initiative?" Unpublished paper, University of California at Berkeley, Graduate School of Education.

———. 2003. "An Evaluation of California's Immediate Intervention/Underperforming Schools Program, II/USP, in Middle Schools." Ph.D. diss., University of California at Berkeley, School of Education.

Goertz, Margaret E., and Allan Odden, eds. 1999. *School-Based Financing*. Thousand Oaks, Calif.: Corwin Press.

Goldhaber, Dan D., and Dominic J. Brewer. 1997. "Why Don't Schools and Teachers Seem to Matter? Assessing the Impact of Observables on Educational Productivity." *Journal of Human Resources* 32(3): 505–23.

Gosa, Travis. 2007. "Oppositional Culture, Hip-Hop, and the Schooling of Black Youth: Hip-Hop's Counter-Narrative and Pro-Schooling Messages." Unpublished paper, Johns Hopkins University, Department of Sociology (May).

Grasso, John, and John Shea. 1979. *Vocational Education and Training: Impact on Youth*. Berkeley, Calif.: Carnegie Council on Studies in Higher Education.

Gray, John. 1990. "The Quality of Schooling: Frameworks for Judgments." *British Journal of Educational Studies* 38(3): 204–33.

Green, Mark, Gail McColl, Robert Nelson, and Christopher Power. 1983. *There He Goes Again: Ronald Reagan's Reign of Error*. New York: Pantheon Books.

Greenberger, Ellen, and Lawrence Steinberg. 1986. *When Teenagers Work: The Psychological and Social Costs of Adolescent Employment*. New York: Basic Books.

Grossen, Bonnie. 2004. "Success of a Direct Instruction Model at a Secondary-Level School with High-Risk Students." *Reading and Writing Quarterly* 20(2): 161–78.

Grubb, W. Norton. 1992. "Postsecondary Vocational Education and the Subbaccalaureate Labor Market: New Evidence on Economic Returns." *Economics of Education Review* 11(3): 225–48.

———, ed. 1995. *Education Through Occupations in American High Schools*, vol. 1, *Approaches to Integrating Academic and Vocational Education*; vol. 2, *The Challenges of Implementing Curriculum Integration*. New York: Teachers College Press.

———. 1996. *Working in the Middle: Strengthening Education and Training for the Mid-Skilled Labor Force*. San Francisco: Jossey-Bass.

———. 2000. "Opening Classrooms and Improving Teaching: Lessons from School Inspections in England." *Teachers College Record* 102(4): 696–723.

———. 2006a. "When Money Might Matter: Using NELS88 to Examine the Weak Effects of School Finance." *Journal of Education Finance* 31(4): 360–78.

———. 2006b. "Dynamic Inequality I: Using NELS88 to Analyze Schooling Outcomes over Time." Unpublished paper, University of California at Berkeley.

———. 2006c. "What Should Be Equalized? Litigation, Equity, and the 'Improved' School Finance." Paper prepared for the Earl Warren Institute on Race, Ethnicity, and Diversity project on "Rethinking *Rodriguez*: Education as a Fundamental Right."

———. 2006d. "Dynamic Inequality II: Modeling Schooling Outcomes over Time with Difference Equations." Unpublished paper, University of California at Berkeley.

———. 2007. "Dynamic Inequality and Intervention: Lessons from a Small Country." *Phi Delta Kappan* 89(2): 105–14.

———. 2008a. "Families and Schools Raising Children: The Inequitable Effects of Family Background on Schooling Outcomes." In *Raising Children: Emerging Needs, Modern Risks, and Social Responses*, edited by Jill Duerr Berrick and Neil Gilbert. New York: Oxford University Press.

————. 2008b. "Multiple Resources, Multiple Outcomes: Testing the 'Improved' School Finance with NELS88." *American Educational Research Journal* 45(1): 104–44.

————. 2008c. "Reforming the Nineteenth-Century High School: 'Weak' and 'Strong' Approaches to Multiple Pathways." In *Multiple Pathways to College and Careers*, edited by Jeannie Oakes and Marisa Saunders. Cambridge, Mass.: Harvard Education Press.

————. 2008d. "SchoolMap! A Developmental System of College and Career Guidance for High Schools." Unpublished paper, University of California at Berkeley.

Grubb, W. Norton, and Associates. 1999. *Honored But Invisible: An Inside Look at Teaching in Community Colleges*. New York: Routledge.

Grubb, W. Norton, and Joseph Flessa. 2006. "A Job Too Big for One: Multiple Principals and Other Nontraditional Approaches to School Leadership." *Educational Administration Quarterly* 42(4): 518–50.

Grubb, W. Norton, Laura Goe, and Luis Huerta. 2004. "The Unending Search for Equity: California Policy, the 'Improved' School Finance, and the *Williams* Case." *Teachers College Record* 106(11): 2081–101 (special issue on *Williams v. State of California*).

Grubb, W. Norton, Luis Huerta, and Laura Goe. 2006. "Straw into Gold, Revenues into Results: Spinning Out the Implications of the 'Improved' School Finance." *Journal of Education Finance* 31(4): 334–359.

Grubb, W. Norton, Heather Kinlaw, Catherine Young, and Linn Posey. 2006. "Dynamic Inequality: Exploring What Schools Do for Low-Performing Students." Unpublished paper, University of California at Berkeley.

Grubb, W. Norton, Claudia Lara, and Susan Valdez. 2002. "Counselor, Coordinator, Monitor, Mom: The Roles of Counselors in the Puente Program." *Educational Policy* 16(4): 547–71.

Grubb, W. Norton, and Marvin Lazerson. 1982. "The Concept of Educational Adequacy in Historical Perspective." In *Adequate Education: Issues in Its Definition and Implementation*. School Finance Project working papers (ERIC ED226 491). Washington: Office of Educational Research and Improvement.

————. 1988. *Broken Promises: How Americans Fail Their Children*. New York and Chicago: Basic Books/University of Chicago Press. (Orig. pub. in 1982.)

————. 2004. *The Education Gospel: The Economic Roles of Schooling*. Cambridge, Mass.: Harvard University Press.

————. 2006. "The Globalization of Rhetoric and Practice: The Education Gospel and Vocationalism." In *Education, Globalization, and Social Change*, edited by Hugh Lauder, Philip Brown, Jo-Ann Dillabough, and A. H. Halsey. Oxford: Oxford University Press.

Grubb, W. Norton, and Stephan Michelson. 1974. *States and Schools: The Political Economy of Public School Finance*. Lantham, Md.: Lexington Books.

Grubb, W. Norton, and Jeannie Oakes. 2007. *"Restoring Value" to the High School Diploma: The Rhetoric and Practice of Higher Standards*. Tempe: Arizona State University, Education Policy Research Unit. Available at: epsl.asu.edu/epru/documents/EPSL-0710-242-EPRU.pdf.

Grubb, W. Norton, and Cary Watson. 2002. "Engagement and Motivation in High Schools: The Multiple Roles of Guidance and Counseling." Unpublished paper prepared for the National Research Council, Committee for Increasing High School Students' Engagement and Motivation to Learn (February).

Guthrie, James. 2004. "Twenty-First-Century Education Finance: Equity, Adequacy, and the Emerging Challenge of Linking Resources to Performance." In *Money, Politics, and Law: Intersections and Conflicts in the Provision of Educational Opportunity*, edited by Karen DeMoss and Kenneth Wong. Larchmont, N.Y.: Eye on Education.

Guthrie, James, and Richard Rothstein. 1999. "Enabling Adequacy to Achieve Reality: Translating Adequacy into State School Finance Distribution Arrangements." In *Equity and Adequacy in Education Finance: Issues and Perspectives*, edited by Helen F. Ladd, Rosemary Chalk, and Janet S. Hansen. Washington: National Academies Press.

Gutiérrez, Kris, Patricia Baquedano-López, and Carlos Tejada. 1999. "Rethinking Diversity: Hybridity and Hybrid Language Practices in the Third Space." *Mind, Culture, and Activity* 6(4): 286–303.

Gutiérrez, Rochelle. 2000. "Advancing African-American, Urban Youth in Mathematics: Unpacking the Success of One Math Department." *American Journal of Education* 109(1): 63–111.

Gutmann, Amy. 1987. *Democratic Education*. Princeton, N.J.: Princeton University Press.

Hakuta, Kenji, and Herlinda Cancino. 1977. "Trends in Second Language Acquisition Research." *Harvard Educational Review* 47: 294–316.

Hanushek, Eric A. 1989. "The Impact of Differential Expenditures on School Performance." *Educational Researcher* 18(May): 45–62.

———. 1997. "Assessing the Effects of School Resources on Student Performance: An Update." *Educational Evaluation and Policy Analysis* 19(2): 141–64.

———, ed. 2006. *Courting Failure: How School Finance Lawsuits Exploit Judges' Good Intentions and Harm Our Children*. Palo Alto, Calif.: Hoover Press.

Hanushels, Eric A., Charles S. Benson, Richard B. Freeman, Dean T. Jamison, Henry M. Levin, Rebecca A. Maynard, Richard J. Murnane, Steven G. Rivkin, Richard H. Sabot, Lewis C. Solmon, Anita A. Summers, Finis Welch, and Barbara L. Wolfe. 1994. *Making Schools Work: Improving Performance and Controlling Costs*. Washington, D.C.: Brookings Institution Press.

Hargis, Charles. 2006. "Setting Standards: An Exercise in Futility?" *Phi Delta Kappan* 87(5): 393–95.

Harkin, Joe, and Pauline Davis. 1996. "The Communication Styles of Teachers in Post-Compulsory Education." *Journal of Further and Higher Education* 20(1): 25–34.

Harr, Jennifer, Tom Parrish, Miguel Socias, Paul Gubbins, and Angeline Spain. 2006. *Evaluation Study of California's High Priority Schools Grant Program: Year 1 Report*. Menlo Park, Calif.: American Institutes for Research.

Harris, Douglas. 2006. "Ending the Blame Game on Educational Equity: A Study of 'High-Flying' Schools and NCLB." EPSL-0603-120-EPRU. Tempe: Arizona State University, Educational Policy Research Unit. Available at: epsl.asu.edu/epru/documents/EPSL-0603-120-EPRU.pdf.

Hart, Betty, and Tod Risley. 1995. *Meaningful Differences in the Everyday Experiences of Young American Children*. Baltimore: Paul Brookes.

Haycock, Kati. 2005. "Closing the Achievement Gap in America's Public Schools: The No Child Left Behind Act." Testimony before the U.S. House of Representatives, Committee on Education and the Workforce.

Heath, Shirley Brice. 1983. *Ways with Words: Language, Life, and Work in Communities and Classrooms*. New York: Cambridge University Press.

Hedges, Larry V., Richard D. Laine, and Rob Greenwald. 1994. "Does Money Matter? A Meta-Analysis of Studies of the Effects of Differential School Inputs on Student Outcomes." *Educational Researcher* 23(3): 5–14.

Henry, Gary T., Charles L. Thompson, Kathleen Brown, Elizabeth Cunningham, Kirsten Kainz, Bianca Montrosse, Adrienne Sgammato, and Yi Pan. 2008. *Final Report of the High School Resource Allocation Study*. Chapel Hill: University of North Carolina, Carolina Institute for Public Policy (February).

Hess, G. Alfred, Jr. 1999. "Understanding Achievement (and Other) Changes Under Chicago School Reform." *Educational Evaluation and Policy Analysis* 21(1): 67–83.

Hess, Robert, and Susan Holloway. 1984. "Family and School as Educational Institutions." *Review of Child Development Research* 7: 179–222.

Heyns, Barbara. 1971. "Curriculum Assignment and Tracking Policies in Forty-Eight Urban Public High Schools." Ph.D. diss., University of Chicago.

———. 1978. *Summer Learning and the Effects of Schooling*. New York: Academic Press.

Hickrod, Alan, Ramesh Chaudhari, Gwen Pruyne, and Jin Meng. 2007. "The Effect of Constitutional Litigation on Educational Finance: A Further Analysis." In *Selected Papers in School Finance, 1995*, edited by William J. Fowler Jr. NCES: 97-536. Washington: National Center for Education Statistics.

Hiebert, Elfrieda, and Barbara Taylor. 2000. "Beginning Reading Instruction: Research on Early Interventions." In *Handbook of Reading Research*, vol. 3, edited by Michael L. Kamil, Peter Mosenthal, Rebecca Barr, and P. David Pearson. Mahwah, N.J.: Erlbaum.

Hightower, Amy, Michael Knapp, Julie Marsh, and Milbrey McLaughlin. 2002. *School Districts and Instructional Renewal*. New York: Teachers College Press.

Hochschild, Jennifer, and Nathan Scovronick. 2003. *The American Dream and the Public Schools*. New York: Oxford University Press.

Hoff, Douglas. 2006. "Reading First Details Sought by Lawmakers." *Education Week*, 11 October.

Hollingsworth, John, and Silvia Ybarra. N.d. "Analyzing Classroom Instruction: Curriculum Calibration." DataWORKS Educational Research. Available at: www.dataworks-ed.com.

Hollins, Etta, and Eileen Oliver. 1999. *Pathways to Success in School: Culturally Responsive Teaching*. Mahwah, N.J.: Erlbaum.

hooks, bell. 1994. *Teaching to Transgress*. New York: Routledge.

House, Ernest. 1998. *Schools for Sale: Why Free Market Policies Won't Improve America's Schools, and What Will*. New York: Teachers College Press.

Howe, Harold. 1993. *Thinking About Our Kids*. New York: Macmillan.

Huefner, Dixie S. 2000. "The Risks and Opportunities of the IEP Requirements Under IDEA '97." *Journal of Special Education* 33(4): 195–204.

Huerta, Luis. 2006. "Next Steps for Results: *Campaign for Fiscal Equity v. State of New York*." *Journal of Education Finance* 3(4): 379–94.

Hughes, Larry W. 1999. *The Principal as Leader*, 2d ed. Upper Saddle River, N.J.: Prentice-Hall.

Hyde, Janet, Sara Lindberg, Marcia Linn, Amy Ellis, and Caroline Williams. 2008. "Diversity: Gender Similarities Characterize Math Performance." *Science* 321(5888): 494–95.

Ingersoll, Richard. 2004. "Why Do High-Poverty Schools Have Difficulty Staffing Their Classrooms with Qualified Teachers?" Washington: Center for American Progress and Institute for America's Future (November).

Irvine, Jacqueline Jordan. 2000. *Black Students and School Failure: Policies, Practices, and Prescriptions*. New York: Greenwood.

Jacob, Brian. 2007. "The Challenges of Staffing Urban Schools with Effective Teachers." *The Future of Children* 17(1): 129–53.

Jencks, Christopher, and Meredith Phillips, eds. 1998. *The Black-White Test Score Gap*. Washington, D.C.: Brookings Institution Press.

Jencks, Christopher, Marshall Smith, Henry Acland, Mary Jo Bane, David Cohen, Herbert Gintis, Barbara Heyns, and Stephan Michelson. 1972. *Inequality: A Reassessment of the Effect of Family and Schooling in America*. New York: Basic Books.

Joreskog, Karl G., and Dag Sorbom. 1979. *Advances in Factor Analysis and Structural Equation Models*. Cambridge, Mass.: Abt Books.

Kaestle, Carl F. 1983. *Pillars of the Republic: Common Schools and American Society 1780–1860*. New York: Hill and Wang.

Kane, Thomas. 2004. *The Impact of After-School Programs: Interpreting the Results of Four Recent Evaluations*. New York: William T. Grant Foundation.

Kannapel, Patricia, Pamelia Coe, Lola Aagaard, and Beverly Moore. 1996. "'I Don't Give a Hoot If Somebody's Going to Pay Me $3,600': Local School District Reactions to Kentucky's High-Stakes Accountability Program." Paper presented to the meeting of the American Educational Research Association, New York.

Kannapel, Patricia, and Stephen Clements. 2005. *Inside the Black Box of High-Performing, High-Poverty Schools*. Lexington, Ky.: Prichard Committee for Academic Excellence.

Kemple, James, Corinne Herlihy, and Thomas J. Smith. 2005. *Making Progress Toward Graduation: Evidence from the Talent Development High School Model*. New York: Manpower Demonstration Research Corporation (MDRC).

Kemple, James, and Jason C. Snipes. 2000. *Career Academies: Impacts on Students' Engagement and Performance in High School*. New York: Manpower Demonstration Research Corporation (MDRC).

Kerchner, Charles Taylor, and Krista Caufman. 1993. "Building the Airplane While It's Rolling Down the Runway." In *A Union of Professionals: Labor Relations and Educational Reform*, edited by Charles Taylor Kerchner and Julia E. Koppich. New York: Teachers College Press.

King, Richard A., and Bettye MacPhail-Wilcox. 1994. "Unraveling the Production Function: The Continuing Quest for Resources That Make a Difference." *Journal of Education Finance* 20(summer): 47–65.

Kirsch, Irwin, John de Jong, Dominique Lafontaine, Joy McQueen, Juliette Mendelovits, and Christian Monseur. 2002. *Reading for Change: Performance and Engagement Across Countries*. Paris: Organization for Economic Cooperation and Development (OECD).

Knapp, Michael, and Associates. 1995. *Teaching for Meaning in High-Poverty Classrooms*. New York: Teachers College Press.

Kohlberg, Lawrence. 1981. *The Philosophy of Moral Development: Moral Stages and the Idea of Justice*. San Francisco: Harper & Row.

Kohn, Melvin. 1977. *Class and Conformity: A Study in Values*. Chicago: University of Chicago Press.

Kohn, Melvin, and Carmi Schooler. 1983. *Work and Personality: An Inquiry into the Impact of Social Stratification*. Norwood, N.J.: Ablex.

Kozol, Jonathan. 1967. *Death at an Early Age: The Destruction of the Hearts and Minds of Negro Children in the Boston Public Schools*. Boston: Houghton Mifflin.

———. 1992. *Savage Inequalities: Children in America's Schools*. New York: Harper Perennial.

Krug, Edward. 1969. *The Shaping of the American High School 1990–1920*. Madison: University of Wisconsin Press

Krugman, Paul. 2007. *The Conscience of a Liberal*. New York: Norton.

Kupermintz, Haggai, and Richard Snow. 1997. "Enhancing the Validity and Usefulness of Large-Scale Educational Assessments: III. NELS: Mathematics Achievement to Twelfth Grade." *American Educational Research Journal* 34(1): 124–50.

Ladd, Helen, Rosemary Chalk, and Janet Hansen. 1999. *Equity and Adequacy in Education Finance: Issues and Perspectives*. Washington: National Academies Press.

Ladner, Joyce. 1995. *Tomorrow's Tomorrow: The Black Woman*. Lincoln: University of Nebraska Press.

Ladson-Billings, Gloria. 1994. *The Dreamkeepers: Successful Teachers of African-American Children*. San Francisco: Jossey-Bass.

Lafer, Gordon. 2002. *The Job Training Charade*. Ithaca, N.Y.: Cornell University Press.

Lambert, Linda. 2002. *The Constructivist Leader*. New York: Teachers College Press.

Lampert, Magdalene. 2001. *Teaching Problems and the Problems of Teaching*. New Haven, Conn.: Yale University Press.

Lankford, Hamilton, and James Wyckoff. 1995. "Where Has the Money Gone? An Analysis of School District Spending in New York." *Educational Evaluation and Policy Analysis* 17(2): 195–218.

Lareau, Annette. 2000. *Home Advantage: Social Class and Parental Intervention in Elementary Education*, 2d ed. Lanham, Md.: Rowan and Littlefield.

————. 2003. *Unequal Childhoods: Class, Race, and Family Life*. Berkeley: University of California Press.

Lauer, Patricia, Motoko Akiba, Stephanie Wilkerson, Helen Apthorp, David Snow, and Mya Martin-Glenn. 2006. "Out-of-School-Time Programs: A Meta-analysis of Effects for At-Risk Students." *Review of Educational Research* 76(2): 275–313.

Lawler, Edward. 1998. *Creating High-Performance Organizations: Practices and Results of Employee Involvement and Total Quality Management in Fortune 1000 Companies*. San Francisco: Jossey-Bass.

Lazerson, Marvin. 1987. *American Education in the Twentieth Century: A Documentary History*. New York: Teachers College Press.

Lazerson, Marvin, and W. Norton Grubb, eds. 1974. *American Education and Vocationalism: A Documentary History, 1870–1970*. New York: Teachers College Press.

LeBlanc, Adrian N. 2003. *Random Family: Love, Drugs, Trouble, and Coming of Age in the Bronx*. New York: Scribner.

Lee, Valerie, and Julia Smith. 1997. "High School Size: Which Works Best and for Whom?" *Educational Evaluation and Policy Analysis* 19(3): 205–27.

Legislative Research Commission. 2006. *Highly-Skilled Educator Program*. Research report 339. Frankfort, Ky.: Program Review and Investigations Committee (November 9).

Leichter, Hope Jensen. 1974. *The Family As Educator*. New York: Teachers College Press.

Lemons, Richard, Thomas Luschel, and Leslie Santee Siskin. 2003. "Leadership and the Demands for Standards-Based Accountability." In *The New Accountability: High Schools and High-Stakes Testing*, edited by Martin Carnoy, Richard Elmore, and Leslie Santee Siskin. New York: Routledge.

Libbey, Heather P. 2004. "Measuring Student Relationships to School: Attachment, Bonding, Connectedness, and Engagement." *Journal of School Health* 74(7): 274–83.

Lindseth, Alfred. 2007. "A Reversal of Fortunes: Why the Courts Have Cooled to Adequacy Lawsuits." *Education Week*, September 12, p. 32.

Lindsey, Randall B., Kikanza Nuri Robins, and Raymond D. Terrell. 2003. *Cultural Proficiency: A Manual for School Leaders*, 2d ed. Thousand Oaks, Calif.: Corwin Press.

Little, Judith Warren. 2006. *Professional Development and Professional Community in the Learner-Centered School*. Washington: National Education Association.

Losen, Daniel, and Gary Orfield, eds. 2002. *Racial Inequity in Special Education*. Cambridge, Mass.: Harvard Education Press.

Loveless, Tom. 1999. *The Tracking Wars: State Reform Meets School Policy*. Washington, D.C.: Brookings Institution Press.

Lowi, Theodore. 1967. "The Public Philosophy: Interest Group Liberalism." *American Political Science Review* 61: 5–24.

———. 1969. *The End of Liberalism: Ideology, Policy, and the Crisis of Public Authority*. New York: Norton.

Lynd, Robert, and Helen Lynd. 1929. *Middletown: A Study in American Culture*. New York: Harcourt, Brace, and World.

MacPhail-Wilcox, Bettye. 1986. "Production Functions Revisited in the Context of Educational Reform." *Journal of Education Finance* 12(2): 191–222.

Macpherson, Crawford Brough. 1977. *The Life and Times of Liberal Democracy*. New York: Oxford University Press.

Marsh, Herbert, and Sabina Kleitman. 2002. "Extracurricular School Activities: The Good, the Bad, and the Nonlinear." *Harvard Educational Review* 72(4): 464–511.

———. 2005. "Consequences of Employment During High School: Character Building, Subversion of Academic Goals, or a Threshold?" *American Educational Research Journal* 42(2): 331–69.

Martin, Edwin W., Reed Martin, and Donna L. Terman. 1996. "The Legislative and Litigation History of Special Education." *Future of Children* 6(1): 25–39.

Mashburn, A.J., R.C. Pianta, B.K. Hamre, J.T Downer, O.A. Barbarin, D. Bryant, M. Burchinal, D.M. Early, and C. Howes. 2008. "Measures of Classroom Quality in Prekindergarten and Children's Development of Academic, Language, and Social Skills." *Child Development* 79(3): 732–49.

Mathis, William. 2003. "No Child Left Behind: Costs and Benefits." *Phi Delta Kappan* 84(9): 679–86.

May, Henry, and Jonathan Supovitz. 2006. "Capturing the Cumulative Effects of School Reform: An Eleven-Year Study of the Impacts of America's Choice on Student Achievement." *Educational Evaluation and Policy Analysis* 28(3): 231–57.

McDonnell, Lorraine M., and Richard F. Elmore. 1987. "Getting the Job Done: Alternative Policy Instruments." *Education Evaluation and Policy Analysis* 9(2): 133–52.

McKnight, Katherine, and Lee Sechrest. 2001. "Evaluation of the Quality of Action Plans." Tucson: University of Arizona, Evaluation Group for the Analysis of Data.

McLaughlin, Milbrey, and Joan Talbert. 2006. *Building School-Based Learning Communities: Professional Strategies*. New York: Teachers College Press.

McNeil, Michelle. 2007. "Tighter Link Sought Between Spending, Achievement in N.Y." *Education Week*, September 4, p. 1, 20.

Meier, Deborah. 1995. *The Power of Their Ideas: Lessons from a Small School in Harlem*. Boston: Beacon Press.

Meyer, Robert. 1981. "An Economic Analysis of High School Education." In *The Federal Role in Vocational Education: Sponsored Research*. Special report 39, ERIC ED230699 (November).

Miles, Karen Hawley. 1995. "Freeing Resources for Improving Schools: A Case Study of Teacher Allocation in Boston Public Schools." *Educational Evaluation and Policy Analysis* 17(4): 476–93.

Miles, Karen Hawley, and Linda Darling-Hammond. 1998. "Rethinking the Allocation of Teaching Resources: Some Lessons from High-Performing Schools." *Educational Evaluation and Policy Analysis* 20(1): 9–29.

Miles, Karen Hawley, and Stephen Frank. 2008. *The Strategic School: Making the Most of People, Time, and Money*. Thousand Oaks, Calif.: Corwin Press/National Association of Secondary School Principals.

Miles, Karen Hawley, and Marguerite Roza. 2006. "Understanding Student-Weighted Allocation as a Means to Greater School Resource Equity." *Peabody Journal of Education* 81(3): 39–62.

Miles, Karen Hawley, Kathleen Ware, and Marguerite Roza. 2003. "Leveling the Playing Field: Creating Funding Equity Through Student-Based Budgeting." *Phi Delta Kappan* 85(2): 114–19.

Miller, Robert, and Brian Rowan. 2006. "Effects of Organic Management on Student Achievement." *American Educational Research Journal* 43(2): 210–53.

Minorini, Paul A., and Stephen D. Sugarman. 1999. "Educational Adequacy and the Courts: The Promise and Problems of Moving to a New Paradigm." In *Equity and Adequacy in Education Finance: Issues and Perspectives*, edited by Helen F. Ladd, Rosemary Chalk, and Janet S. Hansen. Washington: National Academies Press.

Minow, Martha. 1997. *Not Only for Myself: Identity, Politics, and Law*. New York: New Press.

Miron, Gary, Chris Coryn, and Dawn Mackety. 2007. "Evaluating the Impact of Charter Schools on Student Achievement: A Longitudinal Look at the Great Lakes States." Charter School Evaluation Publication. Kalamazoo: Western Michigan University, Evaluation Center (June).

Mnookin, Robert. 1985. *In the Interests of Children: Advocacy, Law Reform, and Public Policy*. New York: Freeman.

Molnar, Alex, David Garcia, Gary Miron, and Shannon Berry. 2007. *Profiles of For-Profit Education Management Organizations: Ninth Annual Report 2006–2007*. EPSL-0708-239-CERU. Tempe: Arizona State University, College of Education, Commercialism in Education Research Unit.

Monk, David H. 1994. "Policy Challenges Surrounding the Shift Toward Outcome-Oriented School Finance Equity Standards." *Educational Policy* 8(4): 471–88.

Monk, David H., and Margaret L. Plecki. 1999. "Generating and Managing Resources for School Improvement." In *Handbook of Research on Educational Administration: A Project of the American Educational Research Association*, 2d ed., edited by Joseph Murphy and Karen S. Louis. San Francisco: Jossey-Bass.

Monk, David H., and Julie Underwood. 1988. *Microlevel School Finance: Issues and Implications for Policy*. Cambridge, Mass.: Ballinger.

Moustafa, Margaret, and Robert Land. 2002. "The Reading Achievement of Economically Disadvantaged Children in Urban Schools Using *Open Court* vs. Comparably Disadvantaged Children in Urban Schools Using Nonscripted Programs." *2002 Yearbook of the Learning, Teaching, and Research Special Interest Group of the American Educational Research Association*, 44–53.

Mukerjee, Diane. 2006. "Why Are African American Students Overrepresented in Behavioral Referral Data at Stoneman Elementary School?" Unpublished paper. University of California at Berkeley, School of Education.

Murnane, Richard J., and Frank Levy. 1996. "Evidence from Fifteen Schools in Austin, Texas." In *Does Money Matter?*, edited by Gary Burtless. Washington, D.C.: Brookings Institution Press.

Murnane, Richard J., John Willett, and Katherine P. Boudett. 1995. "Do High School Dropouts Benefit from Obtaining a GED?" *Educational Evaluation and Policy Analysis* 17(2, Summer): 133–48.

Murphy, Joseph, and Phillip Hallinger. 1993. "School Restructuring: Assessing the Progress." In *Restructuring Schools: Learning from Ongoing Efforts*, edited by Joseph Murphy and Phillip Hallinger. New York: Teachers College Press.

Murray, Sheila, William Evans, and Robert Schwab. 1998. "Education Finance Reform and the Distribution of Education Resources." *American Economic Review* 88(4): 789–812.

Nasir, Na'ilah, Ann Jones, and Milbrey McLaughlin. Forthcoming. "School Connectedness for Students in Low-Income High Schools."

National Center for Educational Evaluation and Regional Assistance (NCEER). 2008. *Reading First Impact Study: Interim Report.* Washington: Institute of Education Sciences (IES).

National Center on Education and the Economy. 1990. *America's Choice: High Skills or Low Wages!* Washington, D.C.: National Center on Education and the Economy.

———. 2007. *Tough Choices or Tough Times: The Report of the New Commission on the Skills of the American Workplace.* New York: Wiley.

———. 2008. *Tough Choices for Tough Times: The Report of the New Commission on the Skills of the American Workforce.* Washington, D.C.: National Center on Education and the Economy.

National Education Association. 1894. *Report of the Committee of Ten on Secondary School Studies.* New York: American Book Company.

National High School Center. N.d. *Easing the Transition to High School: Research and Best Practices to Support High School Learning.* Available at www.betterhighschools.org/docs/NHSC_TransitionsReport.pdf.

National Institute for Literacy. 2003. *Putting Reading First: The Research Building Blocks for Teaching Children to Read.* Available at: www.nifl.gov/partnershipsforreading/reading _first.html.

National Research Council (NRC). Committee on Increasing High School Students' Engagement and Motivation to Learn. 2004. *Engaging Schools: Fostering High School Students' Motivation to Learn.* Washington: National Academies Press.

Nelson, F. Howard, Rachel Drown, Ed Muir, and Nancy Van Meter. 2001. "Public Money and Privatization in K–12 Education." In *Education Finance in the New Millennium: AEFA 2001 Yearbook*, edited by Stephen Chaikind and William J. Fowler. Larchmont, N.Y.: Eye on Education.

Newman, Fred M., Betty Ann Smith, Elaine Allensworth, and Anthony S. Bryk. 2001. "Instructional Program Coherence: What It Is and Why It Should Guide School Improvement Policy." *Educational Evaluation and Policy Analysis* 23(4): 297–321.

Nichols, Joe D. 2004. "An Exploration of Discipline and Suspension Data." *Journal of Negro Education* 73(4): 408–23.

Nickell, Stephen. 2004. "Poverty and Worklessness in Britain." *Economic Journal* 114: C1–25.

Nisbett, Richard. 1998. "Race, Genetics, and IQ." In *The Black-White Test Score Gap*, edited by Christopher Jencks and Meredith Phillips. Washington, D.C.: Brookings Institution Press.

Noddings, Nel. 1992. *The Challenge to Care in Schools: An Alternative Approach to Education*. New York: Teachers College Press.

Noguera, Pedro A. 2003. *City Schools and the American Dream: Reclaiming the Promise of Public Education*. New York: Teachers College Press.

Nussbaum, E. Michael, Laura Hamilton, and Richard Snow. 1997. "Enhancing the Validity and Usefulness of Large-Scale Educational Assessments: IV. NELS88 Science Achievement to Twelfth Grade." *American Educational Research Journal* 34(1): 151–73.

Oakes, Jeannie. 1985. *Keeping Track: How Schools Structure Inequality*. New Haven, Conn.: Yale University Press.

———. 2004. "Education Inadequacy, Inequality, and Failed State Policy: A Synthesis of Expert Reports Prepared for *Williams v. California*." *Teachers College Record* 106(10): 1889–1906.

Oakes, Jeannie, John Rogers, and Martin Lipton. 2006. *Learning Power: Organizing for Education and Justice*. New York: Teachers College Press.

Oakes, Jeannie, and Marisa Saunders. 2008. *Multiple Pathways to College and Careers*. Cambridge, Mass.: Harvard Education Press.

Oakes, Jeannie, Molly Selvin, Lynn Karoly, and Gretchen Guiton. 1992. *Educational Matchmaking: Academic and Vocational Tracking in Comprehensive High Schools*. Berkeley: National Center for Research in Vocational Education.

O'Brien, Daniel. 1998. "Family and School Effects on the Cognitive Growth of Minority and Disadvantaged Elementary School Students." Working paper. Dallas: University of Texas, Green Center for the Study of Science and Society.

O'Brien, Thomas V. 2007. "What Happened to the Promise of *Brown*? An Organizational Explanation and an Outline for Change." *Teachers College Record* 109(8): 1875–1901.

O'Day, Jennifer, and Catharine Bitter. 2003. *Evaluation Study of the II/USP and the High-Achieving/Improving Schools Program of the Public Schools Accountability Act of 1999: Final Report*. Palo Alto, Calif.: American Institutes for Research (AIR).

Odden, Alan R., ed. 1992. *Rethinking School Finance: An Agenda for the 1990s*. San Francisco: Jossey-Bass.

———. 1999. "Improving State School Finance Systems: New Realities Create Need to Reengineer School Finance Structures." Consortium for Policy Research in Education Occasional Paper Series OP-04.

———. 2001. "The New School Finance: Providing Adequacy and Improving Equity." *Journal of Education Finance* 25(4): 467–87.

Odden, Alan R., and Carolyn Busch. 1998. *Financing Schools for High Perfor-*

mance: Strategies for Improving the Use of Educational Resources. San Francisco: Jossey-Bass.

Organization for Economic Cooperation and Development (OECD). 2000. *Literacy in the Information Age: Final Report of the International Adult Literacy Survey.* Paris and Ottawa: OECD/Statistics Canada, Ministry of Industry.

————. 2001. *Knowledge and Skills for Life: First Results from PISA 2000.* Paris: OECD.

Office of the Inspector General. 2006. *The Reading First Programs Grant Application Process: Final Inspection Report.* ED-OIG/I13-F0017. Washington: U.S. Department of Health and Human Services.

Offices of Research and Education Accountability. 2006. *State Approaches to Improving Tennessee's High-Priority Schools.* Nashville, Tenn.: Comptroller of the Treasury (December).

Olson, Lynn. 2005. "Calls for Revamping High Schools Intensify." *Education Week,* January 26.

Payne, Charles M. 1997. "'I Don't Want Your Nasty Pot of Gold': Urban School Climate and Public Policy." WP-97-8. Evanston, Ill: Northwestern University, Institute of Policy Research.

Payne, Charles M., and Mariame Kaba. 2001. "So Much Reform, So Little Change: Building-Level Obstacles to Urban School Reform." *Journal of Negro Education* 2: 37–58.

Perkinson, Henry. 1995. *The Imperfect Panacea: American Faith in Education.* New York: McGraw-Hill.

Peterson, Bob. 1999. "Survival and Justice: Rethinking Teacher Union Strategy." In *Transforming Teacher Unions: Fighting for Better Schools and Social Justice,* edited by Bob Peterson and Michael Charney. Milwaukee: Rethinking Schools.

Phillips, Meredith, James Crouse, and John Ralph. 1998. "Does the Black-White Test Score Gap Widen After Children Enter School?" In *The Black-White Test Score Gap,* edited by Christopher Jencks and Meredith Phillips. Washington, D.C.: Brookings Institution.

Phillips, Meredith, Jeanne Brooks-Gunn, Greg Duncan, Pamela Klebanov, and Jonathan Crane. "Family Background, Parenting Practices, and the Black-White Test Score Gap." In *The Black-White Test Score Gap,* edited by Christopher Jencks and Meredith Phillips. Washington, D.C.: Brookings Institution Press.

Pole, J. R. 1994. *The Pursuit of Equality in American History.* Berkeley: University of California Press. (Orig. pub. in 1978.)

Pollock, Mica. 2004. *Colormute: Race Talk Dilemmas in an American School.* Princeton, N.J.: Princeton University Press.

Pope, Denise. 2001. *"Doing School": How We Are Creating a Generation of Stressed-Out, Materialistic, and Miseducated Students.* New Haven, Conn.: Yale University Press.

Power, Clark. 1985. "Democratic Moral Education in the Large Public High School." In *Moral Education: Theory and Application*, edited by Marvin Barkowitz and Fritz Oser. Hillsdale, N.J.: Erlbaum.

Pressman, Jeffrey L., and Aaron Wildavsky. 1979. *Implementation: How Great Expectations in Washington Are Dashed in Oakland: Or, Why It's Amazing That Federal Programs Work at All, This Being a Saga of the Economic Development Administration as Told by Two Sympathetic Observers Who Seek to Build Morals on a Foundation of Ruined Hopes.* Berkeley: University of California Press.

Puma, Michael, Nancy Karweit, Cristofer Price, Anne Ricciuti, William Thompson, and Michael Vaden-Kiernan. 1997. *Prospects: Final Report on Student Outcomes.* Washington: U.S. Department of Education, Planning and Evaluation Service.

Purkey, Stewart C., and Marshall Smith. 1983. "Effective Schools: A Review." *Elementary School Journal* 83(4): 436–52.

Quint, Janet. 2006. *Meeting Five Critical Challenges of High School Reform.* New York: Manpower Demonstration Research Corporation (MDRC).

Quint, Janet, Howard Bloom, Alison R. Black, LaFleur Stephens, and Teresa Akey. 2005. *The Challenge of Scaling Up Educational Reform: Findings and Lessons from First Things First.* New Work: Manpower Demonstration Research Corporation (MDRC).

Raudenbush, Stephen, Randall P. Fotiu, and Yuk Fai Cheong. 1998. "Inequality of Access to Educational Resources: A National Report for Eighth-Grade Math." *Educational Evaluation and Policy Analysis* 20(4): 253–67.

Ready, Douglas. 2008. *Class-Size Reductions: Policy, Politics, and Implications for Equity.* Equity Matters Research Review 2. New York: Columbia University, Teachers College, Campaign for Educational Equity (April).

Redding, Sam, and Herbert Walberg. 2007. *Handbook on Statewide Systems of Support.* Lincoln, Ill.: Center on Innovation and Improvement, Academic Development Institute.

Resnick, Lauren, ed. 1989. *Knowing, Learning, and Instruction: Essays in Honor of Robert Glaser.* Hillsdale, N.J.: Erlbaum.

Resnick, Michael D., P. S. Bearman, R. W. Blum, K. E. Bauman, K. M. Harris, J. Jones, J. Tabor, T. Beuhring, R. E. Sieving, M. Shew, M. Ireland, L. H. Bearinger and J. R. Udry. 1997. "Protecting Adolescents from Harm: Findings from the National Longitudinal Study on Adolescent Health." *Journal of the American Medical Association* 278: 823–32.

Reubens, Beatrice. 1974. "Vocational Education for All in High School?" In *Work and the Quality of Life*, edited by James O'Toole. Boston: MIT Press.

Rice, Jennifer. K. 1999. "The Impact of Class Size on Instructional Strategies and the Use of Time in High School Mathematics and Science Courses." *Educational Evaluation and Policy Analysis* 21(2): 215–29.

Robinson, Glen E. 1990. "Synthesis of Research on the Effects of Class Size." *Educational Leadership* 47(7): 80–90.

Roe, Emery. 1994. *Narrative Policy Analysis: Theory and Practice*. Durham, N.C.: Duke University Press.

Romo, Harriet, and Toni Falbo. 1996. *Latino High School Graduation: Defying the Odds*. Austin: University of Texas Press.

Rose, Mike. 2006. *Possible Lives: The Promise of Public Education in America*. New York: Penguin Books.

Rosenbaum, James. 2001. *Beyond College for All: Career Paths for the Forgotten Half*. New York: Russell Sage Foundation.

Rosenbaum, James, Regina Deil-Amen, and Ann Person. 2006. *After Admission: From College Access to College Success*. New York: Russell Sage Foundation.

Rothstein, Richard. 2004. *Class and Schools: Using Social, Economic, and Educational Reform to Close the Black-White Achievement Gap*. New York: Economic Policy Institute.

Rowan, Brian. 1990. "Commitment and Control: Alternative Strategies for the Organizational Design of Schools." In *Review of Research in Education* 16, edited by Courtney Cazden. Washington, D.C.: American Educational Research Association.

Rowan, Brian, Steven T. Bossert, and David C. Dwyer. 1983. "Research on Effective Schools: A Cautionary Note." *Educational Researcher* (April): 4–31.

Roza, Marguerite, and Karen H. Miles. 2002. "Moving Toward Equity in School Funding Within Districts." Providence, R.I.: Annenberg Institute for School Reform, Brown University. ERIC Document ED473712.

Roza, Marguerite, and Paul Hill. 2006. "How Can Anyone Say What's Adequate if Nobody Knows How Money Is Spent Now?" In *Courting Failure: How School Finance Lawsuits Exploit Judges' Good Intentions and Harm Our Children*, edited by Eric Hanushek. Palo Alto, Calif.: Hoover Press.

Rubin, Donald B. 1987. *Multiple Imputation for Nonresponse in Surveys*. New York: Wiley.

Rumberger, Russell, and Jim Connell. 2007. "Strengthening School District Capacity as a Strategy to Raise Student Achievement in California." Policy brief for EdSource, "Getting from Facts to Policy: A Policy Convening" (October 19). Sacramento, Calif.: University of California at Santa Barbara, School of Education.

Rumberger, Russell, and Patricia Gándara. 2004. "Seeking Equity in the Education of California's English Learners." *Teachers College Record* 106(10): 2032–56.

Rumberger, Russell, and Katherine Larson. 1998. "Student Mobility and the Increased Risk of High School Dropout." *American Journal of Education Research* 107: 1–35.

Rumberger, Russell, and Greg Palardy. 2005. "Test Scores, Dropout Rates, and Transfer Rates as Alternative Indicators of High School Performance." *American Educational Research Journal* 42(3): 42.

Samuels, Christina. 2007. "Experts Eye Solution to 'Fourth-Grade Slump.'" *EducationWeek*, September 12.

————. 2008. "Embracing 'Response to Intervention.'" *EducationWeek*, January 23.

Sandel, Megan. 2002. "The Impact of the Physical Condition of School Facilities on Students' Short-Term and Long-Term Health." Available at "Decent Schools for California" page of Morrison & Foerster LLP website: www.decentschools.com/expert_reports/sandel_report.pdf.

Saxe, Geoffrey B., Steven R. Guberman, and Maryl Gearhart. 1987. "Social Processes in Early Number Development." Monograph 216. *Monographs of the Society for Research in Child Development* 52(2): 160–63.

Schlossman, Stephen. 1976. "Before Home Start: Notes Toward a History of Parent Education in America, 1897–1929." *Harvard Educational Review* 46: 436–67.

Schneider, Barbara, and David Stevenson. 1999. *The Ambitious Generation: American Teenagers, Motivated But Directionless.* New Haven, Conn.: Yale University Press.

Schoenfeld, Alan. 2006. "What Doesn't Work: The Challenge and Failure of the What Works Clearinghouse to Conduct Meaningful Reviews of Studies of Mathematics Curricula." *Educational Researcher* 35(2): 13–21.

Schorr, Lisbeth. 1998. *Common Purpose: Strengthening Families and Neighborhoods to Rebuild America.* New York: Doubleday.

Schweinhart, Lawrence J., Jeanne Montie, Zongping Xiang, Steven W. Barnett, Clive R. Belfield, and Milagros Nores. 2005. *Lifetime Effects: The High/Scope Perry Preschool Study Through Age Forty.* Monographs of the High/Scope Educational Research Foundation 14. Ypsilanti, Mich.: High/Scope Press.

Scott, Janelle. 2008. "Managers of Choice: Race, Gender, and the Political Ideology of the 'New' Urban School Leadership." In *School Choice Policies and Outcomes: Philosophical and Empirical Perspectives on Limits to Choice in Liberal Democracies*, edited by Walter Feinberg and Christopher Lubienski. Albany: State University of New York Press.

Scott-Jones, Diane. 1984. "Family Influences on Cognitive Development and School Achievement." *Review of Research in Education* 11: 259–304.

Scrivener, Susan, and Jenny Au. 2007. *Enhancing Student Services at Lorain Community College: Early Results from the Opening Doors Demonstration in Ohio.* New York: Manpower Demonstration Research Corporation (MDRC).

Secretary's Commission on Achieving Necessary Skills. 1991. *What Work Required of Schools: A Scans Report for America 2000.* Washington, D.C.: U.S. Governmental Printing Office.

Seltzer, Michael, Kilchan Choi, and Yeow M. Thum. 2003. "Examining Relationships Where Students Start and How Rapidly They Progress: Using New Developments in Growth Modeling to Gain Insight into the Distribution of Achievement Within Schools." *Educational Evaluation and Policy Analysis* 25(3): 263–86.

Seltzer, Michael H., Ken A. Frank, and Anthony S. Bryk. 1994. "The Metric Matters: The Sensitivity of Conclusions Concerning Growth in Student Achievement to Choice of Metric." *Educational Evaluation and Policy Analysis* 16(1): 41–49.

Seyfarth, John T. 1999. *The Principal: New Leadership for New Challenges*. Upper Saddle River, N.J.: Prentice-Hall.

Shapson, Stan M., Edgar N. Wright, Gary Eason, and John Fitzgerald. 1980. "An Experimental Study of the Effects of Class Size." *American Educational Research Journal* 17(2): 141–52.

Shavelson, Richard, and Lisa Towne, eds. 2002. *Scientific Research in Education*. Washington: National Academies Press/National Research Council, Committee on Scientific Principles for Education Research.

Shulman, Lee. 1987. "Knowledge and Teaching: Foundations of the New Reform." *Harvard Educational Review* 57: 1–22.

Siegel, Dorothy, and Norm Fruchter. 2002. "Final Report: Evaluation of the Performance-Driven Budgeting Initiative of the New York City Board of Education, 1997–2000." New York University, Institute for Education and Social Policy (February).

Singer, Judith. 1998. "Using SAS PROC MIXED to Fit Multilevel Models, Hierarchical Models, and Individual Growth Models." *Journal of Educational and Behavioral Studies* 24(4): 323–55.

Singleton, Glen, and Curtis Linton. 2006. *Courageous Conversations About Race: A Field Guide for Achieving Equity in Schools*. Thousand Oaks, Calif.: Corwin Press.

Sipe, Cynthia. 1996. *Mentoring: A Synthesis of P/PV's Research, 1988–1995*. Philadelphia: Private/Public Ventures.

Sirin, Selcuk. 2005. "Socioeconomic Status and Academic Achievement: A Meta-Analytic Review of the Research." *Review of Educational Research* 75(3): 417–53.

Skiba, Russell, Robert Michael, Abra Carroll Nardo, and Reece Peterson. 2002. "The Color of Discipline: Sources of Racial and Gender Disproportionality in School Punishment." *Urban Review* 34(4): 317–42.

Slaughter, Diana, and Edgar Epps. 1987. "The Home Environment and Academic Achievement of Black American Children and Youth: An Overview." *Journal of Negro Education* 56(1): 3–20.

Slavin, Robert. 2003. "A Reader's Guide to Scientifically Based Research." *Educational Leadership* 60(5): 12–16.

Snipes, Jason, Fred Doolittle, and Corinne Herlihy. 2002. *Foundations for*

Success: Case Studies of How Urban School Systems Improve Student Achievement. Washington, D.C.: Council of the Great City Schools.

Snow, Catherine, Susan M. Burns, and Peg Griffin. 1998. *Preventing Reading Difficulties in Young Children*. Washington: National Academies Press.

Solorzano, Daniel. 2001. "Critical Race Theory, Racial Micro-Aggressions, and the Experience of Chicana and Chicano Scholars." *Qualitative Inquiry* 8(1): 23–44.

Solorzano, Daniel, Miguel Ceja, and Tara Yosso. 2000. "Critical Race Theory, Racial Micro-Aggressions, and Campus Racial Climate: The Experiences of African American College Students." *Journal of Negro Education* 69(1–2): 60–73.

Speck, Marsha. 1999. *The Principalship: Building a Learning Community*. Upper Saddle River, N.J.: Prentice-Hall.

Spillane, James. 2006. *Distributed Leadership*. San Francisco: Jossey-Bass.

Spillane, James, Richard Halvorson, and John Diamond. 2001. "Investigating School Leadership Practice: A Distributed Perspective." *Educational Researcher* 30(3): 23–28.

Spillane, James, and Charles Thompson. 1997. "Reconstructing Conceptions of Local Capacity: The Local Education Agency's Capacity for Ambitious Instructional Reform." *Education Evaluation and Policy Analysis* 19(2): 185–203.

Sprague, Jeffrey R. 2004. "Improving School Climate with Schoolwide Positive Behavior Supports." Utah Personnel Development Center. Available at: www.updc.org/library/speducator/multimedia/pdf/Sprague11-04.pdf.

Springboard Schools. 2006. *Minding the Gap: New Roles for School Districts in the Age of Accountability*. San Francisco: Springboard Schools.

Stecher, Brian, and George Bohrnstedt. 2002. *Class Size Reduction in California: Findings from 1999–2000 and 2001–2002*. Palo Alto, Calif.: Ed Source.

Stern, David. 1999. "Improving Pathways in the United States from High School to College and Career." In *Preparing Youth for the Twenty-First Century: The Transition from Education to the Labor Market*. Paris: Organization for Economic Cooperation and Development (OECD).

Stone, Clarence. 2001. *Building Civic Capacity: The Politics of Reforming Urban Schools*. Lawrence: University Press of Kansas.

Straus, Anselm, and Juliet Corbin. 1990. *Basics of Qualitative Research: Grounded Theory Procedures and Techniques*. Newbury Park, Calif.: Sage Publications.

Supovitz, Jonathan. 2006. *The Case for District-Based Reform*. Cambridge, Mass.: Harvard Education Press.

Tharp, Roland, and Ronald Gallimore. 1988. *Rousing Minds to Life: Teaching, Learning, and Schooling in Social Context*. New York: Cambridge University Press.

Thompson, David, and Faith Crampton. 2002. "The Impact of School Finance Litigation: A Long View." *Journal of Education Finance* 27: 783–815.

Thompson, Gail. 2004. *Through Ebony Eyes: What Teachers Need to Know But Are Afraid to Ask About African-American Students*. San Francisco: Jossey-Bass.

Timar, Thomas, and Kris Kim. 2008. "State Strategies to Improve Low-Performing Schools: California's High-Priority School Grants Program." *Teachers College Record* 106(11).

Tinto, Vincent. 1993. *Leaving College: Rethinking the Causes and Cures of Student Attrition*. Chicago: University of Chicago Press.

Townsend, Barbara. 2000. "The Disproportionate Discipline of African-American Learners: Reducing School Suspensions and Expulsions." *Exceptional Children* 66(3): 381–91.

Truman, David. 1951. *The Governmental Process: Political Interests and Public Opinion*. New York: Knopf.

Trelease, Jim. 2007. "Will Changing the Teacher Change the Scores?" (Orig. pub. in 2005.) Available at: www.trelease-on-reading.com/whatsnu_tu toring-nclb.html.

Tyack, David. 1974. *The One Best System: A History of American Urban Education*. Cambridge, Mass.: Harvard University Press.

———. 2004. *Seeking Common Ground: Public Schools in a Diverse Society*. Cambridge, Mass.: Harvard University Press.

Tyack, David, and Larry Cuban. 1995. *Tinkering Toward Utopia: A Century of Public School Reform*. Cambridge, Mass.: Harvard University Press.

U.S. Department of Education. 1999. *Twenty-First Century Skills for 21st Century Jobs: A Report of the United States Department of Labor, Department of Commerce, Department of Education, and National Institute For Literacy*. Washington, D.C.: U.S. Governmental Printing Office.

U.S. General Accounting Office (U.S. GAO). 1997. "School Finance: State Efforts to Reduce Gaps Between Poor and Wealthy Districts." Washington: U.S. GAO.

Valenzuela, Richard. 1999. *Subtractive Schooling*. Albany: State University of New York Press.

Varenne, Hervé, and Ray McDermott. 1998. *Successful Failure: The School America Builds*. Boulder, Colo.: Westview Press.

Verrilli, Caitlin. 2004. "Political Implosions: The Bush Administration's War on Section 8." *Columbia Political Review* 4(2): 16–17.

Verstegen, Deborah. 1998. "The Relationship Between School Spending and Student Achievement." *Journal of Education Finance* 24(2): 243–62.

Vinovskis, Maris. 1999. "Do Federal Compensatory Education Programs Really Work? A Brief Historical Analysis of Title I and Head Start." *American Journal of Education* 107: 187–209.

Vonnegut, Kurt. 1952. *Player Piano*. New York: Charles Scribner's Sons.

Wagner, Christopher. 2006. "The School Leader's Tool for Assessing and Improving School Culture." *Principal Leadership* (high school edition) (December): 41–423.

Wallerstein, Judith, Julia Lewis, and Sandra Blakelee. 2000. *The Unexpected Legacy of Divorce: A Twenty-five-Year Landmark Study*. New York: Hyperion.

Warren, John, and Melanie Edwards. 2005. "High School Exit Exams and High School Completion." *Educational Evaluation and Policy Analysis* 27(1): 53–74.

Wasik, Barbara, and Robert E. Slavin. 1993. "Preventing Early Reading Failure with One-to-One Tutoring: A Review of Five Programs." *Reading Research Quarterly* 28(2): 178–200.

Weinstein, Rona. 2002. *Reaching Higher: The Power of Expectations in Schooling*. Cambridge, Mass.: Harvard University Press.

Welner, Kevin, and Don Weitzman. 2005. "The Soft Bigotry of Low Expenditures." *Equity and Excellence in Education* 38: 242–48.

Wheeler, Rebecca. 2007. "Code-Switching: Insights and Strategies for Teaching Standard English in Dialectically Diverse Classrooms." Unpublished paper. Christopher Newport University, Newport News Va. Available at: www.agi.harvard.edu/Search/download.php?id=127.

Wilkins, Amy, and the Education Trust staff. 2006. "Yes We Can: Dispelling Myths About Race and Education in America." Washington: Education Trust (September).

Williams, Gwendolyn. 2005. "Leading from Personal Experience: Autobiography as a Foundation for Developing African American Teacher Leadership." In *Making Equity Explicit in Inquiry*, edited by Tom Malarkey. Berkeley, Calif.: National Writing Project. Available at: www.nwp.org/cs/public/download/nwp_file.

Willis, Paul. 1977. *Learning to Labor: How Working-Class Kids Get Working-Class Jobs*. Farnborough, U.K.: Saxon House.

Wilson, Pat, Prisca Martens, and Poonam Arya. 2005. "Accountability for Reading and Readers: What the Numbers Don't Tell." *Reading Teacher* 58(7): 622–31.

Wiltz, Nancy, and G. Pat Wilson. 2006. "An Inquiry into Children's Reading in One Urban School Using SRA Reading Mastery (Direct Instruction)." *Journal of Literacy Research* 37(4): 493–528.

Wise, Arthur. 1979. *Legislated Learning: The Bureaucratization of the Classroom*. Berkeley: University of California Press.

Woody, Elisabeth L., Melissa Buttles, Judith Kafka, Sandra Park, and Jennifer Russell. 2004. *Voices from the Field: Educators Respond to Accountability*. Berkeley: University of California, Policy Analysis for California Education.

Yair, Gad. 2000. "Not Just About Time: Instructional Practices and Productive Time in Schools." *Educational Administration Quarterly* 36(4): 485–512.

Yatvin, Joanne. 2002. "Babes in the Woods: The Wanderings of the National Reading Panel." *Phi Delta Kappan* 83(5): 364–69. Available at: www .pdkintl.org/kappan/k0201yat.htm.

Yinger, John, ed. 2004. *Helping Children Left Behind: State Aid and the Pursuit of Educational Equity*. Cambridge, Mass.: MIT Press.

Young, I. Marion. 1990. *Justice and the Politics of Difference*. Princeton, N.J.: Princeton University Press.

Yudoff, Mark, David Kirp, Betsey Levin, and Rachel Moran. 2002. *Educational Policy and the Law*, 4th ed. Belmont, Calif.: West/Thomson Learning.

Zirkel, Shelly. 2005. "Ongoing Issues of Racial and Ethnic Stigma Fifty Years After *Brown v. Board*." *Urban Review* 37(2): 107–25.

———. Forthcoming a. "Creating More Effective Multiethnic Schools and Classrooms." *Review of Educational Research*.

———. Forthcoming b. "The Influence of Multicultural Practices on Student Outcomes and Intergroup Relations." *Teachers College Record*.

Zuckerbrod, Nancy. 2008. "Six States to Design Own Plans for Fixing Schools." *Washington Post*, July 1.

INDEX

Boldface numbers refer to figures and tables.

education management organizations (EMOs), 234, 271–74

Education Trust, 280, 318n8, 347n23

Edwards, M., 327n22

effective schools, studies of, 49–50

efficiency, 270

Elementary and Secondary Education Act (2001). *See* No Child Left Behind (NCLB) Act (2001)

Elementary and Secondary Education Act (ESEA) (1965), 245, 252, 282

Eliot, C., 351n7

Elk Grove Unified School District, 235

Elliott, M., 50, 51, 327n23

Elmore, R., 320n17

ELS (Education Longitudinal Study) (2002), 55

Emery, K., 350n3

EMOs (education management organizations), 234, 271–74

employment, and education, 102

engagement, of students, 120, 186, 216–17. *See also* student connectedness to schooling (SCS)

England, grant-maintained schools, 238

English language learners (ELL): as family background measure, 95; instructional approach, 193–94; linguistic rights litigation, 254; mistreatment of, 108; performance gap, 144; school outcomes, 103

enrichment activities, 183, 196

equality and equity: of access to education, 92, 134, 138; definition and conceptions of, 10–13, 132, 134–43, 154–57; funding, 88–89, 132, 136, 142; litigation, 256–62; political vs. economic, 135

equal opportunity, 134–39, 142–43

Esping-Anderson, G., 319n11

evaluation, of intervention programs, 195–200

exclusion, 143

expenditures per pupil: and school re-sources, 39–40, 77, 78–79, 87; and test scores, 7; total in public elementary and secondary schools, **3**; trends, 5; in urban vs. suburban schools, 35–36; and vocational tracking, 79

Experience and Education (Dewey), 8

extracurricular activities: class differences in participation, 100; and educational aspirations, 117; gender differences in participation, 123; and school outcomes, 32; and student connectedness to schooling, 58, 115; and test scores, 117

facilities, 2, 35, 36

fact transmission teaching, 319n15

family background: data sources, 93; family composition, 95, 96–97, 102–4, 107; and growth trajectories, 164–67; historical observations of influence, 91–92; impact over time, 147; inequality of, 44–45, 164–67; and math scores, 50, 100; measurement, 49, 94–97; NELS88 data, 57; policy issues, 94, 111–12; qualitative analysis, 98–99, 101; racial-ethnic characteristics, 104–11; research considerations, 93–94; and school outcomes, 27, 46, 97–98, 168, 302–3; and student connectedness to schooling, 41, 120–21, 127. *See also* parents

family income, 44, 96, 120

family intervention programs, 143–44

family literacy programs, 221, 284

family structure, 95, 96–97, 102–4, 107

federal funding, 82, 87, 248–52

female-headed households, 96–97, 102–3, 121

Ferguson, A., 109

Ferguson, R., 29, 327n23

Finland, intervention efforts, 173, 240

First Things First, 72, 89, 173

foreign-born students. *See* English language learners (ELL)

313–14; litigation for equity, 262–66; model of, 45–49; NELS88 measures, 56–58; overall effects, 59–60; research considerations, 5–10, 25–26, 49–52; and school outcomes, 27–29, 53–54, 58–59, 61–72, 79, 167–68, 171–72, 294–99; and student connectedness to schooling, 47, 121–23, 127; students as, 41, 43, 114; in urban and low-income districts, 35–36; variance over time, 167–69, 315–16; waste of, 29–36. *See also* funding

restructuring, 191, 235, 276

revenues, 35, 45, 46. *See also* funding

Rice, J., 61

Risley, T., 331*n*7

Roe, W., 320*n*5

role models, 107, 223

Rose, M., 274

Rose v. Council for Better Education, 260

Rothstein, R., 280

Rowan, B., 225, 329*n*5

Rowland Unified School District, 235

Roza, M., 321*n*6, 329*n*7, 348*n*2

Rumberger, R., 70, 119, 144, 326*n*16

Saks, D., 321*n*10

salaries, teacher: expenditures per pupil impact, 78; and federal funding, 82; NELS88 data, 56; as proxy for teacher quality, 213; and school outcomes, 61, 73; and state funding, 81; in urban vs. suburban districts, 36

San Diego, school choice programs, 72

San Diego Unified School District, 235

San Francisco Unified School District, school-level intervention analysis, 177–84, 233–34

SAT scores, 118

Savage Inequalities (Kozol), 2

Saxe, G., 100

SBB (school-based budgeting), 31, 38, 237–39

scarring, 109–10

S-CHIP (State Children's Health Insurance Program), 281

Schoenfeld, A., 331*n*8

school-based budgeting (SBB), 31, 38, 237–39

school-based management, 237

school changes, 97, 103, 121

school choice, 72, 268, 271–74

school culture: in chain or charter schools, 272; and internal accountability, 83–84; racial-ethnic issues, 109; and school outcomes, 65–66, 70, 71, 214–15; support for minority students, 220–21, 223–24; urban schools, 107

school-level policies and reform: effective resources, 213–17; natural experiments, 210–13; racial-ethnic issues, 193–94, 217–24, 227, 277; reorganization as learning community, 224–29; research considerations, 207–10

school lunches, 193

school psychologists, 194

school reform: approaches, 74–75; based on funding increases, 88–89; current climate, 75–76; vs. general reform, 279; inconsistent implementation, 34; natural experiments, 210–13; new public narrative for, 112; test score vs. progress improvement, 71–72, 75; wasteful spending, 30. *See also* specific reforms

Scott, J., 350*n*3

SCS (student connectedness to schooling). *See* student connectedness to schooling (SCS)

Seattle School District; Parents Involved in Community Schools, Inc. v., 335*n*6

Sechrest, L., 342*n*2

second-chance (remedial) programs, 31, 63, 74–75, 150, 177–78. *See also* intervention

segregation, 108, 142, 256–58